Foucault and Heidegger

Critical Encounters

Alan Milchman and Alan Rosenberg
Editors

Contradictions, Volume 16

University of Minnesota Press
Minneapolis
London

"Heidegger and Foucault: Escaping Technological Nihilism" first appeared in *Philosophy and Social Criticism* 13, no. 2 (1987); copyright Sage Publications Ltd.; reprinted with permission. "From Foucault to Heidegger: A One-Way Ticket?" first appeared in *Research in Phenomenology* 21 (1991); reprinted with permission of the publisher, Humanities Press, Inc.

Published by the University of Minnesota Press
111 Third Avenue South, Suite 290
Minneapolis, MN 55401-2520
http://www.upress.umn.edu

Library of Congress Cataloging-in-Publication Data

Foucault and Heidegger : critical encounters / Alan Milchman and Alan Rosenberg, editors.
p. cm. — (Contradictions ; v. 16)
Includes bibliographical references and index.
ISBN 0-8166-3378-9 — ISBN 0-8166-3379-7 (pbk.)
1. Foucault, Michel. 2. Heidegger, Martin, 1889–1976. I. Milchman, Alan, 1940– II. Rosenberg, Alan, 1939– III. Series: Contradictions (Minneapolis, Minn.) ; 16.
B2430.F724 F683 2003
193—dc21

2002155364

Printed in the United States of America on acid-free paper

12 11 10 09 08 07 06 05 04 03 10 9 8 7 6 5 4 3 2 1

Foucault and Heidegger

Contradictions

Edited by Craig Calhoun, Social Science Research Council

Volume 16 Alan Milchman and Alan Rosenberg, editors, *Foucault and Heidegger: Critical Encounters*

Volume 15 Michael D. Kennedy, *Cultural Formations of Postcommunism: Emancipation, Transition, Nation, and War*

Volume 14 Michèle H. Richman, *Sacred Revolutions: Durkheim and the Collège de Sociologie*

Volume 13 Pierre-André Taguieff, *The Force of Prejudice: On Racism and Its Doubles*

Volume 12 Krishan Kumar, *1989: Revolutionary Ideas and Ideals*

Volume 11 Timothy Mitchell, editor, *Questions of Modernity*

Volume 10 Giovanni Arrighi and Beverly J. Silver, *Chaos and Governance in the Modern World System*

Volume 9 François Dosse, *History of Structuralism, Volume 2: The Sign Sets, 1967–Present*

Volume 8 François Dosse, *History of Structuralism, Volume 1: The Rising Sign, 1945–1966*

Volume 7 Patricia Hill Collins, *Fighting Words: Black Women and the Search for Justice*

Volume 6 Craig Calhoun and John McGowan, editors, *Hannah Arendt and the Meaning of Politics*

Volume 5 Gérard Noiriel, *The French Melting Pot: Immigration, Citizenship, and National Identity*

Volume 4 John C. Torpey, *Intellectuals, Socialism, and Dissent: The East German Opposition and Its Legacy*

Volume 3 T. M. S. Evens, *Two Kinds of Rationality: Kibbutz, Democracy, and Generational Conflict*

Volume 2 Micheline R. Ishay, *Internationalism and Its Betrayal*

Volume 1 Johan Heilbron, *The Rise of Social Theory*

Contents

Acknowledgments

We want to acknowledge the enormous importance of the thinking of Michel Foucault and Martin Heidegger, the fecundity of which is amply demonstrated by the essays contained in this volume.

We want to thank the contributors to this volume for their enthusiasm and patience throughout the long process from conception to fruition.

Finally, we want to thank Morris Rabinowitz, whose technical assistance was invaluable to us both.

Toward a Foucault/Heidegger *Auseinandersetzung*

Alan Milchman and Alan Rosenberg

Continental philosophy is riven by a great divide. One tradition, whose foremost representative is Jürgen Habermas, seeks to complete the unfinished project of modernity, based on the concept of reason that it has enshrined. The other tradition, among whose foremost representatives are Martin Heidegger and Michel Foucault, wants—according to Habermas himself—"to advance Nietzsche's program of a critique of reason," in the case of Heidegger through a destruction of metaphysics, in the case of Foucault through a destruction of historiography.[1] Yet notwithstanding the connection between their respective projects, as well as the very different philosophical trajectories of these two thinkers, thus far only one volume in the English language has been devoted to a confrontation between Foucault and Heidegger.[2] Despite the enormous and growing interest in these two thinkers, and in their profound impact on the way we think today (marked by a succession of volumes and essays devoted to each of them), what has been lacking is a critical encounter or *Auseinandersetzung* between Foucault and Heidegger. Yet, the links, as well as the fault lines, between these two thinkers constitute a missing piece of the philosophical trajectory of the twentieth century. It is our contention that the thinking of both Foucault and Heidegger, and the compelling philosophical questions that preoccupied them, can be greatly illuminated by such a critical encounter. Our aim is to begin to investigate the matrix of thinking that is revealed, to explore the new horizons that are opened, when Foucault and Heidegger encounter one another.

Martin Heidegger and Michel Foucault are among the most important figures in the tradition of continental philosophy in the twentieth century. Thus, in his history of modern German philosophy, Herbert Schnädelbach asserts that Heidegger's *Being and Time,* together with Wittgenstein's *Tractatus,* and Lukács's *History and Class Consciousness,* are "the most influential philosophical writings of this century."[3] Moreover, Jürgen Habermas, probably the most renowned philosopher in Germany today, as well as a harsh critic of Heidegger and his philosophical legacy, has nonetheless acknowledged the daring originality of *Being and Time,* a pathbreaking work that recast the themes of hermeneutics, phenomenology, and pragmatism so as to "bring them into a postmetaphysical historicizing overcoming of the philosophy of subjectivity. . . . From today's standpoint, Heidegger's new beginning still presents probably the most profound turning point in German philosophy since Hegel."[4] Meanwhile, the imprint of Heidegger's *Denken* on the writings of many of the most important contemporary philosophers is palpable: Gadamerian hermeneutics, Rorty's new pragmatism, Levinas's phenomenology, Derridean deconstruction, and Lyotard's postmodern rejection of metanarratives are all indebted in manifold ways to the thinking of Martin Heidegger.

Foucault's influence on contemporary thought has also been great. Describing the impact of Foucault on the French philosophical scene, dominated by phenomenology and Marxism in the 1960s, François Dosse has argued that Foucault "dealt a final blow to the phenomenological project and to the pretensions of a philosophy sitting somewhere above the tussle of the empirical sciences. . . . He blamed philosophy for being too strictly academic, and for systematically avoiding Kant's question of knowing what our current reality is. Foucault opened his inquiry up to new objects and displaced the phenomenological perspective of an interiorized description of lived experience, to which he preferred bringing problematized social practices and institutions to light."[5] Indeed, there are few issues in philosophy and social theory that have not been profoundly affected by Foucault's wide-ranging research projects. He has left his mark on psychology as well as ethics, on politics as well as epistemology. The work of the later Foucault on "governmentality" has reconfigured the debate on the meaning of the political. Research on madness, penology, and medicine has been transformed by his writings. Moreover, according to Didier Eribon: "Ten years after the death of Michel Foucault, his *oeuvre* has remained at the forefront of intellectual life, both in France, and in many parts of the world. Without risk of error, it can be said that it has dominated the decade now ending, just as it dominated the prior decade."[6] Indeed, contemporary philosophy and social theory have been visibly affected by what has been called "the Foucault effect."

Beyond the impact of each of these two thinkers on contemporary philosophy, the linking of their names raises the question of the possible influence of Heidegger on Foucault. Indeed, Foucault on several occasions acknowledged his intellectual debt to Heidegger. Thus, in a 1982 interview, when asked about "intellectual influences" on his own thinking, Foucault said that Heidegger was an "overwhelming influence," "but no one in France has ever perceived it."[7] Moreover, in his final interview, just before his death in 1984, Foucault revealed that

> [f]or me Heidegger has always been the essential philosopher. I began by reading Hegel, then Marx, and I set out to read Heidegger in 1951 or 1952; then in 1952 or 1953—I don't remember anymore—I read Nietzsche. I still have here the notes I took when I was reading Heidegger. I've got tons of them! And they are much more important than the ones I took on Hegel or Marx. My entire philosophical development was determined by my reading of Heidegger. I nevertheless recognize that Nietzsche outweighed him. I do not know Heidegger well enough: I hardly know *Being and Time* nor what has been published recently. My knowledge of Nietzsche certainly is better than my knowledge of Heidegger. Nevertheless, these are the two fundamental experiences I have had. It is possible that if I had not read Heidegger, I would not have read Nietzsche. I had tried to read Nietzsche in the fifties but Nietzsche alone did not appeal to me—whereas Nietzsche and Heidegger: that was a philosophical shock! But I have never written anything on Heidegger, and I wrote only a very small article on Nietzsche; these are nevertheless the two authors I have read the most.[8]

This statement has become canonical for those who grapple with the question of the relationship between Foucault and Heidegger. Indeed, in the present volume, Hubert Dreyfus, Steven Hicks, Michael Schwartz, Leslie Thiele, and William Spanos all cite portions of this interview, interpreting it in diverse ways. In our own reading of Foucault's comment, we are struck by the fact that Nietzsche seems more important to him than Heidegger, whom he acknowledges he does not know very well. Indeed, Heidegger's role seems to have been to initiate Foucault's confrontation with Nietzsche, the direct impact of which was enormously significant.

Yet, Foucault's own words would seem to clearly direct us to the nature of the "critical encounters" between Foucault and Heidegger that the essays in this volume will instantiate: the *influence* of Heidegger on Foucault. However, as we will argue, the focus of these critical encounters should *not* be the impact of Heidegger on Foucault, the traces of Heidegger in the Foucauldian text. There are several factors that we believe should direct us *away* from a reading of Foucault that focuses on his purported intellectual debt to Heidegger.

With respect to the voluminous notes on Heidegger to which Foucault refers in his final interview, they are nowhere to be found. Jean Zoungrana, who has written the most detailed and substantive analysis of the place of Heidegger in the Foucauldian corpus thus far, acknowledges that the Centre Michel Foucault in Paris does not have them.[9] But quite apart from the existence of such notes, in contrast to the considerable presence, for example, of Kant or Nietzsche throughout Foucault's writings and interviews, there is very little evidence of the direct textual influence of Heidegger in Foucault's writings, save in his very earliest texts, his long introduction to Ludwig Binswanger's *Dream and Existence* (1954) and his *Mental Illness and Personality* (1954).[10] In both of these texts, the presence of Heidegger is overwhelming, albeit a Heidegger understood as providing an existential anthropology, with its constituent subject. Foucault is most explicitly concerned with Heidegger at this early stage in his thinking, when he had yet to free himself from a phenomenological and transcendental perspective, and, therefore, a reading of Heidegger that privileged the *anthropological.*

Of course, one cannot reduce the question of the influence of one thinker on another to the actual discussion of, or frequency of references to, that thinker's work. In the history of philosophy, influence is not reducible to explicit mention or reference. Thus, Jean Zoungrana, as well as several of the contributors to this volume, makes the case for Heidegger's impact on Foucault in both his later and his early writings, and this despite the paucity of explicit references to him. Moreover, in the case of Heidegger's purported influence on Foucault, specific cultural-political factors may have intervened to prevent its acknowledgment. Thus, Jacques Derrida has claimed that while the shadow of Heidegger is present in French philosophy in the 1960s and 1970s, it was systematically obscured: "I suggested in a note somewhere in *Psyché* (in *Désistance*) that for a quarter century, Heidegger was never named in any book by those who, in France, were forced to recognize in private or in public much later that he had played a major role in their thought (Althusser, Foucault, Deleuze, for example)."[11] Are Foucault's comments in his final interview such an acknowledgment of Heidegger's profound, albeit hidden, influence on his thinking? Paul Rabinow, for one, is unconvinced: "The few scattered comments in the later years are, I am convinced, the product of our encounters more than anything else. . . . Foucault's encounter with Heidegger was in the existential Dasein stage; no doubt he read everything else and learned things from this great philosopher but he was certainly no Heideggerian."[12]

To return to Foucault's own statements, in his interviews, about Heidegger's impact on him, we also cannot ignore what we would term Foucauldian irony, his propensity to provoke, and even scandalize; his tendency to both self-mockery and hyperbole. The "link" between Heidegger and Foucault is one that those who come after them will forge, and in so doing will open new paths of thinking, but it may not be the link of "overwhelming influence" to which Foucault's words seemingly direct us. In his discussion of the way the fold and unfold animate Foucault, Gilles Deleuze has, perhaps, set us on the right path:

> If the fold and the unfold animate not only Foucault's ideas but even his style, it is because they constitute an archaeology of thought. So we are perhaps less surprised to find that Foucault encounters Heidegger precisely in this area. It is more an encounter than an influence, to the extent that in Foucault the fold and the unfold have an origin, a use and a destination that are very different from Heidegger's.[13]

Indeed, focusing on the influence of Heidegger on Foucault seems to ineluctably put us on a one-way street, in which it is difficult for Foucault's own thinking to emerge from the shadow of Heidegger's *Denken.* The result is a reading in which Foucault emerges as a disciple of Heidegger's, someone who is read through Heideggerian lenses. Just such a focus has become the canonical reading of Foucault's relationship to Heidegger. However, we agree with Michael Kelly when he says that "when Foucault is linked too strongly to Heidegger, whether early or late, his relevance for the understanding of the notion of critique in ethical, political, and social theory may be reduced accordingly."[14] Moreover, we believe that this is the case wherever the link between these two thinkers is conceived primarily in terms of the influence of Heidegger on Foucault. The outcome, it seems to us, is a disservice to both thinkers, obscuring their originality, and an obstacle to the confrontation that can assure that their thinking lives, not just in historical tomes, but in the strife over how we are to live our own individual and cultural-political lives. Even Jean Zoungrana, who has sought the traces of Heidegger in the Foucauldian text itself and whose readings yield important insights, nevertheless explicitly rejects a reading that would "Heideggerianize or Heideggerize Foucault," that would "make him a Heideggerian" or "a disciple of Heidegger."[15] Instead, Zoungrana concludes that Heidegger's influence on Foucault, which he believes to be much more profound than we do, "has functioned as an invitation to think with Heidegger, but beyond Heidegger."[16]

This task of thinking with, but beyond, as a feature of the contact between these two thinkers may provide one way to articulate an important facet of the "critical encounter," the *Auseinandersetzung*, between Foucault and Heidegger that we seek to provoke with the essays contained in this volume. Indeed, the very term "critical encounter" can only approximate the nature of the engagement we want to stimulate between Foucault and Heidegger. What is at issue is most certainly an encounter or engagement, one that entails both a confrontation and an exchange; one that proceeds through both dialogue and strife. Indeed, this latter, the agonal moment, seems to be integral to such a critical encounter. Clearly, we are far removed from influences and the history of ideas here. Indeed, while in the case of Heidegger and Foucault the influence could only have been of the former on the latter, a critical encounter, as we conceive it, is not subject to the rules of chronology or biography, but rather can assume the form of a confrontation between an earlier and a later thinker. Thus, whereas an intellectual history could only focus on the possible impact of Heidegger on Foucault, a critical encounter will entail a concern with the impact of Foucault on Heidegger, no less than that of Heidegger on Foucault.

It is our contention that we can best unpack the meaning of the term *critical encounter*, explicate its various elements, by advertence to the German word *Auseinandersetzung*. If we have recourse to a

German word, it has nothing to do with Heidegger's own outrageous claim that to do philosophy one must speak German, or to any metaphysical privileging of the German language. Rather, it is the strangeness of the German word to an Anglophone ear, a word that resonates with a variety of meanings, each of which is integral to the concept of critical encounter, that makes it so serviceable here. Through a "reading" of the word *Auseinandersetzung,* we hope to make clear the stakes of this Foucault/Heidegger encounter. Heidegger himself utilizes the word *Auseinandersetzung* to translate Heraclitus's *polemos* in his 1934 lecture course, *Introduction to Metaphysics.* Heraclitian *polemos* is confrontation, "a strife that holds sway before everything divine and human, not war in the human sense."[17] But as Heidegger points out in his parenthetical addition to the text as published in 1953, "Confrontation does not divide unity, much less destroy it. It builds unity; it is the gathering *(logos). Polemos* and *logos* are the same."[18] For Heidegger, Heraclitian *polemos* must be distinguished from "polemic *[Polemik],*" as he informs us in an appendix to his Nietzsche lectures of 1936–37; and "Only in *Auseinandersetzung* does a productive interpretation arise."[19]

Indeed, in seeking to initiate an *Auseinandersetzung* between Foucault and Heidegger, we are following the very philosophical practice of our two protagonists themselves. Both Heidegger's and Foucault's own engagement with the philosophical tradition entailed *Auseinandersetzungen,* which were a hallmark of their respective paths of thinking. Heidegger's confrontations or *Auseinandersetzungen* with the pre-Socratics, Plato, Aristotle, Kant, Hegel, Schelling, Hölderlin, and Nietzsche constitute the distinctive pathmarks that have shaped his *Denken.* Thus, according to Theodore Kisiel, Heidegger's breakthrough, in the years 1921–24, to the problematic leading to *Being and Time* proceeded through what can be "initially described as the 'confrontation of the ontological tradition,'" in the figure of Aristotle, through which "the Aristotelian texts are stretched well beyond the deconstructive exercise that we would expect from Heidegger's methodology at this stage, so that they are made to yield a plethora of constructive insights as well."[20] With respect to *Being and Time* itself, Kisiel persuasively argues that it proceeds through three distinct drafts: "As we progress from one draft to another, as we move from 1924 to 1925 to 1926, the dominant question becomes in turn 'What is history?,' 'What is being?,' 'What is time?,' with the other two however always lurking in the backround."[21] For each of these successive drafts, there is a dominant philosophical figure with whom Heidegger is engaged in an *Auseinandersetzung,* Dilthey, Husserl, and Kant respectively. Meanwhile, as Charles Scott has pointed out, for Heidegger, *Auseinandersetzung* "has special significance in his lectures on Nietzsche in which Nietzsche appears as an opponent in a struggle over what is most essential for thought. . . . I wish to emphasize that for Heidegger this confrontation—this *Auseinandersetzung*—is the site in which the thinking of Nietzsche, the thinking of Heidegger, and the self-determination of both their thinking take place."[22] Plato, the Epicureans, the Stoics, the Cynics, Kant, and Nietzsche play a comparable role in the shaping of the Foucauldian corpus. Indeed, Foucault's inquiry into the meaning of critique, and his re-posing of the question "What Is Enlightenment?" constitutes just such a confrontation or critical encounter with Kant, while the last two volumes of *The History of Sexuality,* together with his lectures on *parrhésia* at Berkeley and his final lecture course at the *Collège de France* on *Le courage de la verité,* constitute a model of *Auseinandersetzung* with Socratic, Platonic, and Greco-Roman thought.

Yet, as we have pointed out, Foucault's writings are sparse in their references to Heidegger, while Heidegger was no doubt completely unaware of Foucault. Silence, however, should not be taken as absence, as evidence that a confrontation or *Auseinandersetzung* is not possible. In addition to the claims of several of the contributors to this volume that Foucault's own silence in his major works concerning Heidegger should not obscure the existence of a profound confrontation with him, Kevin Hill has argued that in Foucault's archaeological works, such as *The Order of Things* and *The Archaeology of Knowledge,* "though Heidegger is seldom explicitly named in these contexts, a comparison of these passages with the central views of *Being and Time* strongly suggests that it is primarily Heidegger that Foucault has in mind."[23] Moreover, Lucien Goldmann had already made a classic and powerful case for the existence of an *Auseinandersetzung* even where the participants are silent on the very existence of one another's work. Thus, Goldmann has argued that the important passages in Heidegger's *Being and Time* that focus on the "reification of consciousness" constitute a hidden discussion—we would say *Auseinandersetzung*—with Georg Lukács's *History and Class Consciousness,* despite the lack of any direct reference to the latter:

"Most likely this is a discussion between two fundamental books which, moreover, represent an analogous turning-point, while each being entirely opposed to each other."[24] Such confrontations, the silence of the participants notwithstanding, are an important feature of the history of philosophy and can guide us as we embark on a Foucault/Heidegger *Auseinandersetzung.*

Nor is the fact that both its participants are dead an obstacle to the kind of *Auseinandersetzung* we are proposing to initiate between Foucault and Heidegger. Inasmuch as the kind of confrontation for which we are calling is not situated on the terrain of the history of ideas and need not follow the conventions of chronology, a posthumous *Auseinandersetzung* is particularly apposite. The *Auseinandersetzung* between Martin Heidegger and Theodor W. Adorno orchestrated by Hermann Mörchen provides a case in point. While Adorno confronted Heidegger on several occasions, most notably in his *Jargon of Authenticity,* these confrontations were not *Auseinandersetzungen,* but rather polemics, in which denunciation was the dominant motif. Yet through a subtle and insightful reading of both of these thinkers, Mörchen, a student of Heidegger's, has fashioned an *Auseinandersetzung* beyond Adorno's polemic and Heidegger's own absolute silence regarding Adorno, a critical encounter in which the thought of each participant is enhanced, and in which a genuine communication is achieved.[25] We believe that such a communication can also be achieved through a posthumous confrontation between Foucault and Heidegger.

If we now want thinking to proceed on the basis of an *Auseinandersetzung* between Foucault and Heidegger, it is because we believe the several constitutive elements of such a confrontation can make a signal contribution to what Foucault designated as a historical ontology of our present.

One such element of an *Auseinandersetzung* is that it is through a dialogue with what is "other" that it is possible to define what is one's own. Thus, it is through the encounter with the thought of the other that one's own thinking emerges. Heidegger insisted on precisely this facet of *Auseinandersetzung* in his 1942 lecture course at the University of Freiburg, *Hölderlin's Hymn "The Ister"*: "The appropriation of one's own *is* only as the encounter *[Auseinandersetzung]* and guestlike dialogue with the foreign."[26] The encounter we envisage is, therefore, one of the ways in which the thinking of both Heidegger and

Foucault can emerge in its own self-determination, displaying its immanent tendencies and possibilities.

An *Auseinandersetzung* as dialogue with the other does not aim at agreement, a definitive conclusion, or a synthesis of positions. It is an engagement in which differences appear and are sharpened, in which questions are posed, not answered. It is a confrontation in which issues are problematized, in which thinking is interrogated, as Foucault says. That is why Foucault is so wary of anything that smacks of "any totalization—which would be at once *abstract* and *limiting*," whereas his concern is "to *open up* problems."[27]

Moreover, another aspect of such an *Auseinandersetzung* is that it actively involves the "reader," and not just the thinkers whose *Denken* is at stake. As Charles Scott has asserted:

> It constitutes a process, a performative exchange, in which the reader must also engage if he or she is to "understand" what is happening. In this engagement, we can say descriptively, a connecting distance occurs; one stands over against the other; a decisive difference is achieved as the thinkers come into contact by means of thinking. It is a clash of thoughtful moving forces, a *Streit*, Heidegger says, a thoughtful confrontation of minds at odds with one another in their separate enactments.[28]

This strife, this agonism, which is a feature of such a confrontation, "does not work toward resolution but toward a preservation of difference and opposition—an en-countering—in thought."[29]

Thus, a related dimension of *Auseinandersetzung* is that, as Charles Scott has said:

> it thus has the force of connection, gathering, and binding together and suggests, like the word de-cision, both division and relation. In *Auseinandersetzung* separate ways of thinking belong together in their opposition and difference. *Auseinandersetzung* is decisive for thought. It itself provides a *logos* for thought and gathers or binds together in differences what belongs together in separation.[30]

However, this very gathering and binding together in differences also indicates how far removed is an *Auseinandersetzung* from a polemic, with its connotations of savage criticism and complete rejection. For Foucault, polemics are "a parasitic figure on discussion and an obstacle to the search for truth,"[31] whereas the confrontation with another's thought should entail "the serious play of questions and answers, in the work of reciprocal elucidation [in which] the rights of each person are in some sense immanent in the discussion. They depend only on the dialogue situation."[32] Such a dialogue, which is a hallmark of an *Auseinandersetzung,* has nothing in common with the action of the polemicist:

> The polemicist . . . proceeds encased in privileges that he possesses in advance and will never agree to question. On principle, he possesses rights authorizing him to wage war and making that struggle a just undertaking; the person he confronts is not a partner in the search for truth, but an adversary, an enemy who is wrong, who is harmful and whose very existence constitutes a threat. For him, then, the game does not consist of recognizing this person as a subject having the right to speak, but of abolishing him, as interlocutor, from any possible dialogue.[33]

Heidegger echoes Foucault's concern when he insists that "*Auseinandersetzung* is not fault-finding *[Bemängelung].*"[34] Rather, "The sharpness of *Auseinandersetzung* is here only possible when it is accompanied by a fervent affinity *[Verwandtschaft],* by a yes to the essential *[Ja zum Wesentlichen].*"[35] Thus, beyond the separation and difference that is brought out, an *Auseinandersetzung* also forges links between the modes of thinking that confront one another.

Both that aspect of an *Auseinandersetzung,* in which an encounter or confrontation need not lead to resolution, in which differences and not only relations are posited, like that other facet, in which questions are posed, not answered, in which experience is problematized, not reconciled, clash with some of the dominant motifs in Western thought, which in its quest for Truth has privileged resolution of issues and answers to questions. In that tradition, strife and conflict do not instantiate differences so much as resolve them; they do not accentuate oppositions so much as attenuate and reconcile them. And one's interlocutor is not a partner with whom one engages in a dialogue, but rather an enemy to be crushed.

Auseinandersetzung not only tolerates the tension between division and relation, but revels in it. Its conception of strife and agonism seeks not the calm of rational consensus, but the exhilaration of questioning and problematizing experience and thinking. That questioning and problematization is one of the aims of the critical encounters between Foucault and Heidegger to which this volume is dedicated.

Finally, we want to argue that an *Auseinandersetzung* between Heidegger and Foucault presupposes that the work of these two thinkers remains alive, that it is not a finished project, the *True* meaning of which it is the task of interpreters to explain and reveal. Rather, the critical encounter, as we conceive it, entails a vision of a philosophy that continues to develop even after the death of the philosopher; a vision consonant with Heidegger's insistence that his thinking is constituted by "ways, not works" *(Wege—nicht Werke)*,[36] as well as by Foucault's own injunction that his thinking be used as a "tool box." Thus, Foucault insisted that "[a]ll my books . . . are, if you like, little tool boxes. If people want to open them, use them, use a particular sentence, idea, or analysis like a screwdriver or wrench in order to short-circuit, disqualify or break up systems of power, including eventually the very ones from which my books have issued . . . well, all the better!"[37] Moreover, Foucault also saw each book as transitional, "a book which enables me, which I hope will enable me, to go further," insisting that with none of them had he "already got to the point of arrival."[38] What is striking in the vision of both these thinkers is the rejection of any conception that their works are finished, that the questions they have asked are in any sense definitively answered, that there is a single way to read them, together with the injunction to blaze new trails and invent new tools.

Let us now briefly indicate some of the specific possibilities and lines of inquiry opened up by a Foucault/Heidegger *Auseinandersetzung*.[39] One such line of inquiry concerns the relationship of each of these two thinkers to the work of Friedrich Nietzsche. The thinking of both Foucault and Heidegger has been profoundly marked by their own very different confrontations with Nietzsche.

Foucault sees Nietzsche's invocation of the death of God as both more radical than that of Hegel or Feuerbach, and as the end of metaphysics: "For Hegel, Reason takes the place of God, and it is the human spirit that develops little by little; for Feuerbach, God is the illusion that alienates Man, but once rid of this illusion, it is Man who comes to realize his liberty; finally, for Nietzsche, the death of God signifies the end of metaphysics, but God is not replaced by man, and the space remains empty."[40] If one takes the notion of the "death of God" as an example of disruptive wisdom, then what makes Nietzsche more disruptive than his predecessors is that he doesn't replace God with another metaphysical construct, such as Reason or Man, but rather rejects the possibility of any transcendental whatsoever. In place of metaphysics, Foucault argues that Nietzsche ascribed to philosophy a new objective: genealogy. Moreover, it was precisely Nietzsche, he asserts, who freed him from his earlier commitment to dialectic and historicism: "As for the actual influence Nietzsche has had on me, I would find it difficult to specify, because I am, precisely, aware just how deep it has been. I shall simply say that I remained ideologically 'historicist' and Hegelian until I read Nietzsche."[41]

Heidegger, too, engages in an *Auseinandersetzung* with Nietzsche throughout his *Denkweg*. However, where Foucault sees Nietzsche's thinking as the end of metaphysics in the sense of a radical break with the Western metaphysical tradition, Heidegger has claimed that Nietzsche's thinking can be seen as the end of metaphysics only in the sense that it constitutes the "fulfillment of modern metaphysics."[42] Heidegger's view of Nietzsche's thinking as the completion of Western metaphysics rests on his conviction "that behind Nietzsche's exceedingly sharp rejection of the Cartesian *cogito* stands an *even more rigorous commitment* to the subjectivity posited by Descartes."[43] Moreover, according to Heidegger, "[w]ithout being sufficiently aware of it, Nietzsche agrees with Descartes that Being means 'representedness,' a being established in thinking, and that truth means 'certitude.'"[44] Based on what he sees as the inner connection of Descartes to Nietzsche, Heidegger can conclude that Nietzsche "takes the fundamental position of modern metaphysics as absolutely certain and stakes everything on the priority of man as subject. Of course, the subject is now conceived as will to power."[45]

Beyond the interpretation of Nietzsche, the very different readings of that thinker proffered by Foucault and Heidegger are indicative of other fault lines that the kind of critical encounter we are proposing will expose. Among them are the question of being, the *Seinsfrage*, which, in its different formulations preoccupied Heidegger throughout his life; the question of technology, which is a leitmotiv of Heidegger's thinking after the turn; and the issues of power and subjectivation, which so preoccupied Foucault.

One set of fault lines to be examined in any such critical encounter was opened up by Foucault's comments, among the few explicitly directed to the Heideggerian *Denkweg*, that

> [f]or Heidegger, it was through an increasing obsession with *techné* as the only way to arrive at an understanding of objects, that the West lost touch with Being. Let's turn the question around and ask which techniques and practices form the Western concept of the subject, giving it its characteristic split of truth and error, freedom and

> constraint. I think that it is here that we will find the real possibility of constructing a history of what we have done and, at the same time, a diagnosis of what we are.[46]

What Foucault first problematizes here is Heidegger's reading of the history of being as one of *Seinsvergessenheit* (forgottenness of being), with its implication that being has an essence, one that has been forgotten through the development of Western *Technik*, and its culmination in the reign of *das Ge-Stell* (technological enframing). Whether being *(Sein)* precedes thinking for Heidegger, or it is, as Hubert Dreyfus has contended, "short for the understanding of Being, the truth of Being or the meaning of Being,"[47] remains a hotly debated topic. And while it seems clear that in his magnum opus, *Being and Time,* Heidegger claims that there are ahistorical features to *Dasein,* "Existentials," including a receptivity to being, the later Heidegger seems rather to have focused on the historical constitution of the various *Daseine.* Nonetheless, on precisely this complex of issues, one of the stakes in any Foucault/Heidegger *Auseinerandersetzung,* it is worth pondering Dreyfus's conclusion:

> In the last analysis Foucault is more radical than Heidegger, in that, consistent with his opposition to *all* totalising, he avoids any account of what human beings essentially are and are called to do, whether that be Nietzsche's call to constant self-overcoming or Heidegger's claim that Being demands total receptivity. Although Foucault does attempt to be receptive to the problematisations in our current practices "through which being offers itself as having to be thought," he does not claim that in so doing he is fulfilling his human essence.[48]

Foucault's own contribution to the question of being leads him to focus his attention on the issue of problematizations: "It was a matter of analyzing, not behaviors or ideas, nor societies and their 'ideologies,' but the *problematizations* through which being offers itself to be, necessarily, thought—and the *practices* on the basis of which these problematizations are formed."[49] Foucault tracked down these problematizations and their attendant practices in the processes of normalization, the epistemic rules that shape discourse, in discipline and in the practices of the self, all of which constitute the bases for what he sees as the history of the present, and a diagnosis of what we are.

In addition, Foucault seeks to shift the focus of thinking from a preoccupation with how *techné* (know-how or competency) makes objects or beings "show up," with, for example, how the reign of *das Ge-Stell* makes objects show up as *Bestand* (standing reserve), to how the subject is itself constructed by our historically variable techniques or technologies. Heidegger has provided us with perhaps the most far-reaching inquiry into the different ways in which entities *(Seiende)* "show up" in the several epochs of being, thereby exposing the impact of modern technology in all its ramifications to our glance. Heidegger's focus, then, is on how modern technology makes nature and objects show up through a "challenging" *(Herausforden)* and "ordering" *(Bestellen)*. In an important sense, we have scarcely begun to explore all the dimensions of this complex of issues opened up by Heidegger's meditation on *Technik,* inasmuch as a number of texts from the 1940s that elaborate on this question have only recently been published or still await publication in the Heidegger *Gesamtausgabe.* Foucault, by contrast, shifts the focus from the way nature and objects show up in the different epochs of being, with their respective *Techné,* and more specifically under the sway of modern technology, to the ways the subject is constituted by those very technologies, both technologies of domination and technologies of the self. Foucault's concern, then, is with the historically variable and contingent modes of subjectivation, and, perhaps most important of all, the possibilities of new modes of subjectivation that are not yet, that must first be invented. Indeed, this is the way we read Foucault's provocative statement, at the conclusion of *The Order of Things,* that "man is an invention of recent date. And one perhaps nearing its end."[50] Man, in the form of the humanist subject, is a mode of subjectivation no older than the Classical age (sixteenth to seventeenth century), and will give way to new forms of subjectivation.

A Foucault/Heidegger *Auseinandersetzung* would also explore what seem to us the profound implications of Foucault's comments on philosophy's relation to its own classical past. In answer to the question of whether the care of the self in the Greco-Roman sense can be updated to confront contemporary problems, Foucault responded:

> Nothing is more foreign to me than the idea that, at a certain moment, philosophy went astray and forgot something, that somewhere in its history there is a principle, a foundation that must be rediscovered. I feel that all such forms of analysis, whether they take a radical form and claim that philosophy has from the outset been a forgetting, or whether they take a much more historical viewpoint and

> say, "Such and such a philosopher forgot something"—neither of these approaches is particularly interesting or useful. Which does not mean that contact with such and such a philosopher may not produce something, but it must be emphasized that it would be something new.[51]

What Foucault seems to problematize here is the Heideggerian concept of *Widerholung* (retrieval or repetition), and Heidegger's preoccupation with *Ursprunglich* or originary thinking, and its possible return. Foucault, especially the later Foucault, is as preoccupied with the ancients as is Heidegger (even if Foucault focuses on Socrates/Plato and on the Hellenistic thinkers, while Heidegger is more concerned with Aristotle and the pre-Socratics). Nonetheless, Foucault does not share Heidegger's concern with the originary, and a seeming focus on regeneration or refoundation, insisting instead that "you can't find the solution of a problem in the solution of another problem raised at another moment by other people."[52] Thus, Foucault quite deliberately eschews any nostalgia for the Greeks at the very moment that he is most concerned with their thinking, so that his turn to antiquity is, indeed, an aspect of his history of the present, and not, as often seems the case for Heidegger, a yearning for a rebirth.

Another complex of issues raised by a Foucault/Heidegger *Auseinandersetzung* concerns the role of ethics. The later Foucault conceives of ethics as a *rapport à soi,* a kind of self-problematizing or interrogation of oneself, which involves one's ethical substance, that part of our behavior that is problematized, one's mode of subjectivation, the self-practices that one performs, and the telos, or form of ethical subject that one seeks to become. Thus conceived, ethics plays a predominant role in the last stage of the Foucauldian path of thinking. Despite his focus on *Dasein's* being-in-the-world, and being-with-others *(mitsein),* Heidegger has always insisted that ethics has its basis in value, which is itself rooted in a metaphysic of the subject. Thus, critics of Heidegger have often claimed that the absence of an ethics was the mark of his nihilism, leaving him incapable of opposing Nazism. However, Heidegger has always insisted that, far from being a basis upon which one can resist nihilism, ethics, by virtue of its link to a metaphysic of the subject and the will to power, is itself fatally linked to nihilism. Moreover, Heidegger has claimed that categories such as justice, for example, with which he is indeed concerned, are not ethical concepts at all, but are rather ontological, in that they name being with reference to the articulation of beings.

Finally, a Foucault/Heidegger *Auseinerandersetzung* can hardly avoid the vexing question of the political issues with which they have contended. In his Paris lectures on *The Philosophical Discourse of Modernity,* Jürgen Habermas has sought to directly link Heidegger and Foucault not merely philosophically, but also in terms of the political implications of their thinking. For Habermas, the antifoundationalism, the rejection of the ahistorical humanist subject that is a hallmark of the thinking of both Heidegger and Foucault, links them as nihilistic thinkers. Moreover, the nihilism attributed to each of them has sinister political overtones: in the case of Heidegger, it is seen as a key to his surrender to the lure of Nazism; for Foucault, it purportedly renders him incapable of providing any philosophical basis for the defense of the values of modernity. In this volume, both Jana Sawicki and Steven Hicks focus on the question of nihilism in Heidegger and Foucault. The issue of nihilism is, of course, a contentious one, with both Heidegger and Foucault providing us with different meditations linking modern nihilism to the very humanism and metaphysic of the subject that Habermas champions. However, while Heidegger's critique of humanism becomes integral to his critique of modern technology, the reign of *das Ge-Stell,* which for him enframes modernity, Foucault makes a sharp distinction between humanism and key aspects of modernity. Thus, for Foucault, it is necessary to distinguish humanism and the Enlightenment, the philosophical ethos he describes "as a permanent critique of our historical era."[53] Thus, Foucault celebrates that facet of modernity he links to Kant and the Enlightenment, enshrined in the task of a permanent critique of ourselves, and which he rigorously distinguishes from disciplinarity, normalization, and technologies of domination. Heidegger, by contrast, envisages a seamless web consisting of humanism, the Enlightenment, and modern technology as the hallmarks of a nihilistic world, which is shaped by a "*disempowering of the spirit,*" and its "dissolution" as a fount of creativity and dynamism.[54]

Beyond the confrontation between Foucault and Heidegger over their very different evaluations of modernity and its immanent tendencies, which certainly has a political dimension, it seems that a Foucault/Heidegger *Auseinandersetzung* cannot avoid the issue of these two thinkers' very different political commitments and engagements. Heidegger's politics in the early 1930s were linked to those of right-wing revolutionaries such as Ernst Jünger and Carl Schmitt, and his entanglement with Nazism and the Hitler state—however short-lived it may have been—is indisputable.[55] Foucault's political commitments, by contrast, were all on the left, first as a student in the Communist Party, then as a Maoist sympathizer, later in movements aimed at the reform of psychiatric and penal institutions, and finally in the struggle for gay rights. One of the issues raised by a philosopher's political engagements is the question of the relationship between biography and philosophy, between life and works, a matter that has had a particular impact on the recent evaluation of Heidegger.[56] Foucault himself weighed in on this question in a 1983 interview, and thereby helped to illuminate this issue in a way that has a profound impact on how one envisages an *Auseinandersetzung.* Acknowledging Habermas's observations on the impact that Heidegger's Nazism had on him, Foucault pointed out that he had recently had a similar experience "with Max Pohlenz, who heralded the universal values of Stoicism all his life," and yet insisted in 1934 on the intimate link between "true humanism" and the "*Führersideal.*"[57] Yet, for Foucault, Pohlenz's despicable political behavior did nothing to condemn Stoicism. Foucault's argument is especially pertinent here:

> But I think we must reckon with several facts: there is a very tenuous "analytic" link between a philosophical conception and the concrete political attitude of some one who is appealing to it; the "best" theories do not constitute a very effective protection against disastrous political choices; certain great themes such as "humanism" can be used for any end whatever—for example, to show with what gratitude Pohlenz would have greeted Hitler.[58]

It is precisely the complexity and tenuousness of this link between philosophy and politics and the nonreducibility of the one to the other that should guide us when we confront the very different political engagements of Foucault and Heidegger.

Nonetheless, that very complexity has been ignored, particularly in the case of Heidegger, both by those who have argued that Heidegger's Nazism was extrinsic to his philosophy and who claim that philosophy and politics must be kept separate, and by those who have claimed that Heidegger's *Denken* is directly tied to a fascist worldview and that his philosophy can be dismissed as a manifestation of his Nazism. The claim of the later Foucault that philosophy is a way of life, an art of living, means that, for him, there can be no absolute separation between life and thought: "[A]t every moment, step by step, one must confront what one is thinking and saying with what one is doing, with what one is."[59] However, one's life, one's ethos, understood—in Foucault's terms—as "a manner of being,"[60] is not exhausted by a specific political choice. In the case of Heidegger, his life is not reducible to his decision to accept the *Rektorat* and to join the Nazi Party. And given Foucault's strictures on the tenuousness of the link between a "philosophical conception" and a "concrete political attitude," philosophy cannot be reduced to politics.

Nevertheless, if philosophy cannot be reduced to politics, neither can a link between the two be ignored. Thus, Richard Wolin has argued that "Heidegger's involvement with National Socialism—which was of the order of deep-seated, existential commitment—was far from being an adventitious, merely biographical episode. Instead, it was *rooted in the innermost tendencies of his thought*."[61] While Wolin goes on to assert that "[t]his claim in no way entails the assumption that Nazism is somehow a necessary and inevitable outgrowth of the philosophy of *Being and Time*,"[62] he does assert that Nazism "stood in an 'essential' relationship to his philosophical project as a whole."[63] While this claim has been forcefully challenged by a number of interpreters,[64] and specifically in this volume by William V. Spanos and Leslie Paul Thiele, beyond the issue of the connection between Heidegger's politics and his philosophy, it nonetheless raises the question: can we take Heidegger's ideas seriously *if* he was a Nazi? After all, the thrust of Wolin's, and most recently Johannes Fritsche's, claims, quite apart from the cogency of their readings, is that we need not, indeed probably should not, take Heidegger seriously as a thinker; that his *Denken* is fatally compromised by "his" Nazism. This is particularly an issue on the political and cultural Left, where ever since the publication of Victor Farías's *Heidegger and Nazism*, as William Spanos points out in his essay in this volume, "'Heidegger' and 'Foucault' have come to be represented by the Left as incommensurably opposed to one another, indeed as a binary opposition in which the latter has been privileged over the former." Such a view constitutes a formidable obstacle to precisely the *Auseinandersetzung* between Foucault and Heidegger for which we are calling. On this point, too, Foucault's comments seem pertinent: "I have never been too concerned about people who say: 'you are borrowing ideas from Nietzsche; well Nietzsche was used by the Nazis, therefore.'"[65] Despite the distinction between being *used* by the Nazis (Nietzsche) and *being* a Nazi (the claim made about Heidegger), the thrust of Foucault's argument nonetheless is relevant to the Heidegger case as well: "The key to the personal poetic attitude of the philosopher is not to be sought in his ideas, as if it could be deduced from them, but rather in his philosophy-as-life, in his philosophical life, his ethos."[66] One could, therefore, conclude that there was, indeed, a powerful link between Heidegger's ethos—short-lived or not—and Nazism, without that vitiating the importance of his ideas; without that leading to the conclusion that we need not, or should not, read Heidegger or that we cannot, or must not, take his philosophical ideas seriously.

The germ for such an *Auseinandersetzung* as we envisage already exists. In addition to Kevin Hill's essay, already mentioned, both Jana Sawicki and Rudi Visker have confronted Heidegger and Foucault in essays reprinted in the present volume. Moreover, Hubert Dreyfus inaugurated just such an *Auseindersetzung* in his now classic essay, "Being and Power," which he has expanded for the present volume by considering the many responses that it has provoked. The inclusion of this prehistory of a confrontation beween Foucault and Heidegger sets the stage for the thoroughgoing *Auseinandersetzung* that we seek to orchestrate.

We now want to turn to the actual contributions to this volume, a brief overview of which will provide an indication of the possibilities to be opened up by a Foucault/Heidegger *Auseinandersetzung*. We have already pointed to Foucault's own statement, in his final interview, to the effect that for him Heidegger had been "the essential philosopher." It is not surprising that those comments would shape the *Auseinandersetzung* between Foucault and Heidegger, though, as we have already indicated, they may constitute a woodpath, a *Holzweg,* to use a Heideggerian trope, which despite a promising beginning may compel us to retrace our steps, and even lead nowhere. Nonetheless, they provide a link between our two thinkers, and—as we have already indicated—constitute a focal point for several of the essays in this volume, having acquired something of a canonical status.

Hubert Dreyfus provides a substantially revised version of his classic interpretation of Heidegger and Foucault, in which he points to the parallels between being in Heidegger and power in Foucault. Moreover, Dreyfus claims that there are important links between Heidegger's vision of modernity shaped by a tendency toward a "total ordering in technicity," what he terms "total mobilization," and Foucault's vision of modernity shaped by a "totalizing tendency of disciplinary power as 'normalization.'" These parallels notwithstanding, Dreyfus also signals the difference between Heidegger's emphasis on how "things," objects, show up, as opposed to Foucault's focus on how subjects are constituted, in different epochs or regimes. In Dreyfus's view, the later Foucault's emphasis on a self-overcoming for its own sake is indicative of the fact that "although the structure of Foucault's thought is thoroughly Heideggerian, Nietzsche won out in the end."

Meanwhile, both Jana Sawicki and Steven Hicks wrestle with the issue of nihilism in Heidegger and Foucault. Sawicki finds the claim that each of these two thinkers is a nihilist because of their respective assaults on humanism to be "misguided": "Neither Foucault nor Heidegger is a nihilist, but for different reasons." Heidegger links nihilism to calculative thinking, to which he provides an alternative: meditative thinking. Foucault escapes nihilism because he does not totalize the reign of modern technology, but rather focuses only on "particular practices within it." Starting from Nietzsche's meditation on nihilism, Hicks finds Heidegger falling into a "passive nihilism," while Foucault, by contrast, seems to slip into an "incomplete nihilism," from which he is perhaps rescued by his commitment to a life of continual self-overcoming. For Hicks, "a critical, dialogic encounter between Nietzsche, Heidegger, and Foucault . . . is needed to point the way 'out of the abyss' of our current cultural dilemmas to a 'new and different way of thinking and being'—a way that leads beyond nihilism."

Ladelle McWhorter contests what she sees as the dominant reading of Heidegger and Foucault, in which it is claimed that the former believes in the primacy of the subject, while the latter denies there is anything like a subject at all. Instead, McWhorter maintains that a "convergence between the two philosophers can usefully and fruitfully occur," provided we develop "a reading of Foucault that dispels the widely held idea that he repudiates the notion of subjectivity *in toto* and a reading of Heidegger that does not take the analytic of Dasein to be ahistorical." Thus, for McWhorter, to think with both these philosophers is to affirm history above essence.

Both Béatrice Han and Michael Schwartz grapple with the relation of the early Foucault (especially the Foucault of *The Order of Things*) to Heidegger. Han focuses on the relation of both these thinkers to

Kant, and his invention of "transcendental finitude." While according to Han, both Heidegger and Foucault see Kant's Copernican turn as trapped within a vicious circle in which transcendental finitude is "dependent on hidden empirical determinations which themselves are then (wrongly) taken as foundational," Heidegger, too, ends up making a priori claims about the possibility of knowledge, thereby replicating the very logic of Kant's Copernican turn, and Foucault does no better in overcoming what Han sees as his hopeless blurring between two forms of finitude, "in which empirical limitations are made to count as transcendental conditions of possibility." For Han, we cannot be happy with either Heidegger's or Foucault's response to this dilemma: the mystical turn of the former or the genealogical turn of the latter. While acknowledging that "Foucault's project in *The Order of Things* is decisively Heideggerian," Schwartz goes on to argue that Foucault sees Heidegger's history of being as an example of a quest for origins, with its foundational overtones, and seeks to "distance archaeological analysis from the history of Being." This step will allow Foucault to explore new lines of thought informed by his critical encounter with Heidegger, and put the analyses of epistemes in *The Order of Things* behind him.

If Schwartz emphasizes the tension between Foucault, especially the later Foucault, and the Heidegger of the history of being, Stuart Elden focuses on the parallels between Heidegger, particularly the later Heidegger, and the Foucault of the genealogies. While Heidegger after the turn rejects the Kantianism of *Being and Time* and "becomes a historical ontologist," Foucault's genealogical turn means that his project should not be read—as it most often is—as a historical sociology, but rather as a historical ontology.

Leslie Paul Thiele insists on the links between Foucault and Heidegger in the realm of moral and political judgment. While both Foucault and Heidegger "provide us with the resources for prudential thought and action," Thiele argues that each rejects the "axiomatic ethics or politics of first principles" that is constitutive of Western political philosophy. Instead, they each "implicitly highlight the importance of moral and political judgment by providing compelling narratives that foster its cultivation." In addition to opening the space for the production of "a viable (anti)foundation for prudential ethico-political life," a Foucault/Heidegger *Auseinandersetzung,* which eschews the quest "to get them right in a biographical or exegetical sense," will allow us to "combine Foucauldian surface with Heideggerian depth, genealogical insight with ontological wisdom," in the service of creating ethically and politically informed narratives.

William Spanos argues that "Heidegger's ontological and Foucault's sociopolitical orientation toward post-Enlightenment modernity 'belong together,' not in a dialogic harmony, but in strife . . . as *polemos* that *always already* opens out (dis-closes what is latent but in some degree or other invisible to each's discourse) rather than closes down by way of a decisive victory of one over the other." For Spanos, "the planetary technology of power" that shapes Western modernity is neither the consequence of philosophy, as Heidegger claims, nor of the episteme of the Enlightenment, as Foucault argues: "It is, rather, as a reading of Heidegger with Foucault or Foucault with Heidegger suggests, the consequence of both." And the point of departure for the later triumph of these tendencies is to be found, according to Spanos, in tendencies—both philosophical and sociopolitical—that go back to ancient Rome.

Rejecting an exercise in intellectual history, Edith Wyschogrod reads Foucault and Heidegger by seeing "each thinker as questioner of the other." Moreover, both of these thinkers are particularly concerned with the act of questioning itself. In her staging of a Foucault/Heidegger *Auseinandersetzung,* Wyschogrod emphasizes both thinkers' immersion in ancient thought and early Christianity. For Wyschogrod, both Foucault and Heidegger, in very different ways, embody an "askesis of self-transformation," not an asceticism linked to Christianity, but a shaping that both frees "knowledge and truth from embedded contexts of repressive epistemological constraints and their ancillary ethical implications," and permits "a bringing of corporeality cogently into the open."

Rudi Visker also seeks to avoid the history of ideas: "Instead of searching, in the tradition of a comparative study, for parallels between Foucault and Heidegger, I would rather establish where those texts already deconstruct themselves." Because, for Foucault, every discourse lays down its own order of truth, and there is no truth outside of discourse, Visker claims that there is no clear basis upon which a critique of a given order can be mounted, unless it is a rejection of any and all order whatsoever, in the name "of a sort of primordial spontaneity of a body which does not have to be bridled by any order." Heidegger, by contrast, according to Visker, "does not abandon the notion of order, but deepens it and gives the process of ordering a name," "*a-letheia,*" thereby providing an answer to Foucault's impasse.

Charles E. Scott provocatively links Heidegger's meditation on "*Geist*" and "*phusis*" to "physicality," and then shows how Foucault's own focus on physicality is "in concert with significant aspects of Heidegger's thinking in striking ways." Moreover, according to Scott, Heidegger's subversion of the priority of subjectivity permits us to see how Foucault provides "an alternative to a position that privileges a historicized subjectivity." In the end, "both Heidegger's and Foucault's thought lift the burdens of eternity and universality from thought and allow in the process of thinking the, for Western thought, strange lightness of open encompassment." One facet of the "camaraderie" between Foucault's and Heidegger's thought, which is a leitmotiv of Scott's essay, lies in the way that Heidegger's own tendencies to apodictic pronouncements have been softened by his *Auseinandersetzung* with Foucault; Heidegger's *Denken* has incorporated a fragility, a lightness, a luminosity, that is not only absent from most readings, but that also owes a great deal to Foucault.

The essays collected in this volume constitute a beginning, an opening, to a Foucault/Heidegger *Auseinandersetzung*. Beyond the several facets of what we have designated as an *Auseinandersetzung,* agonism, openness, questioning, problematization, in contrast to the canons of intellectual history, which privileges exegesis, or polemic, which seeks victory over an opponent, the specific parameters of the encounter between Foucault and Heidegger should be expanded to include a more far-reaching confrontation over the political commitments of each and their relationship to their projects as a whole. Similarly, the questions raised by both thinkers' engagement with the ancients should be deepened and expanded. While both these issues are touched on in this volume, our efforts to solicit essays specifically devoted to these two questions came up short. The very different notions of history and philosophy in Heidegger and Foucault each deserve the detailed attention of scholars, as well.

Perhaps especially important is another issue that has arisen in the first stages of this Foucault/Heidegger *Auseinandersetzung*. We are speaking of a pronounced tendency to incorporate one more binary opposition into the very heart of the ongoing *Auseinandersetzung,* a binary opposition so firmly rooted in the tradition of Western thinking that it is taken-for-granted: that between *surface* and *depth*. In the case of the Foucault/Heidegger *Auseinandersetzung,* this manifests itself as the opposition between Foucault's purported focus on the ontic level, in contrast to Heidegger's privileging of the ontological level. Too often, the result is a tendency to have Heidegger provide the ontological "depth" needed to ground Foucault's ontic focus. Given our philosophical propensity to attempt to penetrate beneath the "surface," to reach the "depth," a propensity enshrined in our ordinary language, where, for example, one refers to a "deep" thinker, in contrast to a "superficial" one, it is not surprising to see this privileging of the ontological over the ontic transmogrified into a contrast between a focus on surface and depth in the thinking of Foucault and Heidegger.

Yet Heidegger, recognizing that this very tendency has its probable inception in one facet of Platonic metaphysics, spent his whole life seeking to reorient thinking away from its quest for foundations. Indeed, though the terminology changes, Heidegger always retains his early focus on "facticity" and "factical life." For his part, Foucault wanted not to reverse the terms of this binary opposition between surface and depth, privileging the surface, but to *bypass* it entirely. For him, surface folds into depth, and depth into surface, like a Möbius strip. If one theme of the Foucault/Heidegger *Auseinandersetzung* staged in these pages has been the danger of the kind of thinking based on binary oppositions that has haunted the West, perhaps the next stage of this confrontation can begin by exploding the binary opposition between surface and depth.

Notes

1. Jürgen Habermas, *The Philosophical Discourse of Modernity: Twelve Lectures* (Cambridge: The MIT Press, 1987), 254.

2. See Stuart Elden, *Mapping the Present: Heidegger, Foucault, and the Project of a Spatial History* (London: Athlone, 2001).

3. Herbert Schnädelbach, *Philosophy in Germany: 1831–1933* (Cambridge: Cambridge University Press, 1984), 1.

4. Jürgen Habermas, "Work and Weltanschauung: The Heidegger Controversy from a German Perspective," in *The New Conservatism: Cultural Criticism and the Historians' Debate* (Cambridge: The MIT Press, 1989), 142–43.

5. François Dosse, *History of Structuralism,* vol. 1, *The Rising Sign, 1945–1966* (Minneapolis: University of Minnesota Press, 1997), 41.

6. Didier Eribon, *Michel Foucault et ses contemporains* (Paris: Fayard, 1994), 18.

7. Rux Martin, "Truth, Power, Self: An Interview with Michel Foucault, October 25, 1982," in *Technologies of the Self: A Seminar with Michel Foucault,* ed. Luther H. Martin, Huck Gutman, and Patrick H. Hutton (Amherst: University of Massachusetts Press, 1988), 12–13.

8. Michel Foucault, "The Return of Morality," in *Politics, Philosophy, Culture: Interviews and Other Writings, 1977–1984* (New York and London: Routledge, 1990), 250.

9. Jean Zoungrana, *Michel Foucault un parcours croisé: Lévi-Strauss, Heidegger* (Paris: L'Harmattan, 1998), 279.

10. This latter volume was then reworked by Foucault and published as *Mental Illness and Psychology* in 1962. It is this version that was subsequently translated into English, though over the objections of its author.

11. Jacques Derrida, "Politics and Friendship: An Interview with Jacques Derrida," in *The Althusserian Legacy*, ed. E. Ann Kaplan and Michael Sprinker (London and New York: Verso, 1993), 190.

12. Paul Rabinow, private communication to the editors, 13 September 1998. The encounters to which Rabinow refers were the discussions in Berkeley between Foucault, Hubert Dreyfus, and himself.

13. Gilles Deleuze, *Foucault* (Minneapolis: University of Minnesota Press, 1988), 129.

14. Michael Kelly, introduction to *Critique and Power: Recasting the Foucault/Habermas Debate* (Cambridge: The MIT Press, 1994), 9.

15. Ibid., 199.

16. Ibid., 290. Zoungrana's emphasis on the influence of Heidegger on Foucault was preceded by Hubert L. Dreyfus and Paul Rabinow's insistence that Heidegger was influential in the development of Foucault's thinking. See Hubert L. Dreyfus and Paul Rabinow, *Michel Foucault: Beyond Structuralism and Hermeneutics* (Chicago: University of Chicago Press, 1983). Moreover, Foucault himself acknowledged the significance of Dreyfus and Rabinow's claim: "Of course it was quite true. . . . " (Martin, "Truth, Power, Self," 12). This link seems to clash with Dosse's claim that Foucault dealt a final blow to the phenomenological project, out of which Heidegger's own *Denken* emerged. However, when we realize that Foucault's own indebtedness to the tradition represented by Bachelard, Cavaillès, and Canguilhem had its basis in their rejection of Cartesianism, and that Heidegger's *Denkweg* was shaped both by his own deconstruction of Descartes and a break with Husserl in large part provoked by the latter's own rootedness in Cartesianism, it is possible to reconcile Dosse's claim with that of Dreyfus and Rabinow.

17. Martin Heidegger, *Introduction to Metaphysics*, trans. Gregory Fried and Richard Polt (New Haven and London: Yale University Press, 2000), 65. This translation, with its careful attention to philosophical terminology and conceptualization and its German-English glossary, allows the Anglophone reader far better access to Heidegger's thinking than the earlier one by Ralph Manheim.

18. Ibid. In translating Heraclitus's fragment 80, Heidegger links "confrontation," "setting-apart-from-each-other," and "bringing-together" as all within the purview of *Auseinandersetzung*. Ibid., 177.

19. Martin Heidegger, *Nietzsche: Der Wille zur Macht als Kunst, Gesamtausgabe*, (Frankfurt am Main: Vittorio Klostermann, 1985), 43:279 and 275. We are grateful to Gregory Fried for pointing out these two passages. See Gregory Fried, *Heidegger's Polemos: From Being to Politics* (New Haven and London: Yale University Press, 2000), 16–17.

20. Theodore Kisiel, *The Genesis of Heidegger's Being and Time* (Berkeley and Los Angeles: University of California Press, 1993), 225.

21. Ibid., 313.

22. Charles E. Scott, "On Thinking," in *Interrogating the Tradition: Hermeneutics and the History of Philosophy*, ed. Charles E. Scott and John Salis (Albany: State University of New York Press, 2000), 50.

23. Kevin Hill, "Foucault's Critique of Heidegger," *Philosophy Today* (winter 1989):

334. Hill does not indicate why, if Heidegger was the object of criticism in these Foucauldian texts, there is not extensive reference to him.

24. Lucien Goldmann, *Lukács and Heidegger: Towards a New Philosophy* (London: Routledge & Kegan Paul, 1977), 29. Goldmann's insistence on an absolute opposition between Heidegger and Lukács, which is not a facet of *Auseinandersetzung,* would seem to be dictated by his own adherence to Lukács's view that Heidegger was an imperialist or fascist thinker, and hence the confrontation between Heidegger and a Marxist could not have been agonal, but rather would have to have taken modern war as its model.

25. See Hermann Mörchen, *Macht und Herrschaft im Denken von Heidegger und Adorno* (Stuttgart: Klett-Cotta, 1980), and Hermann Mörchen, *Adorno und Heidegger: Untersuchung einer philosophischen Kommunikationsverweigerung* (Stuttgart: Klett-Cotta, 1981).

26. Martin Heidegger, *Hölderlin's Hymn "The Ister"* (Bloomington and Indianapolis: Indiana University Press, 1996), 142. Here, Heidegger is speaking of Hölderlin's own dialogue with Pindar. We are indebted to Will McNeill, "*Heimat*: Heidegger on the Threshold," in *Heidegger toward the Turn: Essays on the Work of the 1930s*, ed. James Risser (Albany: State University of New York Press, 1999) for the above reference, and to the dimension of *Auseinandersetzung* as a dialogue with what is foreign, though McNeill's focus is on the concept of *Heimat,* whereas we wish to emphasize the facet of dialogue or encounter with the other as a hallmark of thinking.

27. Michel Foucault, "Politics and Ethics: An Interview," in *The Foucault Reader,* ed. Paul Rabinow (New York: Pantheon Books, 1984), 375–76.

28. Scott, "On Thinking," 50.

29. Ibid.

30. Ibid., 50–51.

31. Michel Foucault, "Polemics, Politics, and Problematizations," in Rabinow, *The Foucault Reader,* 382.

32. Ibid., 381.

33. Ibid., 382.

34. Heidegger, *Nietzsche: Der Wille zur Macht als Kunst,* 277.

35. Ibid.

36. Heidegger links this vision explicitly to his own emphasis on *Auseinandersetzung.*

37. Michel Foucault, "From Torture to Cellblock" in *Foucault Live: Collected Interviews, 1961–1984,* ed. Sylvère Lotringer (New York: Semiotext(e), 1996), 149. This was said in 1975. Three years later, Foucault reiterated and elaborated on this same point: "I write things which seem usable. In a word, usable in a different way, by different people, in different countries in certain cases" (Michel Foucault, "Michel Foucault and Zen: A Stay in a Zen Temple [1978]" in *Religion and Culture,* ed. Jeremy R. Carrette [New York: Routledge, 1999], 111).

38. Michel Foucault, "Who Are You, Professor Foucault?" in *Religion and Culture,* 87.

39. In "Foucault's Critique of Heidegger," Kevin Hill focuses on several issues, among them death, hermeneutics, finitude, history, and the possibility of an ethics, though less from the perspective of an *Auseinandersetzung,* as we conceive it, than from that of a critique of Heidegger, especially as it is to be found in the early writings of Foucault.

40. Michel Foucault, "Philosophy and the Death of God," in *Religion and Culture,* 85.

41. Michel Foucault, "Who Are You, Professor Foucault?" 97. Nietzsche's impact, to which we have already pointed in discussing Foucault's final interview and its now canonical statement on the influence of Heidegger is perhaps best captured in this striking formulation of Foucault's: "I am simply Nietzschean, and I try to see, on a certain

number of points, and to the extent that it is possible, with the aid of Nietzsche's texts—but also with anti-Nietzschean theses (which are nevertheless Nietzschean!)—what can be done in this or that domain" (Michel Foucault, "The Return of Morality," 251). With all due regard for the Foucauldian irony, to which we have called attention and which seems present in his claim to be "simply Nietzschean," the profound impact of Nietzsche on Foucault is substantiated by the repeated and detailed references to Nietzsche throughout Foucault's writings. For a detailed account of the impact of Nietzsche on Foucault, see Michael Mahon, *Foucault's Nietzschean Genealogy: Truth, Power, and the Subject* (Albany: State University of New York Press, 1992).

42. Martin Heidegger, *Nietzsche,* vol. 4, *Nihilism* (San Francisco: Harper & Row, Publishers, 1982), 138. This is Heidegger's 1940 lecture course on "European Nihilism."

43. Ibid., 123.

44. Ibid., 129.

45. Ibid., 130.

46. Michel Foucault, "Subjectivity and Truth," in *The Politics of Truth,* ed. Sylvère Lotringer (New York: Semiotext(e), 1997), 178–79.

47. Hubert L. Dreyfus, "On the Ordering of Things: Being and Power in Heidegger and Foucault," in *Michel Foucault, Philosopher,* trans. Timothy J. Armstrong (New York: Routledge, 1992), 81.

48. Ibid., 92–93.

49. Michel Foucault, *The Use of Pleasure,* vol. 2 of *The History of Sexuality* (New York: Vintage Books, 1990), 11.

50. Michel Foucault, *The Order of Things: An Archaeology of the Human Sciences* (New York: Vintage Books, 1994), 387.

51. Michel Foucault, "The Ethics of the Concern for Self as a Practice of Freedom," in *Foucault Live,* 443–44.

52. Michel Foucault, "On the Genealogy of Ethics," in Dreyfus and Rabinow, *Michel Foucault,* 231. Kevin Hill also points to what he sees as Foucault's criticism of Heidegger's preoccupation with origins, with the result that "Heidegger can only despair that we are not *yet* ready to understand our origin, which now gets projected into the indefinite future . . . which Foucault believes can never come" (Hill, "Foucault's Critique of Heidegger," 340).

53. Michel Foucault, "What Is Enlightenment?" in Rabinow, *The Foucault Reader,* 42.

54. Martin Heidegger, *Introduction to Metaphysics,* 47.

55. For an overview of Heidegger's ontological politics in this period, see Alan Milchman and Alan Rosenberg, "Resoluteness and Ambiguity: Martin Heidegger's Ontological Politics, 1933–35," in *The Philosophical Forum* 25, no.1 (fall 1993):72–93.

56. For a discussion of the ramifications of Heidegger's entanglement with Nazism and its impact on the way we read him, see Alan Milchman and Alan Rosenberg, "The Philosophical Stakes of the Heidegger Wars, Part I: Methodologies for the Reading of Heidegger," in *The Journal of Value Inquiry* 27 (1993):509–20; and "The Philosophical Stakes of the Heidegger Wars, Part II: Ethical and Political Ramifications of the Reading of Heidegger," in *The Journal of Value Inquiry* 28 (1994):443–54.

57. Michel Foucault, "Politics and Ethics: An Interview," 373–74.

58. Ibid., 374

59. Ibid.

60. Ibid., 377.

61. Richard Wolin, *The Politics of Being: The Political Thought of Martin Heidegger* (New York: Columbia University Press, 1990), 66.

62. Ibid.

63. Ibid., 8. This conclusion is expressed even more forcefully and on the basis of an

extremely close reading of the text of *Being and Time* by Johannes Fritsche: "[O]ne can hardly imagine a philosophical work that leads into National Socialism more directly than Heidegger's *Being and Time*." See Johannes Fritsche, *Historical Destiny and National Socialism in Heidegger's "Being and Time"* (Berkeley and Los Angeles: University of California Press, 1999), 140.

64. See, for example, Fred R. Dallmayr, "Ontology of Freedom: Heidegger and Political Philosophy," in *Polis and Praxis: Exercises in Contemporary Political Theory* (Massachusetts: The MIT Press, 1984); Fred Dallmayr, *The Other Heidegger* (Ithaca and London: Cornell University Press, 1993); William V. Spanos, *Heidegger and Criticism: Retrieving the Cultural Politics of Destruction* (Minneapolis and London: University of Minnesota Press, 1993); and Leslie Paul Thiele, *Timely Meditations: Martin Heidegger and Postmodern Politics* (Princeton, New Jersey: Princeton University Press, 1995).

65. Foucault, "Politics and Ethics," 374.

66. Ibid.

"Being and Power" Revisited

Hubert L. Dreyfus

At the heart of Heidegger's thought is the notion of being, and the same could be said of power in the works of Foucault. The history of being gives Heidegger a perspective from which to understand how in our modern world *things* have been turned into *objects*. Foucault transforms Heidegger's focus on *things* to a focus on *selves* and how they became *subjects*.[1] And, just as Heidegger offers a history of being, culminating in the technological understanding of being, to help us understand and overcome our current way of dealing with things as objects and resources, Foucault analyzes several regimes of power, culminating in bio-power, to help us free ourselves from understanding ourselves as autonomous subjects and disciplined bodies.

These rough parallels suggest that it might be illuminating to see how far the comparison of Heidegger's "Being" with Foucault's "Power" can be pushed. Do these terms designate equivalent functions? Do Heidegger's epochs in his history of being match Foucault's regimes in his genealogy of power? To what extent do their interpretations of our history lead these thinkers to criticize our current cultural condition in similar ways? What does each see as the danger? How does each envisage resistance? And do these thinkers differ in any important ways?

After all, Heidegger's early support of National Socialism and his later recommendation of political passivity seem totally opposed to Foucault's emphasis on social freedom and his political activism. Obviously Heidegger is some sort of conservative and Foucault is clearly on the Left. But lest the striking difference between Heidegger's and Foucault's political attitudes make my project seem hopelessly misguided, we must remember Foucault's comment on Heidegger in his last interview:

> For me Heidegger has always been the essential philosopher. . . . My entire philosophical development was determined by my reading of Heidegger. But I recognize that Nietzsche prevailed over him.[2]

This last remark of Foucault's, when his immanent death freed him to tell the truth even in Paris, forces us to ask how Foucault, in spite of his radically different political ethos, could nonetheless claim, in some important sense, to have once been a Heideggerian.[3] But we also need to ask in what sense Nietzsche prevailed in the end.

The Functioning of Being and Power

It is important to realize at the outset that for Heidegger, being is not a substance or a process. Being, in early Heidegger, is "that on the basis of which beings are already understood."[4] One might say that a culture's understanding of being is its style of life manifest in the way its everyday practices are coordinated. A culture's understanding of being allows people and things to show up *as* something; in Homeric Greece, for example, people showed up as heroes or slaves and things as flashing up to be admired, whereas in the Middle Ages, people were understood as saints or sinners and things were creatures to be mastered and interpreted.

Put generally, the shared practices into which we are socialized provide a background understanding of what counts as things, what counts as human beings, and what it makes sense to do, on the basis of which we can direct our actions toward particular things and people. Thus the understanding of being creates what Heidegger calls a clearing *(Lichtung)* in which things and people can be encountered. Heidegger calls the unnoticed way that the clearing both limits and opens up what can show up and what can be done its "unobtrusive governance" *(Waltens)*.[5]

For Heidegger the history of being in the West has been the history of misunderstandings of the clearing. From the pre-Socratic era on, philosophers have sensed that something beyond ordinary beings was responsible for their existence as anything, but since the clearing, like the illumination in a room, must always stay in the background—or, as Heidegger puts it, withdraw—to do its job of letting things show us, philosophers since Plato have replaced the clearing with a highest being that is the ground of beings and the source of their intelligibility. For Plato the highest being was The Good; for Aristotle, The Unmoved Mover; for Christians, The Creator God; and, after the Enlightenment, it was man himself. Heidegger calls all these attempts to replace the clearing with a "beingest being" onto-theology.[6] We will see later that, according to Foucault, power has suffered a parallel misunderstanding.

Indeed, many of Foucault's difficult remarks concerning power make sense if we take him to be getting at a social clearing, with an emphasis on the way the everyday practices of individuals and groups are coordinated so as to produce, perpetuate, and delimit what people can think, do, and be. For Foucault, power, like Heidegger's being, is no fixed entity or institution, but is incarnated in historical social practices. "One needs to be nominalistic," he tells us. "Power is not an institution, and not a structure; neither is it a certain strength we are endowed with; it is the name that one attributes to a complex strategical situation in a particular society."[7] This strategical situation arises from specific individuals and groups opposing one another. These actions, taken together, open a social space in which people, things, and the real are defined. Like the clearing in Heidegger's account, power is productive. Foucault tells us: "[P]ower produces; it produces reality," that is, it governs what things and people show us *as* and what it makes sense to do.[8]

Thus, for Foucault, power, as opposed to violence, controls actions while nonetheless leaving them free:

> Power is exercised only over free subjects, and only insofar as they are free. By this we mean individual or collective subjects who are faced with a field of possibilities in which several ways of behaving, several reactions and diverse comportments may be realized.[9]

Like Heidegger, Foucault speaks of this nonviolent way of guiding action as a mode of governance:

> Basically power is less a confrontation between two adversaries or the linking of one to the other than a question of government. . . . To govern, in this sense, is to structure the possible field of action of others.[10]

One might say, paraphrasing Heidegger, that power is that on the basis of which human beings already understand each other. As Foucault puts it:

> In the idea of governmentality, I am aiming at the totality of practices, by which one can constitute, define, organize, instrumentalize the strategies which individuals in their liberty can have in regard to each other.[11]

Since Foucault is not interested in how *things* show up but exclusively in *people,* "Power," which is normally used to describe the way governments *govern* people's actions, seems an appropriate, if perhaps misleading, name for what controls the way people understand themselves and others. It should be clear that some type of power in this ontological sense is essential to any society. According to Foucault, "A society without power relations can only be an abstraction."[12]

Seinsgeschichte and Genealogy

For everyday practices to give meaning to people's lives and unite them in a community, something must collect the scattered practices of the group, unify them into coherent possibilities for action, and hold them up to the people. People can then act and relate themselves to each other in terms of this exemplar. Heidegger calls an object that performs this function a work of art. To illustrate an art work working, Heidegger cites the Greek temple. The temple held up to the Greeks what counted as real, Heidegger says, and so established meaningful differences such as victory and disgrace, in respect to which the Greeks could orient their actions.

Generalizing the idea of a work of art, Heidegger holds that "there must always be some being in the open [the clearing], something that is, in which the openness takes its stand and attains its constancy."[13] Let us call such special things cultural paradigms. A cultural paradigm is any being in the clearing that discloses a new world or, by refocusing the current cultural practices, discloses the current world anew. Heidegger mentions five types of cultural paradigms—works of art, acts of statesmen, nearness of a god, sacrifice of a god, and the words of a thinker. For brevity's sake, we shall concern ourselves only with the thinker's words.

The thinker, by being receptive to the current practices (both central and marginal), is able to reconfigure the practices by making the marginal central and the central marginal, and so bring about a new shared style or understanding of being. Heidegger calls the new beginning a founding leap—an *Ur-sprung*—that, by taking up marginal practices from the past, opens a new clearing:

> [T]his unmediated character of a beginning, the peculiarity of a leap out of the unmediable, does not exclude but rather includes the fact that the beginning prepares itself for the longest time and wholly inconspicuously.[14]

For Heidegger, the words of the thinker as a cultural paradigm are an inexhaustible object of interpretation, not because the thinker was a genius or the text too full of meanings, but rather because there is a necessary absence in the text. Just because the thinker manifests the current understanding of being, he names what is so pervasive and embodied it cannot be made fully explicit. The new understanding of being thus pervades the work without being thematized. What is important is the way the thinker's words are *attuned* to the background understanding. Heidegger's clearest formulation of this difficult claim is in his essay "Reflection in Metaphysics":

> The thinking of thinkers is neither something going on in "heads" nor is it the product of such heads. One can always consider thought historiographically in accordance with such viewpoints, and appeal to the correctness of this consideration. However, one does not thus think thinking as the thinking of being. Recollection of the history of being returns to the claim of the soundless voice of being and to the manner of its attuning.[15]

The thinker's unthought, as Heidegger calls it, is not a positive, but a hidden truth. Rather, the text manifests a necessary structural absence.

> The thinker can never himself say what is most of all his own. It must remain unsaid, because what is sayable receives its determination from what is not sayable. (77–78)

Heidegger adds:

> The historicity of a thinker, which is not a matter of him but of being, has its measure in the original loyalty of the thinker to his inner limitation. *Not* to know this inner limitation, not to know it thanks to the nearness of what is unsaid and unsayable, is the hidden gift of being to the rare thinkers who are called to the path of thought. (78)

There is, then, no hidden truth to explicate; the understanding of being, the background intelligibility, the attunement or style of the age, is on the surface in all of its practices. The thinker in his receptivity experiences what is going on in the practices and is able in his work to focus that style, but unlike a lucid agent, a thinker is never able to articulate explicitly what he is doing. Yet precisely because his work can change the understanding of being, a thinker is more effective than the most persistent agent. Likewise, the interpreter or preserver who returns to such founding thinkers can, by taking up practices from the heritage in a new way, contribute to changing the present practices.

Foucault in "What Is an Author?" holds a view remarkably close to Heidegger's when he rejects commentary and introduces what he takes to be the right kind of return to the text of a founder of a domain of discursivity:

> If we return, it is because of a basic and constructive omission, an omission that is not the result of accident or incomprehension. . . . It is always a return to a text in itself, specifically, to a primary and unadorned text with particular attention to those things registered in the interstices of the text, its gaps and absences.[16]

Foucault also sees the effect such an interpretation can produce:

> It follows naturally that this return . . . constantly introduces modifications and that the return to a text is not a historical supplement that would come to fix itself upon the primary discursivity and redouble it in the form of an ornament which, after all, is not essential. Rather, it is an effective and necessary means of transforming discursive practice. (135)

Yet, Foucault seems to agree with Nietzsche and argue against Heidegger when he says, in "Nietzsche, Genealogy, History," that genealogy absolutely "opposes itself to the search for 'origins'"[17] But, in fact, what Nietzsche rejects as origins is the idea that there is a rich truth that the thinker understood that the commentator must make more explicit, which both Heidegger and Foucault reject. When Foucault rejects commentary, he follows Nietzsche in proposing a return to the point of emergence *(Entstehung),* which Foucault defines as "the entry of forces . . . the leap from the wings to the center stage" (84). This corresponds almost exactly to Heidegger's account of the origin of the work of art as an *Ur-sprung,* an originating leap—a leap a thinker's thought brings about when, in that thinker's saying, marginal practices become central and central practices marginal so that the understanding of being is re-gestalted. Foucault's account simply sounds like a more violent version of Heidegger's when he says:

> If interpretation were the slow exposure of the meaning hidden in an origin, then only metaphysics could interpret the development of humanity. But if interpretation is the violent or surreptitious appropriation of a system of rules, which in itself has no essential [i.e., intrinsic] meaning, in order to impose a direction, to bend it to a new will, to force its participation in a different game, and to subject it to secondary rules, then the development of humanity is a series of interpretations. (86)

These similarities between Heidegger and Foucault should not surprise us since it is the Hegelian/Gadamerian notion of the continuous, mediated, unfolding from the origin of some positive cultural or personal identity that Foucault is opposing here—a metaphysical construct first defined and opposed by Heidegger. The notion of the origin as an originating leap, with its account of the emergence of incommensurate worlds, is meant precisely to reject this Hegelian teleological view of the implicit truth gradually becoming explicit.

But there is, nonetheless, at this stage, a real difference between Foucault and Heidegger. Heidegger holds two theses Foucault rejects. The first is that an originating leap can give a culture its identity, so that we in the West received our "historical essence"[18] at the time of the Greek temple. Second, Heidegger holds that a culture unifies itself each time there is a new beginning. He thinks that struggle is always stabilized and focused in a world with an overall style, a world that, for a limited time, gathers together all of the culture's "paths of destiny." On Foucault's reading of himself and Nietzsche, there is no such tendency to stability:

> The purpose of history, guided by genealogy, is not to discover the roots of our identity, but to commit itself to its dissipation. It does not seek to define our unique threshold of emergence, the homeland to which metaphysicians promise a return; it seeks to make visible all of those discontinuities that cross us.[19]

> [Historical] emergence designates a place of confrontation, but not as a closed field offering the spectacle of a struggle among equals. Rather, as Nietzsche demonstrates in his analysis of good and evil, it is a "non-place," a pure distance, which indicates that the adversaries do not belong to a common space.[20]

The main difference between Heidegger and Foucault, then, is that Foucault sees Nietzsche as affirming a continual instability in the practices defining both the self and the culture, while Heidegger points to the importance of a nonmetaphysical but nonetheless essential tendency in the practices to gather into stable, unified worlds—a tendency that he calls appropriation *(Ereignis)*.

Foucault accepts a Nietzschean emphasis on dispersion, but he is also pulled toward a Heideggerian account of gathering when he talks, for example, of the totalizing tendency of a carceral society. Once we realize that, in passages like the above, Foucault is arguing primarily against Hegel and not Heidegger, we will be prepared to understand how the Heideggerian picture of the way marginal practices coalesce to form stable unities comes more and more to dominate Foucault's account of the history of the West. Indeed, if we set aside the question of how stable cultural practices *naturally* are—a question on which, if it makes any sense, Foucault and Heidegger deeply differ—and ask how stable the practices of an epoch *can in fact become,* we will find Foucault's view approaching Heidegger's, as the two thinkers focus their analysis on the understanding of being characteristic of modernity.

The History of the Present

Both Heidegger and Foucault, no doubt influenced by Nietzsche, begin their account of our history with a prehistory in pre-Socratic Greece. Heidegger devotes many pages to showing that, although the pre-Socratics did not think about the clearing, they did not deny it either. They sensed that showing up or presencing depended on what was absent or withdrawn, and truth was understood as unconcealment. But this understanding was lost when Plato took the Good to be the purely present ground of everything, and truth to be the correspondence of theoretical propositions to an independent reality.

Foucault, too, points to the emergence of theory among the Greeks as the great turning point in our history. The pragmatic and poetic discourse of early Greek civilization was destroyed by the rise of theoretical truth: "The Sophists were routed . . . [from] the time of the great Platonic division onwards, the [Platonic] will to truth has had its own history."[21] This change in the style of the practices presumably altered all aspects of Greek life. For example, Foucault tells us that "[T]he West has managed . . . to annex sex to a field of rationality. . . . [W]e are accustomed to such 'conquests' since the Greeks."[22]

According to Heidegger, in the next major stage, the Roman understanding of beings as finished works *(res)*—produced rather than coming-forth *(physis)* or being-brought-forth *(poesis)*—set up the possibility of the medieval world of hierarchically ordered substances produced by a creator God.

Foucault has less than Heidegger to say about Greek *philosophy,* but he has much more to say about how the Self was produced, worked over, and administered in antiquity.[23] He also gives, at the beginning of *Discipline and Punish,* his own brief description of the stage of hierarchical, top-down monarchical power.

Finally, Heidegger's and Foucault's concerns converge upon the transformation that issues in modernity, our current understanding of things and human beings. In his account of modernity, Heidegger begins by telling us that "[m]etaphysics grounds an age, in that, through a specific interpretation of what is, and through a specific comprehension of truth it gives to that age the basis upon which it is essentially formed."[24] Foucault says more narrowly: "In any given culture and at any given moment, there is only one episteme that defines the conditions of possibility of all knowledge whether expressed in a theory or silently invested in a practice."[25]

The two thinkers' parallel view of the history of the West comes into sharp focus when we compare Heidegger's account of the origin of the notion of man in his essay, "The Age of the World Picture," with Foucault's account in *The Order of Things.* Both view the interest in representation in the thought of the classical age as showing the emergence of a new style of practices and as the crucial but unstable beginning of modernity—a starting point that is not yet clear about its radically new subject-centered understanding of being. Both agree, too, that this understanding first becomes explicit in Kant's interpretation of *man,* and finally works itself out in our contemporary technological understanding of being and of bio-power.

Heidegger tells us of a radical transformation in our understanding of being that took place in the seventeenth century. The change was implicit in Descartes's introduction of representation. Kant then made Descartes's unthought explicit in the centrality of his notion of *Vorstellung.* The age of representation differs in fundamental ways from all other ages: "What is, in its entirety, is now taken in such a way that it only is in being to the extent that it is set up by man, who represents and sets forth."[26]

> To represent means to bring what is present at hand before oneself as something standing over against, to relate it to oneself, to the one representing it, and to force it back into this relationship to oneself as the

> normative realm. . . . What is decisive is that man himself expressly takes up this position as one constituted by himself and that he makes it secure as the footing for a possible development of humanity.[27]

Foucault emphasizes that for Kant, since man objectifies everything, he also objectifies himself. So, for Foucault, "Man appears in his ambiguous position as an object of knowledge and as a subject that knows."[28]

Both agree that, with Kant, man becomes the source of the meaning of everything and so philosophy becomes anthropology. In Heidegger's terms:

> [Anthropology] designates that philosophical interpretation of man which explains and evaluates whatever is, in its entirety, from the standpoint of man and in relation to man.[29]

> Anthropology is that interpretation of man that already knows fundamentally what man is and hence can never ask who he may be.[30]

For Foucault, philosophy, which Kant claimed to have awakened from its dogmatic slumber, thus falls into an anthropological sleep.

Both Heidegger and Foucault reach rhetorical heights as they look forward to the end of the humanistic understanding of being. Heidegger says:

> Man cannot, of himself, abandon this destining of his modern essence or abolish it by fiat. But man can, as he thinks ahead, ponder this: Being subject as humanity has not always been the sole possibility belonging to the essence of historical man, . . . nor will it always be.[31]

Foucault writes:

> As the archaeology of our thought easily shows, man is an invention of recent date. And one perhaps nearing its end. If those arrangements were to disappear as they appeared . . . then one can certainly wager that man would be erased, like a face drawn in sand at the edge of the sea.[32]

But not long afterward each thinker realized that man was, indeed, being erased, but that this posthumanism was not the liberating development each had expected. Strangely, in this case as in many others, Foucault seems to have repeated Heidegger's mistakes, even though by the time Foucault wrote, Heidegger had already corrected them.

Our Contemporary Understanding of Being/Power

In "The Age of the World Picture," Heidegger illuminates our current understanding of being by looking at one of its greatest achievements, *scientific research.* His account of modern scientific practices is similar to Thomas Kuhn's in *The Structure of Scientific Revolutions.* What Heidegger calls research resembles what Kuhn calls normal science. Research operates by setting up a *total* interpretation of some region of reality and then attempts to show that the anomalies that emerge can be fitted into this total account. Heidegger's researchers, like Kuhn's normal scientists, keep busy by taking for granted that their general plan is correct; that the anomalies it reveals have no truth to tell, so that in the end they must all be brought under the projected total order. Thus, scientific research is made possible by Descartes's unthought, fully focused in Kant, that rationality consists in human beings imposing a total, systematic order on all that is. Heidegger calls this totalizing understanding of being *technological.* I will call it *technicity* to distinguish the style of the practices from the technological devices these practices produce and sustain.

Like many current critics of the modern age, Heidegger at first failed to distinguish the modern epoch that was coming to an end from the beginning of the postmodern epoch. Thus he was for a time under the illusion that the danger of technicity was that people were dominating everything and exploiting all beings for their own satisfaction, as if man were a subject in control and the objectification of everything were the problem. Thus Heidegger says in 1940:

> Western history has now begun to enter into the completion of that period we call the *modern,* which is defined by the fact that man becomes the measure and the center of beings. Man is what lies at the bottom of all beings; that is, in modern terms, at the bottom of all objectification and representability.[33]

By 1946, however, Heidegger saw that the modern understanding of being was coming to an end, that exploitation and control were not the subject's doing, and "man" never was anything but an effect of other forces:

> Even this, that man becomes the subject and the world the object, is a consequence of technology's nature establishing itself, and not the other way around.[34]

Thus, in his final analysis of technicity, Heidegger is critical of those who, still caught in the subject/object picture, think that technicity is dangerous because it embodies instrumental reason. Technicity, he insists, is "something completely different and therefore new."[35]

To bring out the new flexibility technicity reveals, Heidegger describes the electricity produced by the hydroelectric power station on the Rhine:

> The revealing that rules throughout modern technology has the character of a setting-upon, in the sense of a challenging-forth. That challenging happens in that the energy concealed in nature is unlocked, what is unlocked is transformed, what is transformed is stored up, what is stored up is, in turn, distributed, and what is distributed is switched about *ever anew.*[36]

Heidegger's intuition is that everything is being turned into resources that are subject to endless disaggregation, distribution, and reaggregation so as to order and optimize everything. But we can see now that electricity is not a perfect example of technological stuff since it ends up finally being turned into light, heat, or motion to satisfy some subject's desire. It does not capture the idea that the practices are switched about ever anew, nor that they are, as Heidegger says, "driving on to the maximum yield at the minimum expense."[37]

Thus, as soon as he sees that information is truly endlessly transformable, Heidegger switches to computer manipulation of information as his paradigm.[38] The goal of technicity, Heidegger then tells us, is more and more flexibility and efficiency simply for its own sake. There is no longer, as there was in Kant, an onto-theological center that provides a goal for all activity. There is ordering, but no orderer. Heidegger calls this new way of being of beings standing-reserve *(Bestand).* He says:

> Everywhere everything is ordered to stand by, to be immediately at hand, indeed to stand there just so that it may be on call for a further ordering. Whatever is ordered about in this way has its own standing. We call it the standing-reserve.[39]

We might simply say that things are being revealed as resources.

Heidegger seems to waver on the question of whether, as technicity reaches its final stage, it will accentuate subjects and objects or eliminate them.

> The subject-object relation thus reaches, for the first time, its pure "relational," i.e., ordering, character in which both the subject and the object are sucked up as standing-reserves. That does not mean that the subject-object relation vanishes, but rather the opposite: it now attains to its most extreme dominance.[40]

In the end, however, Heidegger seems clearly to hold that technicity can treat people and things as resources to be enhanced without setting meaning-giving subjects over against objectified things. A year after his remark about subjects and objects reaching extreme dominance, however, Heidegger appears to retract his view about objects at least, in his observation that nature has become "a system of information," and that a modern airliner is not an object at all, but just a flexible and efficient cog in the transportation system.[41] Passengers are presumably not autonomous subjects either, but resources recruited by the tourist industry to fill the planes. Heidegger concludes: "Whatever stands by in the sense of standing-reserve no longer stands over against us as object."[42]

Foucault, in the social realm, like Heidegger thinking of natural things, went through a stage, expressed in *Madness and Civilization,* where he thought the problem was that some groups dominated and excluded others. He announces dramatically:

> The life of unreason no longer manifests itself except in the lightning-flash of works such as those of Hölderlin, . . . of Nietzsche, or of Artaud . . . resisting by their own strength that gigantic moral imprisonment which we are in the habit of calling . . . the liberation of the insane.[43]

Foucault felt he had to expose this sinister repression and liberate the repressed. Later, however, he realized that repression, calling for liberation, was not the problem. He rejected

> the idea that underneath power with its acts of violence and its artifice we should be able to recuperate things themselves in their primitive vivacity: behind the asylum walls, the spontaneity of madness; through the penal system, the generous fever of delinquence; under the sexual interdiction, the freshness of desire.[44]

For Foucault, postmodern power is not an instrument of exclusion, but a pervasive pressure toward ever greater inclusion. Its disciplinary practices do not serve to objectify, exclude, coerce, or punish, but rather to order and enhance life. Power creates docile bodies and self-absorbed subjects, so as to produce ever greater welfare for all. The resulting practices embody what Foucault calls *bio-power.*

> It is a power working to incite, reinforce, . . . optimize, and organize the forces under it: a power bent on generating forces, making them grow, and ordering them, rather than one dedicated to impeding them, making them submit, or destroying them.[45]

Foucault, in a variation on Heidegger's account of research, sees that our current practices, supposedly grounded in sciences such as social psychology, produce anomalies such as delinquents, and then take every anomaly, every attempt to evade them, as an occasion for further intervention to bring the anomalies under scientific norms. All this is done, of course, for the anomaly's own good, so that, ideally, everyone gladly accepts this intervention. Heidegger emphasized the tendency toward total ordering in technicity by calling it "total mobilization"; Foucault refers to the totalizing tendency of disciplinary power as "normalization." He speaks of "new methods of power whose operation is not ensured by right but by technique, not by law but by normalization, not by punishment but by control."[46]

Normalization is, of course, more than socialization into norms. Socialization into norms is the universal way the understanding of being or power governs the actions of the members of any society. In the new arrangement that has emerged more and more clearly since the classical age, however, norms are progressively brought to bear on all aspects of life. Apparently, what makes normalization different (and dangerous) for Foucault is that it expands to cover *all* practices. Similarly, Heidegger, quoting Nietzsche, says, "the wasteland *grows.*" Both see that there is something new and peculiar about the way, in modernity, that individuation and totalizing go hand in hand. Heidegger notes:

> Certainly the modern age has . . . introduced subjectivism and individualism. But it remains just as certain that . . . in no age before this has the non-individual in the form of the collective, come to acceptance as having worth. . . . It is precisely this reciprocal conditioning of one by the other that points back to events more profound.[47]

And Foucault, after discussing the way pastoral power takes care of each individual, says:

> I think that the main characteristic of our political rationality is the fact that this integration of the individuals in a community or in a totality results from a constant correlation between an increasing individualization and the reinforcement of this totality.[48]

In *Discipline and Punish,* Foucault explains the way postmodern power is something entirely new. Unlike monarchical power, whose exercise was top down, centralized, intermittent, highly visible, extravagant, and stable; postmodern power is bottom-up, diffuse, continuous, invisible, operating in the micro-practices, and constantly on the move colonizing new domains. In *The History of Sexuality*, vol. 1, Foucault adds:

> Power's condition of possibility . . . must not be sought in the primary existence of a central point, in a unique source of sovereignty from which secondary and descendent forms would emanate. . . . Power is everywhere; not because it embraces everything, but because it comes from everywhere.[49]

This raises a puzzling question: When Foucault describes power as "coming from everywhere" is he describing power in general, i.e., the social clearing, or is he describing bio-power, which is uniquely discrete, continuous, and bottom-up?

This seeming problem is cleared up, I think, if we remember Heidegger's account of onto-theology. Like the understanding of being, power always, in fact, "comes from everywhere," in that it is embodied in the style of everyday practices. But what these background practices have made possible up until recently is monarchical and state-juridical power, i.e., power administered from above. As Foucault puts it:

> At bottom, despite the differences in epochs and objectives, the representation of power has remained under the spell of monarchy. In political thought and analysis, we still have not cut off the head of the king. Hence the importance that the theory of power gives to the problem of right and violence, law and illegality, freedom and will, and especially the state and sovereignty. (88–89)

But now, Foucault tells us, things have changed. Just as for Heidegger technicity, by treating everything as resources, levels being to pure ordering and so gets rid of onto-theology—the idea that some entity is the ground of everything—so bio-power reveals the irrelevance of questions of the legitimacy of the state as the source of power. Foucault says:

> To conceive of power [in these terms] is to conceive of it in terms of a historical form that is characteristic of our societies: the juridical monarchy. Characteristic yet transitory. For while many of its forms have persisted to the present, it has gradually been penetrated by quite new mechanisms of power that are probably irreducible to the representation of law. (89)

That is, just as for Heidegger total mobilization cannot be understood by positing subjects and objects, so normalization bypasses the state and works directly through new sorts of invisible, precise, continuous practices of control Foucault calls micro-practices.

The everyday person-to-person power relations whose coordination produces the style of any regime of power are, indeed, everywhere. But in earlier regimes of power there were no micro-practices. Only disciplinary power works meticulously by ordering every detail. So, while for Foucault *all* forms of power are bottom-up and the understanding of power as emanating from the sovereign or the state misses this important fact, nonetheless bio-power is bottom-up in a new and dangerously totalizing way, so that understanding power on the model of the power of the king or the state (the equivalent of onto-theology) now covers up an important change in how our practices are working.

We can sum up the many parallels in the structure of Heidegger's and Foucault's thought in a list of the equivalencies between the technical terms each has developed (my gloss in parentheses):

Basic Methodological Terms

(An understanding of reality in the practices)	
Being	Power
(begins with a leap of marginal practices to center)	
Origin *(Ur-sprung)*	Emergence *(Entstehung)*
(and then is stabilized into a series of disclosive spaces)	
Epochs	Regimes
(that must be described historically in order to free us from our current style.)	
Recollection	Genealogy

The Last Two Stages in the History of Being and Power

(Enlightenment/Modernity)	
Age of the World Picture	Age of Man
(Postmodernity)	
Technicity	Bio-power

How Our Current Stage Works

(The style of the practices)	
Challenging forth	Discipline
(results in flexible, disaggregated, optimized things and people)	
Standing reserve	Docile bodies
(making possible the total ordering of everything for the sake of more ordering.)	
Total Mobilization	Normalization

What Resists and Why

Heidegger and Foucault are clear, then, that what is uniquely dangerous in our current practices is not that they exploit nature or that they are repressive and/or illegitimate. According to Foucault, our current society becomes more oppressive as it becomes more protective of rights and more permissive and productive. Heidegger, on his part, distinguishes the current problems of technology—ecological destruction, urbanization, nuclear danger, and so forth—from the devastation that would result if technicity enabled us to solve all such problems:

> What threatens man in his very nature is the . . . view that man, by the peaceful release, transformation, storage, and channeling of the energies of physical nature, could render the human condition, man's being, tolerable for everybody and happy in all respects.[50]

Heidegger and Foucault also agree that, once we get over onto-theology and cut off the head of the king, a critique of techno/bio-power does not need to lead us to oppose the use of technological devices, nor specific welfare practices. Heidegger is clear that it is the *essence of technology* (the technological understanding of being, i.e., technicity) not *technology* that causes our distress. That technicity can be disassociated from technological devices is clear if one looks at contemporary Japan, where a traditional, nontechnological understanding of being—or perhaps better, no single understanding of being at all, but a pluralistic understanding of multiple realities—exists alongside the most advanced high-tech production and consumption.

Heidegger's goal is to enable us to use technological devices, but by thinking the history of the West, to free ourselves from technicity. He claims:

> We can use technical devices as they ought to be used . . . and also deny them the right to dominate us, and so to warp, confuse, and lay waste our nature [as disclosers and preservers of worlds].[51]

Foucault, like Heidegger, is, of course, not opposed to modern welfare techniques, such as specific practices like mass vaccination. Late Foucault even suggests ways to improve the welfare state, but he *is* opposed to taking for granted that welfare practices, based on the social sciences, should, in the name of efficiency and order, be extended without critical questioning to all aspects of our lives.

Neither Heidegger nor Foucault think that we can resist techno/bio-power directly because what ultimately needs to be resisted is not particular technologies, nor particular strategies, but a tendency in the practices toward ever greater order and flexibility. Our current epoch in the history of being, as Heidegger would put it, or our current regime in the history of rationality, according to Foucault, can only be resisted by first showing that it is not inevitable but is an interpretation of reality, and second by connecting our current style with our current discomfort. Only then will we be motivated to resist by taking up marginal practices that have escaped or successfully resisted the spread of techno/bio-power.

Characteristically, Foucault is concerned solely with the current danger to people, while Heidegger focuses on what is happening to things. Each sees what is endangered as, at the same time, a source of resistance. Middle Heidegger's basic idea is that the historical essence of Western human beings is that they are essentially world disclosers. That is, we in the West received our identity in the fifth century B.C. when the practices became coordinated in such a way as to produce a single style for all beings. We then became disclosers of a series of total worlds, in a series of reconfiguration in which marginal practices became central and central practices became marginal. Given our need to be disclosers, or at least articulators and preservers of worlds, we can see that for middle Heidegger the greatest danger is the way modern world-picturing has worked itself out in technicity as a *total* mobilization that tends toward the elimination of all marginal practices. All practices that are inflexible and inefficient are either trivialized and rejected or transformed into efficient ones. So, for example, we are led to feel that friendship is old-fashioned and inefficient and that we need to turn to networking, or we tend to think that, when we go backpacking in the wilderness, we are wasting our time unless we do so to be more adaptable and efficient when we get back. Thus, according to Heidegger, technicity eliminates the marginal practices on the basis of which new worlds could be disclosed and dooms us to what Nietzsche already saw as the eternal return of the same. On this view, all we can do to resist technicity is to preserve the marginal practices and wait for a new cultural paradigm, which Heidegger sometimes calls a new god.

For later Heidegger, however, there is more we can do. The gathering of local practices around things such as a jug of wine or a family meal produces temporary, self-enclosed, local worlds that resist the totalizing and dispersing effects of the flexible and efficient ordering demanded by technicity. Thus cultivating what Albert Borgmann calls focal practices gives a new center, or better new centers to our lives.[52] Heidegger holds that by "here and now fostering . . . the saving power [of the] humble things," human beings can still be world disclosers and preservers, only they would be opening local, temporary worlds rather than a single total one.[53]

It is a striking, surprising, and little-noticed fact that in the late fifties, when Heidegger was writing about things, he hardly mentions being at all.[54] Presumably, when he was thinking of modes of resistance to technicity, Heidegger came to see that there is an essential antagonism between a unified understanding of being and local worlds. Of course, he always realized that there would be an antagonism between the style of a whole epoch and things that could only be brought out in their ownness in a style different from the dominant cultural style. Such things would inevitably be dispersed to the margins of the culture. There, they would shine in contrast to the dominant style, but would have to resist being considered irrelevant or even wicked. Indeed, if there is a single understanding of being, even those things that come into their own in the dominant cultural style will be inhibited as centers of local worlds. Already in his "Thing" essay, Heidegger goes out of his way to point out that, even though the original meaning of *thing* in German is a gathering to discuss a matter of concern to the community, in the case of the thing setting up a local world, the gathering in question must be self-contained. The focal occasion must determine which community concerns are relevant, rather than the reverse.[55]

Given the way local worlds establish their own internal coherence and sense of relevance that resists any imposition from outside, there is bound to be a tension between any glorious cultural paradigm that establishes an understanding of being for a whole culture and the humble inconspicuous things. The shining of the former would wash out the shining of the latter. The tendency toward one unified world would impede the gathering of local worlds. Given this tension, Heidegger abandoned in a late seminar what, in his middle period, he had considered to be his crucial contribution to philosophy: the notion of a single understanding of being and the correlated notion of the ontological difference between being and beings. He remarks that "from the perspective of appropriation it becomes necessary to free thinking from the ontological difference." He continues, "From the perspective of appropriation, [the gathering that brings things into their own] shows itself as the relation of world and thing, a relation which could in a way be understood as the relation of being and beings. But then its peculiar quality would be lost."[56] What presumably would be lost would be the self-enclosed local character of the worlds opened by things. It follows that, as disclosers of worlds in the plural, the only comprehensiveness we can hope to achieve is our openness to dwelling in many worlds and the capacity for moving among them. Only such a capacity allows us to see the dangers of technicity and yet have a genuinely positive relationship to it.[57]

Like Heidegger abandoning talking of being, as Foucault works out his final ideas on how to resist bio-power, he becomes more interested in saving the self from becoming a subject and less interested in power per se. Thus, in a typical retrospective reinterpretation, he begins his essay "The Subject and Power" by saying: "I would like to say, first of all, what has been the goal of my work during the last twenty years. It has not been to analyze the phenomena of power, nor to elaborate the foundations of such an analysis. My objective, instead, has been to create a history of the different modes by which, in our culture, human beings are made subjects."[58] The moral seems to be that, when one is looking for marginal practices that could support resistance to a dominant epoch of the understanding of being or a dominant regime of power, rather than thinking of resistance as the preparation of a new total epoch or regime that is dawning, as both Heidegger and Foucault once did, one should think of the marginal as what resists *any* unified style of being or power. One will seek to preserve not new forms of being or power, but local things and individual selves. Thus in the last works of Heidegger and Foucault the discussions of epochal understandings of being and regimes of power appropriately disappear.

Foucault, then, bases resistance on the self. He finds in antiquity a practice in terms of which to question the direction our current practices are taking, and to resist this trend. He explains:

> [In antiquity] it was a matter of knowing how to govern one's own life in order to give it the most beautiful form possible (in the eyes of others, of oneself, and of the future generations for whom one could serve as an example).[59]

He proposes "opposing to categories of the 'law' and of 'prohibition' those of the 'art of living,' 'techniques of self,' and 'stylization of existence.'"[60] Foucault grounds resistance in these "practices of creativity."[61] In the end, he thus embraces a kind of Nietzschean constant overcoming for its own sake. He offers "a critical philosophy that seeks the conditions and the indefinite possibilities of . . . transforming ourselves."[62] This is the sense in which, although the structure of Foucault's thought is thoroughly Heideggerian, Nietzsche won out in the end.

Conclusion

So now we come to the important difference between Heidegger's and Foucault's ontologies. For Heidegger, the basic way the background practices work is by appropriation, gathering so as to bring things into their own. Human beings, as world disclosers, must respond to and preserve this gathering. For Foucault, on the contrary, the background practices reveal, as they do for Nietzsche, a constantly shifting struggle. Receptivity makes no sense; one must actively engage in the struggle.

Thus, finally, when it comes to the difficult normative question, just why we should resist at all, Heidegger and Foucault take quite different paths, each of which has its advantages and drawbacks. Heidegger, as we have seen, claims that the human essence is to be receptive to the way the background practices gather to disclose new worlds. Foucault explicitly denies any appeal to our human essence—even the weak claim that our essence is to be receivers and preservers of worlds. This saves Foucault from any form of essentialism, but, of course, denies him any account of why bio-power should generally be felt as distressing. So, in contrast to Heidegger, he holds that human beings must resist the current form of power without being able to give an argument for why totalization is especially dangerous. Since Foucault holds that no form of power is without its problems, he adopts an attitude he calls "hyper- and pessimistic activism."[63]

There is, nonetheless, an important kind of resistance these two thinkers share. Thinking the history of being, for Heidegger, and the genealogy of regimes of power, for Foucault, opens a space for critical questioning by showing that our understanding of reality need not be defined by techno/bio-power—that we need not be dominated by the drive to order and optimize everything. Thus an understanding of our historical condition weakens the hold our current understanding has on us and makes possible disengagement from the direction our practices are taking. Both thinkers were once prophets of the dawning of a new world, but both gave up that stance. They both came to share later Heidegger's modest claim:

> The thinking in question remains unassuming because its task is only of a preparatory, not of a founding character. It is content with awakening a readiness in man for a possibility whose contour remains obscure, whose coming remains uncertain.
>
> Thinking must first learn what remains reserved and in store for thinking to get involved in. It prepares its own transformation in this learning.[64]

Or, as Foucault put it in an interview:

> My role . . . is to show people that they are much freer than they feel, that people accept as truth, as evidence, some themes which have been built up at a certain moment during history, and that this so-called evidence can be criticized and destroyed.[65]

He wanted, he said, "to participate in the difficult displacement of forms of sensibility."[66]

Thus both thinkers emphasize the thinker's ability to enable us to think differently and thereby to get into a free relationship with what both regard as the unique danger posed by our current practices.

Notes

1. "For Heidegger, it was through an increasing obsession with *techné* as the only way to arrive at an understanding of objects that the West lost touch with Being. Let's turn the question around and ask which techniques and practices form the Western concept of the subject." Jeremy R. Carrette, ed., *Religion and Culture Michel Foucault* (New York: Routledge, 1999), 161.

2. Michel Foucault, "Final Interview," *Raritan* (summer 1985):8. "Le Retour de la morale," interview by Gilles Barbadette, *Les Nouvelles* (28 June 1984). The full quotation reads as follows: "Heidegger has always been for me the essential philosopher. I started by reading Hegel, then Marx, and I began to read Heidegger in 1951 or 1952; then in 1952 or 1953, I no longer remember, I read Nietzsche. I still have the notes I took while reading Heidegger—I have tons of them!—and they are far more important than the ones I took on Hegel or Marx. My whole philosophical development was determined by my reading of Heidegger. But I recognize that Nietzsche prevailed over him. I don't know Heidegger well enough: I practically don't know *Being and Time* nor the things recently published. My knowledge of Nietzsche is much greater. Nevertheless, these were my two fundamental experiences. I probably wouldn't have read Nietzsche if I hadn't read Heidegger. I tried to read Nietzsche in the fifties, but Nietzsche by himself said nothing to me. Whereas Nietzsche and Heidegger—that was the philosophical shock! But I've never written anything on Heidegger and only a very short article on Nietzsche. I think it's important to have a small number of authors with whom one thinks, with whom one works, but on whom one doesn't write. Perhaps someday I'll write about them, but at that point they will no longer be instruments of thought for me."

In case, for any reason, this last interview be considered unreliable, there are other scattered references to Heidegger in the interviews and lectures that make the same point. For example, when asked about the intellectual influences on his thought, Foucault said, "I was surprised when two of my friends in Berkeley wrote something about me and said that Heidegger was influential. Of course, it was quite true, but no one in France has ever perceived it" ("Truth, Power, Self: An Interview," in *Technologies of the Self,* eds. Luther H. Martin, Huck Gutman, and Patrick H. Hutton [Amherst: University of Massachusetts Press, 1988], 12), And there is Foucault's appraisal of Heidegger as "the kind [of philosopher] who opens up new avenues of thought" (Carrette, *Religion and Culture Michel Foucault,* 86).

Many, though not all, of my revisions of my original Being and Power paper are implicit answers to Paul Rabinow's rather indirect objections to my thesis that we can learn a great deal about these two thinkers by working out the structural parallels in their thinking; see Paul Rabinow, "Modern and Countermodern: Ethos and Epoch in Heidegger and Foucault," in *The Cambridge Companion to Foucault,* ed. Garry Gutting (Cambridge: Cambridge University Press, 1994).

3. In contrasting himself with Laing, Foucault remarks: "He was a Sartrean, I a Heideggerian" (*Michel Foucault: Remarks on Marx, Conversations with Duccio Trombadori,* trans. R. James Goldstein and James Cascaito [New York: Semiotext(e) Foreign Agents Series, 1991], 72.

4. Martin Heidegger, *Being and Time* (New York: Harper & Row, 1962), 25–26.

5. Martin Heidegger, "Letter on Humanism," in *Basic Writings* (New York: Harper and Row, 1977), 212.

6. Martin Heidegger, "The Onto-Theo-Logical Constitution of Metaphysics," in *Identity and Difference* (New York: Harper and Row, 1969).

7. Michel Foucault, *The History of Sexuality,* vol. 1, *An Introduction* (New York: Vintage Books, 1980), 93.

8. Michel Foucault, *Discipline and Punish: The Birth of the Prison,* trans. Alan Sheridan (New York: Pantheon, 1977), 194.

9. Michel Foucault, "The Subject and Power," in *Michel Foucault: Beyond Structuralism and Hermeneutic,* ed. Hubert Dreyfus and Paul Rabinow (Chicago: The University of Chicago Press, 1983), 221.

10. Ibid.

11. Michel Foucault, "The Ethic of Care for the Self as a Practice of Freedom," in *The Final Foucault,* ed. James Bernauer and David Rasmussen (Cambridge: MIT Press, 1988), 19.

12. Foucault, "The Subject and Power," 222–23.

13. Martin Heidegger, "The Origin of the Work of Art," in *Poetry, Language, Thought,* trans. Albert Hofstadter (New York: Harper and Row, 1971), 61.

14. Ibid., 76.

15. Martin Heidegger, "Reflection in Metaphysics," in *The End of Philosophy* (New York: Harper and Row, 1973), 77.

16. Michel Foucault, "What Is an Author?" in *Language, Counter-Memory, Practice,* ed. Donald F. Bouchard (Ithaca: Cornell University Press, 1977), 134.

17. Michel Foucault, "Nietzsche, Genealogy, History," in *The Foucault Reader,* ed. Paul Rabinow (New York: Pantheon, 1984), 77.

18. Heidegger, "Letter on Humanism," 222.

19. Foucault, "Nietzsche, Geneology, History," 95.

20. Ibid. 84–85.

21. Michel Foucault, *The Discourse on Language* (New York: Pantheon Books, 1972), 218–19.

22. Foucault, *The History of Sexuality,* 1:78.

23. Foucault, *The History of Sexuality,* vol. 3, *The Care of the Self,* trans. Robert Hurley (New York: Vintage Books, 1988).

24. Martin Heidegger, "The Age of the World Picture," in *The Question Concerning Technology and Other Essays,* trans. William Lovitt (New York: Harper and Row, 1977), 115.

25. Michel Foucault, *The Order of Things* (New York: Vintage Books, 1973), 168.

26. Heidegger, "The Age of the World Picture," 129–30.

27. Ibid., 131–32.

28. Foucault, *The Order of Things,* 312.

29. Heidegger, "The Age of the World Picture," 133.

30. Ibid., 153.

31. Ibid.

32. Foucault, *The Order of Things,* 387.

33. Martin Heidegger, *Nietzsche,* vol. 4, *Nihilism* (New York: Harper and Row, 1982), 28. Italics mine.

34. Martin Heidegger, "What Are Poets For?" in *Poetry, Language, Thought,* 112.

35. Martin Heidegger, "The Question Concerning Technology," in *The Question Concerning Technology and Other Essays,* trans. William Lovitt (New York: Harper and Row, 1977), 5.

36. Ibid., 16. Italics mine.

37. Ibid., 15.

38. See Martin Heidegger, "On the Way to Language" (1959), in *On the Way to Language,* trans. Peter D. Hertz (New York: Harper and Row, 1971), 132. See also Martin Heidegger, "Memorial Address" (1959), in *Discourse on Thinking,* trans. John M. Anderson and E. Hans Freund (New York: Harper, 1966), 46.

39. Heidegger, "The Question Concerning Technology," 17.

40. Martin Heidegger, "Science and Reflection," *The Question Concerning Technology and Other Essays,* 173.

41. Heidegger, "The Question Concerning Technology," 23.

42. Ibid., 17.

43. Michel Foucault, *Madness and Civilization* (New York: Vintage Books, 1973), 278.

44. Michel Foucault, "The End of the Monarchy of Sex," interview by Bernard-Henri Lévy, *Le Nouvel Observateur* (12 March 1977). Reprinted in *Foucault Live* (New York: Semiotext(e), 1989), 149.

45. Foucault, *The History of Sexuality,* 1:136.

46. Ibid., 89.

47. Heidegger, *The Age of the World Picture,* 128.

48. Michel Foucault, "The Political Technology of Individuals," in *Technologies of the Self,* 161–62.

49. Foucault, *The History of Sexuality,* 1:93.

50. Heidegger, "What Are Poets For?" 116.

51. Heidegger, "Memorial Address," 54.

52. See Albert Borgmann, *Technology and the Character of Contemporary Life* (Chicago: University of Chicago Press, 1984).

53. Heidegger, "The Question Concerning Technology," 33.

54. With one exception that I know of, where, when he is speaking of mortals, Heidegger reverts to the language of *Being and Time.*

55. Martin Heidegger, "The Thing," in *Poetry, Language, Thought.* To put this in terms of meals, it helps to remember that, in Virginia Woolfe's *To the Lighthouse,* arguments about politics brought in from outside almost ruin Mrs. Ramsey's dinner. The dinner only works when the participants become so absorbed in the food that they stop paying attention to external concerns and get in tune with the actual occasion. The

same thing happens in the film *Babette's Feast.* The members of an ascetic religious community go into the feast resolved to be true to their dead founder's principles and not to enjoy the food. Bickering and silence ensue until the wine and food make them forget their founder's concerns and attune them to the past and present relationships that are in accord with the gathering.

56. Martin Heidegger, *On Time and Being,* trans. Joan Stambaugh (New York: Harper Torchbook, 1972), 37.

57. For more on this subject, see Hubert L. Dreyfus and Charles Spinosa, "Highway Bridges and Feasts: Heidegger and Borgmann on How to Affirm Technology," in *Man and World* 30 (1997):159–77.

58. Foucault, "The Subject and Power," 208.

59. Michel Foucault, "The Concern for Truth," interview by François Ewald, *Le Magazine Littéraire* (May 1984). Reprinted in *Foucault Live,* 298.

60. Ibid.

61. Michel Foucault, "On the Genealogy of Ethics," in *Michel Foucault: Beyond Structuralism and Hermeneutics,* ed. Hubert Dreyfus and Paul Rabinow (Chicago: The University of Chicago Press, 1983), 237.

62. Michel Foucault, "About the Beginning of the Hermeneutics of the Self" (1980), in Carrette, *Religion and Culture Michel Foucault,* 161.

63. Foucault, "The Subject and Power," 232.

64. Martin Heidegger, "The End of Philosophy and the Task of Thinking," in *Basic Writings,* ed. David Krell (New York: Harper and Row, 1977), 378–79.

65. Michel Foucault, "Truth, Power, Self," 10.

66. Michel Foucault, "Questions of Method," in *The Foucault Effect,* ed. Graham Burchell, Colin Gordon, and Peter Miller (Chicago: The University of Chicago Press, 1991), 83.

Heidegger and Foucault: Escaping Technological Nihilism

Jana Sawicki

Critics of the Enlightenment faith in reason, science, and human progress are often accused of irrationalism, pessimism, and nihilistic despair. It is sometimes assumed that if one is not an unequivocal defender of reason, science, or technology, then one is against them. Thus, two twentieth-century continental critics, Martin Heidegger and Michel Foucault, have attained notoriety for their respective critiques of modern technology and humanism.

In a thought-provoking passage from his "Letter on Humanism" Heidegger aptly characterizes the situation of cultural critics like himself and Foucault when he says:

> People . . . immediately assume that what speaks against something is automatically its negation and that this is "negative" in the sense of destructive. . . . We pitch everything that does not stay close to the familiar and beloved positives into the previously excavated pit of pure negation which negates everything, ends in nothing, and so consummates nihilism. . . . But does the "against" which a thinking advances against ordinary opinion necessarily point toward pure negation and the negative? . . . only when one posits in advance what is meant by the "positive" and on this basis makes an absolute and absolutely negative decision about the range of possible opposition to it. Concealed in such a procedure is the refusal to subject to reflection this presupposed "positive" in which one believes himself saved. (*LH*, 226–27)[1]

The "presupposed positive" that Heidegger subjected to reflection was modern humanism. In his own histories of the "truth of Being," the later Heidegger linked the autonomous development of a calculative, technological thinking to metaphysical humanisms that placed the human subject at the center of reality and history and sought in it an absolute foundation for knowledge and values.[2] Heidegger engaged in what he referred to as a "meditative thinking," a recollection *(Andenken)* of Being, which might prepare the way for an alternative to modern humanism, and which, in his words, might "realize the proper dignity of man" (*LH,* 210). More recently, in the works of Michel Foucault we find another critique of modern humanism. This time humanism is linked to the emergence of the human sciences and to a set of autonomous disciplinary technologies that make them possible. Foucault also uses history to criticize the present although his histories are not histories of the truth of Being, but histories of the apparatuses of "power/knowledge."

Of course, Heidegger and Foucault each address different domains. Heidegger focuses on the domination of nature by the natural sciences. His documents are classic texts in the history of Western metaphysics (and later, the poetry of Hölderlin). In contrast, Foucault writes histories of the human sciences and of the institutions in which they are embedded. His documents are the relatively obscure documents of the social historian, e.g., administrative treatises, architectural plans, case studies, hospital records—not canonical texts. Yet, despite these differences (and others I will address later), Heidegger and Foucault utilize similar analytical and critical strategies. Both confront similar criticisms as well. In particular, because they both reject the traditional epistemological appeal to a Cartesian subject, their respective critiques of modern culture have been judged groundless. Indeed, both have been charged with nihilism.[3]

In what follows I will assess their respective positions vis à vis nihilism. In the final analysis I will argue that the charge of nihilism is misguided in both cases, but for different reasons. This will require (1) laying out their respective positions on the autonomy of technology, especially as they are related to the critiques of humanism; and (2) challenging the most recent account of the nihilism of Heidegger and Foucault found in the writings of Hubert Dreyfus.

The Autonomy of Technology

As I have indicated, both Heidegger and Foucault operate with the thesis that technology is "autonomous." Because the autonomy thesis is frequently interpreted as the exaggerated and mysterious claim that technology has become a Frankensteinian monster with a life of its own, it is important to clarify its significance.

In general, the belief that technology is autonomous consists of two interrelated claims. First, it is a denial of the standard definition of technology as a neutral instrument, that is, as a neutral means to some humanly defined end. Second, it involves the quite plausible suggestion that the process and direction of technological development is in some respects independent of human control. Thus it is often related, but not necessarily committed, to a version of technological determinism that asserts that the use of certain instruments and techniques determines the nature and direction of future scientific research or social practices. As we shall see, neither Heidegger nor Foucault is a technological determinist; however, both do isolate technological trends.

Heidegger on Autonomy and Humanism

How are these claims embodied in Heidegger's philosophy of technology? In "The Question Concerning Technology" Heidegger rejects the instrumental definition of technology because it fails to capture the "essence" of modern technology. For Heidegger, essential or "true" definitions characterize a phenomenon "ontologically," that is, in relation to a tacit set of shared background practices, prevailing ways of speaking and doing, that make our understandings and interactions with things and people possible. Heidegger is, to borrow Hubert Dreyfus's distinction, a "practical" as opposed to a "theoretical holist" since he does not think that this background of practices can be wholly represented as a system of beliefs or an explicit set of rules.[4] Heidegger asserts: "Technology is therefore no mere means. Technology is a way of revealing."[5] It is a background of habits, customs, and skills against which objects appear as usable.

In particular, modern technology, which Heidegger contrasts with premodern handicraft technologies (e.g., the windmill, the old wooden bridge), reveals nature as "standing reserve" *(Bestand)*. It is a way of revealing that "orders," "calculates," "pursues," "sets upon," "challenges forth," "unlocks," "transforms," "stores up," and "entraps" nature (*QT*, 14–16). The paradigmatic expression of the modern technological relationship to nature is the hydroelectric plant, which according to Heidegger, unlike the premodern "old wooden bridge," transforms the river into a "water-power supplier" (*QT*, 16).

Perhaps the most paradoxical move in Heidegger's analysis of technology is his claim that modern physics is the tool of technology. This amounts to an inversion of the standard idealist view of technology as the tool of science, as applied science. From Heidegger's ontological point of view, physical science does not precede and found modern technology (although it does precede it historically); to the contrary, technology is "ontologically prior" to science. In other words, scientific theorizing is fundamentally inseparable from practices of ordering and controlling. In effect, he reverses the traditional relationship between theory and practice, claiming that in the modern age the theoretical attitude is rooted in a more primordial technological involvement with things at the level of our everyday practices.

Furthermore, as a way of revealing, technology provides the sciences with a calculable and orderable domain of objects. Heidegger writes:

> Modern science's way of representing pursues and entraps nature as a calculable coherence of forces. Modern physics is not experimental physics because it applies apparatus to the questioning of nature. The reverse is true. Because physics, indeed already as pure theory, sets nature up to exhibit itself as a coherence of forces calculable in advance, it orders its experiments precisely for the purpose of asking whether and how nature reports itself when set up this way. (*QT*, 21)

Here Heidegger describes scientific theory as an aggressive, manipulative, and productive practice of control.[6] Thus, he collapses the distinction between theory and practice.

This picture of scientific inquiry as an aggressive and relentless objectification of the real coincides with an even more fundamental event in the advent of modern technology, i.e., the emergence of an understanding of reality as a "world picture." With the emergence of Cartesian philosophy, reality becomes a representable object for a knowing subject.[7] For the first time human beings view themselves as standing over and against a world that is totally depictable (if not yet totally depicted), becoming both objects in the picture and subjects for whom it is a picture. Indeed, Heidegger claims that the idea that reality is a picture for a subject leads to the very problems of relativism and subjectivism that Cartesianism was designed to conquer in its search for an absolute foundation. Once the world becomes a picture, it can be contemplated and compared to other possible world pictures (or, in contemporary discussions, "conceptual schemes"). The search for the most adequate picture, and hence the search for an absolute set of criteria for judging between competing representations of reality, is one that only makes sense within the confines of the age of the world picture. By granting priority to the background practices in which human beings dwell, Heidegger is attempting to circumvent this problematic altogether.[8]

This brings us to the second feature of Heidegger's autonomy theses, namely the issue of human control over technology. It also raises the issue of Heidegger's rejection of humanism. Heidegger asks:

> Who accomplishes the challenging setting upon through which what we call the real is revealed as standing-reserve? Obviously, man. To what extent is man capable of such a revealing? Man can, indeed, conceive, fashion, and carry through this or that in one way or another . . . but man does not have control over unconcealment itself, in which at any given time the real shows itself or withdraws . . . the unconcealment itself, within which ordering unfolds, is never a human handiwork, anymore than is the realm man traverses every time he as a subject relates to an object. (*QT*, 18)

Here Heidegger asserts that the idea that the mark of the human is the rational ordering and controlling of reality is itself not something that anyone or any group has consciously chosen. The ideas that reality is an object for human control and technology merely a human instrument are themselves examples of the technological thinking that dominates the modern age. Although we *do* decide whether any given representation of reality is true or false, or how any particular thing is to be used, which representations come up as candidates for truth or falsity, which questions are taken seriously, and the very fact that beings are revealed as things for use, are not themselves up for choice.[9] The background against which objects appear is neither wholly graspable nor intentionally constituted. It is, instead, a forgotten horizon of historically transmitted practices and beliefs that we take for granted.

In the *Discourse on Thinking* Heidegger addresses this unchosen, autonomous feature of technology when he says: "Whenever we plan, research, and organize, we always reckon with conditions that are given." In "The Question Concerning Technology" he uses the term "enframing" *(Gestell)* to describe the essence of modern technology; it is "the way in which the real reveals itself as standing reserve" (*QT*, 23). Moreover, "enframing" represents a "destining" of revealing insofar as it "pushes" us in a certain direction. Heidegger does not regard destining as determination (he says it is not a "fate which compels"), but rather as the implicit project within the field of modern practices to subject all aspects of reality to the principles of order and efficiency, and to pursue reality down to the finest detail. Thus, insofar as modern technology aims to order and render calculable, the objectification of reality tends to take the form of an increasing classification, differentiation, and fragmentation of reality. The possibilities for how things appear are increasingly reduced to those that enhance calculative activities.

Heidegger perceives the real danger in the modern age to be that human beings will continue to regard technology as a mere instrument and fail to inquire into its essence. He fears that all revealing will become calculative and all relations technical, that the unthought horizon of revealing, namely the "concealed" background practices that make technological thinking possible, will be forgotten. He remarks:

> The coming to presence of technology threatens revealing, threatens it with the possibility that all revealing will be consumed in ordering and that everything will present itself only in the unconcealedness of standing-reserve. (*QT*, 33)[10]

Therefore, it is not technology, or science, but rather the essence of technology as a way of revealing that constitutes the danger; for the essence of technology is *existential,* not technological.[11] It is a matter of how human beings are fundamentally oriented toward their world vis à vis their practices, skills, habits, customs, and so forth. Humanism contributes to this danger insofar as it fosters the illusion that technology is the result of a collective human choice and therefore subject to human control.[12]

Nevertheless, having denied that we control modern technology Heidegger does not want to lapse into nihilism. In his characteristically enigmatic fashion, he quotes Hölderlin: "But where danger is, grows / The saving power also" (*QT*, 34). I will address the nature of this hope and ask whether it is justified in my conclusion. In the meantime, let us turn to Foucault's account of technology and humanism.

Foucault on Autonomy and Humanism

The theme of technology first appears in Foucault's relatively recent history of punishment, *Discipline and Punish.* In this book, Foucault maps the emergence of a new form of power, disciplinary power, which takes the form of a technology of the body, and which he locates at the "microlevel" of society in prisons, schools, hospitals, factories, and so forth. Foucault describes this technology thus:

> There may be a "knowledge" of the body which is not exactly the science of its functioning, and a mastery of its forces that is more than the ability to conquer them; this knowledge and this mastery constitute . . . the political technology of the body.[13]

Here, a technology is described that is both a mode of knowledge and a form of power, i.e., "power/knowledge."

Because power/knowledge is the key concept in Foucault's philosophy of technology, it will serve as the basis for my comparison of Foucault and Heidegger. Just as Heidegger was able to capture the essence of modern technology and to reveal the inadequacies of the instrumental definition of technology only by relating it to a shared background of practices, Foucault isolates the technologies of power/knowledge (he also refers to them as the "disciplines" or "disciplinary technologies") not by writing an internal history of either the human sciences or prisons, but by analyzing the human sciences and penal law in relation to a matrix of nonscientific practices and discourses. It is significant in this light that Foucault locates the practices of power/knowledge at the "microlevel" of society, for by this term he wants to refer to the diffuse, deep, and often hidden character of the practices he describes. Foucault writes:

> This technology is . . . rarely formulated in continuous, systematic discourse; it is often made up of bits and pieces; it implements a disparate set of tools or methods. In spite of the coherence of its results, it is generally no more than a multiform instrumentation. Moreover, it cannot be localized in a particular type of institution or state apparatus. For they have recourse to it. . . . But, in its mechanisms and its effects it is situated at a quite different level. What the institutions operate is, in a sense, a micro-physics of power, whose field of validity is situated . . . between these great functionings [i.e., the institution] and the bodies themselves. (*DP,* 26)

Power/knowledge apparatuses are located "right down into the depths of society" within and between individuals, bodies, gestures, dispositions, techniques and so forth (*DP,* 27).

Isolating this level of micro-practices enables Foucault to highlight features of social phenomena such as delinquency and deviancy that are obscured in psychological or sociological studies operating at the level of individual or group intentions within institutions. For example, in *Discipline and Punish* he isolates latent functions of the prison and delinquency as well as the dysfunctionality of practices of punishment in order to focus on other functions that the prison has served.

Furthermore, Foucault's critique of the human sciences, which, he claims, are inseparable from disciplinary technologies, is not based on the assumption that they are false. Instead, he investigates the power of discourses that are regarded as true. But more than this, like Heidegger, he wants to describe how it was that certain questions became important, how an entire domain of true-or-false statements (that were taken as serious scientific hypotheses and played a role in public policy) were produced. Foucault does not question science or technology in terms of traditional epistemology, but in terms of their relations to other practices. In other words, he is not interested in assessing the correctness of scientific representations, but rather in analyzing the social effects of our taking them so seriously. One distinguishing feature of Foucault's analyses is that he does not simply *refer* to background practices; instead he *describes* them in concrete detail.

How is the autonomy thesis embodied in Foucault's account of power/knowledge? First, he claims, power and knowledge are not external to one another. The power of technology does not result from an application of previously established scientific knowledge. On the contrary, the knowledge that Foucault describes takes the form of technical control. Disciplinary technologies are not simply neutral instruments; they are inextricably linked to practices of domination.

Second, the form of power exercised through such knowledge is not primarily repressive. It is productive. Indeed, productivity is the distinguishing feature of modern technologies of the body as compared to those of the sovereign power that preceded it. Modern technologies do not control the body by conquering it (as did the techniques of torture and execution under sovereign power), but by simultaneously rendering it more useful and docile. Foucault describes the emergence of the disciplines thus:

> This historical moment of the disciplines was the moment when an art of the human body was born which was directed not only at the growth of its skills, nor at the intensification of its subjection, but at the formulation of a relation that in the mechanism itself makes it more obedient as it becomes more useful and conversely. What was

> then being formed was a policy of coercions that act upon the body, a calculated manipulation of its element, its gestures, its behavior. The human body was entering a machinery of power that explores it, breaks it down and rearranges it. (*DP*, 137–38)

Thus, disciplinary techniques compose a micro-physics of power that relies on a knowledge of the body that renders it calculable and manipulable in much the same way as Heidegger depicts physics as setting up and setting upon nature.

Foucault locates specific events in the history of disciplinary technology that make the constitution of the individual possible: a new distribution of bodies in space brought about through the use of architectural designs and an overall analysis of spaces; a new coding of activity that regulates movements, imposes timetables, correlates body and gestures (writing) and body and object (rifle drills), i.e., a series of techniques for training the body. In addition, techniques of surveillance, documentation, organization, administration, and examination emerge that increase the visibility of the individual and make possible an increasing normalization and standardization of the population. In particular, Foucault isolates techniques of examination such as comparison, measurement, differentiation, and classification that issue in normalizing judgments and thereby facilitate the discovery of the "abnormal." The more abnormal the individual, the more individuated he or she is likely to become, and the more likely the abnormal type itself to become the subject of further scientific inquiry.[14]

Hence, not only are the disciplinary technologies of power/knowledge not neutral, they "push" inquiry in the direction of isolating abnormalities that require further inquiry. Hence, they produce objects for the human sciences. One could describe disciplinary technologies in the terms Foucault uses to describe the project of Bentham's Panopticon, i.e., as a "laboratory of power . . . [in which] knowledge follows the advances of power, discovering new objects of knowledge over all the surfaces on which power is exercised" (*DP*, 204). Indeed, Bentham's Panopticon might be said to occupy a role in Foucault's history of power/knowledge analogous to that of Heidegger's world picture. Both represent the emergence of the ideal of a perfectly systematized, regulated whole.

As we have seen, Heidegger regards modern technology as ontologically but not historically prior to the rise of modern physics. In contrast Foucault's technologies are among the historical conditions that make the emergence of the human sciences possible. However, like Heidegger, Foucault accords methodological primacy to the domain of practice, collapsing the distinction between theory and practice altogether insofar as he treats scientific discourses themselves as practices that produce effects of power in the social field. The term "power/knowledge" itself is *designed* to undercut the rigid distinction between theory and practice and thereby to focus our attention on how theoretical formulations embody relations of power.

Turning to the third way in which Foucault's account of power/knowledge employs the autonomy thesis brings us to the issue of humanism and the control of technology. Foucault gained notoriety for his rejection of humanism, particularly phenomenological and existential versions, with their recourse to a constitutive subject. Why does he reject it? The reasons are methodological and strategic. In the first place, because he wants to describe the processes through which the modern subject (epistemological, moral, and empirical) has been constituted, he suspends the use of humanistic assumptions in his own research. Moreover, Foucault thinks that humanistic discourses that place the human subject at the center of reality or history fail to grasp the extent to which the subject is decentered and without privileged access to its own springs of action or to the effects of its acts in the social field. Finally, Foucault wants to analyze the power effects of humanistic discourses that seek an emancipatory and essentialist knowledge of the human by showing how humanism, as an ideology of progress and reform, masks the oppressive effects of the human sciences by diverting attention away from the practices that he describes.

For example, in *Discipline and Punish* Foucault describes the introduction of the "soul" of the criminal into criminological discourse as a humanistic strategy that masks the simultaneous emergence of dominating technologies of the body. On the concept of the soul are built domains of analysis (e.g., subjectivity, personality, consciousness), techniques and discourses (e.g., psychopathology, psychoanalysis), and the moral claims of humanism. Thus, the humanity the human sciences aim to understand and to liberate through self-understanding is itself the effect of techniques of subjection that preceded it.[15]

Operating without humanistic assumptions allows Foucault to reveal the oppressive effects of practices that are more often regarded as beneficial or benign, to investigate the patterning of the unintended or overlooked consequences of individual or collective practices and programs, and to isolate the technologies of disciplinary power. The search for techniques and strategies of power/knowledge replaces the search for a subject of history; for these strategies are not reducible to the intentions of a class or group. They are intentional but not subjective. Foucault describes them as strategies without subjects in which the "logic is perfectly clear, the aims decipherable, and yet . . . no one is there to have invented them, and few who can be said to have formulated them" (*HS*, 95). Foucault's technologies of power function anonymously in much the same way as Heidegger's account of enframing suggests modern technology prevails. As the Heidegger of *Being and Time* might have said, they are implemented by no one and everyone.

So, just as Heidegger prefers to write histories of the truth of Being rather than histories of the progress of knowledge, Foucault writes histories of the techniques of power/knowledge rather than histories of humanistic reform. Both refuse to operate with humanistic assumptions. Both portray the rise of modern technology (which, as we have seen, they focus differently) as beyond human control.

As I have indicated, this emphasis on autonomy coupled with the charge that they reject humanism have opened both of these cultural critics to the charge of nihilism. Most recently, Hubert Dreyfus has attempted to save Heidegger from nihilism by suggesting that in his later writings on art Heidegger refers to a level of human practices that still remain beyond the grasp of modern technology.[16] In the same vein, Dreyfus fears the nihilistic implications in Foucault's view that "physical reality, the body and history are whatever we take them to be."[17] "Nihilism," according to Dreyfus's definition, is the view that there are no meaningful differences between people and things.[18] Dreyfus claims that to escape nihilism, one must ground one's critique on an account of what human beings really are—on humanism. But is either Heidegger or Foucault a nihilist? Is Dreyfus's strategy for saving Heidegger from nihilism either warranted or effective? To answer these questions we must turn to Heidegger's and Foucault's respective responses to the dangers of modern technology.

"Where danger is, grows / The saving power also." Thus Heidegger enigmatically indicates there is hope that all thinking in the modern age will not be reduced to technological thinking, or human beings reduced to "standing reserve." Heidegger bases his hope on two ways of responding to modern technology. First, he calls for "releasement toward things" *(Gelassenheit)*. "Releasement" connotes a serene disposition toward the real, a suspension of calculative thinking that enables one to direct attention to the concealed background of practices that ground the modern way of revealing, and that have significance that is neither recognized nor realized in the present. It issues in the cultivation of an egolessness, a sense of both the richness and the limits of the project to master nature that reigns in modern science. Finally, releasement involves a "meditative thinking" that does not counsel direct intervention, but rather, having directed attention to the concealed ground of the technological way of revealing, waits for the emergence of an alternative to the prevailing configurations of practices that compose modern technology. In other words, if the essence of modern technology is not technological but existential, that is, a matter of how human beings in their social practices are primarily oriented to their world (e.g., as knowing subjects), then, if the technological way of revealing is understood as merely one way of taking up a range of possibilities that are themselves not chosen but received, they may hope that by slowing down and reflecting on the process of calculative thinking, they will prepare the way for the emergence of other possible relationships to Being (*QT*, 33). Hence, attaining this new self-understanding requires a historical thinking that frees us from the sense that our current practices are necessary and opens up new ways of understanding, new ways of living.

Heidegger also responds to the danger of technology by reviving the premodern understanding of technology as craft or art *(techne)*. His reference to the Greek definition of *techne* as a form of *poiesis* (bringing forth) may be interpreted in several ways. An interpretation that links his method to Foucault's would suggest that Heidegger refers to premodern technology simply to highlight and circumscribe modern technology and thereby release us from its grasp. But there is also a basis in Heidegger's writings for interpreting the revival of *techne* as a call for us to supplement and enrich modern technological ways of revealing with those of an artful praxis that is both technical and contemplative. As Don Ihde has pointed out, artistic technologies reveal objects without reducing them to serviceability. They defamiliarize the real and utilize imagination to proliferate the possibilities for how things can appear.[19]

Hubert Dreyfus offers an interesting variation on the above interpretations in order to rescue Heidegger from nihilism. He calls it Heidegger's "religious form of resistance to nihilism."[20] Dreyfus claims that the later Heidegger appeals to the remnants of a premodern understanding of Being that persist in the concealed and inarticulable background of practices in the modern age. He states:

> Nontechnological micro-practices, if they still exist at all, are hard to discern, not because they are so pervasive as to be ineffable, or so numinous as to be unreachable—they were once palpably present in cultural exemplars such as the Greek Temple—but because they are dispersed by the objectifying practices which have had such success since the Enlightenment.[21]

According to Dreyfus, the fact that we resist modern technology at all can be explained only if we assume that such remnants persist. What makes this appeal religious is the fact that all we can do is "hope that the micro-practices excluded by technology will find a new focus in a new paradigm."[22] This paradigm (the postmodern equivalent of the Greek temple) presumably will be grounded in some authentic view of humanity, i.e., something "specific that we are."[23]

Although there is much in Dreyfus's rather forced reading of Heidegger with which I agree, I have strong reservations about this account of Heidegger's hope. First, it opens him (and Heidegger) to the charge of romanticism. What is the basis for the claim that premodern technology is ontologically distinct from modern technology? That our hopes lie only in the premodern practices of contemporary Western society?[24]

It is noteworthy that Heidegger himself never addressed the present in such a way as to make a case for the persistence in our background practices of a premodern way of revealing. Indeed, some Heidegger scholars would rejoice at this lacuna in his corpus since it could be interpreted as promoting the sort of humanism and subjectivism that Heidegger rejects. Heidegger repeatedly emphasized our inability to will the appearance of a new epoch of Being and regarded combative efforts to resist technology as just further examples of it.

Dreyfus makes much of Heidegger's reference in "The Question Concerning Technology" to the saving power in "little things." "Little things" may indeed refer to ways of thinking and doing that are not technological. Yet, I find no basis for the interpretation of these ways of thinking and doing as more authentically human. When Heidegger invokes authenticity, he usually is referring to our role as questioners of Being. What makes us human appears to be nothing more specific than being the kinds of beings who put Being into question. Over and above this, we are the practices that constitute us and our world. Heidegger questions technology to achieve a clearer understanding of what we are doing, to focus our practices in a different way. If more people were to question and to live with their questions, technological thinking might be slowed down and the saving power fostered. Thus the aims of Heidegger's critical project are rather modest—more modest than even Dreyfus's interpretation suggests.

Left without an appeal to anything specific that we are, does Heidegger succumb to nihilism? I think not. Charging Heidegger with nihilism begs the question; for, after all, he is attempting to dissolve the problem of nihilism altogether. (He is also trying to reveal the danger of nihilism that is harbored in our current situation.) It is Heidegger's contention that the Cartesian search for an absolute foundation in the subject of knowledge is itself at the root of the relentless quest for certainty and for mastery that characterizes modernity and culminates in a nihilism in which all of our options increasingly become technological and all of our values instrumental. Heidegger's notion of the "ontological difference," i.e., the difference between the clearing and what shows up in it, guarantees his escaping nihilism, for it guarantees that there are other possibilities for self-understanding (and for understanding nature) to be attained through meditative thinking.

The fact is that we cannot master Being, nor can we know in advance which relationships to Being are salvific. Understanding this does not lead to nihilism, but rather to the commitment to cease the project of mastering Being and experiment with alternative modes of questioning, knowing, and living that are made possible through the disposition of releasement.

Dreyfus begs the question as well when he would have Heidegger escape nihilism by appealing to the very sort of humanism that he rejects, one that attempts to ground a way of life in some objective account of what human beings really are.[25]

Foucault offers a strategy of resistance to the practices of power/knowledge that can escape the charge of nihilism (and romanticism). To be sure, as we have seen, he also stresses the autonomous, nonneutral, and undesirable features of the technologies that he describes. He rejects humanistic assumptions and emphasizes the lack of human control over history. Moreover, from Dreyfus's perspective he appears to be even more nihilistic insofar as he identifies processes through which human beings have been constituted by these technologies.

Dreyfus's (and Paul Rabinow's) fear that Foucault may not escape the charge of nihilism is the result of his tendency to overextend the range of Foucault's project and to conflate several distinctions that should be made between him and Heidegger (as Dreyfus interprets him). One difference between them is that Foucault is not a holist. He is a relational analyst who analyzes phenomena like punishment in relation to a domain (i.e., technologies of the body) that has been obscured in traditional humanist histories of progress and reform. His philosophy of technology is particularistic. He does not attempt to provide a general account of the practices that compose the "essence" of modern technology, but rather specific histories of technological practices that have been overlooked in traditional accounts of modern forms of power. He simply identifies particular practices in the present, the assumed value of which he is skeptical, and traces their lines of descent in Nietzschean fashion. He utilizes history to reveal the contingency of present practices and categories associated with them, to denaturalize them. He puts into question modern notions of self, society, and history by showing how they have been constituted. Such questioning is not tantamount to prescribing an ontology, either antihumanist or humanist. He questions much of what we assume to be real, necessary, or universal. As one commentator recently remarked, Foucault's histories are not

> histories of things, but of the terms, categories and techniques through which certain things become at times the focus of a whole configuration of discussions and procedure . . . and his aim is not to "ground" the experience of things but to denaturalize, defamiliarize and distance us from it, and hence to question its *raison d'être*.[26]

So, Foucault's histories are designed to make the present seem less inevitable. It is within this contingent aspect of history that Foucault places his hope. Accordingly, freedom lies not in the discovery of essential features of the human situation, in complete mastery of reality, or in releasement, but rather in "rebelling against the ways in which we are already defined, categorized and classified" by the dominating technologies of power that he describes.[27]

The reason Foucault's account of technology appears to be antitechnological in a more global sense is that he begins with a diagnosis of some particular injustice in the present and then uses a historical narrative to reveal its origins. It is a mistake to read his histories as Whig histories in reverse. That they may appear to be such is due to the fact that the point in the present toward which his histories lead is itself one where domination and a malevolent use of technology is found. Thus, there is no reason to assume that technologies of power/knowledge do not also have beneficial features. It is just that Foucault does not focus on them.

Finally, Foucault's rejection of humanism and the ideology of progress does not romanticize the past. His accounts of premodern technologies are not nostalgic but strategic. And, as I have suggested, one might say the same of Heidegger's. The description in *Discipline and Punish* of the sovereign's bloody spectacle at the scaffold is designed to limit the temporal range of disciplinary power. He neither condemns the past in an effort to justify the present, nor romanticizes it in an effort to criticize the present.

Neither Foucault nor Heidegger is a nihilist, but for different reasons. Heidegger escapes by linking nihilism to calculative thinking and by providing, in turn, an alternative form of thinking, meditative thinking, through which we can uncover meaningful alternatives to present ways of being. Foucault escapes because he is not offering a diagnosis of the whole of modern technology, or of its overall direction, but rather of particular practices within it. The practices of power/knowledge do not form a systematic whole, but are instead *diffused* throughout the social body. (In contrast, Dreyfus describes Heidegger's salvific premodern practices as dispersed by those of modern technology.) Foucault is inventing instruments for identifying and combating the undesirable effects of specific practices while maintaining a skeptical attitude about the control he has over them.

In one of his last interviews Foucault referred to himself as a "hyperactive pessimist." He remarked: "My point is not that everything is bad, but that everything is dangerous. . . . If everything is dangerous, then we always have something to do."[28]

This brings me to the key differences between Heidegger and Foucault. Having suggested that these social critics share analytic and critical strategies, it is imporant to acknowledge these differences. Hyperactive pessimism is not a self-description that Heidegger would ever have embraced. Indeed, Heideggerian *Gelassenheit* has a much more serene, quietistic tone. Moreover, Heidegger's preoccupations with canonical texts in the history of metaphysics, his frequent references to uprootedness, loss of tradition, to the destiny of the German people and language, his use of the language of grace, and finally, his dogged avoidance of politics contrast sharply with Foucault's active and willful images of combat, resistance, and struggle and his blatant disregard, even irreverence, for tradition. These differences in style and content are significant, for Heidegger would no doubt have regarded Foucault's specific practices of revolt as further examples of a Nietzschean will to power, of technological thinking. While Foucault tries to turn thinking into exercises of power, Heidegger counsels the cultivation of meditative thinking that prepares us for the coming of another epoch of Being. Heidegger states:

> Philosophy will be able to bring out no direct change in the present condition of the world. This applies . . . to all merely human thought and endeavor. Only a God can save us. The sole possibility that remains is to prepare the attitude—through thought and poetry—for the appearance of the God.[29]

Unlike Heidegger, the later Foucault does not find in art a source of redemption. To the contrary, it is simply another arena of struggle. Heidegger's ambiguous remarks regarding resistance to the dangers he describes are too passive for a Foucauldian. In contrast, Foucault's questioning is offered as an active mode of resistance that directly confronts particular practices of domination wherever they arise. Among these practices are those (like Dreyfus's and the early Heidegger's) that attempt to "ground" a particular path by appealing to some positive account of who we are. In the final analysis, it is the specific, concrete, and unambiguously active nature of Foucault's critique that recommends it over Heidegger's. Foucault holds on to his hope without anticipating the emergence of a better time, basing it instead on the many sites of resistance to forms of domination in the social body.

Notes

1. Martin Heidegger, "Letter on Humanism," *Basic Writings*, ed. David Krell (New York: Harper & Row, 1977). Hereafter cited in the text as *LH*.

2. Heidegger uses many terms to refer to the subject of his inquiry, e.g., "meaning of Being," "clearing," "lighting," "Nothing." For present purposes we can define it as an inarticulable shared background of practices within which things appear as intelligible. David Hoy aptly defines it as "a hidden context that makes particular contents evident" ("The Unthought and How to Think It," paper presented at the meeting of the American Philosophical Association, Sacramento, Calif., 25 March 1982, 13).

3. See the following: Hubert Dreyfus, "Holism and Hermeneutics," *Review of Metaphysics* 34 (September 1980): 3–23; Hubert Dreyfus and Paul Rabinow, *Michel Foucault: Beyond Structuralism and Hermeneutics* (Chicago: University of Chicago Press, 1983), 86–89, 205. By "nihilism" here I mean the belief that there are no absolute foundations for our choices and thus no meaningful differences between one course of action and another.

4. Dreyfus, "Holism and Hermeneutics," 7–12.

5. Martin Heidegger, "The Question Concerning Technology," in *The Question Concerning Technology and Other Essays,* translated and introduction by William Lovitt (New York: Harper and Row, 1977), 12. Hereafter cited in the text as *QT.*

6. In another essay, "Science and Reflection," Heidegger concludes that the relationship of science to the real is not merely a passive contemplation, but rather an act of aggression. Thus, the real "becomes surveyable and . . . secured in its objectness. From this there result spheres or areas of objects that scientific observation can entrap after its fashion." He continues: "Entrapping representation, which secures everything in that objectness which is thus capable of being followed out, is the fundamental characteristic of the representing through which modern science corresponds to the real." See *The Question Concerning Technology and Other Essays,* 155–82, esp. 168.

7. Heidegger comments: "What is, in its entirety, is now taken in such a way that it first is in being and only is in being to the extent that it is set up by man, who represents and sets forth. Wherever we have the world picture, an essential decision takes place regarding what is, in its entirety. The Being of whatever is, is sought and found in the representedness of the latter." ("The Age of the World Picture," in *The Question Concerning Technology and Other Essays,* 115–54, esp. 129–30.)

8. Cf. Charles Guignon, *Heidegger and the Problem of Knowledge* (Indianapolis: Hackett Publishing Co., 1983), 192ff, for a similar discussion of how Cartesian "subjectivism" leads to relativism.

9. Cf. Joe Rouse, "Heidegger's Later Philosophy of Science," *Southern Journal of Philosophy* 23 (spring 1985):75–92, esp. 77, for a similar analysis of Heidegger's account of technology as destiny.

10. Martin Heidegger, "Memorial Address," in *Discourse on Thinking,* trans. John M. Anderson and E. Hans Freund (New York: Harper & Row, 1966), 46.

11. Don Ihde makes a similar point in "Heidegger's Philosophy of Technology," in *Technics and Praxis* (Holland: D. Reidel Publishing Co., 1979), 113.

12. In "The Age of the World Picture," Heidegger links humanism with the ideas of the individual or collective subject and thus with the modern problematic of individualism versus communalism; see 133ff.

13. Michel Foucault, *Discipline and Punish,* trans. Alan Sheridan (New York: Random House, 1977), 26. Hereafter cited in the text as *DP.*

14. He comments: "In a disciplinary regime . . . individualization is 'descending': as power becomes more anonymous and more functional, those on whom it is exercised tend to be more strongly individualized. . . . In a system of discipline, the child is more individualized than the adult, the patient more than the healthy man, the madman and the delinquent more than the normal. . . . All the sciences, analyses, or practices employing the root 'psycho' have their origin in the historical reversal of the procedures of individualization" (*DP,* 193).

15. The word "subjection" *(asujetissement)* has a double meaning for Foucault here, referring to both the production of an object for scientific study (in this case a subject) and to political subjection.

16. Dreyfus, "Holism and Hermeneutics," 21.

17. Dreyfus and Rabinow, *Michel Foucault,* 205.

18. Dreyfus, "Holism and Hermeneutics," 3.
19. See Ihde, *Technics and Praxis*, 129.
20. Dreyfus, "Holism and Hermeneutics," 22ff.
21. Ibid., 22.
22. Ibid., 23.
23. Ibid., 21.
24. Heidegger, of course, had a complex relationship to romanticism. A treatment of it would take me beyond the scope of this essay. Nevertheless, one might recall that he often lamented the loss of rootedness in tradition. In his last interview he commented: "I know that all that is great and essential originated from the fact that man had a home and was rooted in tradition." ("Only a God Can Save Us: *Der Spiegel*'s Interview with Martin Heidegger," trans. M. P. Allen and J. D. Caputo in *Philosophy Today* 20 [1976]: 279ff.)
25. In his excellent study *Heidegger and the Problem of Knowledge*, Charles Guignon makes a similar point when he states: "The measure of the truth of Heidegger's phenomenology is not whether it offers us a correct representation of who and what we are. The measure of truth lies in the way our lives are enriched and deepened through these descriptions" (250). Here, of course, truth is understood as unhiddenness or openness, not as correctness.
26. John Rajchman, "The Story of Foucault's History," *Social Text* (spring 1984): 8.
27. Ibid., 15.
28. Michel Foucault, afterword to Dreyfus and Rabinow, *Michel Foucault*, 232.
29. Heidegger, "Only a God Can Save Us," 279ff.

Nietzsche, Heidegger, and Foucault: Nihilism and Beyond

Steven V. Hicks

In the view of many, we are living in a period of philosophical disintegration and drift, one largely shaped by the three thinkers discussed in this study, Nietzsche, Heidegger, and Foucault. All three see in modern Western culture a tendency toward destruction and decline. Thus Nietzsche writes:

> Disintegration characterizes this time, and thus uncertainty: nothing stands firmly on its feet or on a hard faith in itself; one lives for tomorrow as the day after tomorrow is dubious. Everything on our way is slippery and dangerous, and the ice that still supports us has become thin. (*WP*, § 57)[1]

Echoing these Nietzschean sentiments, Heidegger claims that our modern Western culture is "an age of consummate meaninglessness" in which man "stretches his essence thin, flattens it, and loses it" (*N*, 3:163 and 4:146).[2] And Foucault characterizes it in terms of "an immense expanse of shade . . . [which] is really a bottomless sea" (*OT*, 211).[3]

It seems doubtful that Nietzsche, Heidegger, and Foucault would have had such a profound impact on contemporary thinking if they were simply wrong. They obviously struck a nerve in contemporary culture. Their influence and the need to analyze what they said would seem to arise from modernity itself—a period in both philosophy and the broader culture marked by social, political, economic, and technological tensions. In what follows, I shall investigate why these thinkers have had such an influence and propose a way out of the dilemmas they uncover. In particular, I will argue that, like Nietzsche, both Heidegger and Foucault "plumb the depths of nihilism" and attempt to open a way "out of the abyss to a new and different way of thinking and being"—a way that can transcend nihilism.[4]

A common thread connecting the diverse views of Nietzsche, Heidegger, and Foucault is the belief that nihilism is the result of various forms of concealment and "forgetfulness" inherent in the history of the West. These forms of concealment range from the suppressed genealogy behind our moralistic modes of interpretation (Nietzsche) to the "withdrawal of the question of Being" in Western metaphysics (Heidegger), to the subtle forms of domination and hidden constellations of power that make up our inherited identity and commitments (Foucault). Despite the differences in their approaches, all three stress the "curative" properties of unconcealment and aim to overcome nihilism by disclosing the original experiences of it that have been covered up in and by the Western philosophical tradition. Foucault and Heidegger, in particular, find the most effective early expression of this "uncovering" in Nietzsche's writings.

As Heidegger reads it, the nihilism that Nietzsche feared and wanted to overcome—the sense of emptiness and purposelessness, the experience of the exhaustion of meaning, the decline of the uppermost values, the devotion to frenzied consumption, domination, materialism, and war—is the direct result of the metaphysics underlying Western history (cf. *N*, 1:156–57). By metaphysics, Nietzsche understands the acceptance of a "two-world" view, i.e., the acceptance of a "true" or transcendent world that is, in some sense, higher than the natural world, and that ultimately devalues the natural world. This devaluation eventually leads to the idealization of asceticism, which in turn leads to nihilism, when the values enshrined by metaphysics ultimately collapse under the weight of the contradictions and inconsistencies inherent in the "ascetic ideal." Thus Nietzsche aims to overcome nihilism by overcoming metaphysics; and this he attempts to accomplish, in part at least, through his genealogical analysis of morality (which uncovers the meaning of the ascetic ideal) as well as through his doctrines of "eternal recurrence" (which rules out a "true" or transcendent world) and "will to power" (which provides the principle for a new, nonascetic mode of valuation).[5] Similarly, in the writings of

Foucault, Nietzsche appears as a source for the overcoming of the same tradition of Western metaphysics that Heidegger discusses. "But the end of metaphysics," Foucault adds, "is only the negative side of a much more complex event in Western thought," namely, "the appearance of man" and the human sciences (*OT,* 317). In this context, Foucault writes:

> It is easy to see why Nietzsche's thought should have had, and still has for us, such a disturbing power when it introduced in the form of an imminent event, the Promise-Threat, the notion that man would soon be no more—but would be replaced by the superman; in a philosophy of the [Eternal] Return, this meant that man had long since disappeared and would continue to disappear, and that our modern thought about man, our concern for him, our humanism, were all sleeping serenely over the threatening rumble of his non-existence. (*OT,* 322)

In what follows, I shall first focus on Nietzsche's understanding of nihilism. I will then examine the impact of Nietzsche's views on the Heideggerian and Foucauldian reflections on nihilism.

Nietzsche and the Problem of Nihilism

Several kinds of nihilism are distinguished in Nietzsche's writings. This is not unusual, given his belief that "only what has no history has a fixed definition" (*GM,* 2: § 13).[6] In his drawing of these distinctions, however, it becomes apparent that Nietzsche's attitude toward the issue of nihilism is ambivalent at best. On the one hand, Nietzsche places himself squarely in a Central European debate about the ills of modern society, a debate that can be traced back to F. H. Jacobi in 1799, who first used the term "nihilism" in his attacks on Fichte's idealism. This was a debate in which many, including Nietzsche, were in broad agreement about the basic diagnosis of the problem, while disagreeing sharply about the prescribed treatment, as well as the prognosis. The basic diagnosis was that life in the modern world lacked a kind of coherence, unity, purpose, and meaningfulness that life in previous societies (e.g., ancient Greece) had possessed.[7] As a consequence of the loss of an integrated civic life (with which individuals could identify), the loss of faith in God, or industrialization and depersonalization (which reduced individuals to cogs in a purposeless machine), the prevailing mood in the modern era is one of despair over the emptiness and triviality of human existence—the "meaninglessness of events" (*WP*, § 599). Thus Nietzsche, along with other participants in this debate, feared an approaching period of nihilism, the seeds of which had already been sown in nineteenth-century Europe: "What I relate is the history of the next two centuries. I describe what is coming, what can no longer come differently—*the advent of nihilism*" (*WP*, preface, § 2). Nietzsche grasped with prophetic insight the imminent "crisis of reason," i.e., the imminent collapse of the traditional epistemological and metaphysical supports of the values to which modern humans had committed themselves. He saw on the modern horizon a moral or axiological nihilism (i.e., the belief that moral standards and norms cannot be justified by rational argument) as well as a metaphysical or epistemological nihilism (i.e., the claim that there are, ultimately, no truths). "What does nihilism mean? *That the highest values devaluate themselves.* The aim is lacking; 'why?' finds no answer" (*WP*, § 2). Moreover, Nietzsche was appalled at the consequences that he believed would follow once everyone had become fully aware of the implications of this "collapse." "If nothing is true, then everything is permitted" (*GM*, 3: § 24). Contemplating the collapse of the traditional supports of values, the mounting belief in the Darwinian notion of the relentless evolution of the species (which blurred the distinction between human and animal), and the uncritical faith in the human species' unchecked technological capabilities, Nietzsche expected disaster: "Our whole European culture has been moving as towards a catastrophe, with a tortured tension that is growing from decade to decade" (*WP*, preface, § 2). He boldly predicted that power politics, decadence, "constructs of domination," and "vicious wars" would be the wave of the future (see *WP*, § 12; and *EH*, 783).

Yet paradoxically Nietzsche claims that the route from this "disintegration" to a "new mode of life" leads through an even more radical and thoroughgoing form of nihilism: nihilism as "a divine way of thinking" (*WP*, §§ 14–15), a "pathway to a Yes" (*WP*, § 1041). This is the "strong" or "perfect" nihilism that Nietzsche affirms and which, he claims, has sufficient strength to accept "perspectivism"—the doctrine that any belief is just an interpretation of the world from a particular point of view, there being no objective authority for values (cf. *WP*, §§ 22, 481, 567, 602, 616, and 1055).[8] Moreover, it is an "active" nihilism that has the necessary resolve to set or revaluate all of the "highest" prevailing values to date (cf. *WP*, §§ 2, 3). "Such an experimental philosophy as I live anticipates experimentally even the possibilities of the most fundamental nihilism, but this does not mean that it must halt at a negation, a No, a will to negation"; rather, under the right conditions, it can lead to what he calls a "Dionysian yes-saying to the world as it is, without subtraction, exception, or exemptions" (*WP*, § 1041). As Heidegger rightly observes, Nietzsche's preferred rubrics for his own philosophy are "nihilism," on the one hand, and "revaluation of all values hitherto," on the other (*N*, 4:9). Yet Nietzsche's self-described "radical nihilism" (e.g., with regard to truth) seems to threaten the coherence of his critique of traditional morality as well as his "transvaluation of values." Somehow these two (positive and negative) aspects of his philosophy must be held together in a coherent way.

The clue to resolving this dilemma, I shall argue, turns on recognizing the link between nihilism and the ascetic ideal. Let me elaborate.

Nietzsche articulates at least three forms of nihilism: weak or passive nihilism (cf. *WP*, § 22), incomplete nihilism (cf. *WP*, § 28), and complete/strong/active (or classic) nihilism (cf. *WP*, §§ 23, 28, 55, 1055). Only the latter—the "classic or active nihilism"—is identified by Nietzsche with his own philosophy (and described as "a phenomenon of strength and of heightened power of spirit" that is capable of overcoming the weak or incomplete forms of nihilism; cf. *WP*, § 14). By "weak" or "passive" nihilism, Nietzsche has in mind, first, the all-too-common psychological experience of weariness, discouragement, sense of insecurity, and defeat. This is the experience of the disillusioned individual who has lost faith in the efficacy of traditional values and who cannot bear this life of pain and suffering without the hope and promise of a better or "truer" world—an ultimate order or ready-made purpose "out there" giving us direction in terms of goals, moral imperatives, and so forth (cf. *WP*, § 12).[9] Nietzsche suggests that this weak or passive nihilism is originally derived from certain religious views (Buddhist, Hindu, and especially Christian) that hold that the world we live in has no ultimate reality or worth, and that our seeming knowledge of it and attachment to it are illusory and invalid (cf. *GM*, 3: § 27; *WP*, § 5). The world of our everyday life is without sense or point—a vale of tears, a ceaseless alteration of birth, death, and rebirth—and if we wish salvation, it is salvation from this world that we seek.[10] Nietzsche frequently identifies this nihilism of weakness or emptiness with pessimism or "the loathing of existence . . . the conception of this existence as a punishment to be borne to the end . . . the belief in the identity of existence and indebtedness."[11] This "pessimism of weakness" received its most sophisticated and influential philosophical articulation in the work of Schopenhauer, who basically argued that "the *only* kind of role available for a human is that of one or another kind of victimization or frustration."[12] But Nietzsche claims that Schopenhauerian pessimism, like Christian optimism, ultimately entails a form of nihilism (of weakness or passivity), for both are committed to the view that this world, our world of everyday life—the only one there is—is worth nothing (cf. *WP,* §§ 2–4). "Since both Schopenhauer and Christianity agree that *this* world is not to be affirmed, they are really instances of the same kind of weakness, and the difference in their metaphysical views (that the Christian thinks the underlying *reality* of the world, God, is to be affirmed while Schopenhauer thinks this underlying reality, the Will, is to be negated) is irrelevant."[13]

"Incomplete nihilism" is described by Nietzsche as a "stage" of transition "in the midst of which we live" (*WP,* §§ 13, 28). In this state of transition, modern (late nineteenth-century) humans have found the will to negate more fully and meaningfully to deepen the problem, but they have not yet found "the strength to revaluate values and to deify and affirm the apparent world of becoming [our everyday world] as the only one" (*WP,* § 585). This incomplete nihilism, or "nihilism of negativity," is exemplified in a number of social and political movements—socialism, anarchism, "free spiritism," atheism, and so forth—that flourished in Central Europe and Russia in the 1850s and 1860s (cf. *WP,* §§ 51, 82, 125).[14] What was common among these diverse groups was a negative or destructive attitude toward the body of traditional moral, political, and religious teachings and beliefs, which these nihilists felt were confusing, obscure, old-fashioned, and anti-progressive. Political nihilism or anarchism is perhaps best represented by the character of Bazarov in Turgenev's *Fathers and Sons* (1862), who claims "to believe in nothing" (cf. *WP,* § 82; cf. also Nietzsche's "Letter to Gast," 10 November 1887, cited by Kaufmann in his note to *WP,* § 82). Atheistic nihilism is best represented either by Feuerbach (cf. *GM,* 3: § 3) or by the character of Ivan ("If God is dead, everything is permitted") in Dostoevsky's *Brothers Karamazov* (cf. *WP,* §§ 51, 82, 125). While often claiming to believe in nothing, Nietzsche argues that these incomplete nihilists actually believed in (i.e., had uncritical faith in) a crudely materialistic (or positivistic) interpretation of "science."[15] Most of them believed that "science"—broadly construed to include evolution, socialism, utilitarianism, free-marketism, and so forth—would fill the place left empty by traditional moral and religious beliefs. And while Nietzsche viewed the "emancipation of science from moral and religious purposes" as "a very good sign" (*WP*, § 63), he claims that these political and atheistic nihilists still derive an "old-fashioned metaphysical comfort" from a "beyond"—a "true world" in contrast to which the world we actually live in is devalued (*WP*, §§ 30, 37). "Having unlearned one faith," incomplete nihilists "follow the old habit and seek *another* authority that can *speak unconditionally* and *command* goals and tasks" (*WP*, § 20). One dogmatic faith simply replaces another.

What both non-Nietzschean forms of nihilism share is the belief that there "ought" to be some ultimate order or ready-made purpose from without—a "real" or "true" world that bestows value and purpose on this one. Moreover, both "weak" and "incomplete" nihilists express despair (or in some way devalue the natural world) when no ultimate purpose from without is found. What Nietzsche's "active" or "complete" nihilism claims is that precisely this attitude—the state of mind which demands that there be a ready-made purpose from without—needs to be overcome. In overcoming this belief in a "true world" or one metaphysically preferable to this one, Nietzsche argues, the grounds for pessimism and despair are removed. Thus Nietzsche rejects a nihilism which denies this world and affirms another "true" world (which is "nothing"); Nietzsche says that a nihilism which recognizes that there is no "being" or "thing-in-itself"—no metaphysically preferable world alternative—and which celebrates this as the principle of a new beginning, is a "pathway to a new mode of life" (cf. *WP*, §§ 54, 112, 1041).

What complicates Nietzsche's attempt to open this "new pathway to a Yes" is the powerful hold that he thinks the ascetic ideal still exercises over humanity. Indeed, Nietzsche goes so far as to claim that the only dominant (culture-wide) ideal developed so far in human history has been the ascetic ideal; and hence the ultimate logical conclusion of human history is "the advent of nihilism" (*WP*, preface, §§ 2–3). Why has the ascetic ideal triumphed? Why has it led inevitably to the weak and incomplete forms of nihilism that Nietzsche feared?

In the *Genealogy of Morals,* Nietzsche devotes what is perhaps his most sustained and sophisticated philosophical analysis to answering these questions. While the intricacies of his genealogical analysis are beyond the scope of this discussion, the gist of his argument is well worth considering. According to Nietzsche, there has never been a real alternative to the ideal of asceticism. Moreover, any meaning for life is better than none—people would rather "will nothing than not will at all" (*GM*, 3: § 28). While its message may be that this world—our everyday life—has no value and ought therefore to be denied, the ascetic ideal still gives us a feeling that there is, after all, something worth living for, something that can satisfy our psychological need for a sense of effectiveness and power in the world (even if this feeling of effectiveness is attained through "dishonest" ascetic means of self-denial, self-mortification, and devaluation of the natural world). From a "cosmic" point of view, Nietzsche claims that the "self-contradiction" represented by the ascetic ideal is that it, in fact, is a disguised form of the "will-to-preservation-of-life" (*GM*, 3: § 13). This disguised or concealed form of the "will-to-preserve-life" is shown by Nietzsche to develop genealogically through a number of distinct early phases and separate strands, including (1) the struggle between certain historical modes of valuation based on class membership: noble/priestly/slave; (2) the slave reversal of values (based on resentment, imaginary revenge, invention of "evil" as a category, and so forth); (3) the origin of a "bad conscience" as "consciousness of guilt"; and (4) the priestly interpretation of suffering as the result of one's "guilty" or "sinful" nature. The final genealogical "synthesis" is that modern "complex" of "morality" (or moral mode of evaluation) based on the priestly valuation-plus-interpretation, which *both* gives suffering a meaning (e.g., "you suffer because you are guilty") *and* initiates a process of excess "debauchery" of feelings—a spiral of feelings of guilt, ascetic practices, sense of sin— which (temporarily, at least) numbs the suffering (*GM*, 3: § 19). For a long time, the life-denying ascetic ideal actually served a life-enhancing function: it worked to overcome depression and disgust with life, it spurred our willingness to go on, to keep acting, to keep willing. In short, it gave humanity a sense of power—a feeling that we could take on more suffering and endure it. Yet if the ascetic ideal was the best way up to Nietzsche's time of satisfying the psychological need for a sense of power and effectiveness in the world, why did he claim that the ascetic ideal had failed and was leading to (passive/incomplete) nihilism?

This question brings us to what Nietzsche says is the most "terrifying" aspect of the ascetic ideal (*GM*, 3: § 27). For it is a peculiar problem of the ascetic ideal that, while it cultivates truthfulness and introspection (e.g., Christian confession about self and world), it is "a form of valuation which requires its devotees to make claims and have beliefs that won't stand up to truthful introspective scrutiny (such as that moral action arises from altruistic sources)."[16] Hence it "dissolves" itself (*GM*, 3: § 27). More precisely, it destroys what is "exoteric" in the ideal—viz., the comforting illusions, the life-enhancing exteriors, the other-worldly myths, "the lie involved in the belief in God"—while clinging to the life-denying "esoteric" remanents of the ideal (*GM*, 3: § 27). "The awe-inspiring catastrophe of two thousand years of training in truthfulness" is that humanity can no longer get what it really needs from the ascetic ideal—a feeling of power and effectiveness in the world—except by denying or ignoring the truth (*GM*, 3: § 27). And those with a "will-to-truth" cannot simply go back to an explicit acceptance of the ascetic ideal once they accept the "truth" that their "will-to-truth" is itself an expression of the ascetic ideal. Psychologically, one would feel foolish rather than powerful embracing a life-denying ideal once one accepted the truth that one's real motive for embracing it was to get a sense of power and vitality necessary to feel better about life, and thus to continue living.[17] Hence the need for a new ideal.

The problem, according to Nietzsche, is that there have been no alternatives. "Science," "knowledge," "art," "traditional atheism," "free spiritism," and "utopian" political movements are all bound up with the ascetic ideal in complex and subtle ways (*GM*, 3: §§ 5, 23–25). They all embody what Nietzsche terms the "will-to-truth": the faith in truth as having an unconditional value; the commitment to "truth at any price"; the belief in the overriding importance of "being scientific," and so forth. This "unconditional will to truth," Nietzsche says, is simply the latest expression of "faith in the ascetic ideal itself, even if as an unconscious imperative" (*GM*, 3: §§ 23–24). It is not the practice of science or the capacity of human knowledge to inform us of the truth that is at issue. It is the uncritical commitment to the absolute value of truth—along with all of the self-denial involved with that commitment—that Nietzsche equates with the ascetic ideal.[18] Science, traditional atheism, and utopian socialism all involve themselves in various forms of asceticism—e.g., denying oneself the comforting belief in an afterlife, taking a stand against natural desires and practical inclinations, and so forth. And they typically do this *not* to make life worth living, but just for the sake of truth. Thus utopian political movements see this life as valuable only in terms of some unrealized (and probably unrealizable) future state of affairs (e.g., the "worker's state") which involves sacrifice and self-denial here and now (e.g., embracing the next "five-year plan"). Traditional atheism condemns the comforting illusion but without condemning that which condemns life, viz., the moral values generated by the ascetic ideal (cf. Feuerbach's attempt to save Christian ethics by abandoning or naturalizing its transcendentalist metaphysics).[19] Science's striving after "objectivity" (i.e., truth about the world as it is "in itself") requires its practitioners to adopt an attitude of "disinterested" objectifying investigation: holding oneself back from imposing an interpretation on results, refraining from allowing one's interests to play a role in determining the outcome of investigation. This is a case of a (relatively close) approximation in the cognitive sphere to the ascetic ideal (e.g., directing human energies back against themselves). While it has important uses and is successful in certain contexts, and while Nietzsche has no objection to science as an activity, what it doesn't give us is a new or "counter-ideal" to the ascetic ideal, i.e., a set of positive values for human life.

Paradoxically, then, Nietzsche's "radical nihilism" (e.g., regarding truth) remains committed to the search for truth, and even praises this commitment, but only in the service of an ideal that enhances life rather than devaluing it. But which ideal? To date, Nietzsche argues, there are no counter-ideals that can function as "life-promoting, life-preserving, species-preserving, perhaps even species-cultivating" alternatives to the heretofore dominant ascetic ideal (*BGE*, § 4). Moreover, humanity desperately needs such an alternative ideal, for Nietzsche thinks that his genealogical investigation has uncovered the concealed "danger" modern humans face from the harmfulness of the ascetic ideal and its eventual demise. It will be increasingly difficult for people in the modern world to avoid realizing that traditional moral beliefs (as grounded in the ascetic ideal) are false. The dissolution of these beliefs will lead to serious cultural dislocation and general social malaise: nihilism will be the result of the self-dissolution of previously accepted values (cf. *WP*, §§ 2, 3, 12).[20] Certainly, the sorry state of world affairs since Nietzsche "disclosed" the pending "demise of the ascetic ideal"—a world increasingly oriented toward consumption, domination, and war—offers little reason to think he was wrong.

To sum up: having uncovered the "meaning of the ascetic ideal" and its relation to the genealogy of morality, and having argued that the imminent demise of the ascetic ideal portends the "advent of nihilism," Nietzsche struggles in various works to generate some content for a "life-affirming" counterideal. For example, he talks in terms of "wedding the bad conscience to all unnatural inclinations" (*GM,* 2: § 24); he recommends reinterpreting "objectivity" as an ideal, e.g., by allowing as many different perspectives on and affects about a thing to arise as possible while still retaining "mastery over the Pro and Contra of one's affects" (*GM,* 3: § 12); and he advocates "renaturalizing" the ascetic ideal so that it does not turn the activity of valuing, which is necessary for life, against life (*WP,* § 915). Moreover, his celebrated doctrines of "will to power" and "eternal recurrence" are clearly attempts to formulate affirmative ideals that will not tempt people (à la the ascetic ideal) to disesteem human life by contrasting it with something eternal, unalterable, and intrinsically good (i.e., a "true world"), and which will not provide humanity with an instrument for the impoverishment, stagnation, and debasement of life. Yet for all of his efforts, Nietzsche finds that the values by which his own genealogical discourse is structured—the desire to get a more honest account of the origin of values, the drive to provide a "truer" account of morality than the Christian-ascetic—are the very ones his analysis puts in question. Genealogical knowledge is also characterized by a "faith" in the overriding value of truth. Thus Nietzsche recognizes the continuing presence of the ascetic ideal in his own genealogical thought. As such, the "curative" properties of his genealogical interpretation vis-à-vis the ascetic ideal are "tainted" by the presence of the ascetic ideal in his attempts to overcome it. The values in question—faith in truth, honesty, and so forth—are probably not avoidable in any serious philosophical inquiry, but Nietzsche thinks we can no longer pursue truth in service of the ascetic ideal without running the risk of nihilism. Therefore, a big issue is whether his "genealogy" can propel itself beyond itself in its genealogical knowledge of its own ascetic ideal and create conditions for the emergence of nonascetic successor ideals in whose service we could actually pursue truth. If the answer is yes, then the ground for the Western ascetic ideal (and for nihilism) will gradually fall away. If the answer is no, then "philosophers of the future" will continue to work in service of the ascetic ideal (and hence nihilism) until such time as they can commend some opposed alternative (nonascetic/life-affirming) ideal to universal attention.

Nihilism and the Withdrawal of Being: Heidegger

In his lectures on Nietzsche, Heidegger poses the following question: In Nietzsche's philosophy, *"which for the first time expresses and thinks nihilism as such, is nihilism overcome or is it not?"* (*N*, 4:200). Heidegger's direct answer: Nietzsche's philosophy is "nihilism proper," and this implies not only that Nietzsche's philosophy does not overcome nihilism, but also that "it can never overcome it" because "it is the ultimate entanglement in nihilism" (*N*, 4:203). Despite Nietzsche's valiant efforts to formulate a nonascetic/antinihilistic ideal in terms of which humanity could affirm rather than devalue the natural world, Heidegger argues that Nietzsche fails precisely because he "posits new [nonascetic] values from the [perspective of] will to power" (*N*, 4:203). According to Heidegger, this is simply the "culmination" of the history of traditional (productionist) metaphysics, which, in turn, results in the very nihilistic "constructs of domination" that Nietzsche feared the most. "Such utterly completed, perfect nihilism is the fulfillment of nihilism proper" (*N*, 4:203). Why does Heidegger claim that Nietzsche's philosophy is the ultimate "fulfillment" of nihilism and not its overcoming?

Heidegger believes that Nietzsche's doctrines of "will to power" and "eternal recurrence" are themselves metaphysical doctrines; that is to say, they are intended as answers to traditional metaphysical questions concerning essence and existence. As such, Heidegger argues, they are connected to the whole history of nihilism and to the modern technological/productionist attitude toward the world which that history entails. Let me enlarge on this.

As we have seen, Nietzsche basically understands traditional metaphysics as the acceptance of a "true" or transcendent world that ultimately devalues this (ordinary, everyday) world. This eventually leads to the idealization of asceticism, which in turn leads to nihilism when the values propped up by metaphysics and its ascetic ideal are devalued. Nietzsche aims to overcome nihilism and asceticism by overcoming metaphysics, and this he attempts to do, in part at least, by means of his doctrines of will to power (which provides the basis for a new kind of valuation) and eternal recurrence (which rules out a "true" or transcendent world). Heidegger argues, however, that these supposed nonascetic doctrines are themselves thoroughly metaphysical since they claim to offer Nietzsche's answer to the old question concerning the "Being of beings": "will to power" is the ultimate essence of the world under the mode of existence of "eternal recurrence" (cf. *N*, 2:203).[21]

Strictly speaking, Heidegger's claim that these central Nietzschean doctrines are themselves metaphysical is not quite fair. In numerous passages Nietzsche claims to have shown how all metaphysical doctrines are part and parcel of the "history of an error," which his own perspectivism supposedly overcomes (see *TI*, 485–86).[22] Moreover, he often claims to have reduced "fundamental problems of philosophy" to problems of "psychology" (*BGE*, § 23). Thus one might defend Nietzsche against Heidegger by arguing that Nietzsche's nonascetic, antinihilistic ideals of "will to power" and "eternal recurrence" do not have the suspect features of traditional metaphysics or cosmology (as Heidegger charges), but are more akin to psychology.[23] For example, we might read Nietzsche's claim that the world is will to power under the mode of eternal recurrence as primarily a perspectival (imaginative, metaphorical) construction of the world from the viewpoint of Nietzsche's alternative (nonascetic) values. That is to say, we might interpret it psychologically as an attempt to project onto the world the kinds of things that Nietzsche values most. For example, we might interpret his "world is will to power" claim as a generalization of the drive or desire for power and a feeling of effectiveness in the world; we might view it as basically a glorification of the (psychological) drive that aims to affirm or find value in life through overcoming obstacles and enhancing one's own will-to-life (cf. *BGE*, §§ 188, 257). Or alternatively, we might view it as a psychological strategy of sorts for not turning the activity of valuing, which is necessary for and directed by life, against life (à la the ascetic ideal); or we might view it as a tactic for increasing our effectiveness in the world without having to deny or ignore the truth of the world (as one would have to do to get a feeling of effectiveness from the ascetic ideal). Similarly, we might interpret the doctrine of eternal recurrence not as a cosmological theory, but as a kind of psychological test of one's underlying attitudes toward the world. We might interpret "eternal recurrence" as an imaginative, metaphorical attempt to take the willingness to relive one's life over and over as the measure of the affirmation (or positive value) one places on one's actual (nonrecurring) life. As an imaginative psychological strategy for finding intrinsic value in life—that is, for valuing the process of living as an end and not as a means to an end beyond itself—it is part of Nietzsche's alternative to the ascetic ideal.[24] Thus as regards both the "will to power" and "eternal recurrence," we might defend Nietzsche by arguing that his alternate ideals belong more to psychology than to metaphysics or cosmology, and as such, they don't provide a basis for the reappearance of the ascetic ideal and nihilism (cf. *BGE*, § 23). These alternative ideals, we might argue, help transform "the nay saying" of the ascetic ideal into a "yea saying" by the "transvaluation of founded [metaphysical] meaning into meanings that are created and affirmed in the midst of no [fixed, transcendent] meaning at all."[25]

This response, however, only succeeds in postponing Heidegger's real objection. For according to Heidegger, psychology (and indeed, all of the human sciences) are caught up in the web of traditional metaphysical thinking. As such, "Nietzsche's 'psychology' is simply coterminous with metaphysics. . . . [it] lies grounded in the very essence of modern metaphysics" (*N*, 4:28). Heidegger argues that "modern" metaphysics is defined precisely by the fact that "man becomes the measure and center of beings," and this, in turn, results in the modern technological understanding of beings as objects for use and control, or as Heidegger says, entities wholly present as "standing-reserve" *(Bestand)* (*QT*, 17).[26] This extends even to human beings themselves, who are increasingly transformed by the "human sciences" (and their technological systems) into "resources" for objectification and control (cf. *N*, 4:234–45). Here, Heidegger anticipates Foucault's claim that modern technological systems attempt to make human beings wholly present as "bio-power," or subjects completely present for surveillance and control via the disciplinary practices of institutions (psychological, juridical, carceral) whose aim is to "normalize" human life.[27] Thus from Heidegger's perspective, the actual nihilism Nietzsche feared—"annihilation, spreading violence," and so forth—is evoked by the preponderance, in the modern world, of this productionist, technological "objectification of being," and by "the complete ordering of all beings in the sense of a systematic securing of stockpiles" for further technological usage, control, and domination (*N*, 4:229–34). "The relentlessness of [this] usage extends so far . . . that the abode of Being—that is, the essence of man—is omitted; man is threatened with the annihilation of his essence, and Being itself is endangered" (*N*, 4:245). Ironically, Heidegger argues, it was precisely Nietzsche's "proposing of Being as a value posited by the will to power" that led to this "final [nihilistic] step of modern metaphysics, in which Being comes to appear as will to power" (*N*, 4:234). Simply put, Nietzsche's doctrine of the will to power succeeds in reducing the whole question of Being to the status of a value; and this completes the "metaphysics of subjectivity" initiated by Descartes, which in turn results in a "blindness" to the whole question as to what Being itself is. This "blindness to Being," Heidegger argues, is at the root of all nihilism and is connected to the modern technological/productionist attitude toward the world (cf. *N*, 4:231–32). Why does Heidegger make this claim?

Heidegger believes that metaphysics is essentially the history of Being, a history in which Being discloses itself as withdrawn in "default" or concealed (cf. *N*, 4:230–32). He basically reads the whole history of Western philosophy as the history of Being and its gradual self-concealment. In this context, Heidegger praises Nietzsche for his insight into "the basic development" of that history: "In his [Nietzsche's] view it is nihilism. . . . The phrase 'God Is Dead' is not an atheistic proclamation; it is a formula for the fundamental experience of an event in Occidental history" (*N*, 1:156). Heidegger even suggests that Nietzsche came close to recognizing (albeit opaquely) that the fundamental question of Being had been "omitted," forgotten, or suppressed within the metaphysical tradition of previous philosophy, and that this "omission of the default of Being in its unconcealment" is the very "essence of nihilism" (cf. *N*, 4:230–32). For example, when Nietzsche denies truth or refers to Being as "an empty fiction" (see *TI*, 481), Heidegger claims that he is actually experiencing and expressing the "nothing" or "omission" of Being itself in the history of Western philosophy, which is tantamount to nihilism:

> By nihilism Nietzsche means the historical development, i.e., the event that the uppermost values devalue themselves, that all goals are annihilated. . . . There is no longer any goal in and through which all the forces of the historical existence of peoples can cohere and in the direction of which they can develop; no goal of such a kind . . . [that can] by virtue of its power conduct *Dasein* (humanity) to its realm in a unified way and bring it to creative evolution. (*N*, 1:156–57)

It is Nietzsche's "veiled" recognition of the omission of Being that inspires Heidegger to struggle to recover a sense of Being or acknowledge the mystery of "Being as Being"; and this means (among other things) "allowing Being to rein in all its questionableness . . . persevering in the question of Being," i.e., promoting the recognition that the question of Being can never be closed off and that genuine thinking must remain open to the possibility that ever new, more primordial determinations of Being may be disclosed (*N,* 4:201).

Admittedly, previous philosophers claimed to be concerned with the question of Being as such, and not just with this or that particular kind of being or aspect of being. But according to Heidegger, their attempts to ascertain the "Being of beings" actually covered up or helped to conceal the "persevering" or "primordial" question of Being itself (cf. *N,* 4:201). Previous philosophers tended to take for granted a certain understanding of Being—as, e.g., a permanent or "enduring presence," or something simple, identifiable, and available for objective discovery and control—which they then failed to recognize as such (*N,* 2:200). According to Heidegger's reading of the history of philosophy, Plato initiated the move toward a "productionist metaphysics" by transforming the question of Being into beingness: a transcendent or permanently present form *(eidos)* that makes things (beings in the world of sense) possible (cf. *N,* 1:151–210). Aristotle expanded this productionist attitude by arguing that for something "to be" means for it to be caused, effected, or produced. This productionist model of Being continued to develop in late classical times where "to be" meant to be the effect of some cause, and "causing" meant to work upon something, to effect it, to make it. In medieval times, God became identified with the Being of entities and was depicted as an all-powerful causal agent who planned, calculated, and produced "the relatively stable and independent presence" of entities.[28] A decisive transformation in the metaphysical model occurs with the "subjectivistic turn" of Descartes. For with Descartes humanity claimed for itself the role of God—the underlying substance or grounding support at the foundation of things—and thus entered into a *"new freedom of self-assured self-legislation"* (*N,* 4:100). The human being *(Dasein)* is transformed into a subject, and from now on the decision as to what is to count as a being comes to rest with the human being: "to be" means to be the object of a self-certain subject (cf. *N,* 4:86). Only what can be represented to the cognizing subject as indubitable counts as a being.

Human beings thus establish themselves in "a position of dominance" in relation to everything that is (*N*, 4:100).

According to Heidegger, however, the final and decisive transformation of the subjectivistic productionist model occurs with Nietzsche himself, who changes "the determination of the being of entities from objectivity—the re-presentability of entities of the self-certain subject—to value—the capacity for entities to contribute to the subject's limitless Will to Power."[29] Heidegger attributes to Nietzsche the "consummation" of subjectivistic (productionist) metaphysics: "to be" now means to be set-there *(zugestellt),* not merely as a pregiven object for a self-certain subject, but as a disposable *(verfügbar)* product of the human will (cf. *N,* 3:6–8).[30] With Nietzsche, "to be" means to be valuable for increasing the human will's "will to will," i.e., its aimless striving after ever more power-striving (cf. *N,* 4:248). "To be" means to be "generated by and for the Will to Will: human willing as that which causes, effects, and makes possible all things."[31] With his doctrine of will to power, Nietzsche thus affirms "the predominance of beings [i.e., human beings] over against Being" (*N,* 3:6).

Here again, one might raise objections to Heidegger's equating of Nietzsche's doctrine of will to power with the metaphysics of subjectivity. After all, Nietzsche often attacked Descartes's "ego cogito" as a logical or linguistic fiction (cf. *BGE,* §§ 16, 54). Yet according to Heidegger, Nietzsche still follows Descartes's lead in making human beings the subject or foundation of things. Unlike Descartes, however, Nietzsche's subject is not a fixed mental substance, but the body interpreted as a center of instincts, drives, affects, and sublimations, i.e., as will to power. Heidegger claims that this "body as given" idea still involves Nietzsche in a "fixity" that brings him into the philosophy of presence: "Nietzsche argues that being is as fixated, as permanent" (*N,* 2:200). And this forced sense of presence, Heidegger thinks, leads to the dangers of "radical objectifiability" and to the "disposability of beings," i.e., treating beings as nothing but objects of use, control, and management.[32] Moreover, like its Cartesian counterpart, the Nietzschean subject reins supreme over the whole of beings and posits "the measure for the beingness of every . . . being" (*N,* 4:121).[33] In claiming that "truths are illusions" and that "Being is an empty fiction," Nietzsche "fashions for the subject an absolute power to enjoin what is true and what is false" and hence to define what it means "to be" or "not to be" a being (*N,* 4:145). According to Nietzsche, what is true—what has being—is that which serves the interest of the subject whose essence is will to power (in the mode of existence of eternal recurrence; cf. *N*, 2:203). Being is thus reduced to the status of a value or a "condition of the preservation and enhancement of the will to power" (*N*, 4:176). This is why Heidegger considers Nietzsche the "consummation," and not the overcoming, of Western metaphysics: by reducing Being to a value, the doctrine of will to power makes the nihilism of the metaphysical tradition (the assumption that Being itself is nothing and the human will everything) a matter of philosophical principle.[34] Thus Nietzsche's "counter-ideals" of will to power and eternal recurrence, far from overcoming nihilism, actually express or exemplify the loss of any sense of Being, or the withdrawal of Being itself, in favor of beings (i.e., products of human will). As Heidegger reads him, Nietzsche understands Being in terms of value (or what is useful for enhancing the human will) because Being itself has totally withdrawn in default. And this brings to completion traditional metaphysics, which, according to Heidegger, is the history of Being in its withdrawal. As Heidegger sees it, Nietzsche's metaphysics of will to power is "the most extreme withdrawal of Being" and thus "the fulfillment of nihilism proper" (*N*, 4:204, 232). So Nietzsche brings to completion, in his denial of Being, the very nihilism he wanted to overcome.

Far from twisting free of the ascetic ideal, Heidegger claims, Nietzsche's doctrine of will to power actually provides the basis for its most complete expression in the modern "secularized" ascetic "will-to-control" everything. In other words, instead of seeking salvation in a transcendent world by means of ascetic self-denial—the aspect of metaphysics that Nietzsche most obviously rejects—salvation is now, Heidegger claims, sought "exclusively in the free self-development of all the creative powers of man" (*N*, 4:89). This unlimited expanding of power for power's sake parallels in many ways what Nietzsche characterized as the most terrifying aspect of the ascetic ideal: the pursuit of "truth for truth's sake." It is, according to Heidegger, the "hidden thorn" in the side of modern humanity (cf. *N*, 4:99). This "hidden thorn" expresses itself variously in the Protestant "work ethic" and in the "iron cage" of bureaucratic-technological rationality (discussed in the works of Max Weber); it also expresses itself in the various power aims of modern scientific/technological culture as well as in the frenzied impulse to produce and consume things at ever faster rates.

Heidegger even suggests that Nietzsche's own figure of the Overman *(Übermensch)* foreshadows the calculating, technological attitude of modern secularized asceticism: "His Overman [stands] for the technological worker-soldier who would disclose all entities as standing-reserve necessary for enhancing the ultimately aimless quest for power for its own sake."[35] This emerging technological human, grounded in a control-oriented anthropocentrism, compels entities to reveal only those one-dimensional aspects of themselves that are consistent with the power aims of a technological/productionist culture. Instead of dwelling and thinking in a world unified by what Heidegger metaphorically terms the "fourfold of earth and sky, gods and mortals," impoverished modern technocrats occupy a world "bereft of gods" in which thinking becomes calculating, and dwelling becomes tantamount to the "technological domination of nature" and what Nietzsche calls "the common economic management of the earth" in which "mankind will be able to find its best meaning as a machine in the service of this economy" (*WP*, § 866). Thus citizens come to be viewed primarily as consumers, wilderness is looked upon in terms of "wildlife management areas," and genuine human freedom is "replaced by the organized global conquest of the earth, and the thrust into outer space" (*N*, 4:248). As Heidegger sees it, "our era entertains the illusion that man, having become free for his humanity, has freely taken the universe into his power and disposition" (*N*, 4:248).

In summary, Nietzsche tried to combat the nihilism of the ascetic ideal (e.g., the collapse of the Christian table of values) by bringing forth new nonascetic values that would enhance rather than devalue humanity's will to power. According to Heidegger, however, instead of overcoming nihilism, Nietzsche simply reinforced it. By characterizing Being as an "empty fiction" and "the last smoke of a vaporized reality" (*TI*, 2:2, 481), and by degrading it to the status of a value for enhancing the subject's will to power, Nietzsche loses any sense of Being as such. For him it is a mere nothing, a "nihil." And this brings to completion the "fundamental movement" of history in the West, which is nihilism: the withdrawal of Being itself and the consequent focus on beings as objects for "consolidating the power of Will and for expanding it out beyond itself" in an ever-increasing spiral.[36] As Heidegger sees it, this "eternally recurring" will to power, or "will to will," is a will-to-control that only reinforces the nihilism Nietzsche feared: the loss of meaning or direction, the devaluation of the highest values, the "constructs of domination," and the devotion to frenzied consumption and production.

Where to now? How can humanity find its way out of this "age of accomplished destitution," "the epoch of the concealment of Being in the unconcealment of beings in the form of will to power" (*N*, 4:248)? Here Heidegger calls for a new way of thinking—a meditative way as opposed to a calculative way—that places itself into "tarrying inherence in the midst of the self-veiled truth of Being" and that "lets entities be" (*N*, 4:233). In other words, as opposed to the power-oriented ways of objectifying, "entrapping" *(Nachstellen),* and "enframing" *(Ge-stell),* things in the "external" world (and the "internal" one as well) as "resources" for mastery and control, Heidegger advocates a way of thinking and existing in the "openness" of Being so that entities can manifest themselves in various appropriate ways (cf. *QT,* 15, 19). By contrast, "technological humanity fills up that openness with methodological projects which compel entities to manifest themselves in a one-dimensional way" only, e.g., as calculable resources (cf. *QT,* 21).[37] Heidegger insists that any discussion of Being itself must always remain interrogative, open to the possibility that more primordial and ever new dimensions of Being may always be disclosed. As opposed to the egoism, power drive, and self-centeredness that Heidegger sees as hallmarks of modernity, he calls instead for keeping alive and open the question of Being as such, uncovering original experiences of it that have been concealed by the metaphysical tradition in the West, and promoting the recognition that the question of Being can never be closed off. In a word, Heidegger aims at a recovery of the sense or mystery of Being, which at the very least means a sense of power that cannot be brought under the control and mastery of technological humanity (cf. *N*, 4:239–45). Such a recovery would also involve a recovery of the original and nonmetaphysical sense of truth *(aletheia)* as the unconcealment of Being, and a revised conception of human beings *(Dasein)* as "shepherds of the mystery of Being, keepers of the house of Being," i.e., as those whose essential role is to "let the Being of beings disclose itself," instead of insisting on the mastery and control of beings in accord with the technological nihilism that Heidegger considers the "completion" of metaphysics.[38]

Heidegger recognizes the possible "abstractness" of his concern with "heeding the Being of Being" and "responding to the call of unconcealment" (cf. *N*, 4:224–30; *QT,* 19). He is also aware of the danger that his "call" will be misinterpreted as a kind of neoromantic (or even neo-Luddite) attempt to escape the complexities of contemporary life by either glorifying some idyllic pastoral way of life (e.g., that of the Schwarzwald peasant) or reveling in "the absurd wish to revive what is past" (*QT*, 22). Admittedly, many passages in his works tend to support such a misinterpretation.[39] Yet Heidegger presents his own philosophical analysis, not as a rejection of modern science or technology per se, but as a "preparation" of sorts for a more "fundamental ontology" that will help supply some missing account of Being that he believes has been concealed or covered over by the modern technological/scientific obsession with calculating, identifying, and ordering nature exclusively as a "system of information" and "standing reserve" (cf. *QT*, 23). In his later works, he tends to characterize his analysis more in terms of an "interrogative" approach that focuses on intensifying the enigma of Being and promoting the recognition that this enigma can never be completely resolved or pigeonholed into the "dry," "monotonous," and sometimes "oppressive" categories of a technological, power-oriented culture (cf. *QT*, 17). As technology and science become increasingly important in our lives, Heidegger seeks a serious "meditative" way of thinking about questions of technology, science, and culture that is not itself driven by the self-same "entrapping," "ensnaring," or "enframing" way of disclosing things—"that setting-upon which sets upon man"—characteristic of technological culture (cf. *QT*, 20). He also seeks a way of thinking that is open to a transformation of our current power-oriented cultural reality and that goes beyond "thinking [exclusively] in terms of values and calculation."[40] In short, he seeks a transformation in our sense of reality that would allow us to "affirm the unavoidable use of technical devices, and also deny them the right to dominate us" (*DT*, 54).[41]

Thus we might conclude that what Heidegger's philosophy offers us is a (Nietzsche-inspired) genealogical interpretation of the meaning of the (post-Nietzschean) secularized ascetic "will-to-control," which he (Heidegger) thinks can be accounted for, in part at least, by "telling a story of the progressive narrowing, leveling, and totalizing of the West's understanding of being."[42] As Heidegger sees it, our current technological understanding of being thinks of everything in terms of values and calculations—as resources to be stockpiled, used, and then discarded. Moreover, it seeks "to order everything so as to achieve more and more flexibility and efficiency" simply for the sake of flexibility and efficiency: its only goal is "optimal ordering, *for its own sake*."[43] In uncovering this peculiar and dangerous aspect of our current technological understanding of being—namely, that "calculative thinking may someday come to be accepted and practiced *as the only* way of thinking"—Heidegger seeks not to oppose technology, but to promote an understanding of being that necessarily involves mystery and receptivity and is sensitive to those aspects of things that can never be completely articulated, dominated, or controlled (*DT*, 56).[44] This transformation in our understanding of Being will, Heidegger hopes, enable us to remain open "to the meaning hidden in technology, *openness to the mystery*" and grant us "the possibility of dwelling in the world in a totally different way . . . [a way in] which we can stand and endure in the world of technology without being imperiled by it" (*DT*, 55). In urging us to rethink our dominant technological understanding of Being, Heidegger aims to reawaken what he sees as our essential receptivity to understanding Being as a mysterious and measureless source of meaning that both creates and sustains us.

Does Heidegger's philosophy succeed in opening up a new possibility of "being with beings" that does not diminish them to calculable "presences" for use, control, and management?[45] Does it disclose any new cultural paradigms or shared meaningful concerns? Does it open up new ways of acting and relating to things that could elicit our commitments, give our lives intrinsic meaning, and provide us with a new ground and foundation—a new rootedness in nature and our local surroundings (cf. *DT*, 55–56)?[46] Does it succeed in initiating a "recoiling" transformative movement of thought that will excite and elicit new cultural possibilities and lead people away from technological nihilism back to a new cultural wholeness and unity?[47] Certainly the complexities of Heidegger's earlier views (e.g., his analysis of the mortal temporality of *Dasein* and the ek-stasis that it constitutes), as well as the obscurity of some of his later claims (e.g., his call for a "releasement" toward things *(Gelassenheit)* and an open resoluteness to "let beings be"), have led many to question the viability of his project. Given our interest in Heidegger's relation to Nietzsche and Foucault, however, I shall conclude by focusing on a somewhat narrower question. In trying to overcome the nihilism of technological thinking and the obsession with mastery and control that, he thinks, drives modern civilization, has Heidegger in fact relapsed into the passive "nihilism of emptiness" or "pessimism of weakness" that Nietzsche feared would come to dominate modernity? Foucault's implied answer, in part at least, is yes.

Nihilism and the Arrangements of Power: Foucault

At first glance, the shift from Heidegger's analysis to Foucault's seems abrupt. In contrast to the seriousness and quasi-religious tone of Heidegger's thought, one encounters in Foucault a Nietzschean playfulness and even irreverence; one finds (as with Nietzsche) an emphasis on experimental thinking with a "hammerlike" style, continuous references to the body and its desires and affects, and an almost Dionysian invocation of revelry and intoxication: "the explosion of man's face in laughter, and the return of masks" (*OT,* 385). Moreover, like Nietzsche, Foucault focuses on issues of power and the arrangements of power; he offers genealogies of "epistemic and volitional capacities" and a "genealogy of truth" in which the concepts of history and truth are analyzed in terms of the "war and struggle" of different "wills to power" attempting to subdue different institutions or disciplines for their own purposes—each will attempting to impose a certain interpretation on history, to make history a certain kind of thing.[48] In his genealogical approach (which comes directly from Nietzsche), Foucault questions modern notions of self, society, punishment, and history by showing how they have been constituted and by tracing their lineages. Moreover, he identifies particular practices of power and knowledge in the present (the assumed value of which he puts in question), and he uses a genealogical analysis to reveal the contingency of the present practices (and concepts associated with them) in order to demystify or "denaturalize" them.[49] In this way, he claims (like Nietzsche) to reject all essentialist "metaphysical" assumptions (e.g., about what is real and universal) and to be radically pluralistic about the existence of different kinds of interpretive strategies. Indeed, Foucault accepts much of Nietzsche's "perspectivist" claims about the radical interpretability of the world: the world is infinitely interpretable; it never comes to a final point; there is not always a clear distinction between truth and falsity or truth and illusion; truth and illusion may always be intermixed; there is no such thing as a "fixed" or "essential" object (e.g., the body) that you can end your analysis with—analysis can always go further. Yet despite his apparent anarchistic claims concerning truth, knowledge, and power, and despite the extreme vertigo caused by the perspectivist claim that "everything is just an interpretation," Foucault, like Nietzsche, does not wish to "halt at a negation, a No, a will to negation," but instead points the way to a new beginning, a "pathway to a new mode of life," albeit one where "the markings are often unclear and the course unfinished" (see *WP*, § 1041).[50] In particular, Foucault offers a strategy of resistance to traditional arrangements of power and knowledge, and he makes a number of innovative claims concerning the "critical/curative" properties of genealogy and the "stylization of freedom," e.g., that freedom means being able to resist a given social definition or "essence" that is put on one by others (refusing an economic, juridical, or even sexual identity that's given to one).[51] In this regard, Foucault can even be shown to fit in with a certain positivistic tradition in French philosophy (cf. Sartre). Finally, with Foucault we encounter a lingering Nietzschean problem with respect to the issues of truth and "transvaluation," viz., how can Foucault combine a genealogical view about the historical constitution of forms of knowledge with some nonrelativistic "curative" view that allows for strategies of resistance and innovative claims concerning freedom, but does not commit him to traditional (essentialist, dogmatic) doctrines of truth?

For all of his debt to Nietzsche, Foucault's main influence vis-à-vis the issue of nihilism is Heidegger's suggestion that the post-Nietzschean secularized will to power—the ascetic will-to-control—manifests itself not only in the external world (by, for example., transforming beings into "standing reserve") but in the internal one as well: transforming human beings into "resources" (or "bio-power") available for the totalizing power aims of a technological culture (cf. *N*, 4:240–45).[52] But where Heidegger tends to see the nihilism of the post-Nietzschean situation as describable primarily in terms of an all-encompassing but ultimately meaningless "will-to-will" (leading humanity to disclose entities as raw material for use and control), Foucault sees in technological nihilism an important change in the character of power itself. In the disciplinary practices and imperatives of technological systems, "power itself . . . seeks invisibility and the objects of power—those [human subjects] on whom it operates—are made the most visible. It is this fact of surveillance, constant visibility, which is the key to disciplinary technology."[53] In analyzing the "disciplinary practices" of such modern institutions as the asylum, the prison, the reformatory, and the factory, as well as such domains as sexuality and the use of pleasure, Foucault goes further than Heidegger in uncovering the surreptitious dimensions of technological nihilism. According to Foucault, the power relations at work in the institutions of modernity are both "intentional and nonsubjective" (*HS*, 1:94). Why speak of "intentionality without a subject, a strategy without a strategist?" According to Dreyfus and Rabinow, there is an internal logic of sorts to the disciplinary practices of modern technological systems:

> There is a push towards a strategic objective, but no one is pushing. The objective emerged historically, taking particular forms and encountering specific obstacles, conditions and resistances. Will and calculation were involved. The overall effect, however, escaped the actors' intentions, as well as those of anybody else. As Foucault phrased it, "People know what they do; they frequently know why they do what they do; but what they don't know is what what they do does."[54]

Put differently, under the guise of helping people achieve normalcy, modern institutions subject people to constant surveillance and disciplinary control; in addition, human sciences such as psychology and sociology are enlisted in this effort to disclose everything possible about the "normal" person so that men and women can be properly adjusted "to the imperatives of the technological system, which itself lies hidden in the apparently beneficial institutions carrying out the disciplinary training needed to keep the system going."[55] Such "systems" tend to take on an autonomous life of their own, where the only goal is to preserve and enhance the power relations and practices at work in the institutions of modernity. Foucault thus takes the nihilism disclosed in Heidegger's reading of the post-Nietzschean technological era one step further: humans are revealed not just as resources for the "total mobilization" of ultimately meaningless power aims, but as subjects completely present for surveillance and disciplinary control. Moreover, Foucault shows that and how the power arrangements at work in this new disclosure of humanity tend to conceal themselves; and what is made manifest by these hidden power relations are the disciplinary practices and institutions whose aim is to "normalize" and "standardize" human life.[56]

Like Heidegger, Foucault also sees these power arrangements and technological systems of modern institutions as embedded in an "inarticulable" shared background of practices—what Heidegger terms a "clearing"—which contains a concealed epistemic content or understanding of being within which particular events become evident and things and people appear as intelligible.[57] This shared background of habits, customs, and skills, against which objects and people appear as meaningful and usable, is never itself fully accessible to reflection or wholly representable as a system of beliefs and rules.[58] It is more of a historically transmitted "horizon" that we have inherited, which we largely take for granted and which we do not completely control. Like Heidegger, Foucault thinks that there is something slightly askew about the tacit background practices and prevailing ways of speaking and doing that have been transmitted to us. Both philosophers view our fundamental orientation toward the world—our modern "clearing"—as nihilistic in that it emphasizes the dominance (and even autonomy) of calculative, technological thinking; and both link this "autonomy of technology" to "metaphysical humanism" (or the modern metaphysics of subjectivity), which places the human subject "at the center of reality and history" and which seeks in it an absolute foundation for knowledge and value.[59]

As we have seen, Heidegger's approach to dealing with the problem of nihilism focuses more on analyzing the history of Western metaphysics (culminating in Nietzsche) to show how all modern thinking comes to be "consumed in ordering," how all valuing is reduced to the instrumental, how all of our options become increasingly technological, and how all revealing presents itself "only in the unconcealedness of standing reserve" (*QT,* 33). His "curative" strategy focuses more on cultivating a "meditative thinking" or "recollection" *(Andenken)* of Being that renounces the modern quest for certainty and mastery of Being and prepares the way for alternative modes of knowing and living that may, in his words, let "man see and enter into the highest dignity of his essence" (*QT,* 32). Foucault's analysis is less totalizing than Heidegger's. He does not attempt to provide a general account of the beliefs and practices that compose the "essence" of modern technology, nor does he attempt to ground an alternative way of life on some objective account of what human beings essentially are.[60] Instead, Foucault's analysis focuses more on specific histories of institutions and the particular practices within their technological systems that, he thinks, have been largely overlooked in traditional accounts of power and authority (cf. *DP,* 23–24). For example, he documents the records of hospitals and reformatories, the case studies and treatises of the human sciences, and so forth, in an attempt to uncover the hidden forms of disciplinary "power-knowledge" and "technologies of the body" located at the "micro-level" of social institutions (cf. *DP,* 26–27).[61] Foucault traces the histories of the techniques and apparatus of power-knowledge "right down into the depths of society," by isolating the "latent functions" of such institutions as the school, the prison, and the factory, and by highlighting the "dysfunctionality" of such practices as punishment and education in order to focus on the other functions that these "disciplinary techniques" have surreptitiously served, for example, rendering bodies docile, obedient, and useful. Thus Foucault hopes to uncover the side-effects of power arrangements and domains of disciplinary practices (e.g., psychoanalysis) that are usually regarded as benign or beneficial (cf. *DP,* 26–27; 135–69).[62]

Foucault also offers us a "curative" strategy of resistance to particular practices of "power-knowledge" that he hopes will provide an alternative to technological nihilism and that may someday, as Heidegger puts it, restore "the proper dignity of humanity."[63] By advocating a strategy of rebellion against the often malevolent ways in which we have already been defined, categorized, and normalized by the dominating technologies of power of modern institutions, Foucault may also hope to show that the undesirable effects of specific disciplinary practices are not necessarily inevitable, and that resistance may point the way to more beneficial alternative features of technological systems—features about which Foucault has surprisingly little to say.

To paraphrase Foucault, we might conclude that it is with the experience of both "Nietzsche and Heidegger . . . in that region where the gods have turned away, where the desert is increasing" that Foucault's own critical project begins (*OT,* 334). In an often quoted interview, Foucault even says the following:

> For me Heidegger has always been the essential philosopher. . . . My entire philosophical development was determined by my reading of Heidegger. I nevertheless recognize that Nietzsche outweighed him. . . . [T]hese are the two fundamental experiences I have had. It is possible that if I had not read Heidegger, I would not have read Nietzsche. I had tried to read Nietzsche in the fifties but Nietzsche alone did not appeal to me—whereas Nietzsche and Heidegger: that was a philosophical shock![64]

Why a "philosophical shock"? The answer, in part, may be that from Foucault's perspective, Heidegger's insightful reading of Nietzsche and the problem of nihilism is itself too ascetic. Heidegger's emphasis on "silence" as proper to *Dasein's* being, his frequent use of quasi-religious (even Schopenhauerean) terms of "grace" and "call of conscience," his many references to the destiny of the German *Volk,* his avoidance of politics and the serious "quietistic" tone of Heideggerian *Gelassenheit* are all reminiscent of the life-denying ascetic ideal Nietzsche sought to avoid.[65] Moreover, Foucault seems to join with Derrida and other "neo-Nietzscheans" in regarding Heidegger's idea of "letting Being be"—his vision of those who have left traditional metaphysics behind and with it the obsession with mastery and technology that drives contemporary civilization—as too passive or apathetic a response to the legitimate problems of post-Nietzschean nihilism that Heidegger's own analysis uncovers.[66] Here we have arrived at a key difference between Heidegger and Foucault: for Foucault, Heidegger takes insufficient account of the playful and even irreverent elements in Nietzsche and of Nietzsche's critique of the dangers of the ascetic ideal. Foucault joins with other new Nietzscheans in promoting, as an alternative to Heideggerian *Gelassenheit,* the more Nietzschean vision of "playing with the text"—which in Foucault's case means promulgating active and willful images of resistance and struggle against particular practices of domination, rebellion against "micro-powers," and blatant disregard for tradition (cf. *DP,* 27).[67] This context-specific, unambiguously confrontational nature of Foucault's critique of the forms of domination and technologies of power lodged in modern institutions offers a more Nietzsche-like response than the one Heidegger offers to the nihilistic problems of Western civilization. As Foucault sees it, the lessons Heidegger would have us draw from Nietzsche throw us back to the passive "nihilism of emptiness" that Nietzsche feared. While not predicting the emergence of better times, Foucault tries to offer a better (less passive, less ascetic) model for reforming our "background practices" and for cultivating an affirmative attitude toward life that he and other neo-Nietzscheans think may be "our only chance to keep from extinguishing life on earth altogether."[68]

At this juncture we should ask whether the lessons that Foucault would have us draw from Heidegger's account of technology also hark back to another "incomplete" form of nihilism that Nietzsche equally feared: the "nihilism of negativity." Certain passages in Foucault would suggest as much. In one of the later interviews, Foucault refers to himself as "a hyperactive pessimist" who avoids apathy by seeing *everything* as "dangerous" precisely because all systems of power, all forms of social and political organization, can inhibit struggle and militate against their contestation.[69] And in a manner reminiscent of the Russian nihilism Nietzsche rejects, Foucault says: "Writing interests me only in the measure that it incorporates the reality of combat, as an instrument, a tactic, a spotlight. I would like my books to be like surgeons' knives, Molotov cocktails, or galleries in a mine, and, like fireworks, to be carbonized after use."[70] In underscoring the agonal nature of his work, Foucault shares with Nietzsche an almost tragic glorification of struggle in the face of overwhelming forces (of nihilism). Yet contra Nietzsche, much of Foucault's analysis of the mechanisms and arrangements of "power-knowledge" undercuts the possibility of formulating positive, alternative ideals for a better future. As one commentator points out, Foucault's understanding of modern power, as "ubiquitous, inescapable, stemming from [miro-levels] below, and productive of our very identity," rules out any "opiate belief in absolute emancipation":

> In the modern world the most insidious forms of power are shown to be productive forces engaged in the subjectification of their participant victims. Modern power not only restricts, it incites—and does so by means of administering over the self-definition of its subjects. . . . [A]n escape from [such] subjectification is impossible. Resistance to its forces remains the only alternative. . . . [T]here is no realm of freedom in which we may escape power to assert our nature: we might change our positions on the web [like a captured fly], but there is no jumping off.[71]

Hence, the only "ethico-political choice" we have, one that Foucault thinks we must make every day, is simply to determine which of the many insidious forms of power is "the main danger" and then to engage in an activity of resistance in the "nexus" of opposing forces.[72] "Unending action is required to combat ubiquitous peril."[73] But this ceaseless Foucauldian "recoil" from the ubiquitous power perils of "normalization" precludes, or so it would seem, formulating any defensible alternative position or successor ideals. And if Nietzsche is correct in claiming that the only prevailing human ideal to date has been the ascetic ideal, then even Foucauldian resistance will continue to work in service of this ideal, at least under one of its guises, viz., the nihilism of negativity. Certainly Foucault's distancing of himself from all ideological commitments, his recoiling from all traditional values by which we know and judge, his holding at bay all conventional answers that press themselves upon us, and his keeping in play the "twists" and "recoils" that question our usual concepts and habitual patterns of behavior, all seem a close approximation, in the ethico-political sphere, to the idealization of asceticism.

What may save Foucault from this charge is the following. Like Nietzsche and Heidegger, Foucault tends to see his own critical project as the "unfolding of a space in which it is once more possible to think" and the marking of "a threshold beyond which contemporary philosophy can begin . . . again" (*OT*, 342). Having argued in a Nietzschean fashion that humanity has no fixed essence or intrinsic identity waiting to be realized, Foucault rejects moralizing standards and codes and thinks that "the alternative to passive nihilism" entails an "artistic perspective": a political analogue of sorts to Nietzsche's "philosophical and aesthetic life of continual self-overcoming."[74] "One struggles because the uncontested life is deemed not worth living."[75] But what does one struggle toward?

Here Foucault seems less interested in defining a purpose for "incitation and struggle" than underscoring its "potential creativity": bringing into the struggle "as much gaiety, lucidity and determination as possible."[76] Given his belief that even our modern discourses of liberation, rights, and humanism are all deeply entangled in the inarticulable and inescapable background "web" of power practices, Foucault's only option to passive nihilism seems to be "the perpetuation and amelioration of the conditions that make struggle itself possible."[77] And this political task of promoting the "pathos of struggle" functions as an alternative to the ascetic ideal: creating and maintaining "many sites of resistance" to the numerous forms of domination, exploitation, and subjectification present in the social and political body.[78] Admittedly, the "pathos of struggle" has a strong (and from a Nietzschean perspective, a possibly suspect) negative component: struggling against any system of constraints or technologies of power that prevent individuals (affected by the systems) from having "the possibility of altering them" or "the means of modifying" them.[79] As an ethico-political ideal, the "pathos of struggle" would call for the negation of all political, social, and cultural conditions that preclude the possibility of struggling to change these conditions. As Foucault writes, "perhaps one must not be for consensuality, but one must be against nonconsensuality."[80] But it would also contain an affirmative component as well, a "struggle for" something: "Minimally, it will be a struggle for the establishing of conditions in which self-creation is made possible, in which the assertion of individuality and otherness is viable."[81] As with Nietzsche's alternative ideals (of "recurrence" and "will to power"), the final trajectory of the "pathos of struggle" remains undetermined. It can't tell us beforehand what our goals should be, only that (a) the conditions of their conception and articulation must remain "polymorphous" and "unhierarchical," and that (b) whatever they are, they should remain rooted in gratitude and service to life—"a joyful . . . creative, and self-constituting engagement"—rather than resentment against it.[82] But as with Nietzsche's nonascetic ideals, the "pathos of struggle" might also supply *some* affirmative content as well: the doing of what is necessary to affirm your creative freedom and enhance the ongoing process of self-definition and social definition (within the constraints of not excluding or disempowering the viable "other"). For example, overcome the oppression of your present situation if it prevents you from getting a sufficient sense of power and effectiveness in relation to life except by devaluing life.[83]

In a manner somewhat reminiscent of Schiller's attempt to instill an "aesthetic education" in humanity to promote political freedom, we might view Foucault as attempting to instill an "agonistic education"—a will to struggle within "an overarching aesthetics of life"—to prepare "the ground for, and manifest, our creative freedom."[84] According to Foucault, glimpses of freedom and creation of the self as a "work of art" are prompted by continuous acts of resistance and political struggle that serve to loosen the hold of those vast matrices of disciplinary power and technologies of the body that threaten to overwhelm and homogenize us (cf. *HS,* 2:10–11).[85] As Foucault sees it, then, a will to struggle, an "aesthetic agonism," becomes the defining characteristic and alternate (nonascetic) ideal that allows us to best live out our "unresolved existence"—surrounded by ubiquitous, inescapable power arrangements and tottering on the abyss of nihilism.

Does Foucault's "pathos of struggle" offer humanity a viable alternative—or what Nietzsche terms "an opposing will that might express an *opposing ideal*" (*GM,* 3: § 23)—to the present nihilistic conditions that both Foucault and Heidegger think characterize our modern technological era? Or is the "pathos of struggle" simply one further example of the post-Nietzschean "will-to-control," and hence of the technological frame of mind, which both philosophers think threatens the human race with annihilation? A convincing answer to these questions has yet to be given. As a down payment toward an answer, however, let me close with the following observations.

First, we might begin by rejecting a central component of Heidegger's argument against Nietzsche, namely, that in attempting to counter the spiritual corruption of the modern era, Nietzsche's philosophy culminates in a vain desire, rooted in the same nihilistic tendencies Nietzsche sought to overcome, for a "supreme form of mastery. . . . [for] making human power over the world absolute."[86] Contra Heidegger, we might try to argue that a careful examination of the "pathos" of the Nietzschean "exaltation of the will" shows that it eschews all such absolute "power trips" and technologies of control in favor of a "free-spirited skepticism," an internal sobriety (culminating, for example, in the highly prized Nietzschean value of "being-able-to-hold-silent" [*GM*, 1: §§ 9–10]), and an "intellectual conscience" that, in Nietzsche's words, remains open to "this whole marvelous uncertainty and rich ambiguity of existence" (*GS*, § 2). These "rare and identifying marks" of the higher human being—marks that Nietzsche says "the great majority of people lack" (*GS*, § 2)—bear a striking resemblance to the "saving" qualities that Heidegger says "keep meditative thinking alive" and foster our human receptivity to the few practices in our culture that may (someday) lead to "a new ground and foundation," a new nonnihilistic cultural paradigm, rich enough to give "new content" and meaning to our lives (*DT*, 55–57).[87] The need to safeguard such practices from being totally mobilized as "resources" or "standing reserve" may, in turn, provide a basis for the (nonascetic) politicizing of what both Nietzsche and Heidegger preferred to internalize, namely, the will to struggle. Thus, far from being an instance of the vain desire for mastery and control, we might view Foucault's "pathos of struggle" as a nonascetic creative strategy for preserving and even enhancing those marginal "spaces" and "saving" nontechnological practices within which ongoing struggles for self-creation and dignity can occur—struggles that may help prepare the ground (à la Heidegger) for a new cultural "clearing" that offers meaningful nonnihilistic options. And the imperative to safeguard and enhance the social and political conditions for the flourishing of nontechnological options and marginal spaces of "otherness" may, in turn, provide what many critics find missing in Foucault's account of political judgment, viz., a criterion for evaluating the merits of different forms of struggle and for showing that not all forms of struggle are equally valuable. How far one can push this approach without being charged with essentialism is a good question. Still, it seems to me that a critical, dialogical encounter between Nietzsche, Heidegger, and Foucault, such as the one suggested above, is needed to point the way "out the abyss" of our current cultural dilemmas to "a new and different way of thinking and being"—a way that leads beyond nihilism.

Notes

The research for this project was supported, in part, by a grant from the City University of New York PSC-CUNY Research Award Program. A special thank you goes to James N. Jordan for his editorial comments and suggestions.

1. Friedrich Nietzsche, *The Will to Power*, trans. Walter Kaufmann and R. J. Hollingdale (New York: Viking Press, 1968). Hereafter abbreviated as *WP* and cited by section number. I generally follow the standard translations of Nietzsche and Heidegger listed below, and the alterations I have made are usually minor ones.

2. Martin Heidegger, *Nietzsche*, trans. David Krell, 4 vols. (New York: Harper and Row, 1982). Hereafter abbreviated as *N* and cited by volume and page number.

3. Michel Foucault, *The Order of Things* (New York: Vintage Books, 1973). Hereafter abbreviated as *OT* and cited by page number.

4. Cf. *Nietzsche's New Seas: Explorations in Philosophy, Aesthetics, and Politics*, ed. Michael Allen Gillespie and Tracy B. Strong (Chicago: University of Chicago Press, 1988), 1.

5. See Maudemarie Clark, *Nietzsche on Truth and Philosophy* (Cambridge: Cambridge University Press, 1990), 9.

6. Friedrich Nietzsche, *On the Genealogy of Morals*, "Second Essay," § 13, translated by W. Kaufmann and R. J. Hollingdale, in *Basic Writings of Nietzsche* (New York: Random House, 1968). Hereafter abbreviated as *GM* and cited by essay and section number.

7. See Raymond Geuss's discussion in his introduction to Nietzsche's *Birth of Tragedy and Other Writings*, trans. Ronald Speirs (Cambridge: Cambridge University Press, 1999), xii. See also Friedrich Nietzsche, *Ecce Homo*, trans. Walter Kaufmann, in *Basic Writings of Nietzsche*, 783. Hereafter abbreviated as *EH* and cited by page number.

8. Compare also Friedrich Nietzsche, *Beyond Good and Evil*, §§ 2, 9, 14, 34, translated by Walter Kaufmann in *Basic Writings of Nietzsche*. Hereafter abbreviated as *BGE* and cited by section number.

9. Nietzsche sometimes cites Kant's "postulates of practical reason" (Freedom, God, Immortality) and Hegel's "Absolute" as examples of "weak nihilism" (cf. *GM*, 3: § 1; *WP*, § 1).

10. See Arthur Danto's excellent discussion of philosophical nihilism in *Nietzsche as Philosopher* (New York: Columbia University Press, 1980), 19–35.

11. Friedrich Nietzsche, "Homer's Contest," trans. Maximilian Mügge, in *Early Greek Philosophy and Other Essays* (New York: Russell and Russell, Inc., 1964), 53

12. See Geuss, introduction, xxv.

13. Ibid., xxvi–xxvii.

14. The expression "nihilism of negativity" comes from Danto; see his *Nietzsche as Philosopher*, 29.

15. For example, the character of Bazarov says, "I do not believe in anything," but then asserts "chemists are more valuable than poets."

16. Raymond Geuss, *Morality, Culture, and History: Essays on German Philosophy* (Cambridge: Cambridge University Press, 1999), 21.

17. See Clark, *Nietzsche on Truth and Philosophy*, 184–87, 191–92, 234.

18. See ibid., 184–87.

19. Feuerbach claims that the values embodied in Christian religious tradition are basically the right ones—i.e., both positive and appropriate to human nature—just expressed in an "alienated" form. By contrast, Nietzsche thinks that the "moral values" generated in the genealogical situation of the experience of failure (e.g., the reactive and resentful slave/plebian values) are themselves a form of "counter-nature."

20. See also Geuss, *Morality, Culture, and History*, 178.

21. See Clark, *Nietzsche on Truth and Philosophy*, 9.

22. Cf. Friedrich Nietzsche, "Twilight of the Idols," trans. Walter Kaufmann, in *The Portable Nietzsche* (New York: Viking, 1968). Hereafter abbreviated as *TI* and cited by page number.

23. Cf. Clark, *Nietzsche on Truth and Philosophy*, 205–86.

24. Ibid. Cf. Friedrich Nietzsche, *Thus Spoke Zarathustra*, 3:3, in *The Portable Nietzsche*, trans. Walter Kaufmann. Cf. also Friedrich Nietzsche, *The Gay Science*, trans. Walter Kaufmann (New York: Random House [Vintage], 1974), § 341. Hereafter abbreviated as *GS* and cited by section number.

25. Charles E. Scott, *The Question of Ethics: Nietzsche, Foucault, Heidegger* (Bloomington and Indianapolis: Indiana University Press, 1990), 45.

26. Martin Heidegger, *The Question Concerning Technology and Other Essays*, trans. William Lovitt (New York: Harper and Row, Inc., 1977). Hereafter abbreviated as *QT* and cited by page number.

27. See Michael E. Zimmerman, *Heidegger's Confrontation with Modernity* (Bloomington and Indianapolis: Indiana University Press, 1990), 202–3.

28. See ibid., 171–72.

29. Ibid., 171.

30. Cf. ibid., 172.

31. Ibid., 173.

32. See Scott, *The Question of Ethics*, 115–16, 138.

33. Cf. Clark, *Nietzsche on Truth and Philosophy*, 10.

34. See ibid.

35. Zimmerman, *Heidegger's Confrontation with Modernity*, 173.

36. See ibid., 186–87.

37. Ibid., 181.

38. See Clark, *Nietzsche on Truth and Philosophy*, 8.

39. For example, in "The Question Concerning Technology," Heidegger contrasts the "old wooden bridge" that is built organically into the Rhine River, "joining bank with bank for hundreds of years," with the "monstrousness" of the hydroelectric plant that dams up the river into the power plant, transforming the river into "a water power supplier" (*QT*, 16). In the same work, he also contrasts the old-time forester, "who walks the same forest path in the same way as did his grandfather," with the modern park ranger who "today is commanded by profit-making in the lumber industry, whether he knows it or not." The modern forester is "made subordinate to the orderability of cellulose, which for its part is challenged forth by the need for paper, which is then delivered to newspapers and illustrated magazines. The latter, in their turn, set public opinion to swallowing what is printed, so that a set configuration of opinion becomes available on demand" (*QT*, 18).

40. See Hubert L. Dreyfus, "Heidegger on the Connection between Nihilism, Art, Technology, and Politics," in *The Cambridge Companion to Heidegger,* ed. Charles Guignon (Cambridge: Cambridge University Press, 1993), 307.

41. Martin Heidegger, *Discourse on Thinking,* trans. John M. Anderson and E. Hans Freund (New York: Harper and Row, 1966). Hereafter abbreviated as *DT* and cited by page number.

42. Dreyfus, "Heidegger on the Connection," 314.

43. Ibid., 305–6.

44. As Heidegger sees it, our technological understanding of Being is the cause of much of our cultural discontent. For apart from encountering things and ourselves as resources to be ordered and used, nothing shows up as anything meaningful at all for us, no possibilities for action make sense. To combat the "flatness" and "drabness" of the modern age, people tend increasingly to retreat into "private experiences": voyeuristic entertainment, frenzied consumption, drugs, spectator fads, and so forth. This hardly compensates for the lack of "shared experiences" of great projects that "focus public concerns and elicit social commitment" (see ibid., 292, 307).

45. See Scott, *The Question of Ethics,* 138–40.

46. Cf. also Dreyfus, "Heidegger on the Connection," 309–12.

47. Cf. Scott, *The Question of Ethics,* 158–60.

48. See Michel Foucault, "Truth and Power," in *Power/Knowledge: Selected Interviews and Other Writings,* ed. Colin Gordon (New York: Pantheon Books, 1980), 109–33; and "Nietzsche, Genealogy, History," in *Language, Counter-Memory, Practice,* ed. Donald F. Bouchard (New York: Cornell University Press, 1977), 139–64. Cf. also Scott, *The Question of Ethics,* 94–95.

49. See Jana Sawicki, "Heidegger and Foucault: Escaping Technological Nihilism," *Philosophy and Social Criticism* 13, no. 2 (1987): 169.

50. See also Leslie Paul Thiele, "The Agony of Politics: The Nietzschean Roots of Foucault's Thought," *American Political Science Review* 84, no. 3 (1990): 909.

51. See Michel Foucault, *The History of Sexuality,* vols. 1–3, trans. Robert Hurley (New York: Vintage and Pantheon Books, 1980–87). Hereafter abbreviated as *HS* and cited by volume and page number.

52. See also Michel Foucault, *Discipline and Punishment: The Birth of the Prison,* trans. Alan Sheridan (New York: Vintage Books, 1979), 185–87. Hereafter abbreviated as *DP* and cited by page number.

53. Herbert Dreyfus and Paul Rabinow, *Michel Foucault: Beyond Structuralism and Hermeneutics* (Chicago: University of Chicago Press, 1982), 159.

54. Ibid., 187.

55. Zimmerman, *Heidegger's Confrontation with Modernity,* 203.

56. See ibid., 203.

57. See Sawicki, *Heidegger and Foucault,* 156 and 171; see also Dreyfus, "Heidegger on the Connection," 296.

58. See Sawicki, *Heidegger and Foucault,* 156 and 171.

59. Ibid., 156–57; Dreyfus, "Heidegger on the Connection," 296.

60. See Sawicki, *Heidegger and Foucault,* 168–69.

61. Also cf. ibid., 160.

62. Cf. also ibid., 161–64.

63. Martin Heidegger, "Letter on Humanism," in *Basic Writings,* ed. David Krell (New York: Harper and Row, 1977), 233.

64. Michel Foucault, *Politics, Philosophy, Culture: Interviews and Other Writings, 1977–1984,* ed. Lawrence Kritzman (New York and London: Routledge, 1988), 250.

65. See Scott, *The Question of Ethics,* 175–78; Sawicki, *Heidegger and Foucault,* 170.

66. See Clark, *Nietzsche on Truth and Philosophy,* 19

67. See also Jacques Derrida, *Writing and Difference,* trans. Alan Bass (Chicago: University of Chicago Press, 1978), 278–93; and *Margins of Philosophy,* trans. Alan Bass (Chicago: University of Chicago Press, 1982), 109–36.

68. Clark, *Nietzsche on Truth and Philosophy,* 20.

69. See Michel Foucault, afterword to *Michel Foucault: Beyond Structuralism and Hermeneutics,* 231–32; see also Thiele, "The Agony of Politics," 916.

70. Michel Foucault, "An Interview with Michel Foucault," interview by Jean-Louis Ezine, trans. Renee Morel, *History of the Present* 1 (February 1985): 14.

71. Thiele, "The Agony of Politics," 907–8.

72. Foucault, afterword, 231–32

73. Thiele, "The Agony of Politics," 916.

74. Ibid., 915–16.

75. Ibid., 916.

76. See Foucault, afterword, 222–23; see also "An Interview with Michel Foucault," 14.

77. Thiele, "The Agony of Politics," 918.

78. Cf. Sawicki, *Heidegger and Foucault,* 170; ibid., 919–20.

79. Foucault, *Politics, Philosophy, Culture,* 294–95.

80. Michel Foucault, "Politics and Ethics: An Interview," In *The Foucault Reader,* ed. Paul Rabinow (New York: Pantheon Books, 1984), 379.

81. Thiele, "The Agony of Politics," 919.

82. Cf. Clark, *Nietzsche on Truth and Philosophy,* 245–86; Thiele, "The Agony of Politics," 919–20.

83. See Clark, *Nietzsche on Truth and Philosophy,* 245–86; Thiele, "The Agony of Politics," 921.

84. Thiele, "The Agony of Politics," 920–22. See also Friedrich Schiller, *On the Aesthetic Education of Man in a Series of Letters,* ed. Elizabeth M. Wilkinson and L. A. Willoughby (Oxford: Oxford University Press, 1967), especially "Letters," 1–3, 26–27.

85. Cf. also Foucault, afterward, 237.

86. Peter Berkowitz, *Nietzsche: The Ethics of an Immoralist* (Cambridge: Harvard University Press, 1995), 8–9.

87. The "marginal" practices Heidegger tends to "idealize" are those he thinks direct people away from consumption, manipulation, and "meaningless fragmentation" toward a "gentle communion together in association with all things"—e.g., a "conversation on a country path" with one's colleagues, hiking on a wilderness trail with friends, sampling the local wine, and so forth (see *DT,* 58–90; see also Dreyfus, "Heidegger on the Connection," 310–11, and Scott, *The Question of Ethics,* 202–12). Obviously, much more is required than this to open a possible "clearing release" *(Gelassenheit)* out of our current technological nihilism.

Subjecting Dasein

Ladelle McWhorter

"Das 'Subjekt' ist eine Fiktion," Nietzsche declares in aphorism 370 of *Der Wille zur Macht*. There is no such thing as an ego, a unitary center of personhood that can be appraised and approved for its virtue and wisdom or blamed for its premeditated transgressions and irresponsible beliefs. Subjectivity does not exist. Despite Nietzsche's pervasive influence, however, the question of subjectivity—the ontological nature, the ethical status, and the epistemological significance of the human subject—has been a preeminent theme in Continental philosophy for the entirety of the twentieth century. Virtually all Continental philosophers have found it necessary to address the question. Martin Heidegger and Michel Foucault are not exceptional in that regard. Both thinkers take up the question as a central issue in their work; both have a great deal to say about subjectivity and its philosophical place.

On the face of it, however, the two men's conceptions of subjectivity seem quite divergent, particularly when one looks at the earlier work of Heidegger alongside the later work of Foucault. In *Sein und Zeit,* Heidegger undertakes an analytic of Dasein, a systematic phenomenological investigation of individual human existence, while Foucault (in texts such as *Surveiller et punir,* for example) eschews any such overarching ontological project and pluralizes subjectivity to speak of historically emergent subjectivi*ties*. (And some would say, as a follower of Nietzsche, he goes so far as to debunk and dismantle subjectivity altogether.) If one reads Heidegger as an existentialist through the French existential movement and Foucault as a Nietzschean iconoclast (especially through North American leftist and feminist commentators), there seems to be no ground of comparison. Heidegger, it would seem, believes in the phenomenological and epistemological primacy of the human subject, while Foucault apparently believes that there is no such thing as the subject at all.

To compare Heidegger's and Foucault's understandings of subjectivity, to stage a critical encounter between them on this issue, the first thing that must be done is to put these two philosophers onto some common ground. We can do that by developing a reading of Foucault that dispels the widely held idea that he repudiates the notion of subjectivity in toto and a reading of Heidegger that does not take the analytic of Dasein to be ahistorical. Only then can we usefully compare the two ways of thinking and see how they contrast and what differing effects they might have.

I will begin, then, with Foucault. In the first section of this chapter I will discuss the ubiquitous claim that Foucault repudiates subjectivity as an analytic category and an ontological reality and will put forth an alternative interpretation of his work. In the second section I will discuss the view—put forward by Kevin Hill, for one—that Foucault's account of subjectivity is a direct reaction against Heidegger's work. Then I will begin to develop a reading of Heidegger that distinguishes between Dasein on the one hand and subjectivity on the other and that takes very seriously the import of temporality in Dasein's constitution—my aim here being to bring out a Heideggerian account of Dasein that is historical in some of the ways that Foucault's pluralized subjectivities are historical. In this section I will move toward a way of reading subjectivity in Heidegger's work that focuses on the effects of his discursive practice more than on the assertions that he makes. It is on this ground, I believe—the shifting and perhaps ungrounding ground of discursive effects—that convergence between the two philosophers can usefully and fruitfully occur. In the final section of the chapter, then, I will stage this convergence by turning to the issue of care, a major theme in both thinkers' writings. I will argue that under the theme of care Heidegger's work moves thinking along some of the same paths that Foucault's work tends to move. Differently put, I will argue that both thinkers engage in philosophical practices of care that create some similar philosophical effects, that transform the thinking that goes on in, as, and alongside their texts. I will argue that both are caught up in practices of philosophical self-overcoming that move them and their readers beyond such notions as subjectivity as traditionally conceived. Although their differences are great, I hope to show that the consequences of following their very different paths are in some ways remarkably similar.

The Subject for Foucault

In an interview from the mid-1970s, Foucault discusses his interest in coming to an understanding of the historical emergence of certain categories of human being—such as the madman or the criminal. The emphasis in his discussion, as in his analyses, is not on subjectivity "itself," but rather on history, on emergence and passage; he wants to understand how forms of subjectivities that have not previously existed have come into existence (and how some have passed away). It is in that context that he says:

> I don't believe the problem can be solved by historicising the subject as posited by the phenomenologists, fabricating a subject that evolves through the course of history. One has to dispense with the constituent subject, to get rid of the subject itself, that's to say, to arrive at an analysis which can account for the constitution of knowledges, discourses, domains of objects, etc., without having to make reference to a subject which is either transcendental in relation to the field of events or runs in its empty sameness throughout the course of history.[1]

It is this passage, above all,[2] that has led so many readers to conclude that Foucault takes Nietzsche literally and maintains that there is no such thing as subjectivity.[3] But it is important to note that here, as elsewhere, Foucault is actually making a much more nuanced and strategic (as opposed to ontological) claim. He is actually saying that to understand the emergence of certain forms of subjectivity in history, we have to refrain from presuming that any aspect of subjectivity stands apart from history and preexists its historical "expression" or formation. History—or more precisely historical forces, networks of power relations—must receive complete analytic priority over subjectivity if we are to take the historical emergence of subjectivities like the delinquent or the madman seriously. Therefore, Foucault's analytic demotion of subjectivity, far from being the prelude to dismissing subjectivity altogether, is a way of coming to terms with the reality of subjectivities *as they actually occur and as we experience them.* Subjectivity is not dismissed at all; it takes on central importance as the very reason for Foucault's repudiation of ahistorical categories. As he asserts in a 1983 interview, "[I]t is not power, but the subject, which is the general theme of my research."[4]

Nevertheless, many commentators still object that Foucault is effectively eliminating subjectivity not only as a historical constant, but as the individual human agent. For, if there is no center of identity or selfhood that persists regardless of historical change, there is no agent who can initiate thought and action; what appears as subjectivity is in reality just an effect of historical, social, and political forces and so (as is often concluded) cannot ever act freely, independent of such forces. Linda Alcoff writes,

> [I]t is not simply the transcendental notion of subjectivity that Foucault is opposing, that is, a subject that is transhistorical and universal, but the notion of a subject as a being with a kind of primordial interiority that is autonomous or spontaneous in some ontological sense. This is why Foucault says that historicizing the subject is insufficient and that we must dispense with the constituent subject altogether. . . . What his analysis undermines is the conceptualization of the very internal life of consciousness that has been taken, within the Cartesian tradition, to be the ultimate authority, a level of reality about which we can have more direct knowledge than any other and that generates a knowledge least open to interpretation and illusion.[5]

Not only is Foucault opposing a perhaps questionable philosophical formulation of transcendental subjectivity—a Kantian or Husserlian transcendental ego—but, according to Alcoff, he is also opposing the more usual, commonsense notion of subjectivity as my own inner life, my own sense of myself persisting through time, my own consciousness as distinct from the various experiences that I undergo, and my ability to originate action.

It is this last issue that most distresses Alcoff and many other feminist and leftist commentators.[6] If we adopt Foucault's analysis of subjectivity as a pluralized, historically emergent effect of networks of power, we allegedly lose any claim to freedom or responsibility—in short, we lose agency. As I have argued elsewhere,[7] I believe this understanding and consequent criticisms of Foucault result from a tendency to read passages such as the one quoted above about the role of the concept of subjectivity in various philosophical projects alongside other passages where Foucault is concerned with subjectivities as effects of power. In particular, Alcoff cites an interview from 1983 where Foucault says, "It is a form of power which makes individuals subjects. There are two meanings of the word *subject:* subject to someone else by control and dependence, and tied to [one's] own identity by a conscience or self-knowledge. Both meanings suggest a form of power which subjugates and makes subject to."[8]

Surely the two definitions of the word *subject* that Foucault offers here are uncontroversial. And, while subjection of the first sort does compromise agency, subjection of the second sort is the very basis *for* agency; without conscience or self-knowledge surely responsible decision and action could not occur. What troubles Alcoff and others is the last sentence, wherein Foucault suggests that conscience and self-knowledge are effects of subjugation. If it is the case that power is the source of conscience and self-knowledge, then it would appear that individual selves have no control over their own beliefs and hence their own actions; agency is an illusion.

This conclusion can be avoided, however, if we take very seriously Foucault's account of power. Foucault insists that there is no such thing as power, no entity that stands apart from and causes "its" effects.[9] Power is an event, not a thing. It is not a cause that generates effects external to it. It exists only in its exercise, its occurrence, and it occurs as sets of relations. Within these relations of repeating events, selves (among other beings) form. Selves are events of power and remain always dependent upon repetitions of the power-events that maintain them. Consciences, self-understandings, capacities for judgment and creative practice come to be within these networks of repeating events. Subjugation occurs and subjects emerge, but the power relations that afford these emergences are not therefore external to them. Selves are not constrained by powers external and foreign to them. Relations and networks of power *are* selves, *are* subjects.[10]

The reason many commentators are troubled by Foucault's insistence on seeing subjectivities as "effects" of power is that they fail to revise their conception of power along Foucauldian lines. They persist in understanding power as an entity external to the entities it produces. Therefore they tend to view power as a kind of agent itself, the *real* agent of historical events, one that robs human individuals of their freedom by controlling their behavior and beliefs. In other words, they fail to make the analytic reassignment that Foucault insists upon; they fail to understand subjectivity as historical and then accuse Foucault of simply eliminating *human* subjectivity while promoting the subjectivity of power.

For Foucault the genealogist, all subjectivity is historically emergent. He writes, "Where the soul pretends unification or the self fabricates a coherent identity, the genealogist sets out to study the beginning—numberless beginnings whose faint traces and hints of color are readily seen by an historical eye. The analysis of descent permits the dissociation of the self, its recognition and displacement as an empty synthesis, in liberating a profusion of lost events."[11] This means, of course, that all subjectivity occurs in and as relations of power. But this does not mean that agency is illusory or that individual selves cannot take responsibility, create new things, or deliberately undertake to change themselves and the world around them. The question for Foucault, then, is: How do such beings with these capacities and others come into existence? How have these beings been effected and how do they effect changes in themselves and others? What relations exist between these beings and the systems of knowledge that they produce and that produce them?[12] These questions are thoroughly historical even while they are also thoroughly philosophical. But because subjectivities are historical, because capacities and self-knowledges differ across different subjectivities, the philosophical questions cannot be addressed outside specified historical contexts. How madmen came to exist and engage in practices of self-transformation is a different question from how homosexuals came to exist and engage in practices of self-transformation. There is no answer to the question of how subjectivity comes to exist for the simple reason that there is no such thing as subjectivity per se. There are only madmen and women, delinquents, homosexuals, citizens, Christians, and so on. But these subjectivities assuredly do exist—or at least have existed—and they can be objects of historico-philosophical (or, in other words, genealogical) investigation.

The Subject for Heidegger

All of this would seem to make Foucault's work incompatible with Heidegger's work in *Being and Time.* Indeed, Kevin R. Hill has argued that "[t]hroughout Foucault's early 'archeological' works, *Being and*

Time occupies a central position as an object of criticism."[13] In particular, Hill argues, Foucault is critical of Heidegger's attempt

> to move beyond the everyday to an interpretation of what Dasein really is (even while Dasein attempts to flee this knowledge), i.e., being-toward-death. This core of our being is intended as an ahistorical feature of Dasein which must enter into any of its comportments whatsoever—indeed, it is meant to be *the* transcendental condition for human existence. (335)

If Hill's assessment of Heidegger's project in *Being and Time* is correct, Foucault's abandonment of transcendental explanation and his complete historicization of human subjectivity is utterly irreconcilable with Heidegger's work—whether or not Foucault deliberately criticizes *Being and Time.*

Hill goes on to discuss Foucault's *Birth of the Clinic,* claiming that "[a]ccording to Foucault, prior to the nineteenth century, the concept of death was radically excluded from the concepts of life and nature as a kind of counter-force, and this conceptual structure made medical pathology an unintelligible enterprise" (335). In other words, Hill maintains, human experience of death has varied through history, so in Foucault's view it cannot serve as a constitutive feature of human existence transcendent to history.

Indeed, to this extent at least, Hill is undeniably correct. Foucault does claim in *The Birth of the Clinic* that death is completely reconfigured and realigned in medical discourses at the end of the eighteenth century,[14] and he goes on to claim that this change in the meaning of death is what gives us moderns our understanding of ourselves.[15] He reasserts this same claim in *The Order of Things* when he argues that the modern episteme, which is now in the process of crumbling, is rooted in death: "Is death not that upon the basis of which knowledge in general is possible?"[16] Death, as we understand it and as it figures into our knowledges and practices, is therefore a modern phenomenon, not a transhistorical one. Furthermore, Hill continues, the analytic of finitude that Foucault criticizes in *The Order of Things* "begins with Kant [and] reaches . . . its consummate expression in Heidegger's *Being and Time*" (337). Thus Foucault's announcement of the death of man is, in effect, also an announcement of the death of the kind of philosophical project that *Being and Time* represents.

While Hill's points are important, and he may well be right that one of Foucault's major targets in some of his work—particularly in

The Birth of the Clinic and *The Order of Things*—is the existentialist thought that Heidegger's early writings helped to initiate, the characterization of Heidegger's analytic of Dasein that Hill puts forth is not the only possible interpretation of Heidegger's work, and in fact is not the best interpretation. Far from seeking a transcendental structure or foundation for human being—which is, of course, what Foucault's historicization of subjectivity precludes—Heidegger is seeking a way to think about human existence that does not turn human being into a being-present. An ahistorical characteristic is an ever-present characteristic; it is something that defies temporality or at least that maintains itself in one mode of temporality. Insofar as human being, or subjectivity, has been thought that way, Heidegger's work is destructive of it.[17] Even prior to *Being and Time,* for example in his lecture course from the summer of 1923, Heidegger insists, "Dasein is not a 'thing' like a piece of wood nor such a thing as a plant—nor does it consist of experiences, and still less is it a subject (an ego) standing over against objects (which are not the ego)."[18] The term *Dasein* and the use made of the term *Dasein* are intended to move our thought away from the tradition that seeks transcendental structures. Heidegger writes:

> In choosing a term to designate this region of being and appropriately demarcate it, we have avoided the expression "human Dasein" [human existence], "human being," and will continue to do so. In all its traditional categorial forms, the concept of man fundamentally obstructs what we are supposed to bring into view as facticity. The question "What is man?" blocks its own view of what it is really after with an object foreign to it. (*Ontology,* 21)

And we do not see a departure from this position in *Being and Time.* Heidegger is adamant from the beginning of his analytic of Dasein that "[t]his being . . . never has the kind of being of what is merely objectively present within the world."[19] Just as Foucault announces his opposition to the phenomenological methods that posit an ahistorical subject, Heidegger announces his opposition to the medieval and modern philosophical thinking that substantializes human existence. He opens *Being and Time* with declarations such as this:

> One of our first tasks will be to show that the point of departure from an initially given *ego* and subject totally fails to see the phenomenal content of Da-sein. Every idea of a "subject" . . . still posits the *subjectum (hupokeimenon) ontologically* along with it, no matter how

> energetic one's ontic protestations against the "substantial soul" or the "reification of consciousness." (*B&T,* 43)

For Heidegger, as for Foucault, subjectivity is never treated as a substance, a foundation, or an origin, even when it is treated as a central philosophical issue. Hill may want to argue, as does Michel Haar,[20] that Heidegger fails to think Dasein without surreptitiously positing an ahistorical transcendental feature of human existence, and thus he might argue that Heidegger's work differs from Foucault's in its degree of success; but in aim there is more similarity than difference. Both thinkers are attempting to move away from traditional conceptions of subjectivity and into a way of thinking that disciplines itself to history rather than to transcendental truth.

Furthermore, deathliness is not an ever-present transcendental condition for the possibility of Dasein, as Hill apparently would have it. Dasein's deathliness is its possibility for absence, discontinuity, cessation, passage. Dasein's deathliness is its being in history, its lack of eternality or rest in the self-same. Thinking Dasein's deathliness is thinking its nontranscendentality. Heidegger moreover does not posit a *consciousness* of deathliness as a necessary feature or characteristic of Dasein; Dasein is not given to itself as a subject who has deathliness ever before it as an object. Dasein just *is* deathly and ex-ists in that way of being. Awareness of deathliness also occurs, of course; even consciousness of deathliness may occur. But *consciousness* of deathliness or limit or loss is not what makes Dasein Dasein. In no way, therefore, is deathliness an essentially present thing either in Dasein's being or in Dasein's thinking. Dasein *is* as a being who may not be.

It is certainly a mistake to read Heidegger's analytic of Dasein as an analysis of human subjectivity squarely within the tradition of Descartes and Kant. Heidegger's work is not an extension of that tradition; it is a break from that tradition and a critique of it. Nevertheless, Heidegger was never able to finish the analysis he began in *Being and Time.* Despite his intention to work against the metaphysics of presence and to think Dasein against the long reign of substantial subjectivity, he could not fulfill his aim. Otto Pöggeler, among others, claims that the work was bound to fail, "because its point of departure carried within it the necessity of failure."[21] Despite himself, Pöggeler argues, Heidegger was too foundationalist in orientation, too intent upon wanting-to-ground. He starts with Dasein in an effort to secure or found his investigation into the question of being. Dasein's role in *Being and Time* is to stabilize the *Seinsfrage,* which means Dasein's non-self-identity is perpetually at odds with its function as analytic, phenomenological origin. Pöggeler writes, "Only slowly did Heidegger's thinking relinquish its wanting-to-ground. Experiencing the thrownness of the grounding projection had to be deepened to experiencing the abysmal character of the truth of Being" (130). The problem, according to Pöggeler, lay primarily in Heidegger's use of metaphysical language to undo metaphysical, or representational thinking. As he struggled with the questions his own work was raising, however, Heidegger's language gradually transformed, which made it possible for him to move beyond the quasi-foundationalist tendencies of the analytic of Dasein.

Nonetheless, Pöggeler emphasizes that Heidegger's early work, for all its flaws, does not come to an end in anticipation of the later work; there are not two Heideggers. *Being and Time* fails only on its own most literal terms. Much more importantly, it also succeeds. Its success lies in the fact that it serves as a pathway for Heidegger and for Heidegger's readers through a set of fundamental questions toward a different way of conceiving of those questions in particular and of philosophical practice in general. If we read Heidegger's work as a pathway, as Pöggeler suggests, rather than as a set of assertions and arguments, we will experience it in its eventful occurrence as an unfolding. It is this way of reading, I will argue in the next section, that allows Heidegger's work to move with or at least close to Foucault's.

Care

For Heidegger in *Being and Time,* Dasein is care.[22] Ontically this means that Dasein watches over, protects, repairs, and in general takes care of things and is concerned with and about others and self. All this is because things can decay and break and people can be injured or die. Care bespeaks an alertness to passage and deathliness. But this way of construing care does not constitute an adequate understanding of Heidegger's ontological claim that the being of Dasein is care. Fundamentally and primordially, care is not a project that Dasein inevitably takes on any more than deathliness is fundamentally and primordially an object of cognition. In Heidegger's terms, Dasein is a being that is always concerned about its being; it *is* always as ex-isting. It is a moving toward its own potentiality-for-being (and for nonbeing). Dasein is always ahead of itself, so to speak.[23] It is facticity. Ex-isting is a kind of stretching along, never resting in self-identity. It is this moving-ahead-of-itself in perpetual non-self-identity that is what Dasein *is*.

In this sense, Dasein *is* care—rather than, say, a subjectivity characterized by care or behaving with care. Dasein as care displaces subjectivity as substance with qualities. Dasein is an ever-non-self-identical ex-isting, "itself" only in ever moving beyond itself. This is Heidegger's claim. But more importantly, it is also simultaneously Heidegger's practice. In the process and effort of thinking Dasein as care, that thinking "itself" undoes itself, becomes nonidentical with itself. In this process, Heidegger is caught up in a movement of thinking that necessarily alters the thinking he is engaged in and the agent of that thinking. Within that movement of thinking, our very Cartesian conception of what thinking itself is must give way. For just as being is no longer thinkable in terms of objective presence, thinking is no longer the activity of subjects. Thus, just as subjects (and objects) are not fundamental in Foucault's thinking through the historical constitution of subjectivities, subjects and objects are not fundamental in this Heideggerian analysis of human existence, and through the course of this movement of thinking, subjects and objects lose their power to order our philosophical world.

Here particularly, in his discussion of care, we see the moving of Heidegger's thinking moving ahead of Heidegger's thinking. *What* he thinks is giving way to thinking such that that particular *what* is jeopardized. The effort to think ex-istence beyond the dictates of the Cartesian tradition eventually pushes itself beyond the questions it first poses for itself in order to get underway. For in this diminishing power of Cartesian subjects and objects, this analytic of Dasein, too, gradually loses its power and urgency. As the movement of thinking that is the analytic of Dasein does its work, it violates its own intentional ground. Thinking Dasein as care was, for it, a way, a path as Pöggeler puts it, beyond Dasein. The analytic of Dasein is an incomplete project, because it is a project of self-overcoming. Hence, not only is *Being and Time* about Dasein as care, but Heidegger's *work* in *Being and Time* essentially *is* care, and it is care that makes the thinking of care as conceived in *Being and Time* inessential.

Nevertheless, here Heidegger's work once again appears to be very different from Foucault's. The last of Foucault's books to be published in his lifetime was *Le souci de soi* (The care of the self), a book about ancient practices of self-improvement or self-cultivation.[24] In that text and in numerous interviews and lectures given prior to its publication, Foucault discusses various specialized activities that were intended as forms of personal, subjective strengthening or discipline.[25] These practices were not ordinary, everyday concernful "taking care of things," like Heidegger's descriptions of the ontic expressions of Dasein as care. They were *askeses,* extra-ordinary disciplines that people imposed upon themselves to become better—stronger, better able to govern, more alert, more in tune with divinity—than they were before, activities designed to lift individuals out of average everydayness. Furthermore, Foucault seems favorably disposed toward such practices—not the reinstatement of the specific ancient practices that he examines but the creative undertaking that such practices represent.[26] And all of this seems utterly opposed to anything Heidegger would advocate, judging by passages in *Being and Time* such as the following: "The expression 'care for oneself,' following the analogy of taking care and concern, would be a tautology. Care cannot mean a special attitude toward the self, because the self is already characterized ontologically as being-ahead-of-itself" (*B&T,* 180). What Heidegger means by *Sorge*—an ontological determination of the being of Dasein—and what Foucault means by *souci*—a deliberate practice of self-cultivation—seem analytically incompatible.

Yet I want to argue that while the words are differently employed, in fact the *philosophical* practices that Heidegger and Foucault engage in under the rubric of care and especially under the rubric of thinking care are closely allied. As I have argued above, Heidegger is involved in—caught up in—a self-overcoming movement of thinking that fundamentally alters thinking and selves in ways unforeseeable at that thinking's outset. His work is a path without a defined, stable, static destination. In this respect, what Heidegger does is very similar to what Foucault does and advocates doing when he thinks through self-development and self-constitution in disciplinary practices. As I have argued in detail elsewhere, Foucault sees the practice of philosophy itself as a discipline that functions—or at least can function—as a form of care of the self,[27] as he understands that phrase. To make my point, it will be necessary to offer a brief discussion of the phenomenon that he names "normalization" and of care of the self as normalized practice.

Foucault gives an extensive account of the emergence of normalization in *Surveiller et punir (Discipline and Punish).* He asserts there that normalization is a form of disciplinary power that is pervasive in present-day society and has been prevalent since the nineteenth century.[28] Normalizing disciplinary power is a set of organizational forces that give shape and meaning to virtually every aspect of the modern world. A fundamental rule within normalizing disciplines is the notion that all living things (and many nonliving things and processes) are developmental in their very nature, and their development can be captured and characterized statistically; it can be "normed." Nowadays the technical experts among us norm almost everything—from intelligence quotients to weather patterns. And all of us analyze things and events and assess them with reference to norms. But norms are not taken to be inviolable givens; we know that processes of development can be influenced and redirected in various ways, and new norms can be created. Normalizing power does not simply determine norms and force individuals to approximate them; it is not primarily prohibitive. Rather, normalizing power establishes norms, reformulates entire developmental trajectories, and uses the developmental power it discovers in all things as a medium for re-creating the world.

Foucault's analysis of normalization often presents such networks of power and knowledge as frightening, insidious, and overwhelming. There is no outside to this way of ordering, no counter-order to which we could escape. "Power is everywhere"[29]; "power *is* 'always already there,' . . . one is never 'outside' it, . . . there are no 'margins' for those who break with the system to gambol in."[30] Since subjectivities are formed in history, in networks of power, our very identities are based on normalizing power/knowledge networks; those networks constitute us and hold us firmly in their grip. But Foucault is no fatalist, despite the bleak picture he paints in *Discipline and Punish* and elsewhere. He is a Nietzschean; he is alert, always, to the movements of self-overcoming within all movements, all events and networks of power.

It is this deep and powerful Nietzschean undercurrent in all of Foucault's genealogical work that offsets the threat of fatalistic despair. All things change; nothing retains its identity through time. "The forces operating in history are not controlled by destiny or regulative mechanisms, but respond to haphazard conflicts."[31] Systems of power/knowledge do not simply subsist; to perpetuate themselves they must repeat themselves in exercise from moment to moment. And thus there is always the possibility that they will alter, fail, or realign themselves—in large ways or in small ones. We may not be able to step outside of normalizing power, but normalizing power is, nevertheless, neither monolithic nor eternal. On the contrary, the relations that produce and reproduce it at every turn are ultimately unstable and changeable. "To say that one can never be 'outside' power does not mean that one is trapped and condemned to defeat no matter what."[32]

Nevertheless, to say that systems or networks of power are changeable is also not to say that those sets of relations are subject to any person's control. How conflict or challenges may affect the networks is not completely predictable. However, we know from history that in some instances at least, human beings have developed ways to alter the selves that they have been made to be within the networks of power/knowledge that formed them. Precisely this was what Foucault was studying when he examined the *askesis* of the ancients, their *techne tou biou,* in the last two volumes of the *History of Sexuality* series, *The Use of Pleasure* and *The Care of the Self.* These ancient practices of self-cultivation figured as care demonstrate the possibility that human beings can cultivate themselves as forms of subjectivity. They show that there exists the possibility of intentional creative change, even for what Foucault terms an art of life.

Within normalizing networks of power, in particular, this possibility for intentional creativity looms large. Because of the crucial role of the phenomenon of development within normalizing power/knowledge networks, those networks are especially susceptible to change. Therefore it is possible that we could cultivate selves—types or modes of subjectivity—within normalizing networks of power/knowledge in ways that may be self-violating and thus could break open a new space for new power/knowledge formations. This is, surely, Foucault's aim when he undertakes analyses of such means of self-cultivation from his own position within a normalized society. By studying and attempting such practices, we can turn the energy of developmental normalization against itself by inciting development not along predetermined, normed lines toward a known goal—as disciplinary power always seeks to do—but along developmental lines themselves. We can engage in developmental self-cultivation for its own sake, embrace normalization without embracing the drive for absolute control that normalization has embodied. In other words, we can honor the path without thought of the destination; we can think and act with movements of self-overcoming in the absence of a static objective. This is the direction that Foucault's ethical work in the late 1970s and 1980s clearly points—the development of development beyond the normalized category of development. In short, then, and in words other than his own, Foucault's call for care of the self, his call to an art of existence, is a call to engage—philosophically, practically, bodily—in a rejection of the metaphysics of presence in favor of an embodied affirmation of ex-istence.[33]

Conclusion

As I acknowledged at the beginning of this essay, it may very well seem upon first reading that Foucault's rejection of subjectivity as a primary analytic category and Heidegger's central attention to human experience in his phenomenology of Dasein place these two thinkers in severe opposition. And it is true that their projects are in some respects fundamentally different from one another. A careful reading of both, however, can generate an appreciation for the similarities in their critiques of traditional conceptions of subjectivity and, more importantly, in the effects their work can have on our thinking and even on our embodied experience of ourselves as subjects.

Both philosophers' works effect displacements of subjectivity that can usher in fundamental transformations in thought and life. For Foucault, philosophy is an *askesis,* an exercise of thinking that moves beyond its own ground, that transforms thinking itself.[34] For Heidegger, too, philosophy is an exercise, a movement of thinking that transforms thinking. Regardless of countless differences in emphasis, vocabulary, approach, and simple temperament, therefore, both men practice philosophy as a *way,* a movement that leaves nothing immune from transformation—neither the object of thought, nor thinking's subject, nor the traditions of thinking that set up such categories in the first place. To think with either philosopher is to abandon oneself to movements of self-overcoming that affirm history, passage, and change above stasis and essential identity. However different they may be, these thinkers' paths converge in the nonplace of difference.

Notes

1. Michel Foucault, "Truth and Power," in *Power/Knowledge: Selected Interviews and Other Writings, 1972–1977,* ed. Colin Gordon (New York: Pantheon, 1980), 117.

2. There are other passages, however, that commentators often cite in this connection. Consider, for example, this statement from an interview in 1984: "[The subject] is not a substance; it is a form and this form is not above all or always identical to itself." Michel Foucault, "The Ethic of Care for the Self as a Practice of Freedom," in *The Final Foucault*, ed. James Bernauer and David Rasmussen (Cambridge: MIT Press, 1988), 10.

3. In fact Nietzsche is asserting, quite specifically, that there is no such thing as a unitary Ego. So even his remarks in the aphorisms surrounding #370 need to be seen as something other than a blanket rejection of any notion of human subjectivity or agency whatsoever. It is very important in this discussion to keep careful track of definitions of terms.

4. Michel Foucault, "Afterword: The Subject and Power," in *Michel Foucault: Beyond Structuralism and Hermeneutics*, ed. Hubert L. Dreyfus and Paul Rabinow, 2d ed. (Chicago: University of Chicago Press, 1983), 209.

5. Linda Alcoff, "Feminist Politics and Foucault: The Limits to a Collaboration," in *Crises in Continental Philosophy*, ed. Arleen Dallery and Charles Scott with Holley Roberts (Albany, N.Y.: SUNY Press, 1992), 71.

6. For an example of a leftist critique of the same sort, see Michael Walzer, "The Politics of Michel Foucault," in *Foucault: A Critical Reader*, ed. David C. Hoy (London: Blackwell, 1986), 61.

7. Ladelle McWhorter, *Bodies and Pleasures: Foucault and the Politics of Sexual Normalization* (Bloomington: Indiana University Press, 1999), chapter 3, esp. 74–79.

8. Michel Foucault, "Afterword: The Subject and Power," 212.

9. See, for example, Michel Foucault, "On the Genealogy of Ethics," in Dreyfus and Rabinow, *Michel Foucault: Beyond Structuralism and Hermeneutics*, 219.

10. I have made this point at length in my "Asceticism/Askesis: Foucault's Thinking Historical Subjectivity," in *Ethics and Danger: Essays on Heidegger and Continental Philosophy*, ed. Arleen B. Dallery and Charles Scott, with Holley Roberts (Albany: SUNY Press, 1992), 243–54.

11. Michel Foucault, "Nietzsche, Genealogy, History," in *Language, Counter-memory, Practice*, ed. Donald F. Bouchard (Ithaca: Cornell University Press, 1977), 145–46.

12. For this last question, see especially Michel Foucault, "Technologies of the Self," in *Technologies of the Self*, ed. Luther Martin, Huck Gutman, and Patrick Hutton (Amherst: University of Massachusetts Press, 1988), 18.

13. Kevin R. Hill, "Foucault's Critique of Heidegger," *Philosophy Today* (winter 1989): 334.

14. See Michel Foucault, *The Birth of the Clinic*, trans. A. M. Sheridan Smith (New York: Vintage Press, 1973), 156.

15. See Foucault, *The Birth of the Clinic*, 197, where he writes: "[F]rom the integration of death into medical thought is born a medicine that is given as a science of the individual. And, generally speaking, the experience of individuality in modern culture is bound up with that of death: from Hölderlin's Empedocles to Nietzsche's Zarathustra, and on to Freudian man."

16. Michel Foucault, *The Order of Things* (New York: Random House, 1970), 375.

17. For an extended and very helpful discussion of this whole issue, see François Raffoul, *Heidegger and the Subject* (Atlantic Highlands, N.J.: Humanities Press, 1998).

18. Martin Heidegger, *Ontology—The Hermeneutics of Facticity*, trans. John van Buren (Bloomington: Indiana University Press, 1999), 37. Hereafter *Ontology*.

19. Martin Heidegger, *Being and Time*, trans. Joan Stambaugh (Albany: SUNY Press, 1996), 40. Hereafter *B&T*.

20. See Michel Haar, *Heidegger and the Essence of Man,* trans. William McNeill (Albany: SUNY Press, 1993), esp. xxxiv and 174.

21. Otto Pöggeler, *Martin Heidegger's Path of Thinking,* trans. Daniel Magurshak and Sigmund Barber (Atlantic Highlands, N.J.: Humanities Press, 1987), 144.

22. See Heidegger, *Being and Time,* 178–83.

23. See ibid., 179.

24. Michel Foucault, *The Care of the Self,* trans. Robert Hurley (New York: Pantheon, 1986).

25. See, for example, Michel Foucault, "Technologies of the Self," in *Technologies of the Self,* 16–49; Michel Foucault, "On the Genealogy of Ethics: An Overview of Work in Progress," in *Michel Foucault: Beyond Structuralism and Hermeneutics,* ed. Hubert Dreyfus and Paul Rabinow (Chicago: University of Chicago Press, 1983), 229–52; summaries of the 1982 and 1983 courses at the Collège de France, translated as "Subjectivity and Truth" and "The Hermeneutics of the Subject" in *Ethics: Subjectivity and Truth,* vol. 1 of *The Essential Works of Foucault, 1954–1984,* ed. Paul Rabinow (New York: The New Press, 1997), 87–92 and 93–106, respectively; and Michel Foucault, "Writing the Self," in *Foucault and His Interlocutors,* ed. Arnold Davidson (Chicago: University of Chicago Press, 1997), 234–47; see also Michel Foucault, *Discourse and Truth: The Problematization of Parrhesia,* typescript of the seminar given by Foucault at Berkeley in 1983.

26. In "On the Genealogy of Ethics" in response to a question about the possibility of returning to techniques of the self like those practiced by the ancients, Foucault said, "I think there is no exemplary value in a period which is not our period . . . it is not something to get back to" (see 234). But he goes on to say in the same interview that the ancient practice of an "art of existence" or "art of life" is something worth developing. He says, "From the idea that the self is not given to us, I think there is only one practical consequence: we have to create ourself as a work of art" (237).

27. See my *Bodies and Pleasures,* 186–92.

28. See Michel Foucault, *Discipline and Punish: The Birth of the Prison,* trans. Alan Sheridan (New York: Vintage Books, 1977), 183ff.

29. Michel Foucault, *The History of Sexuality,* vol. 1, *An Introduction,* trans. Robert Hurley (New York: Random House, 1978), 93.

30. Michel Foucault, "Power and Strategies," in Gordon, *Power/Knowledge,* 141.

31. Foucault, "Nietzsche, Genealogy, History," 154.

32. Foucault, "Power and Strategies," 141–42.

33. I argued for this reevaluation of normalization at length in my *Bodies and Pleasures;* see especially chapter 7.

34. See Michel Foucault, *The Use of Pleasure,* trans. Robert Hurley (New York: Pantheon, 1984), 9.

Foucault and Heidegger on Kant and Finitude

Béatrice Han

For Foucault and Heidegger, both the modern quest for transcendental foundations and many of our contemporary epistemic quandaries stem from the Kantian dilemma: in a bereaved world in which God is no guarantor of eternal truths anymore[1] and can only be construed as a postulate, how can a finite being step beyond the boundaries of its empirical limitations and know anything with a legitimate claim to universality? According to Foucault, Kant's bold answer to skepticism consists in *inventing a new form of finitude* (which for ease I shall call "transcendental finitude"[2]). As *The Order of Things* puts it,

> the Kantian critique marks the threshold of our modernity; it questions representation . . . on the basis of its rightful limits. . . . It thus uncovers a transcendental field in which the subject, which is never given to experience (since it is not empirical) but which is finite (since there is no intellectual intuition) determines in its relation to an object = x all the formal conditions of experience in general.[3]

The true purport of the famed "Copernican turn" lies in its attempt to overcome empirical finitude (as expressed by the "limits of representation") via the thematization of the transcendental (the subject as both "finite" and yet "never given to experience"), a move by which the a priori study of our (limited) faculties becomes the starting point for construing the necessary form of our knowledge, thus outlining the conditions of possibility of truth itself.[4] For Foucault, Kant's real genius, then, lies in having reversed the formerly negative meanings of finitude by making the latter foundational at the transcendental level.[5] Indeed, whether religiously understood as the reversed mirror image of God's perfection and the sign/proof of our ontological inferiority (Pascal's view of the "misery of Man without God," Descartes's analysis of the discrepancy between our [almost divine] will and our [merely human] intellect), or cast in more secular terms (Locke's refutation of innate ideas, Hume's criticism of the principle of causality as based on habitual mental associations, not objective necessity), human finitude was a major argument against the ambitions of dogmatism to absolute knowledge.[6] But once transposed as the universal and necessary organization of our faculties, it becomes the precondition of our knowing the world: rather than being mere strictures imposed on him by his mortal nature, man's former limitations can now be construed as a priori foundational in the sense that any epistemic content will have to be mediated through them to be known at all. The empirical forms of our finitude (such as the passivity of our sensibility, the partiality of our will to sensible inclinations, and so forth[7]) are not overcome in the obvious sense that they would be denied,[8] or miraculously bypassed by the shift to a more advanced state of the human race.[9] Kant's more subtle argument is that although it has to be acknowledged as empirically unsurpassable, human finitude should be redefined a priori and therefore understood *positively,* i.e., as what generates the scope of our possible knowledge and ultimately (because it outlines the possibility of rational determination itself) as the cornerstone of our freedom.[10]

Of course, this shift from empirical finitude to its a priori counterpart does not operate without generating its own set of difficulties: as I shall suggest in the first part of this chapter, much of Foucault's early reading of Kant is devoted to showing the unfortunate consequences of the merging by the *Anthropology* of the two understandings of finitude (empirical and transcendental) that the *Critique of Pure Reason* was meant to keep distinct. What emerges, then, is neither the transcendental subject of the *First Critique* nor the noumenal will of the *Second Critique,* but the ambiguous and opaque image of "man" as subject/object,[11] a dangerous figure that the *Order of Things* will redefine as the "empirico-transcendental doublet," following on Foucault's former analysis of the "originary" as a hidden return of the empirical within the transcendental. Although it has never been published, Foucault's *Commentary* can thus be regarded as the prehistory to chapters 7 and 9 of the *Archaeology of the Human Sciences* and fruitfully used to explain Foucault's negative diagnosis of modernity as trapped within the "anthropological sleep," along with his rejection of humanism. Indeed, the blurring of the empirico-transcendental divide within man's "doubles" repeatedly defeats the foundational core of the Kantian strategy by generating a new inability to sustain the a priori perspective necessary for securing a universal epistemic ground. Because of man's dual nature (both transcendental and empirical), the transcendental subject, the former a priori and self-transparent condition of possibility of knowledge, now appears as "already"[12] determined by the empirical background of Life, Language, and Labor. Yet this background eludes him by definition as it constantly withdraws from a field of knowledge that can only be generated by the a priori perspective itself: the thinking subject cannot recapture the moment of its own emergence as a thinking entity without (retro)projecting it in a paradoxical past. This paradox is due to the fact that the ordering of time (as past, present, and future) is itself opened up by the epistemic perspective generated by the subject, and therefore cannot be regarded as an independent succession in which the apparition of the thinking subject could be chronologically dated.[13] From this newly disclosed impossibility for the subject to know the conditions of its own genesis stems a fundamental opacity at the heart of knowledge: transcendental finitude retrospectively appears as dependent on hidden empirical determinations that themselves are then (wrongly) taken as foundational, while conversely anthropology reveals itself as "a transcendental which would like to be true at the natural level."[14] The Copernican turn has become a (vicious) circle, an endless oscillation between the two forms of finitude that revives the threat of skepticism by depriving philosophy of a clear starting point.[15] The analytic of finitude analyzes the various forms of this return of empirical finitude within its transcendental counterpart, the "Cogito and the Unthought" and the "Return of the Origin" being descriptions of failed phenomenological attempts (either from the perspective of the subject or from that of temporality) to recapture this originary level within the transcendental itself, and therefore to restore the pristine clarity of the Kantian beginnings.

Interestingly enough, Heidegger, too, interprets Kant's version of human finitude by tying it to the empirico-transcendental divide and more precisely to the problem of (empirical) passivity and (noumenal) activity, the most basic form of finitude being the absence of a purely spontaneous, creative form of intuition and consequently the necessary receptive character of our sensibility. Like Foucault, he reads the invention of the transcendental and the attempt to overcome empirical finitude by shifting to the level of the a priori as the (aborted) kernels of the Kantian critique[16]: "Kant awoke to the problem of searching for finitude precisely in the pure, rational creature itself, and not first in the fact that it is determined through sensibility."[17] Although they converge in reading Kant's recentering of the three critical interrogations on the question of man's finitude in the *Anthropology* as essential, both authors differ as to the cause of the failure of the Kantian project: whereas Foucault concludes in his *Commentary* that any man-based solution to the problem of finitude was doomed from the start, Heidegger thinks that although Kant saw that the epistemic overcoming of finitude was vital in fighting against skepticism, he shrank back from what would have made such an overcoming actually possible, i.e., his intuition of the originary link between transcendental imagination and time in the first edition of the *Critique of Pure Reason.* From this divergence in diagnosis stem two very different curative strategies: either finding a nonanthropological way of reinterpreting and relativizing transcendental finitude while preserving the foundational perspective itself (which was the aim of the archaeology as the study of the historical a priori), or redefining human finitude itself in such a fashion as to avoid the empirico-transcendental confusions that have plagued the post-Kantians, from the German Idealist tradition to the Husserlian version of phenomenology—which is Heidegger's own ambition in shifting from transcendental philosophy to fundamental ontology.

However, Foucault never mentions Heidegger among his examples of failed phenomenologists, the model of which is clearly Husserl.[18] If he is right in focusing his analysis of modernity on the question of finitude and its overcoming,[19] can we derive from his silence about Heidegger that the latter manages somehow to win free from the analytic of finitude? The obvious answer would be to argue from Heidegger's antihumanism and rejection of any subject-centered approach[20] that he is indeed bound by his very premises to escape the anthropological sleep. However, as indicated above, the true core of the analytic of finitude is the attempt to overcome empirical forms of finitude by shifting to a level at which finitude itself can become foundational (i.e., the a priori), a move that works by prioritizing knowledge over existence and *happens* to be subject-centered in Kant's philosophy (and consequently in most phenomenological attempts), but *needs* not necessarily be so—Dasein's thrownness clearly is another expression of finitude. The real question, then, is not whether Heidegger speaks of "man"—an easily solved matter—but whether, by refocusing his analysis on Being-in-the-world and by shifting from the transcendental to the ontological perspective, he manages to deal successfully with the Kantian problem, i.e., to refute skepticism while acknowledging the limitations of human finitude in such a way as to avoid the recurrence of the empirical within the transcendental. In the second part of this chapter, I shall suggest that much of his early work can be read as addressing the crucial issues highlighted by Foucault's analysis. Indeed, the uncovering of the ontological level might be interpreted as Heidegger's way of taking up the transcendental approach, but in such a manner as to avoid the circularity of the analytic of finitude, the point being to *displace the empirico-transcendental divide itself* and therefore to come up with a renewed understanding of existence. Seen in this light, his strategy consists in acknowledging the traditional limitations of anthropological finitude (such as temporality and death), but by recasting them at the ontological level itself, a move that reestablishes the possibility of an a priori analysis of the structure of existence (fundamental ontology itself) while generating a new understanding of finitude (as defined by the existentials identified and indexed by *Being and Time*). Whether Heidegger succeeds in overcoming the Analytic of Finitude or merely gives the old circle a new twist is the question I shall try to address in my conclusion, along with a more general one: should it appear that we must *perforce* give up such heroic endeavors as Kant's—and subsequently Nietzsche's, and perhaps Heidegger's—how shall we deal with finitude? Is epistemic overcoming a good path in coming to terms with our own condition? Or more radically, is *overcoming* itself a desirable strategy?

Kant occupies a central position in Foucault's archaeology of knowledge for at least two reasons: as indicated at the beginning of chapter 7 of the *Order of Things,* he stands at the brim of two *épistémès,* being the thinker who still focused on representation but brought the classical age to its end by moving from the analysis of ideas to the analytic of their condition of possibility (the transcendental subject itself). But more importantly, Foucault sees in Kant's own philosophical itinerary—especially in the refocusing of the three critical questions on that of "man" in the *Logic*,[21] and therefore in the passage from the *Critique* to the *Anthropology*—the prefiguration of the fate of modernity. As I have tried to show elsewhere,[22] the status of Kant's *Anthropology* itself remains ambiguous since Foucault reads the introduction of a new concept, the "fundamental," as a way to safeguard transcendental finitude from any empirical contamination. To put it briefly, the *Anthropology* differs from the *First Critique* in that it acknowledges our empirical limitations and even sets itself the explicit task of exploring them:[23] in this new context, the "fundamental" protects Kant's earlier foundational aspirations by indicating the need to refer any empirical content to the level of the a priori as its epistemic condition of possibility. For example, the subject is now recontextualized as a "denizen of the world," and therefore appears as limited by the strictures of his mundane existence (having to live in society, being exposed to moral vices, and so forth); but ultimately, the world itself (as the source of man's limitations) can only be thought of *as world* from the transcendental perspective itself.[24] Anthropological finitude is empirically constricting but can only be known as such from an a priori standpoint, a *prioritizing of epistemic intelligibility over causal determination* by which Kant reasserts the primacy of transcendental finitude over its empirical counterpart, thus preserving the possibility of transcendental philosophy.

Yet even so the legacy of the *Anthropology* is highly ambivalent in the sense that the introduction of the fundamental is accompanied with that of another concept, the "originary." A highly paradoxical pairing: whereas the former was meant to preserve the logic of the Copernican turn, the second undermines it by blurring the distinction between the empirical and the a priori so that transcendental finitude loses its stable ground and foundational power, thus opening the door to the oscillations of the Analytic of Finitude, which then would be operative *within* Kant's own work. The thematic of the originary is introduced through a reflection on the relationship between *Geist* and *Gemüt*, the latter being defined as the purely empirical object of psychology, while the former, although it is an empirically given element, generates the possibility of (noumenal) spontaneity. Because of the

Geist, the *Gemüt* "is not only what it is, but what it does with itself."[25] In Kant's terminology, the *Geist* accounts for the "pragmatic" dimension of the *Anthropology* and for the ambivalent status of man as a being that is neither determined by his sensible inclinations, nor identifiable with a pure, angelic will for which the moral law would not even need to be a command: the *Geist* "animates the *Gemüt* through the ideas" (60). In his context, Foucault's crucial move is the identification between the *Geist* and the "enigmatic nature of our reason" (89) mentioned by the "Methodology" in the *Critique of Pure Reason*: "There exists in the faculty of reason a natural desire to venture beyond the field of experience, to attempt to reach the utmost bounds of all knowledge by the help of ideas alone, and not to rest satisfied, until it has fulfilled its course and raised the sum of its knowledge into a self-subsistent systematic whole."[26] The *Geist* would therefore be the dynamic principle in which reason's "metaphysical drive" (as Schopenhauer puts it) originates—in Foucault's terms, "something which would be the kernel of pure reason, the ineradicable root of its transcendental illusions."[27]

However, this generates a major problem in the sense that the *Geist* now indicates the presence *at the transcendental level itself* of an "originary passivity" that Foucault understands as empirically determined (as a "*natural* drive"). Transcendental finitude is suddenly folded back upon man's empirical limitations: "[The *Anthropology*] seems to refer the *Critique,* arrived at its summit, toward an *empirical* region, toward a domain of facts where man would be condemned to a very originary passivity."[28] Like freedom in the *Critique of Practical Reason*—although in a parodic way—the *Geist* is an "originary fact of reason,"[29] i.e., an unknowable given that cannot be rationally accounted for but only retrospectively observed through its effects. Although it generates the drive to knowledge and therefore opens up the transcendental field itself, as the "kernel" of pure reason the *Geist* must remain opaque to reason: it is "the root of the possibility of knowledge. And, by the same token, indissociably present and absent from the figures of knowledge: it is that withdrawal, that invisible and 'visible reserve' in the inaccessible distance of which knowing takes its place and positivity" (56). In other words, because pure reason cannot reflect back on its own origin, the *Geist* is nonhomogeneous to the epistemic space it discloses and cannot be thematized in the terms of the knowing activity it generates: it is, so to speak, the "blind spot" of reason, that which enables it to know but cannot be known per se. For Foucault, the major consequence of this withdrawal is the newly appeared impossibility of any transparent starting point for transcendental philosophy, and therefore the ruin of the foundational ambition formerly expressed by the Copernican shift to the transcendental.[30] Overcoming the limitations of anthropological finitude by shifting to the epistemic primacy of its a priori counterpart is not possible anymore if the latter reveals itself as contaminated from the start by empirical determinations (the *Geist* itself): in Foucault's own words, "the transcendental would suddenly be excluded, and the conditions of experience would finally be referred to the *primary inertia of a nature*."[31] Being the original testimony to the unsurpassability of anthropological finitude, the *Geist* is the first stumbling block in Kant's critical paradise, and therefore the primary figure of the "Return of the Origin."

This paradoxical movement, by which the *Geist* opens up the possibility of human knowledge but necessarily retreats from our epistemic field in the very operation that constitutes it, is considerably expanded on by what Foucault sees as the second figure of the "Return of the Origin," i.e., the "originary" itself. The concept is introduced by a very dense passage:

> [T]hat which, from the point of view of the *Critique*, is an *a priori of knowledge* does not transpose itself immediately in anthropological reflection as an *a priori of existence*, but appears within the density of a becoming where its sudden emergence takes infallibly, in retrospect, the meaning of the already-there. (57)

How should we understand such a "transposition"? The quote clearly refers to a temporalization by which only the transcendental subject can appear within the "*density* of becoming." However, such a temporalization cannot be thought of as homogeneous to chronological time (which is why it is not "immediate" and the originary must appear as an "already there," as if it was in some manner preexisting itself) because from a critical standpoint, *the transcendental subject is the condition of intelligibility of time itself.* Just as the *Geist*, as the origin of reason, had to withdraw from the field of knowledge, in the same way the transcendental subject cannot enter directly the temporal framework it generates. Indeed, the *First Critique* excluded this possibility by providing two models to think of time, either as a pure form of sensibility in the "Transcendental Aesthetics," or as what unites a priori the order of phenomena (physical time) in the "Analogies of Experience." From the critical perspective, then, for an entity to appear as temporal means that it is perceived through the form of time and can be chronologically ordered according to the laws of the understanding: time is not a given, but what constitutes phenomena. Since it is the condition of intelligibility of time itself, the transcendental subject cannot appear within time as an indifferent content—the only subjective element that can be temporally known is the empirical ego. The paradoxical nature of the originary is therefore due to the new necessity for the *Anthropology* of working around this impossibility while leaving the perspective of the transcendental subject for that of "man": the paradox rests on the merging of the two standpoints that the *First Critique* was meant to keep separate, i.e., empirical existence and transcendental determination.[32] Indeed, if the transcendental subject is to know itself as an existing subject (which is the meaning of the passage from the "*a priori* of knowledge" to the "*a priori* of *existence*"), then it must already *exist* prior to being able to know itself; but the fact of its own existence[33] can only be disclosed to it from the point of view of the epistemic framework it generates—and therefore, *retrospectively.* The anthropological paradoxes of the originary are thus caused by the newly appeared ambivalence of man: the originary can only be thought of as "already there" by reference to the empirical time of succession (the "density of becoming"), by which man as an empirical being is determined. But time itself must be referred to the transcendental subject to be understood as such: man may always have been "already there," but the meaning of this "already," i.e., of the succession itself, is dependent on his transcendental capacity as a *knower* whose faculties are the necessary mediation for the formation of any knowledge content. The "suddenness" of the "emergence" Foucault refers to is thus caused by this abrupt shift from the perspective of existence to that of the a priori as its condition of intelligibility—which is also the reason why the transcendental can only be "transposed" as a withdrawing origin, not as a beginning.[34]

The instability of the originary as an epistemic structure results from this oscillation between transcendental finitude (as the a priori framework of intelligibility on the background of which only existence itself can make sense and appear as temporal) on the one hand, and empirical finitude on the other (as the necessity for the subject to exist in order to know anything). As we have seen, it also hinges on the distinction between two kinds of determination, epistemic (man as the transcendental subject, the active condition of possibility of knowledge) and causal (man as passively determined by his own facticity), and plays the one against the other. Although anthropological finitude is chronologically determining, the meaning of the chronology itself can only appear on the background of transcendental determination; but conversely, the need to recast the latter within the element of the former opens up a highly unstable ground (and a possibility that was specifically excluded by the *First Critique*), i.e., the inscription of the a priori within existence itself. This generates endless paradoxes that annihilate the possibility of a clear starting point for human knowledge and reopen the way to skepticism in the sense that retrospection becomes the only way man can reflect on his own duality: because he is his own a priori condition of intelligibility (as transcendental subject), he can only recapture the brute and unaccountable fact of his (empirical) existence as an impossible chronological anteriority that, in turn, can only make sense as such from the transcendental standpoint.[35] Thus,

> the relationship between the given and the *a priori* takes in the *Anthropology* a structure which is the reverse to that which had been set out by the *Critique*. The *a priori* in the order of knowledge becomes, in the order of concrete existence, an *originary* which is not chronologically first, but which, once it has appeared . . . reveals itself as *already there*.[36]

Moreover, this "inversion" opens up the possibility of a transcendental passivity opposed to the spontaneous syntheses of the understanding in the *Critique of Pure Reason*. As Foucault says, "that which is the pure given in the order of knowledge, is illuminated, in reflection on concrete existence, with dim lights which give it the depth of the *already operated-on*."[37] The transcendental subject itself is "already" enmeshed in the passive syntheses of existence: being unable to recapture the moment of its own birth, it cannot play the foundational role it had in the *First Critique* anymore.

As "a being whose enigmatic reality constitutes, *prior to all knowledge,* the order and the connection of what it has to know,"[38] man now appears as the core of the new analytic of finitude, occupying the position formerly attributed to representation by the classical age. Correlatively, the Copernican overcoming of empirical finitude within the element of transcendental philosophy is replaced by endless oscillations between the two forms of finitude. From the point of view of existence, man is finite in the sense that he depends on empirical conditions that he does not master (the *Geist* and the originary in Kant's *Anthropology*, life, language and labour, "those realities that . . . are the foundation of what is given to us and reaches us,"[39] in the *Order of Things*). On the background of this empirical dependence, the critical shift to the transcendental standpoint was meant to reestablish the primacy of transcendental finitude by making the a priori analysis of the subject's faculties the precondition of knowing experience itself: thus, "each of these positive forms [life (the body), language and labor] in which man can learn that he is [empirically] finite *is given to him only against the background of its own* [transcendental] *finitude*."[40] Yet this search for a transcendental foundation is now met only with the anthropological paradoxes of the originary: life, language and labor are not only objects of knowledge, given as such on the foundational background of man's transcendental finitude: "life, language and labour appear as so many 'transcendentals' . . . they are *conditions* of knowledge" (244). Indeed, man can only know himself and the world from his perspective as a living, speaking, and working being—i.e., as "already" existing: "as soon as he thinks, man unveils himself to his own eyes in the form of a being who is already, in a necessarily subjacent density, in an irreducible anteriority, a living being, an instrument of production, a vehicle for words which exist before him" (313). Yet as suggested by the recurrence of the temporal paradoxes ("as soon as," "already"), this new recontextualization of the transcendental subject within the empirical de facto repeats the anthropological structure of the originary and thus ruins the foundational power of transcendental finitude by generating a logical contradiction: the a priori now has to appear within the very element which it was the epistemic condition of possibility of, i.e., experience itself.[41]

As a result, the anthropological turn leaves us in an impossible position, that of looking anew for an a priori foundation for knowledge while the very conditions of possibility of such a demand (having as a pure transcendental ground) have been destroyed by the return of empirical finitude within its transcendental counterpart. For Foucault, this fundamental aporia is what defines the general structure of modernity: on the one hand, "in the very heart of empiricity, there is indicated the obligation to work backwards to an analytic of finitude, in which man's being will be able to provide a [transcendental] foundation . . .

for all those forms that indicate to him that he is not [empirically] infinite."[42] But on the other hand, this Copernican logic is defeated by the anthropological twist: "[N]ow that the site of the analysis is no longer representation but man in his finitude, it is a question of revealing the conditions of knowledge [transcendental finitude] on the basis of (or starting from) the empirical contents given in it [empirical finitude] (319). The former clarity of the empirico-transcendental divide is hopelessly blurred by this reversed interplay between the two forms of finitude, in which empirical limitations are made to count as transcendental conditions of possibility (life, labor, and language as the "quasi-transcendentals"). As the *Commentary* had prophetically phrased it, "anthropology will move indifferently from the problematic of necessity [transcendental finitude as an a priori foundation for knowledge] to that of existence [anthropological finitude]; it will conflate the analysis of conditions [finitude as transcendentally founding] and the interrogation on [empirical] finitude."[43] In this "interminable cross-reference of finitude with itself,"[44] we are left with an irreducible opacity that annihilates the possibility of a sure foundation for knowledge:

> from one end of experience to the other [i.e., experience as (transcendentally) founded or as (anthropologically) determinative], finitude answers itself: it is the identity and the difference of the positivities [as knowledge-contents transcendentally founded on the one hand, and as the positive limitations (Life, Language and Labour) that bear on the transcendental itself because of the dual nature of man on the other] and of their foundation, within the figure of the Same [man as the empirico-transcendental double in whom the two forms of finitude are ultimately merged]. (315)

There is no way man can overcome his empirical limitations by turning them into transcendental conditions of possibility anymore: now understood as originary, the limits of our finitude exceed by definition the scope of our knowledge (the quasi-transcendentals, "in their being, are outside knowledge").[45] Yet the foundational logic of the analytic of finitude requires that we give a clear account for them as clear beginnings—a protean but hopeless task, some of the forms of which Foucault analyzes in the "Cogito and the Unthought" and the "Return of the Origin."[46]

If this dreary diagnosis is correct, what can we do to extricate ourselves from "man" and his doubles? As I suggested before, we might find some hope in the fact that Foucault does not explicitly mention Heidegger among the failed phenomenological attempts to find a way out of the analytic of finitude. Given the latter's rejection of humanism, can we read Foucault's omission as a hint that fundamental ontology could offer us an alternative to the analytic of finitude?[47] As suggested above, Foucault's assessment of the anthropological turn leaves us with three major difficulties: first, the folding back of the a priori on the empirical within the context of "concrete existence," by which the structure of the originary is characterized; second, our inability to think such a temporalization of the transcendental subject with the intellectual tools provided by the *First Critique*; finally, the joint demand and impossibility for man to give an a priori account of his own limitations (mainly encountered in the form of death [life], language, and labor), and therefore to replicate the Copernican turn by mastering again empirical finitude at the transcendental level. Whether Heidegger manages to break free from the anthropological circles or not will depend to a large extent on the answers he can offer to these problems: does he have an understanding of "existence" that would allow him an a priori analysis of its structures, and yet would not merge the transcendental and the empirical? Does he present us with a way to think of time that would solve the paradoxes of retrospection specific to the originary? Can he account for the major forms of our thrownness in a nonempirical way? I shall suggest that his reinterpretation of existence (with the uncovering of a specific level to analyze it, i.e., the *existential* as opposed to the *existentiell*), and more generally the distinction between the ontic and the ontological—along with his intended overcoming of Husserl's "*transcendental* phenomenology" through fundamental ontology—are all various ways in which Heidegger might escape from the analytic of finitude *by displacing the empirico-transcendental divide itself.* Yet before exploring these issues I'll turn to his reading of Kant to preempt a potentially serious objection: what if Heidegger was not aware at all of finitude as a problem? Or if he did not understand finitude by linking it to the Kantian divide between the empirical and the transcendental?

Like Foucault, Heidegger reads Kant's philosophy as an attempt to redefine and overcome human finitude. Unlike Foucault, however, he thinks that had Kant remained faithful to his original insight, his understanding of transcendental imagination could have dealt with human finitude while remaining at the level of the a priori, therefore avoiding the anthropological confusions. The *Critique of Pure Reason* would then have been both the locus of the identification of finitude as a problem and the way to solve it without the need to turn to the *Anthropology.* To put it briefly, for Heidegger[48] Kant's version of finitude lies in the opposition between the passivity of our sensibility and the spontaneity of our understanding, which limits severely the scope of our knowledge by restricting it to actually given phenomena. As defined in the first edition of the *First Critique,* however, transcendental imagination was able to bridge that gap because of its ability to intuit an object without its being present: as a "formative power" *(bildend Kraft),* transcendental imagination was both receptive (in the sense that it needs some original sensuous input) *and* spontaneous (because it can provide a representation of the object even in its absence).[49] However, according to Heidegger, grounding this mediating ability would have entailed a fundamental move from Kant's part—to establish that both time and space as the a priori forms of sensibility on the one hand, and the "I think" of transcendental apperception implicitly involved in any judgment on the other, are dependent on the syntheses of transcendental imagination itself: thus, "the origin of pure intuition and pure thinking as transcendental faculties [would be] shown to be based on the transcendental power of imagination."[50] Following this logic, transcendental imagination would have bridged the initial opposition between passivity and spontaneity while expanding our epistemic abilities (and therefore the limits of our finitude), thus providing Kant with the a priori ground that the originary cannot offer because of its structural instability—hence Heidegger's conclusion: "pure intuition possesses the character of spontaneity. As a pure, spontaneous receptivity, it has its essence in the transcendental power of imagination. As spontaneity, pure thinking must at the same time exhibit the character of pure receptivity."[51]

Interestingly, this early definition of transcendental imagination might have prevented most of the difficulties specific to the analytic of finitude: being both active and passive but also a transcendental faculty, transcendental imagination could have allowed Kant to cast finitude in such a manner as not to include any empirical elements (contrary to what happens in the case of the relationship between reason and the *Geist* identified by Foucault). Moreover, it involves a projective understanding of time that presents an alternative to the two other models provided by the *First Critique* by opening up the possibility of a temporalization of the "I think" that might not meet the chronological paradoxes of the originary. Finally, following through this understanding of time—which according to Heidegger was Kant's most authentic intuition—might have allowed the latter to recover the question of Being, and hopefully to understand existence itself in such a way as to overcome the empirico-transcendental divide.[52] However, on Heidegger's reading Kant "shrunk back from his original intuition" because of the excessive priority he gave to reason, which "was not able to tolerate in proximity to itself . . . the power of imagination, which was reputed to be not only a specifically human faculty, but also a *sensible* one. The problematic of a pure reason amplified in this way must push aside the power of imagination, and with that it really first conceals its [transcendental] essence."[53] Consequently, the second edition of the *Critique of Pure Reason* leaves aside the syntheses of imagination and understands the latter as a sensible faculty, depriving it of its former ability to mediate at a transcendental level between passivity and spontaneity;[54] it also redefines reason as the major and best characteristic of the human mind, following on this the Aristotelian tradition. When years later Kant turned to the *Anthropology* to reformulate his analysis of human finitude, he had no way to connect it back to the transcendental.[55]

Given Kant's failure to deal successfully with the question of human finitude, it is left to Heidegger himself to rethink the latter in his own terms and these, interestingly enough given Foucault's own analysis, include a sharp awareness of the dangers of anthropology:

> anthropological-psychological knowledge is not thereby declared to be "false" . . . but for all its correctness it is not sufficient to hold in view from the start and constantly the problem of Dasein's existence—and that means its finitude."[56]

Like Kant himself, Heidegger acknowledges that finitude is the defining characteristic and central difficulty of our human condition, implicitly expanding on Kierkegaard's and Schopenhauer's analyses:[57] yet although anthropology is correct (in the sense that it gives a good factual account of man's limitations, and thus satisfies the criteria of truth as *homoiosis*), it is not "true" because it misses the ontological dimension of existence and therefore has no access to the fundamentally disclosive dimension of truth as *aletheia*. Relying on anthropology (or psychology) to define finitude would amount to understanding existence as an empirical given. But neither existence nor finitude itself are merely facts—nor, interestingly enough, can they properly be viewed from the standpoint of pure reason: "finitude does not depend simply upon human reason, but instead *its* finitude is perishing, i.e., 'care about the potentiality to be finite.'"[58] Contrary to what was Kant's ambition in the *First Critique,* our finitude cannot be overcome by the shift to the transcendental perspective: reason itself is finite, and the form that Heidegger assigns to its finitude is fundamentally different from those identified by Foucault in the *Anthropology* (the *Geist* as the "root" of pure reason or the originary itself) in the sense that it is not empirical. Indeed, having "care about the potentiality to be finite" is not a factual determination: it is only possible for a being for whom its own being is at issue in the very way it is.[59] In other words, "existing" means having an implicit interpretation of what existing itself means: "[E]xistence is in itself finitude, and as such it is only possible on the basis of the understanding of Being . . . which manifests itself as the innermost ground of human finitude."[60] To understand "care about the potentiality to be finite" properly (i.e., as an existential, and moreover as the structure that unites all the existentials), one must have an ontological comprehension of existence (already called for by the projective notion of "potentiality" anyway), and therefore moved beyond the empirico-transcendental divide itself.

Indeed, if finitude is to be recontextualized, it cannot be done either in the naturalistic way suggested by anthropology, nor according to the a priori logic specific to the Copernican turn: Heidegger's own intuition is that the overcoming of empirical finitude will only work through the reinterpretation of existence in the light of the question of Being. As suggested above, existence cannot be viewed as empirical unless one wants to adopt a deterministic or behaviorist vision of Dasein that would miss its fundamentally self-interpretative dimension. But conversely, it cannot be understood from an a priori perspective because Dasein is never a detached, transcendental starting point: it is "in the world," which means that it always has a precomprehension of Being that is already involved in each and every one of its activities and therefore beyond any complete thematization. To deal with Kant's ambivalent legacy—the Copernican turn, but also the analytic of finitude—one must start from what Kant himself did not thematize, i.e., the link between existence and our understanding of Being:

> [O]nly because the understanding of Being is the most of finitude in what is, can it also make possible the so-called "creative" capacities of the finite human. And only because it occurs within the ground of finitude, does it have the breadth and constancy, but also the concealedness previously characterised.[61]

The first part of Heidegger's answer is clearly a reformulation of Kant's definition of finitude: the necessity for us to move within an understanding of Being we cannot master can be read as *Being and Time*'s equivalent of the *First Critique*'s impossibility of an *intellectus originarius,* i.e., of a purely spontaneous and creative mind (hence, probably, Heidegger's allusion to the "*creative* capacities of the finite human"). The fact that our intellectual and practical horizon is constituted by our understanding of Being is the primary version of our finitude.[62] However, the second part of the first sentence offers Heidegger's own take on the Copernican turn: if we shift to the ontological level, our understanding of being is not only what limits but also what "makes possible" our "creative capacities," since it is only on its background that things can be disclosed to us as what we act upon or as theoretical objects. Although it is the hallmark of our finitude in the sense that it restricts the scope of our knowledge and our actions,[63] our understanding of Being is also the precondition of our knowing anything at all—by which the Kantian analysis of transcendental finitude finds its ontological twist. Indeed, if knowing is possible only on the background of being-in-the-world, then the conditions of possibility of knowledge themselves should not be understood as a priori but as existential, since they now include as their premise the definition of existence as presupposing an interpretation of Being in everything we do. Admittedly, Heidegger's problem in *Being and Time* is wider than the Kantian question of the conditions of possibility of knowledge in the sense that he wants to reconnect theoretical knowledge itself to the unthematized "know-how" of our everyday activities (*Vorhandenheit* is a derived mode from *Zuhandenheit*).[64] But this very width allows him to recast the whole Kantian problematic in a richer context by showing that whatever we can know is given to us as knowable only on the background of our practices, thus healing the Cartesian rift between subject and objects and reinserting the epistemic within the existential.[65] Of course, this generates a new difficulty in the sense that these background practices, like our understanding of Being itself, cannot be thematized exhaustively (the most we can achieve is a partial and progressive clarification), which invalidates the possibility of the clear beginning required by the transcendental philosophy: we may have moved from the circles of the analytic of finitude to the endless spirals of hermeneutics. The obvious answer to this problem would be to drop the foundational logic inherited from Kant; such, however, is not early Heidegger's way. As I shall suggest later, he has another strategy, albeit perhaps not a fully successful one.

The second part of the quote is especially interesting because it seems to give an anticipated answer to the quandaries to the analytic of finitude: what can it mean, indeed, for our understanding of being to occur "within the ground of finitude" and to have "concealedness"? An unfavorable reading would immediately identify this structure with that of the originary itself by interpreting the "ground of finitude" as the empirical constraints that bear upon us, and the concealedness of Being as the anthropological withdrawing of the origin. However, such a reading cannot be right: its occurrence within the ground of finitude is also what gives "breadth" to our understanding of being, i.e., what enables us as doers and knowers. The "concealedness," therefore, cannot be empirical: in fact, it refers to our structural tendency to cover up the question of Being. As Heidegger indicates, "the finitude of Dasein—the understanding of Being—lies in forgetfulness."[66] Yet this forgetfulness is not an ontic failure (such as having a bad memory), but an ontological characteristic—it is "nothing accidental and temporary, but on the contrary is necessarily and constantly formed" (159). Because falling is not an ontic determination (neither "accidental" nor "temporary") but an existential structure of being-in-the-world, the concealedness of Being can be accounted for ontologically, thus avoiding the recurrence of the empirical within the transcendental that was the hallmark of the analytic of finitude. The same strategy is clearly at work in the following passage:

> [A]ll projection—and consequently all of man's creative activity—is *thrown,* i.e, it is determined by the dependency of Dasein on the being already in the totality, a dependency over which Dasein itself does not have control. The thrownness, however, thoroughly masters the being-there as such. . . . This refers . . . to a characteristic of the innermost *transcendental* finitude of Dasein. (161)

Again, this quote could be interpreted uncharitably, as an anthropological inversion of the Copernican turn: what Kant would have seen as transcendental finitude (i.e., "man's creative activity") would then be read as dependent on factual elements (thrownness as "being already in the totality," i.e., as having an understanding of Being we can neither choose nor clarify entirely). But thrownness "thoroughly masters the being-there as such," a statement by which Heidegger rescues fundamental ontology from the paradoxes of the originary: because of the existential dimension of thrownness, "being-there" cannot be understood as an empirical fact, if only in the sense that it involves a stand on what existence is, an auto-interpretative dimension that is the "innermost" meaning of transcendental finitude. What Heidegger is really saying, therefore, is not that we are, in our transcendental finitude, determined by empirical characteristics, but the very opposite, i.e., that these characteristics only make sense from the ontological point of view of transcendental finitude itself.[67] One might be surprised to see Heidegger use the word "transcendental" (especially given his opposition to transcendental phenomenology), but fundamental ontology entails an existential reinterpretation of the concept itself, a point that the *Essence of Reasons* makes abundantly clear : "a philosophy which treats the transcendental as a 'standpoint,' even as an 'epistemological' standpoint, cannot give us any clue to what 'transcendental' means."[68] The key to redefining the transcendental is to start from Dasein's transcendence, and therefore from being-in-the-world itself, not from the transcendental subject as a detached set of faculties.

Heidegger's strategy (i.e., overcoming the empirico-transcendental divide itself rather than trying, as Kant did, to have one form of finitude take over the over) can be tested against the other two key issues left open by the analytic of finitude, i.e., time and death as the major forms of our empirical finitude.[69] Regarding the first point, the problem inherent in the temporalization of the transcendental was that it generated the paradoxes of retrospection specific to the originary. From the (chronological) point of view of empirical time, the subject ought to have a "concrete existence" prior to its knowing anything; but from the a priori perspective, time as a condition of intelligibility of experience was dependent on the transcendental subject, which therefore could only recapture the anteriority of its own existence over its thinking activity as a paradoxical "already there." But Heidegger's understanding of time provides us with at least two ways of displacing the conceptual framework of the problem:[70] first, one might say that the paradox is based on a misleading opposition between empirical and transcendental time. Division two of *Being and Time*[71] makes clear that both notions must be replaced within the ontological context of ecstatic temporality. Time is neither physical succession, as Aristotle claimed,[72] nor pure interiority (Augustine's *tensio animae*), but an ecstatic process generated by Dasein as being in the world.[73] Chronological time is a fallen mode[74] implicitly derived from the authentic temporality that underlies care itself and can be analyzed from the projective ways in which Dasein relates to the nonpossibility of its own death.[75] From this perspective, the anthropological paradoxes are generated by Kant's inability to think of time properly (remember that he "shrunk back" from his original intuition), which itself laid the ground for the analytic of finitude: the retrospection characteristic of the originary can only happen if one treats chronological time as independent from being in the world itself, i.e., if one disregards the ontological connection between time and being. But since time itself is opened up by Dasein as an existing being, it makes no sense to speak of an "already there" prior to Dasein's own existence: being and being in time are synonymous. The second reason why anthropological retrospection is a fictitious projection lies in its implicit dependence on an artificial separation between existence and thought, as if existence was some sort of objective given that could be conceived of independently of Dasein's disclosive abilities. Again, the correct view is that there is no anteriority of existence over thought or vice versa because the very notion of anteriority is derived from the ecstatic dimension of existence itself: therefore, it is pointless to speak of Dasein's "being" prior to its thinking—both are coextensive.

Heidegger's analysis of death gives a slight twist to the same overall strategy. According to the analytic of finitude, death is our utmost limitation in the sense that we can neither control it nor foresee it—as Horace said, "*mors certa, hora incerta*"—and mostly that we can't know it, although our being mortal is the background upon which all knowledge is formed (which is why death is a "quasi-transcendental" for Foucault). Of course, Heidegger does not claim that we can know death—quite the opposite, in fact, death is a "nonrelational possibility." But what he does claim is that death should not be primarily understood from an empirical point of view: if it is the major form of human finitude, it is an *ontological* one. Being-towards-Death is not an ontic "fact" but an existential structure that can be analyzed a priori. Conversely, ontic modalities of relating to death (such as mourning, grieving, and so forth) only make sense on the background of our ontological mode of relating to death (i.e., as authentic or inauthentic, via either resolution or denial). In this regard, Heidegger's brilliant move is to establish that what the metaphysical tradition saw as an empirical stricture can only appear as such on the implicit background of the ontological structure of existence. Moreover, facing death is instrumental in overcoming even some of the ontological limits of our finitude in the sense that owning up to the possibility of one's own death is the way to authenticity,[76] and authenticity itself has to be conquered over other existentials, such as falling, idle talk, curiosity, and so forth. According to this heroic logic, and even at the ontological level itself, death is not purely constrictive but also—provided that we live up to its challenge—the indirect way for us to reach beyond our fallen everyday state.

From a Heideggerian perspective, then, the Kantian diremption between the two forms of finitude, which generated both the Copernican turn (by having transcendental finitude take over its empirical counterpart) and the analytic of finitude (because of the return of the empirical within the transcendental expressed by the originary), might finally be avoided by virtue of the displacement of the empirico-transcendental divide itself. The limitations inherent to human existence are shifted by *Being and Time* from the purely factual to the ontological, a move that prevents the former anthropological confusions by enabling a new analysis of finitude itself. The ontic forms of our finitude (life, language, and so forth) now have an ontological basis (thrownness as the general form of our finitude), which allows them to be rethought ontologically (as Being towards Death or Discourse).[77] In short, Heidegger's answer to the problem of finitude lies in the passage from metaphysics to fundamental ontology—a move that, incidentally, uncovers in advance the unthought of Foucault's analyses of modernity and therefore brings them to completion: indeed, Foucault's main conclusion in the *Order of Things* was that our current aporia stems from the impossibility for man as the empirico-transcendental doublet to provide the required foundation for knowledge. But Heidegger's own study of the history of Western metaphysics shows that the empirico-transcendental dichotomy itself results from a misconception of existence (as opposed to *essentia*) due to the forgetting of the question of Being. Whereas Foucault's analyses establish from the inside the limits of the Copernican turn and of Kant's reinterpretation of metaphysics (as well as that of the Idealist tradition, especially German), Heidegger's recontextualize the whole of the Western tradition from the new perspective generated by fundamental ontology itself.

However, whether this solution is as effective as I have made it seem so far is a touchy question, for at least two reasons: first, in spite of his criticism of Kant's transcendentalism, Heidegger, too, ends up making a priori claims regarding the conditions of possibility of knowledge. Second, although he does displace the empirico-transcendental dichotomy, his shift to fundamental ontology replicates the logic of the Copernican turn in the sense that it still unquestioningly works by prioritizing the perspective of intelligibility over that of factual determinations. Regarding the first point, Heidegger does recognize—and in fact argues against Husserl—that there is no absolute foundation for knowledge in the sense that, as mentioned before, we can't clarify the understanding of being presupposed by our practices: we are always *in medias res*. However, his strategy consists of suggesting that although we can't predict the ontic forms that our finitude will take (i.e., what type of practices we shall be involved in, or how, or when), we can still know a priori its ontological structures, i.e., the existentials themselves. Therefore, we must distinguish between two levels in his discourse: from the perspective of its content, Heidegger fully acknowledges that his ontological version of the hermeneutic circle[78] excludes any transcendental foundation for empirical knowledge. But as far as *form* is concerned, *Being and Time* definitely rests on the claim that such a foundation is possible and legitimate, since it is presented as an analysis of the ontological structures of existence, which views them as both necessary (applying to all forms of Dasein, including the non-man-centered ones[79]) and universal (valid for all times)—which is, *stricto sensu*, the Kantian definition of the a priori.[80] For example, there may be huge cultural differences between various societies, both geographically and historically, but Heidegger assumes that everywhere and at any given time people will care for themselves as beings for whom Being itself is an issue, will have moods, a projective understanding of temporality, and so forth. There may be different ways of caring for oneself in this world, but all of them will make sense as forms of *care*.[81] In this sense, Heidegger implicitly restores for *Being and Time* the same transcendental claims to universality and necessity that were Kant's in the *First Critique*; moreover, he does so by distinguishing again between two levels of analysis and therefore by reintroducing the major form of metaphysical thought—i.e., dichotomy—which brings me to my second point.

Indeed, as I have suggested earlier, Heidegger's way of dealing with apparently ontic forms of finitude (such as death) is to shift to the ontological level and claim that it is only from such perspective (in this case, Being Towards Death) that these forms can make sense as forms of finitude. In other words, it may be the case that Dasein can only be understood from its practices, and that these are severely constricting: but they can only make sense as human, self-interpretative practices on the ontological background of the question of Being. They appear as meaningful practices only if we relate them to the existentials that define the ontological structure of Being in the world. Thus, most female animals protect their young: but what a mother does will only be understood as *a mother's* activity from the perspective of care, for herself (her understanding herself as a mother) and for her baby (leaping in or leaping ahead, for example).[82] To take up the example of death again, as Hegel said before,[83] animals perish, but only human beings die: what really matters in death is not the empirical fact of the cessation of life, but the meanings it may have for an entity who can reflect on the perspective of its own death, and more fundamentally, whose being in the world involves from the start an implicit understanding of its own mortality embodied in its practices (such as avoiding danger, physical hurt, or positively taking care of one's health, staying fit, and so forth). However, the Kantian strategy consisted precisely in claiming that although human beings are (causally) determined by the various empirical forms of their finitude, the latter can be overcome because they are (epistemically) dependent on the transcendental subject in order to be known as such. By moving from death as an ontic fact to Being towards Death as an existential, Heidegger therefore implicitly endorses the emphasis formerly placed by Kant on a priori intelligibility over empirical determinations, while giving the Kantian strategy an even wider scope. Although he rejects the empirico-transcendental divide as implicitly funded on a mistaken conception of existence, he replicates the logic of the Copernican turn by keeping the shift from the post hoc to the a priori, and by making the ontological the condition of intelligibility of the ontic, therefore reestablishing another dual distinction (the ontological difference itself) as the core of his thought.

The crucial question, of course, becomes the following: is Heidegger running from the frying pan into the fire? Is he escaping the (post) Kantian analytic of finitude only to meet his own version of the originary? As far as I can see, at this stage the difficulty does not lie in a return of the ontic within the ontological, but rather with his transcendentalist claims to universality. In spite of his concession to the hermeneutic circle, i.e., that we may not elucidate completely the historical forms that our understanding of being can take, Heidegger still presupposes that whatever the time and place, the understanding of being we have (or shall have) will always be shaped by the existentials defined in *Being and Time*. But how can we be assured of this? How can Heidegger justify that claim? As shown by Lévi-Strauss,[84] there are some societies that do not perceive time as ordered by a continuity between past, present, and future—hence the opposition between "hot" and "cold" cultures, the latter having no cumulative understanding of history. In the same way, the distinction between profane and sacred forms of temporality that is specific to mythical thought[85] is not identical to that between chronological time and authentic temporality. Because it presupposes both apodictic certainty and the possibility of a detached, historical (in other words, transcendental) point of view, Heidegger's very claim that existence has structures that can be analyzed a priori might very well be turned against him, and read as being per se a refutation of the relativist logic of the hermeneutic circle (which he otherwise fully acknowledges and even uses as a strategic weapon against Husserl)—in which case early Heidegger would have, as Kant before him, defeated himself. As I have tried to show elsewhere,[86] Foucault, who also makes the same move by trying to isolate successive historical a priori as epochal conditions of intelligibility, is also met with his own version of the originary in the sense that he can't account for change without having the empirical recur within the transcendental. From this succession of failures, one might conclude that the very logic of the Copernican turn is flawed and must be given up, a point to which I shall return at the end of this chapter.

Does later Heidegger do better? One could indeed claim that although fundamental ontology retains some metaphysical traits because of the implicit transcendentalist claims it involves, the later "history of Being" was meant to avoid such an atemporal and decontextualized perspective (if only by acknowledging and studying the multiplicity of the "epochs" of Being). However, later Heidegger may then be threatened by the second of the dangers of the analytic of finitude, i.e., the return of the empirical. Indeed, if he is to avoid the difficulties inherent in the a priori standpoint of *Being and Time,* he must have an explanation for the manner in which our understandings of being themselves are transformed, i.e., a way to account for historical change. The obvious way to do so would be to claim that some modifications can happen at the ontic level that are so considerable that they act on the very ontological structure of our existence and modify it—for example, the Western understanding of time has been radically modified by Judaism, and later by Christianity. Yet such an explanation would be tantamount to reestablishing the circularity characteristic of the originary in the sense that the conditions of intelligibility would be modified by that which they are supposed to allow us to think, which would negate the very notion of independent epochal conditions—hence, probably, Heidegger's implicit rejection of this "solution." But this (wise) move forces him to give up the possibility of any explanation for historical changes, which are then understood as different (and unaccountable for) "sendings" of Being. Yet the consequence of this turn is that it transforms the history of being into a *transcendental* form of history in the sense that Being has now to be conceived as outside of the historical flow itself, by which later Heidegger runs again into the earlier difficulty of justifying such an a priori standpoint.[87] The obvious answer might be to give up the notion of justification itself altogether with the foundational logic of the Copernican turn: it is clearly the option chosen by Heidegger in his last works. However, this, in turn, entails two dangers: either a purely positivist account of history, in which philosophy has no place, or the mysticism recumbent in Heidegger's final essays on language. Perhaps either of these would be preferable to the aporia of the analytic of finitude—it certainly is the conclusion that both Heidegger and Foucault seem to draw from their previous experiences with transcendentalism, Heidegger by deliberately embracing mystical thought and Foucault with his genealogical turn. But can we be really happy with either of these?[88]

If I may be allowed in my conclusion to turn back on the question with a broader (but admittedly more simplifying) perspective, it seems that until the Kantian turn, the West had come up with at least three possible strategies to try to deal with finitude. One is the exploration of *hybris* as wanting more than the share imparted to us by *moira.* As shown by J. P. Vernant's work on tragedy,[89] the Greek hero transgresses the law given by Zeus to men ("Suffer so that you will understand") and dares to try what the gods themselves cannot do,[90] i.e., to change his destiny: failing to understand, he then suffers more. The tragic way to deal with our limitations is heroic denial, a Promethean rebellion in which human finitude consumes itself in the attempt to reach beyond its own condition. At the opposite end of the spectrum of human action, the second path is the Stoic knowledge and acceptance of fate (later taken up by Christian thinkers like Augustine via such notions as predestination).[91] "Neither a Tragic, nor a Courtesan" said Marcus Aurelius[92]—an equal distance from the hopeless revolt of the hero on the one hand, and a demeaning and slavish attempt to ingratiate oneself with fate on the other: dignity above all. As beautifully expressed by Epictetus, we should remember that we are like actors in a play that we did not choose, having to enact a character that has been arbitrarily assigned to us:[93] the best we can do is to learn to know our part and to use this knowledge to impersonate it better, so that the whole cosmic stage will end up the richer and the more subtle for our small contribution. Conversely, "if you take a part which is beyond your capacity, not only will you perform badly, but you will leave aside the part that you could have filled properly."[94] The very opposite of the tragic hero, the Stoic sage deals with finitude from the inside, by lucidly exploring his limitations and trying to make the best of them: what really matters, then, is not the many constraints that weigh upon us (such as death, illness, pain, loss), but the way we behave toward them. Of course, one may rightly argue that there is still a strongly hybristic element in the Stoic belief in the absolute power of reason (which is exemplified by the Stoic analysis of pain as solely dependent on judgment); yet *hybris* still occupies a much smaller part than in tragedy in the sense that it is now submitted to a higher goal *(ataraxia)* instead of being the defining characteristic of human behavior. More radically, one might point out that the Stoic attitude implicitly rests on the claim that one can accept *any* fate, and thus that there are no limits to the power of human reason, another hybristic claim that in turn presupposes a (rationally unjustifiable) belief in the benevolent nature of the order of things. However, although it is sometimes so hyperbolic as to turn into its very opposite (pride and solipsism, as Hegel saw very well), the Stoic insistence on humility and acceptance of fate still outlines another way of dealing with finitude, through knowledge and restraint, rather than through audacious but unwise action.

The third option differs from the previous two in the sense that it does not share their (explicit or implicit) heroism: it is the humanist mild derision of human failures, a healing tenderness and humorous coming to terms with our limitations—Sganarelle's comic good sense as opposed to Dom Juan's self-consciousness in Molière's play, the sly Goupil of the *Roman de Renard,* Montaigne's lucid criticism but gentle tolerance for the weaknesses of his fellow human beings in the *Essays.* This third manner of approaching finitude also emphasizes acknowledgment of our human limitations, but in a nondramatic way, i.e., via endlessly renewed distance and play: the burlesque exaggerations that make fun of our bodily constraints, the more reflective self-distance of irony, overall the playfulness of someone who allows himself to be strongly affected by the world and by others (contrary to the Stoic), but refuses to take anything in too serious or definite a manner (as opposed to the tragic). Rather than electing to either reject or reinforce his proper place in the course of things, the humorist gives up the very idea of such a fixed cosmic and moral order, and shifts from perspective to perspective, following his moods and the ever changing flux of events. Consequently, he sees things on a smaller scale, for a shorter time, and tries to be receptive to them in more subtle ways, paying attention to the minute details of everyday existence, the "small ironies of life," as Thomas Hardy put it. Humor might be the "politeness of despair," as Vladimir Jankélévitch said, a modest way to deal with life and spare others the sight of one's suffering: but it is also a question of content, not only form. Or rather, a "forme-sens" by which fundamentally sad elements (finitude itself) can be both expressed and played with—a humorous alternative to Dionysian fury or Apollonian wistful dreams.

On this (admittedly sketchy but hopefully helpful) background, the Copernican turn and the Kantian legacy itself (i.e., the analytic of finitude) appear as a revival of the tragic overcoming of finitude, renewed by the incorporation of the Stoic insistence on the power of knowledge and reason—in short, a twist on the first two traditions in thinking of finitude, which pushes them to their utmost limit. The hybristic nature of the critical project shows clearly in the way in which transcendental finitude, having overcome its empirical counterpart via Kant's foundational shift to the a priori, ends up defining the very range of all possible knowledge and action, a claim that neither the tragics nor the stoics had ever dared to make (the first because they never thought it was possible for humans to know their destiny; the second because although our reason is homogeneous in nature to the great Logos of the world, it is incommensurable with it). But for Kant, within the (restricted) scope of experience, human reason is absolutely sovereign. Of course, he never asserted that experience defines everything that can be given to thought (not knowledge), quite on the contrary; moreover, some of the most fundamental elements of human nature (beginning with freedom itself as the "fact of reason") can only be acknowledged in their effects, but not known.[95] Yet insofar as knowledge remains the basis of free agency (as based on rational determination) and the only defense we have against skepticism, transcendental finitude encompasses the whole of our theoretical and practical possibilities, thus being the core of a (prehermeneutic) circle that may not be the only possible one (as Kant says, other rational beings might apprehend reality in very different ways), but still defines, from our point of view, the horizon of all that we shall ever know or do. In this regard, Kant's overcoming of empirical finitude via the invention of the a priori gives man a position and a power that the Greeks never dreamt of, that of the "King," as Foucault says in *The Order of Things*: the center of a purely anthropological stage from which even God has been excluded as supreme Director.[96]

The hybristic character of the Copernican turn becomes more obvious in the later aspirations of German idealism to absolute knowledge or even godhood (as in Schelling), but also, as Foucault and Heidegger saw so clearly, in the renewed attempts of modern thought to keep up with the demands of the analytic of finitude, and therefore to make finitude self-foundational. However, if my previous analyses are right, it should be clear that finitude cannot be understood in this solipsistic way, as its own foundation and the path to its private overcoming. So what ought we do? Or perhaps more aptly, what should we hope for? Although this is far too massive a question for me to address here (if ever!), I might suggest the following: our contemporary understanding of Being has given us the implicit belief and more importantly the practices from which it appears that technological *Macht* is what defines our relationship to the world and to ourselves. But these aspirations to an endless self-overcoming by which human finitude would be transcended in the very operation that makes it reach beyond itself (the implicit optimism of the "theoretical man"[97] now culminating in our reverence for scientific progress) can easily—as Nietzsche himself understood so clearly—lead to nothing but nihilism, a hyper-efficacious but spiritless and valueless dynamic. Since the ubiquitous paths of tragic *hybris* have been trodden anew in so many ways by modernity and, at the end of the day, with so few benefits, perhaps it is time for us to abandon the very idea of an overcoming itself; to break away from the solipsistic circularity of the analytic of finitude by acknowledging that there is no way in which finitude can be self-foundational. Of course, such a recognition of powerlessness reopens the way to skepticism, but the latter need not be the radical pyrrhonism feared so much by the thinkers of the Enlightenment. Perhaps a measured form of skepticism—if truth has "many veils," as Nietzsche said, why shouldn't doubt have many shadows?—along with something of a revival of the tradition left aside by Kant and his followers[98] (humanist good cheer and irony in the face of our limitations) might exhibit, in their small ways, more saving virtues than our past Copernican dreams of power.

Notes

1. Cf. René Descartes to Père Mersenne, 15 April 1630, *Oeuvres et Lettres* (Paris: Gallimard, coll. Pléiade, 1953), especially 933–34.

2. Although Foucault does distinguish between the two forms of finitude (empirical and transcendental) in the *Commentary* (see, for example, 102), the names are of my own choosing. Similarly, the text I refer to henceforth under the name *Commentary* is Foucault's unpublished and unnamed commentary to Kant's *Anthropology*. Along with a translation of the same text (published in France by the éditions Vrin), this commentary was Foucault's complementary doctoral thesis. A copy is still available at the Bibliothèque de la Sorbonne and another one at the Centre Michel Foucault in Paris. All translations here are mine.

3. Michael Foucault, *The Order of Things: An Archaeology of Human Knowledge* (New York: Vintage Books, 1970), 242–43.

4. This transcendental form of analysis is opposed by Foucault (in chapter 7 of *The Order of Things*, 240ff.) to the de facto exploration of our mental abilities performed by Condillac and the Ideologists. This shift from the post hoc to the a priori is the core of transcendental finitude.

5. There are other strategies in the Kantian corpus that are clearly meant to overcome empirical finitude by shifting to a different level. Among these, the distinction between the (Cartesian) *Willkür* and the a priori self-determining *Wille* in the *Critique of Practical Reason*, or Kant's analysis of the sublime in the *Third Critique*, in which the finitude of human imagination is outlined only to be overcome through the revelation of reason's suprasensible power.

6. Descartes, *Meditations on First Philosophy* (Cambridge: Cambridge University Press, 1986); see in particular Meditation 4, "On Error"; cf. Locke, *An Essay Concerning*

Human Understanding (Oxford: Clarendon Press, 1924); cf. Hume, *An Inquiry Concerning Human Understanding* (New York: The Liberal Arts Press, 1955).

7. These empirical forms of our finitude are identified by Foucault in chapter 9 of *The Order of Things* as "Life," "Language," and "Labour." However these empirical limitations are given a "quasi-transcendental" value by the anthropological turn (cf. 244ff), which is the reason why the analytic of finitude is deemed hopeless by Foucault. I shall come back to this point very shortly.

8. This is the reason why Kant disagrees with dogmatic metaphysicians such as Leibniz or Christian Wolff.

9. This is a twist on the Rousseauist notion of "perfectibility" elaborated in the first part of *A Discourse on Inequality* (trans. M. Cranston [Harmondsworth: Penguin Books, 1984]), which Kant takes up in his later essays on history (cf. *On History*, trans. Lewis W. Beck [Indianapolis: Bobbs-Merrill, 1963]).

10. As Kant establishes in the *Second Critique*, free agency (as opposed to animal behavior, or even to human comportment when the agents are "pathologically" determined by their sensuous inclinations) rests on the possibility of rational determination and therefore also on the exercise of our reason in its knowing capacity.

11. Cf. *Commentary*, 23 : the *Anthropology* finds "neither a subject in itself, nor the pure 'I' of synthesis [i.e., of transcendental apperception], but a subject who is object and present only in its phenomenal truth. Yet this object I, given to sense under the form of time, is not foreign to the determining subject, *since at the end of the day it is nothing else than the subject as it is affected by itself*" (my italics).

12. Ibid., 60.

13. This is the core of Derrida's analysis of "primitivity" in his commentary to Husserl's *Origin of Geometry*. See Derrida, *Le problème de la genèse dans la philosophie de Husserl* (Paris: Presses Universitaires de France, 1990).

14. "Philosophie et Vérité," discussion with Alain Badiou, Georges Canguilhem, David Dreyfus, Jean Hyppolite, and Paul Ricoeur, in *Dits et Ecrits* (Paris: Éditions Gallimard, 1995), 1:452; my translation.

15. Interestingly, Foucault expresses this in Kantian terms in an interview with Paul Ricoeur: "[A]s soon as one tries to define an essence of man which could be spelled out from itself [i.e., an empirical knowledge of man, based on observation] and which would at the same time be the foundation of all possible knowledge and of any limit to knowledge, then we are in the middle of a paralogism" (Ibid., my translation). Foucault's favorite example for this (ill-fated) move is Husserl's transcendental phenomenology, and the move from the early analysis of the transcendental ego to the study of the *Lebenswelt*.

16. Thus the three fundamental questions of the "Canon of Pure Reason" ("what can I know, ought to do, hope for") presuppose finitude, since only a finite being would ask questions concerning possibility (what *can* I do, what *should* I do). For an infinite being, the very concept of a possibility without the potential for actualization would not exist—possibility and actualization would be identical (which is the reason why a metaphysician like Spinoza denies the very notion of possibility).

17. Heidegger, *Kant and the Problem of Metaphysics* (Bloomington: Indiana University Press, 1990), 115.

18. The fact that he had a clear knowledge of early Heidegger, however, can be derived from other texts dating from the same period: for example, his long introduction to Ludwig Binswanger's *Dream and Existence* (Seattle: Review of Existential Psychology and Psychiatry, 1986) shows that Foucault was familiar with the fundamental notions of *Being and Time*, such as "being-in-the-world," and moreover that he shared Heidegger's antinaturalistic approach.

19. Many critical questions could be asked at this point, such as the following: in

Foucault's versions of the doubles, is it truly the empirical that recurs under the form of the origin (either as an empirical givenness that determines the transcendental perspective, or as the chronological understanding of time that generates the paradox of the originary subject preexisting itself)? Even if we grant Foucault that any kind of transcendental analysis is bound to encounter forms of givenness and passivity, couldn't the latter be understood at the transcendental level itself, thus avoiding the recurrence of anthropological forms of finitude within the a priori? Moreover, couldn't the a priori be recast in such a way as to avoid the strict empirico-transcendental dichotomy? Much of the later Husserl's work, especially in *Experience and Judgment* (London: Routledge and K. Paul, 1973) on the question of passive synthesis, and *The Crisis of European Sciences and Transcendental Phenomenology; An Introduction to Phenomenological Philosophy* (trans. D. Carr [Evanston, Ill.: Northwestern University Press, 1970]) on the *Lebenswelt* could be read as attempts to address these two points. In the same way, could the temporal self-affection that is operative in the originary be understood as purely transcendental, which again seems to be the point that Husserl is trying to make in the *Phenomenology of Internal Time-consciousness* (The Hague: Nijhoff, 1964)? Since these interrogations (and others) are internal to Foucault's own problematic, however, I shall leave them aside for now.

20. This rejection is clearly shown by his controversy with Husserl on the question of intentionality, especially in the *History of the Concept of Time* (Bloomington: Indiana University Press, 1985), and then in his answer to Sartrian existentialism in the *Letter on Humanism* (published in *Basic Writings from "Being and Time" [1927] to "The Task of Thinking" [1964]*, [London: Routledge & K. Paul, 1978]).

21. Cf. Foucault, *The Order of Things*, 341.

22. Cf. Béatrice Han, *Foucault's Critical Project: Between the Transcendental and the Historical*, trans. Edward Pile (Stanford, Calif.: Atopia, 2002); originally published as *L'ontologie manquée de Michel Foucault* (Grenoble: Éditions Jérôme Millon, 1998).

23. Cf. Foucault, *Commentary*, 61: the *Critique* was "an investigation of what is conditioning in foundational activity," and the *Anthropology* the "inventory of the non-founded in what is conditioned." Whereas the *Critique* was the a priori exploration of our faculties in their foundational use, the *Anthropology* analyzes their various a posteriori misuses.

24. Ibid., 79: the world can be a "source" for knowledge [which therefore is *stricto sensu* limited to the empirical] only "on the background of a transcendental correlation between passivity and spontaneity," i.e., for the transcendental subject as able to make spontaneous judgments based on the basis of the data provided by his sensibility. In the same way, the world can be a "domain" for action [and therefore a limit to what we can do] only "on the background of a transcendental correlation between necessity and freedom" [explained by Kant in the "Third Antinomy"], which accounts for the possibility of any free action at all (my translation, my gloss in brackets).

25. Ibid., 52.

26. Kant, *Critique of Pure Reason*, trans. Norman Kemp Smith (London: Macmillan, 1929), "Canon of Pure Reason," A796/B824.

27. Foucault, *Commentary*, 55.

28. Ibid., 54 (my italics).

29. "The *Geist* is the originary fact which, in its transcendental version, implies that the infinite is never there" (ibid., 55).

30. Cf. Foucault, *The Order of Things*, chapter 9, "The Cogito and the Unthought" (322ff.): this subsection refers to the fact that the more we try to think the conditions of possibility of thought, the more they retreat away from us (in the opacity of the body in Merleau Ponty, for example, or in the passive syntheses of Husserl).

31. Foucault, *Commentary*, 54.

32. Cf. Kant, *Critique of Pure Reason*, "Transcendental Analytic," where Kant mentions two ways of conceiving the relationship between representation and its objects: either the existence of an object makes the latter possible by producing sensuous impressions (causal determination), or the representation itself remains determining a priori with regard to the object, in which case it is the only way to know something as an object (transcendental determination). The *First Critique* is concerned with the second type of determination, which is epistemically constitutive.

33. Of course, one may ask whether "existence" should be understood, as Foucault implicitly does, as *empirical* existence. Foucault very likely derives the notion of an "a priori of existence" (like that of "passive synthesis") from Husserl, more precisely from the *Cartesian Meditations* (The Hague: M. Nijhoff, 1969). But when Husserl speaks of a "concrete" a priori, he does not mean by that an empirical a priori.

34. Contrary to an origin, which cannot be inscribed within human temporality, a beginning is homogeneous to that which it initiates. For example, the invention of writing is the beginning of history (as opposed to prehistoric times); but the creation of the world as narrated in Genesis is (for the believer) an origin.

35. Interestingly enough, Derrida identifies a similar structure in Husserl's thought in his commentary to the *Origin of Geometry*: "primitivity" is the name he chooses to designate the impossibility for the origin to be comprehended within the temporal framework of intelligibility it generates.

36. Foucault, *Commentary*, 60. This temporalization is a self-affection of the subject: however, that such a self-affection should necessarily be thought of as empirical is not as obvious as Foucault suggests—it is one of the major questions of German idealism, especially in Fichte's thought (the "*Ich-Spältung*").

37. Ibid., 60 (my italics).

38. Foucault, *The Order of Things*, 244.

39. Ibid. Cf. also 313: "[M]an is governed by labour, life, and language: his concrete existence finds its determinations in them."

40. Ibid., 314 (my italics and gloss in brackets). The quote goes on as follows: "Moreover, the latter [transcendental finitude] is not the completely purified essence of positivity [i.e., a set of empirical determinations that would be so fundamental and clear ('purified') that we could account for the empirical in a purely positive, i.e., deterministic way: for example having a perfectly clear vision of economic causal networks to account for the production of knowledge], but that upon the basis of which it is possible for positivity to arise [in the sense that positivity as such (i.e., intelligible as positivity) can only appear as founded by transcendental finitude]" (my gloss in brackets).

41. This structure commands the three figures of the origin identified by Foucault, i.e., the *Geist* as the empirical "root" of reason, the originary as the "already there," and life, language, and labor as the "quasi-transcendentals" in *The Order of Things*.

42. Foucault, *The Order of Things*, 315.

43. Foucault, *Commentary*, 105.

44. Foucault, *The Order of Things*, 318.

45. Ibid., 244. The quote goes on to say "but by that very fact are conditions of knowledge," which could be misleading. However, the rest of the text indicates that the only "foundation" the quasi-transcendentals can provide for knowledge is *via* man in his duality, and insist on the impossibility of him having any clear knowledge of himself or the world (and therefore of providing a real foundation).

46. This is the schema that Foucault uses to read most phenomenological trends: transcendental finitude, which formerly defined the conditions of possibility of knowledge, is put back within the context of anthropological finitude, which concerns the ex-

istential conditions of possibility of empirical life. The transcendental subject itself now appears on the background of life, labor, and language. Examples of this would be Husserl's *Lebenswelt,* Merleau-Ponty's "embodied cogito," the later Sartre's definition of consciousness as always confronted with praxis and the practico-inert. Each of these philosophers, in his attempt to deal with the transcendental, is faced with one of the forms of existential finitude ("Life" for Husserl, "Language" for Merleau-Ponty, "Labour" for Sartre). Foucault certainly has a point in identifying the a priori as a crucial node for all three thinkers; whether he is correct in his assessment (which is less severe in the case of Merleau-Ponty) cannot be discussed here for lack of space.

47. I shall focus on Heidegger's early texts because they are the only ones that Foucault clearly knew. However it seems clear from some passages of *The Order of Things* that he also was familiar with Heidegger's later work. For example, the following passage is highly reminiscent of the first part of *What Is Called Thinking:* "[T]he return is posited only in the extreme recession of the origin—in that region where the gods have turned away, where the desert is increasing, where the *technê* has established the dominion of its will" (334). In particular, the idea that the "desert is increasing," especially in the context of a criticism of technology (as self-willing) seems a direct echo of Nietzsche's sentence (commented upon by Heidegger in the above-mentioned text), "the wasteland grows."

48. This reading is strikingly similar to the one that Foucault presents. It is quite likely that the latter was influenced by the publication in French of Corbin's translation of *Kant and the Problem of Metaphysics,* which occurred before he completed *The Order of Things.*

49. This is a feature that Sartre expands upon considerably, especially *The Psychology of Imagination* (London: Methuen, 1972).

50. Heidegger, *Kant and the Problem of Metaphysics,* 95. To summarize quickly Heidegger's argument: both time and the "I think" are shown to be "rooted in transcendental imagination" (95). Thinking is not radically different from intuiting in that it involves a re-presenting *(vorstellen)*: "thinking in the sense of the free-forming and projecting conceiving of something, the original thinking is pure imagining" (105). Moreover, the "I" of the "I think" can only be understood as a unity through the synthetic power of transcendental imagination because the "'I' lies in pure consciousness of the self": this pure consciousness itself is read in phenomenological terms, i.e., as a "preliminary self-orienting towards" (a form of transcendence as self-projecting): thus, "the transcendental power of I projects, forming in advance the totality of possibilities in terms of which it 'looks out,' in order therefore before itself the horizon within which the knowing self . . . acts" (106). Finally, transcendental imagination accounts for the unity of the "I" itself (and not only for the projection of the horizon of possibilities), through the categories (as an "I think substance," and "I think causality," and so forth). As for time, it is an "original representation." Yet for it to be "original" means that it is unifying (and not unified, as empirical contents are): this unification is provided by transcendental imagination as "image-giving imagining" (98). This is accounted for by the analysis of the three syntheses of transcendental imagination (§ 32–34): a) apprehension (taking a likeness), which presupposes the present in the sense that a sequence of nows can only appear as such on the synthetic horizon of presence (each now being taken as actual); b) reproduction (which presupposes the past, because it entails the bringing forth of a past representation); c) recognition (which presupposes the future in that recognition supposes that one is "watching out" for something, as Heidegger puts it, i.e., that one has a preconception of what has to be synthesized through recognition). Therefore transcendental imagination is the "original," i.e., generative power through which time is made possible as a unity/totality within which other intuitions can

be represented: "*the syn- of the totality of time belongs to a faculty of formative intuition*" (98).

51. Ibid., 105.

52. Thus, Kant was right in rejecting the traditional understanding of existence as a predicate (which was central to Descartes's formulation of the ontological argument in the *Fifth Meditation*); unfortunately this promising move away from the logical understanding of existence did not lead him to recast the latter ontologically. In Heidegger's view, Kant remains a metaphysician.

53. Heidegger, *Kant and the Problem of Metaphysics,* 115.

54. Cf. ibid., 111ff.

55. Of course, it may well be the case that Heidegger is reading in his own thought in Kant's philosophy rather than providing an exegesis *stricto sensu,* which casts some doubts as to the effectiveness of such solutions. However, within the framework of Heidegger's reading it seems quite likely that transcendental imagination would have saved us from the anthropological contradictions of the originary.

56. Heidegger, *Kant and the Problem of Metaphysics,* 160.

57. It is clear that Heidegger did not have much esteem for Schopenhauer, as shown by the first volume of the *Nietzsche* lectures (trans. David Krell [San Francisco: Harper and Row, 1979]). Yet finding a solution to the "problem of existence" is the main ambition of Schopenhauer's thought, with fine arts and philosophy being the two major ways of dealing with human finitude and making it bearable (cf. *World as Will and Representation,* trans. E. F. J. Payne [New York: Dover, 1969], supplements, chapter 33). As for the connection between Heidegger and Kierkegaard, compare, for example, the second appendix to Hubert Dreyfus's *A Commentary to Being and Time, Division I* (Cambridge: MIT Press, 1991).

58. Heidegger, *Kant and the Problem of Metaphysics,* 148.

59. Compare: "*[T]he essence of Dasein lies in its existence* . . . . So when we designate this entity with the term 'Dasein,' we are expressing not its 'what' (as if it were a table, house or tree) but its Being. That Being which is an *issue* for this entity in its very being, is in each case mine" (*Being and Time,* trans. John Macquarrie and Edward Robinson [Oxford: Blackwell, 1962], § 9, 67).

60. Heidegger, *Kant and the Problem of Metaphysics,* 157.

61. Ibid., 156.

62. Cf. the introduction to *Being and Time,* § 7, especially 62. Our finitude is also expressed in the fact that we are already caught within the hermeneutic circle, i.e., the fact that any interpretation a) presupposes other interpretations that cannot be entirely clarified and b) changes the very medium it uses (language), i.e., sediments itself as the implicit basis for new interpretations. In this regard, the transcendental dream of an absolute foundation must be forsaken from the start. See also § 32, 189–95.

63. Thus we can't be knights or Samurais anymore.

64. Cf., ibid., § 13, 88 : "[I]f knowing is to be possible as a way of determining the nature of the present-at-hand by observing it, then there must be first a deficiency in our having-to-do with the world concernfully."

65. As indicated above, this move cannot be equated with a reverting to an empirical account of epistemic finitude because existence itself has ontological structures (being-in, being-with, etc.) that the first division of *Being and Time* is meant to clarify.

66. Heidegger, *Kant and the Problem of Metaphysics,* 159.

67. This explains the importance of care as what makes possible such a unified standpoint. In Heidegger's own words, "the progress of existential ontology (÷) takes aim solely at the working out of the unity in the transcendental primal structure of the finitude of Dasein [this unity being care itself]" (ibid., 167).

68. Heidegger, *The Essence of Reasons,* trans. Terence Malick (Evanston: Northwestern University Press, 1969), 41.

69. Hopefully the first one, the problem of the relationship between existence and the empirico-transcendental divide, has been sufficiently expanded on.

70. This displacement is similar to the one performed by Heidegger when answering the skeptic's challenge concerning the existence of the external world in *Being and Time:* Heidegger does not engage in a refutation but shows that the skeptic's point of view is dependent on inadequate premises (because she starts with a detached, Cartesian understanding of the subject, instead of being-in-the-world).

71. Mainly § 65–68.

72. Cf. Aristotle, *Physics IV* (trans. Edward Hussey [Oxford: Clarendon Press; New York: Oxford University Press, 1983]), where time is said to be "the number of movement."

73. Cf. Heidegger, *Being and Time,* 378.

74. Cf., ibid., § 78 and 81.

75. Thus, facing being-towards-death requires three elements: first, grasping the absence of essence that defines Dasein (Dasein as a "null" basis for projection); this means implicitly acknowledging the past (although in a nondeterminative way, cf. Heidegger, ibid., 373). Second, opening a futural dimension by projecting death as a (nonrelational) possibility: Dasein's being is futural. It is only on the background of the future that the other ecstasies make sense to me (I relate to my past by being directed toward my future, which makes me select this or that element, for example). Finally, being open to the present (since I must live and act now as if my death were imminent). Resoluteness reveals the present to me as a situation for choice and action (cf. ibid., 374ff).

76. This is the case because in the light of my awareness of death as the horizon for my possibilities I must act in such a way as to make my life a unified whole.

77. For lack of space I haven't supplied an analysis of language. But it is clear from *Being and Time* that the ontic use of language is in fact dependent on the articulation operated by discourse *(Rede),* which is a replication of Heidegger's move concerning death and Being-towards-Death.

78. See, for example, *Being and Time,* § 2, 28 : "The guiding activity of taking a look at Being arises from the average understanding of Being in which we always operate and *which in the end belongs to the essential constitution of Dasein itself.*" See also § 7, 62, or again § 32, 190: "[I]n interpreting, we do not, so to speak, throw a 'signification' over some naked thing which is present-at-hand, we do not stick a value on it; but when something within-the-world is encountered as such, the thing in question already has an involvement which is disclosed in our understanding of the world, and this involvement is one which gets laid out by the interpretation."

79. This is another replication of a Kantian move, ironically enough: as noted by many commentators (such as Henry Allison, for example, in *Kant's Theory of Freedom* [Cambridge: Cambridge University Press, 1990]), the *Second Critique* is devoted to the analysis of rational creatures, not necessarily human beings.

80. Cf. Kant, *Critique of Pure Reason,* "Analytic of Principles."

81. For example, in a Hindu understanding of Being, caring for the world means protecting all its forms of life, hence practices such as vegetarianism and the absolute rejection of violence. But in the Aztec understanding of Being, caring for the world means preventing its ending, which can only be achieved by feeding the "Fifth Sun" with human blood, hence very different practices, such as ritual wars and human sacrifice.

82. Cf. Heidegger, *Being and Time,* § 26.

83. Heidegger, *Phenomenology of Spirit* (Oxford: Clarendon Press, 1977).

84. Cf. Lévi Strauss, *Race et Histoire* (Paris: Unesco, 1952).

85. This distinction between sacred and profane forms of temporality is analyzed by Mircea Eliade in *Rites and Symbols of Initiation: The Mysteries of Birth and Rebirth* (Woodstock, Conn.: Spring, 1995).

86. Han, *L'ontologie manquée de Michel Foucault,* part 1.

87. On the question of the history of being as transcendental history, see Michel Haar, *La fracture de l'histoire* (Grenoble: Jérôme Millon, 1993).

88. Heidegger's mysticism has been criticized enough. As for Foucault, his genealogy may not be as exempt of a priori claims as he suggests: cf. Habermas's criticism in *The Philosophical Discourse of Modernity* (trans. Frederick Lawrence [Cambridge: Polity, in association with Basil Blackwell, 1987]) and my own book, parts 2 and 3.

89. J. P. Vernant, *Mythe et pensée chez les Grecs: études de psychologie historique* (Paris: Maspéro, 1966).

90. Cf. Homer, *Odyssey* (Oxford and New York: Oxford University Press, 1980), 3:236: "[T]he Gods themselves cannot protect from Death a hero they love, when the pernicious fate *(moira)* has seized him to let him lie in death."

91. One of the first instances is Paul in his Epistle to the Romans, chapters 8, 28, and 30. Augustine expands on this (against the Pelagian heresy) in *De Praedestinatione Sanctorum* and *De Dono perseratione.*

92. *The Thoughts of the Emperor Marcus Aurelius Antoninus* (Medici Society, 1912), 5:28.

93. *The Discourses as reported by Arrian: the Manual, and Fragments,* trans. W. A. Oldfather (Cambridge: Harvard University Press, 1959), 17:213 (French edition): "[R]emember that you are like an actor with the role that the playwright has seen fit to give you. Short, if it is short; long, if it is long. If he wants you to play the part of a beggar, play it well. Do similarly for the part of a cripple, a judge, a private person. It is dependent on you to play the character that has been given to you well. But choosing it belongs to another."

94. Ibid., XXXVII. The good actor must always accept his part: a famous counterexample in the Stoic literature is provided by Nero, who tried to usurp the place of the gods and design his own play (by having Rome burned so that he could compose an elegy, for instance).

95. Cf. Kant, *Critique of Practical Reason* (trans. L. Beck [New York: Macmillan, 1993]), theorem 4.

96. Thus, however important the part played by the ultimate good in the *First Critique* and by faith in *Religion within the Limits of Reason Alone* (New York: Harper, 1960), the existence of God remains a postulate that cannot be theoretically proven.

97. Friedrich Nietzsche, *Birth of Tragedy,* trans. Walter Kaufmann (New York: Vintage Books, 1967), chapters 14 and 15.

98. An exception to this would be Jena Romantics, especially Friedrich von Schlegel, who was very much focused on the question of wit and irony, but in a rather dogmatic and serious manner; cf. *Fragments,* trans. Peter Firchow (Minneapolis: University of Minnesota Press, 1971). On this point, see Philippe Lacoue-Labarthe and Jean-Luc Nancy, *The Literary Absolute: The Theory of Literature in German Romanticism* (Albany: State University of New York Press, 1988).

Epistemes and the History of Being

Michael Schwartz

> *The* question *of the essence of knowledge* is, *everywhere and always, already a thinking* project *of the essence of man and his position within beings, as well as a projection of these beings themselves.*
>
> —Martin Heidegger, *Nietzsche*, vol. 3, *The Will to Power as Knowledge and as Metaphysics*

Foucault was explicit in his last interviews that for him Heidegger was "an overwhelming influence,"[1] "the essential philosopher" who determined his "entire philosophical development."[2] Yet he never wrote an article, let alone a book, about Heidegger; and his published remarks about the thinker who determined his entire philosophical development are few and brief. Nor are Heideggerian themes self-evident in his writings. If we take Foucault at his word about his philosophical roots, we are left to unearth and explicate the Heideggerian dimensions of his thought.[3]

One of the major books in Foucault's oeuvre is his 1966 study *The Order of Things*. As a number of commentators have noted, Foucault's history of epistemes has strong affinities with the unfolding of epochs in the history of Being.[4] To put the matter coarsely, both narrate stages in the rise and subsequent decentering of representation in Western European culture. But even if the content and storyline of the two projects are very close, this leaves unexamined their respective theoretical orientations. For what is an episteme? And how does its level of analysis stand with regard to that of the history of Being? In what follows I address these issues, limiting myself to the task of bringing to light Foucault's critical encounter with Heidegger in *The Order of Things*. I stress those texts of Heidegger's that Foucault would most likely have known, and offer abundant citation to demonstrate Foucault's appropriation and critical reworking of the history of Being. The present essay is commentarial, its approach intertextual.

The Order of Things, as I hope to show, subscribes to Heidegger's claim that knowledge and science have become primary determinants of existence:

> The question of knowledge as such, and of science in particular, is now to assume priority, not only because "science" determines our most proper area of work, but above all because knowledge and knowing have attained an essential power within Western history. "Science" is not simply *one* field of "cultural" activity among others; science is a fundamental power in that confrontation by dint of which Western man is related to beings and asserts himself in their midst.[5]

As expounded here in the 1961 Nietzsche volumes (with comparable remarks having appeared in essays and books published earlier), this thesis would have especially interested Foucault, whose archaeological projects from the *History of Madness* onward were engagements with and within the tradition of the French history and philosophy of science.[6] It is a thesis that could only have reinforced Foucault's sense of the importance of writing a history of epistemes.

Yet, the two thinkers do not proceed to address the question of knowledge in quite the same manner. Heidegger's philosophical "step back" allowed him to survey the regional sciences and their metaphysical groundings while still sounding the question of Being. As we shall see, Foucault, for his part, brackets the Being question and dives more deeply into the epistemic details of first-order scientific inquiry, thereby challenging basic Heideggerian assumptions—even as *The Order of Things* would have been impossible without the history of Being as its model.

Episteme

Toward the end of the original 1966 preface to *The Order of Things*, Foucault explains that

> the present study is, in a sense, an echo of my undertaking to write a history of madness in the Classical age; it has the same articulations in time, taking the end of the Renaissance as its starting-point, then encountering, at the beginning of the nineteenth century, just as my history of madness did, the threshold of a modernity that we have not yet left behind. But whereas in the history of madness I was investigating the way in which a culture can determine in a massive, general form the difference that limits it, I am concerned here with observing how a culture experiences the propinquity of things, how it establishes the *tabula* of their relationships and the order by which they must be considered. I am concerned, in short, with a history of resemblance. . . . The history of madness would be [then] the history of the Other . . . whereas the history of the order imposed on things would be the history of the same—of that which, for a given culture, is both dispersed and related, therefore to be distinguished by kinds and to be collected together into identities.[7]

Foucault is here correlating *The Order of Things* to his earlier study, the *History of Madness* (1961). Both operate with the same periodization of Renaissance, classical, and modern ages; but whereas the *History of Madness* explores "the limit-experience of the Other,"[8] *The Order of Things* is concerned with a culture's sense of order. Foucault explains that this sense of order is governed by an a priori of resemblance that is specific to a particular period, hence it is a "historical *a priori*."[9] And in *The Order of Things,* this historical a priori of resemblance constitutes an episteme: that "epistemological field . . . in which knowledge, envisaged apart from all criteria having reference to its rational value or to its objective forms, grounds its positivity and thereby manifests a history which is not that of its [knowledge's] growing perfection, but rather that of its [historical] conditions of *possibility.*"[10] Foucault's book explicates the successive configurations of this field since the Renaissance.

The Order of Things is accordingly an unconventional history of knowledge. It inspects not so much the accumulated bodies of knowledge as it brings to light the historically changing conditions of such knowledge. Further, inasmuch as the a priori of resemblance coordinates the propinquity of identities for a given culture, Foucault maintains that an episteme "makes manifest the modes of being of order."[11] In *The Order of Things,* knowing is understood to be inextricably woven with and disclosive of modes of being.

It is here instructive to recall that Heidegger, in several passages in his writings from the 1930s onward, took up discussion of the ancient

Greek notion of *epistēmē* (especially in its resonance with *physis*).[12] In "The Question Concerning Technology," he explains that

> From earliest time until Plato the word *technē* is linked with the word *epistēmē*. Both words are names for knowing in the widest sense. They mean to be entirely at home in something, to understand and be expert in it. Such knowing provides an opening up. As an opening up it is a revealing.[13]

Heidegger is retrieving what he takes to be the ontological import of knowing, forgotten in modern metaphysical construals of a subject representing an already constituted object-sphere, but sedimented in the ancient Greek understanding of knowing as involved with the "event" of Being itself. This view of *epistēmē,* as an opening up that is a revealing, complements Heidegger's questioning of the truth of Being and his creative retrievals of the terms of ancient Greek *aletheia*—truth-as-the-unconcealing-of-beings. Metaphysical versions of truth and knowledge, Heidegger argues, always forget Being in concentrating on beings. By reviving what he takes to be the ancient Greek understandings of truth-as-*aletheia* and knowing-as-*epistēmē,* Heidegger is striving to deepen and "overcome" *(Verwindung)* our epistemological habits of thought, pressing metaphysics beyond its reified assumptions toward the question of Being itself.[14]

Not only does Heidegger retrieve *epistēmē* as a knowing that reveals beings, articulating what the conjunction of knowing and being could mean in *The Order of Things,* but he also—to sound once again the terms of Foucault's phrasing—theorizes Being as an a priori that preordinates the likeness and equality among beings. Once again creatively drawing upon Greek deliberations, Heidegger advances that:

> Equality already unfolds essentially in the unconcealed; likeness "is" before we, with our perceiving, *explicitly* view, observe, and indeed consider like things as like. In our comportment towards similar things, equality has already come into view in advance. Equality, Being-alike, as Being—that is, as presence in the unconcealed—is what stands essentially in view, and in such a way that it first brings "view" and "the open" with it, holds them open, and grants visibility of similar beings.[15]

Being is an a priori because in the Opening of Being, similarities among beings always already shine forth.

Heidegger goes on to elucidate that this "*a priori,* when rightly conceived as the previous *[Vor-herige],* first reveals its *time*-ly essence in a more profound sense of 'time,' which our contemporaries do not presently *wish* to see, because they do not see the concealed essential connection between Being and Time."[16] This more profound sense of "time" is, for Heidegger, bound up with history—not history in the sense of a chronology of events and happenings, but history as the previous itself, as the opening, as that which regions.[17] Heidegger contends that "History as Being—indeed, as coming from the essence of Being itself—remains unthought."[18] Up until now "Hegel's history of philosophy is the only philosophical history heretofore, and it will remain the only one until philosophy is forced to think historically—in a still more essential and original sense of that word—taking its own most grounding question [i.e., "what is Being itself?"] as its point of departure."[19] Heidegger's answer to think history-as-Being is *Seinsgeschichte.* The a priori, conceived as the previous, would not be then for Heidegger a constant. Likenesses among beings would have a history.

It would seem that Foucault makes this thought-path the explicit project of *The Order of Things,* conjoining the trope of "Being as the *a priori* of likeness" to that of "History as Being" to advance the study's guiding notion of a "historical *a priori* of resemblance." He takes up Heidegger's retrieval of ancient *epistēmē* as a knowing-that-reveals, only to recast it so that episteme is now to be construed as the historical conditions of knowledge that exhibit the mode of being of order, with this order coming forth via the a priori of resemblance. Although Foucault never said as much, the principal terms of investigation in *The Order of Things* are decidedly Heideggerian.

Even Foucault's construal of the relation between the who and what of knowing finds its precedent in Heidegger, for whom the human knower and the to-be-known are not substantive entities, not ontic constants, but *relata* that are determined by the *relatans* of knowing:

> Formally viewed, knowing consists in the relation of a knower to what is knowable and known. Yet this relation does not lie somewhere indifferently by itself, like the relation of a felled tree trunk in the forest to a rock lying nearby, a relation we may or may not come across. The relation that distinguishes knowing is always the one in which we ourselves are related, and this relation vibrates throughout our basic posture. This basic posture expresses itself in the way we take beings and objects in advance, in the way we have determined what is decisive in our relation to them.[20]

And as articulated a few pages later in the same Nietzsche lecture:

> [F]or what is knowable and what knows are each determined in their essence in a unified way from the same essential ground. We may not separate either one, nor wish to encounter them separately. Knowing is not like a bridge that somehow subsequently connects two existent banks of a stream, but is itself a stream that in its flow first creates the banks and turns them *toward* each other in a more original way than a bridge ever could.[21]

For Heidegger knowing does not connect an already existent knower to an already existent entity-to-be-known, but is what constitutes these poles in the first place. Stated in terms of the history of Being, the who and what of knowing are epochally corevealed in the unconcealing withdrawal of Being.

There would thus be a history of the human knower whose character would be determined in advance by a given culture's mode of knowing. *The Order of Things* takes up this theme. In the Renaissance, knowing is the recognition of the similitudes, with the knower constituted as a designator or interpreter who traces and outlines the correspondences already laid out in God's created world. In the classical episteme, knowing is the representation of tables of identities and differences, with the knower constituted as a subject who grounds the representations that it presents to itself in reestablishing the order of things. And in the modern episteme, the figure of Man emerges as both the knower and what primarily is to be known, as both the subject and object of knowledge, with Man's representations now finding their deeper conditions in life, labor, and language, as these facets of existence are disclosed in new modalities of knowledge. The procedures of knowing proper to each of the epistemes determine the character of the knower.

From the notion of an episteme as the historical a priori of resemblance to the positing of the ways of knowing as prior to and deciding the character of the human knower, Foucault's project in *The Order of Things* is decisively Heideggerian. And yet—and this must be stressed, due to Foucault's great indebtedness to Heidegger—there are subtle and important differences between their two philosophical histories. Contained in *The Order of Things,* I shall attempt to show, is an unannounced critique of the history of Being that is in part empowered by turning Heidegger against Heidegger.

Science and Philosophical Reflection

In the preface to *The Order of Things*, there is a long paragraph that is central to Foucault's self-understanding of his project. I quote it in its entirety:

> The fundamental codes of a culture—those governing its language, its schemas of perception, its exchanges, its techniques, its values, the hierarchy of its practices—establish for every man, from the very first, the empirical orders with which he will be dealing and within which he will be at home. At the other extremity of thought, there are the scientific theories or the philosophical interpretations which explain why order exists in general, what universal law it obeys, what principle can account for it, and why this particular order has been established and not some other. But between these two regions, so distant from one another, lies a domain which, even though its role is mainly an intermediary one, is nonetheless fundamental: it is more confused, more obscure, and probably less easy to analyze. It is here that a culture, imperceptibly deviating from the empirical orders prescribed for it by its primary codes, instituting an initial separation from them, causes them to lose their original transparency, relinquishes its immediate and invisible powers, frees itself sufficiently to discover that these orders are perhaps not the only possible ones or the best ones; this culture then finds itself faced with the stark fact that there exists, below the level of its spontaneous orders, things that are in themselves capable of being ordered, that belong to a certain unspoken order; the fact, in short, that order *exists*. As though emancipating itself to some extent from its linguistic, perceptual, and practical grids, the culture superimposed on them another kind of grid which neutralized them, which by this superimposition both revealed and excluded them at the same time, so that the culture, by this very process, came face to face with order in its primary state. It is on the basis of this newly perceived order that the codes of language, perception, and practice are criticized and rendered partially invalid. It is on the basis of this order, taken as a firm foundation, that general theories as to the ordering of things, and the interpretation that such an ordering involves, will be constructed. Thus, between the already "encoded" eye and the reflexive knowledge there is a middle region which liberates order itself: it is here that it appears, according to the culture and the age in question, continuous and graduated or discontinuous and piecemeal, linked to space or constituted anew at each instant by the driving force of time, related to a series of variables or defined by separate systems of coherences, composed of resemblances which are either successive or corresponding, organized around increasing differences, etc. This middle region, then, in so far as it makes manifest the modes of being of order, can

> be posited as the most fundamental of all: anterior to words, perceptions, and gestures, which are then taken to be more or less exact, more or less happy, expressions of it (which is why this experience of order in its pure primary state always plays a critical role); more solid, more archaic, less dubious, always more "true" than the theories that attempt to give those expressions explicit form, exhaustive application, or philosophical foundation. Thus, in every culture, between the use of what one might call the ordering codes and reflections upon order itself, there is the pure experience of order and its modes of being. The present study is an attempt to analyze that experience.[22]

Foucault is not positing here "regions of thought" as proper to a faculty psychology or a transcendental subjectivity, nor does "regions" refer to the arrangement of social spaces where modes of thinking take place. Here "regions" (perhaps echoing the phenomenological notion of "regional ontologies") conjures a spatial metaphor about the interrelationships among a culture's ways of understanding and knowing, especially as these pertain to that culture's sense of order.

There are three basic regions. The most immediate is where the codes of everyday life manifest a spontaneous but provisional and revisable empirical order. At the other pole is the highest region of thought, philosophical reflection as well as generalizing scientific theories like physics, which attempt to "explain why order exists in general." But what interests Foucault most is the "middle region," which "liberates order itself." Foucault contends that "in so far as this [middle] region makes manifest the modes of being of order, [it] can be posited as the most fundamental of all: anterior to words, perceptions and gestures, which are then taken to be more or less exact, more or less happy, expressions of it." "Anterior" as an attribute of this region shifts the figurative register from the spatial to the temporal. The middle region is "spatially" between the other two regions but also "temporally" prior, because it governs their sense of order.

"Anterior to words, perceptions, and gestures," the middle region is presymbolic. Its most direct expression is that region of thought concerned with resemblance and "closest" to it (perhaps to be understood as this middle region's overlay), namely, the nongeneralizing sciences such as natural history, biology, and economics. These sciences produce bodies of knowledge that revise the sense of order operative in the everyday realm—which is how, in Foucault's understanding, the sciences constitute and orient our ways of existence. The particular sciences therefore receive the greatest measure of attention in *The Order of Things*. But this does not exclude other regions of thought from consideration. For in its attempt to explain a culture's sense of order, the highest region reflects upon and gives indication of this order. It is telling, then, that Foucault does not, as would the traditional philosopher, take up residence in this highest region, so to view the mode of being of order from above, but *as archaeologist goes beneath both these regions of knowing, science and reflection, to ascertain their common ground in the episteme.*

It is of particular note, then, that this line of inquiry was anticipated by Heidegger in his third Nietzsche lecture. As he explains:

> To be able to carry out metaphysical reflection concerning his field, the scientific researcher must therefore transpose himself into a fundamentally different kind of thinking; he must become familiar with the insight that this reflection on his field is *something essentially different* from a mere broadening of the kind of thinking otherwise practiced in research, whether that broadening be in degree and scope, in generalization, or even in what he sees as a degeneration. However, the demand for an essentially different thinking for reflection on a particular field does not signify regulation of the sciences by philosophy but, on the contrary, recognition of the higher knowledge concealed in every science, on which the worth of that science rests. . . . *Science and reflection on the specific fields are both historically grounded on the actual dominance of a particular interpretation of Being, and they always move in the dominant circle of a particular conception of the essence of truth.*[23]

In other words, for Heidegger the interpretation of Being of a given epoch grounds both the regional sciences and reflection upon those sciences. Similarly, for Foucault, an episteme opens the space for and governs the local sciences and philosophical reflection, with both these regions of thought registering the middle region's presymbolic experience of order.

In essays like the "Age of the World Picture" and "Science and Reflection," Heidegger shows how the interpretation of Being of an epoch grounds sciences as diverse as physics, historiography, and linguistics, developing probing and insightful analyses of the procedures and metaphysical assumptions of these areas of inquiry.[24] Yet in comparison to Foucault, he does not advance *detailed analyses* of the sciences he discusses. Although he devotes entire lecture courses to thinkers such as Nietzsche and Hölderlin, Heidegger never would do so for any figure of a regional science, nor for any modern scientific discipline. Heidegger clearly privileges philosophical and poetic thinking over first-level scientific research, envisioning philosophy as the more difficult and greater task: "The transition from scientific thinking to metaphysical reflection is essentially more alien and thus more difficult than the transition from prescientific, everyday thinking to the kind of thinking we do in the sciences. The transition to metaphysics is a *leap*. The transition to science is a steady development of earlier determinations of an already existing way of representing."[25] This leap, moreover, is an ascension, philosophy assuming a "high altitude" stance, as suggested in many Heideggerian texts, like the following from the first Nietzsche lecture:

> In philosophy the Being of beings is to be thought. For philosophy's thinking and questioning there is no loftier and stricter commitment. In contrast, all the sciences think always only of *one* being among others, *one* particular region of beings. They are committed by this region of beings only in an indirect manner, never straightforwardly so. Because in philosophical thought the highest commitment prevails, all great thinkers think the same.[26]

Philosophy's thinking and questioning are defined as the *loftiest,* as the *highest* commitment. In Foucault's scheme, this locates philosophy in thought's highest region, enabling generalizing reflection by establishing a certain distance from what is to be reflected. Heidegger, of course, sees this stance less in terms of traditional notions of reflection and instead as what facilitates our most immediate receptivity and attunement to Being.[27] Although claiming that both science and reflection *(Besinnung)* on science are grounded in a common interpretation of Being, and while, in at least one instance, interjecting that even the great thinkers are influenced by "contemporaries and traditions,"[28] Heidegger focuses on those thinkers he views as having attuned to Being. His "step back" eschews nitty-gritty analysis of the regional sciences and their procedural nuances, because thinkers do not, like scientists, study "*one* being among others," but attune to Being itself, disclosing the interpretation of Being that underwrites each and every scientific discipline.

Viewed in light of Foucault's model of regions, however, Heidegger's approach appears one-sided, privileging higher-level reflection to the exclusion of more detailed and sustained examination of the local sciences, which for Foucault constitute the region of thought that impacts most directly on the everyday experience of order. Heidegger assumes that the thought of the great thinkers of the tradition subsumes and grounds that of the scientist; Foucault, while mindful of philosophical reflection, sees the regional sciences as the surest access to the middle region's sense of order. As he exclaims: "Only those who cannot read will be surprised that I have learned such things [about modern thinking and its problematics] more clearly from Cuvier, Bopp, and Ricardo than from Kant and Hegel."[29] Foucault's archaeology locates itself *below* science and reflection, broadening its approach as compared to what it takes to be the elevated and one-sided stance of philosophy.

All of this, I want to propose, is for Foucault a criticism of the history of Being, which concerns itself exclusively with those great thinkers who purportedly attune to Being. Foucault would seem to be taking up a line of thought inaugurated by Heidegger—that both science and philosophy share a common ground—only to reformulate it as a critique of the high-mindedness of the history of Being.[30]

Two Kinds of Philosophy

The Order of Things, I am suggesting, rewrites the history of Being as an epistemic history of the experience of order. Although Foucault draws heavily upon Heidegger in formulating the very notion of an episteme and its ontological import, he critically reworks his source material. There is at least one text in which this critical encounter with Heidegger finds more explicit expression, an interview titled "What Is a Philosopher?" from 1966, the same year as the publication of *The Order of Things.* Foucault concludes the interview with the following:

> We can envisage, moreover, two kinds of philosopher: the kind who opens up new avenues of thought, such as Heidegger, and the kind who in a sense plays the role of an archaeologist, studying the space in which thought unfolds, as well as the conditions of that thought, its mode of constitution.[31]

As brief as these remarks are, they can, in light of our findings, prove extremely helpful in understanding Foucault's envisioning of the status of his archaeological project in *The Order of Things* and its relation to Heidegger.

First, we need to note that there is a meaningful symmetry of presentation made between the philosopher who founds a new path of thought, as exemplified by Heidegger, and the philosopher as archaeologist, implicitly Foucault himself, who studies and defines the space and conditions of thought. This parallelism of presentation suggests that these two projects are in some way complementary, comparable, or analogous. Second, we need once again to pay heed to Foucault's spatial metaphors—that one mode of philosophizing opens a new *path* of thought, hence is trailblazing, while the other maps the *space* of thinking, with the implication that as a broader project defining the conditions of modern thought in general, archaeology would map the terrain in which the original philosopher forges her path. In other words, Heidegger's history of Being opens up a new avenue of thinking, with archaeology taking up this path, extending and broadening its contours, so to circumscribe the space of modern thinking, including the avenue of thought that was its departure site. Archaeology investigates the wider grounds—the epistemic space—in which not only the regional sciences, but also philosophy take their place.[32]

Although the history of epistemes is a rewriting of the history of being and is impossible without the latter project as its model, it would seem to understand itself as accounting for the space of modern thought in which Heidegger travels. And, to be sure, Foucault's delineation of the modern episteme can be interpreted as locating some of the fundamental questions and topics of the history of Being within the wider space of modern concerns. Three themes stand out.

First, Heidegger takes the thought/unthought trope to be proper to the lineages of great thinkers since antiquity. The history of Being is constructed from those thinkers, those philosophers and poets, who have attuned to Being so that Being speaks through them. In addition, each thinker, in thinking Being, also deposits an unthought to her own thinking, an unthought that only a subsequent great thinker can bring to light. Foucault, in turn, acknowledges that one may indeed think the unthought, but counters that it is a mode of knowing proper and internal to the modern episteme. The modern gap between the "I think" and the "I am," he maintains, necessitates that every act of thinking the unthought—thinking Being, so to speak—can never eliminate this gap, leaving what is newly thought with its own unthought conditions.[33] Furthermore, this movement of thought is by no means restricted to Heidegger's canon of "great thinkers," but is common to both philosophers and regional investigators. From this vantage point, not only would focusing on the great thinkers unnecessarily delimit discussion and analysis of an episteme, but the scenario of a "community" of great thinkers who, by transcending epochal confines, think the unthought of each other, is to misconstrue what is properly the movement of both philosophical and scientific-regional thought *within* (or at least *with regard to*) the space of the modern episteme. Foucault's implicit criticism would be that Heidegger misplaces and projects the thought/unthought trope too broadly onto Western history as a whole.

A second critical point aims at the heart of Heidegger's project—at the presumed loftiness of the Being question. For Heidegger, philosophy has always been addressing, if never explicitly asking, certain principal questions. In the first of the Nietzsche lectures, he distinguishes between the guiding and the grounding questions of Western philosophy.[34] The guiding question, which philosophy has periodically asked, has been: "What is the being?" But the deeper, grounding question of philosophy, never explicitly broached by philosophy, hence philosophy's own founding radical unthought, is: "What is Being itself?" Heidegger's task is to disclose this radical and founding unthought of philosophy, since with "the question of the essence of Being we are inquiring in such a way that nothing remains outside the question, not even nothingness."[35]

Foucault concurs that, at least for us moderns, being has become a principal issue. He even goes so far as to contend that in post-Kantian thinking the question of being has displaced the question of truth.[36] But this is not the same as claiming that being questions have been the unstated backdrop of the tradition all along. That is to say, given the modern episteme, we today may be compelled to ask questions of being—as with Foucault's own seeking of the mode of being of order—but this is not identical to ascribing that question to the suppressed, unthought, or implicit concern of past ages. Moreover, whereas Heidegger sees the grounding question of philosophy as always having been "What is Being itself?" Foucault sees the gap between the "I think" and the "I am" that characterizes the modern cogito as leading "to a whole series of questions concerned with being,"[37] not to one commanding question grasped as the unthought, forgotten, or hidden thematic of the tradition of thought since antiquity.

Third, if to repeat what others have already noted, Foucault would seem to implicate Heidegger's history of Being as falling into the impulsion of the retreat and return of the origin.[38] Heidegger does often seem at various turns in his writing of the history of Being to posit an origin or beginning to the metaphysical tradition, even if this beginning is plural and dispersed among various ancient thinkers. The Foucault of *The Order of Things,* however, is skeptical about all attempts to locate a historical origin, since with ongoing research an even earlier origin will readily come to light, subverting the foundational and essentializing intent of the priorly posited origin. By seeking to locate in ancient philosophy the origins of metaphysics—where metaphysics is construed as founding the nihilistic trajectory of Western history—*Seinsgeschichte* would fall into this self-deluding movement of modern thinking.

In sum, Foucault's presentation of the modern episteme can be interpreted as accounting for the space in which questions and themes basic to Heidegger's history of Being take their place. By situating major tropes of the history of Being in its broader epistemic context, Foucault implies that there is overstatement and a self-imposed narrowness to the Heideggerian project, that Heidegger tends to project specifically modern conditions of thinking and questioning onto Western thought all along.

The Order of Things understands itself as presenting the epistemic context of Heidegger's thought. And yet, if Foucault's own archaeological project is an extension and expansion of the Heideggerian path, how does archaeology stand in the modern episteme? What, in short, would be the conditions of possible knowledge that would enable one to write a history of epistemes?

Archaeology's Unthought

To be sure, nowhere in *The Order of Things* does Foucault broach the issue of how as a whole his version of philosophical history fits into the epistemic space of modern thought. He does assert in several passages that his pursuit of specific topics has been made possible by modernity's epistemological field. Most notably, he acknowledges that the questions he raises about the relation between the being of Man and the being of language are proper to our times.[39] But beyond Foucault's own testimony, there are several ways that the archaeological project can be seen as conforming to the current episteme.

First, Foucault's archaeology of the human sciences is a historical inquiry, so can be grasped as finding its governance in the modern episteme's generative trope of History (218–20). Second, as a mode of philosophical inquiry as well, archaeology can be seen as operating as the Memory that "lead[s] thought back to the question of knowing what it means for thought to have a history," accomplishing this by unearthing the historical conditions of knowing and thinking since the Renaissance (219–20). Third, Foucault's study attempts to disclose the unthought that makes the thought of a historical culture possible, a line of investigation that takes up the modern episteme's trope of thinking the unthought (but without assuming that this trope is internal to premodern procedures of knowing). And fourth, Foucault's archaeology, in seeking to lay bare the mode of being of order, asks an ontological question that as such is properly modern.

Yet despite apparent conformity to the modern episteme, the archaeological project edges beyond the space of thinking that it maps. For example, historical inquiry, as proper to the modern episteme, analyzes empiricities as organic structures that perform a function, where these organic structures form a chronological series based on analogies, thereby constituting an "evolutionary" history. But an episteme is surely not an empiricity. And as the condition of possible knowledge, it is difficult to fathom what it would mean for an episteme to be an organic structure that is functional in a way comparable to, say, a microbe. Nor does archaeology chart a series of historical constellations of knowing that can be seen as "evolving" over time, which would point to some kind of progress in or direction to Reason, contrary to Foucault's own assessment of his project.[40]

Perhaps most pertinent is that archaeology is conducted in *The Order of Things* at the same time as history and philosophy. But, then, as a philosophical history concerned with disclosing the sequence of epistemes since the Renaissance, how could archaeology—as philosophy—situate itself in the space between history and History, so to function as the Memory of thought's history, if it, too, is a history? This seeming conundrum is just one way of noting that *The Order of Things* never defines the specific epistemic conditions of archaeology's status as a new form of philosophical history. But then should it? Or, more to the point, *can* it? According to the dictates of the modern episteme, archaeology as a mode of historical inquiry aspires to know History,[41] but will never close the gap between itself as an exercise in history and History as the condition and receding "source" of all histories. This unbridgeable gap between history and History is nothing other than an instantiation of the thought/unthought trope—that archaeology may be able to disclose the unthought of modern thinking, but can only do so by leaving undisclosed conditions of knowing that make it possible.

Understanding itself as less original but more broadly based than the history of Being, Foucault's project makes no attempt to account exhaustively for its conditions of possibility. The "narrower" if more originary path of thought—the history of being—is contained within the modern episteme, while the "broader" if less originary form of thought—Foucault's own episteme project—necessarily exceeds the space of modern thought that it unveils. Foucault is forthright about the limitations of his project, acknowledging that the "event [of the emergence of the modern episteme], probably because we are still caught inside it, is largely beyond our comprehension."[42] Even as it proclaims great breadth and scope for its analyses, *The Order of Things* does not assert the certainty of its findings, nor does it propose some final, fixed Archimedean vantage point from which henceforth to conduct philosophical history. (In this respect it is noteworthy that Foucault quickly adopted the analysis of discursive practices in lieu of the historical study of epistemes.)[43]

What the study does afford Foucault is the ability to sidestep some of the pitfalls he sees in other modern projects, as with positing a founding origin to one's historical narrative. All well and good. But then in the end, for all its theoretical reworking of and challenge to the Heideggerian project, just how different are the particulars of Foucault's account from those of the history of Being? To explore this would require an extensive analysis of the detailed content of their respective philosophical histories, a task that far exceeds the present study. What we can do, in bringing this essay to a close, is briefly to consider how Foucault views the relation of words and things as well as the "schema" of time and space, as these are terms central to his analysis of an episteme. And this will lead us into some concluding reflections on modern finitude.

Words and Things, Time and Space

With regard to explicating a culture's way of knowing, Foucault submits that the conjunction of words and things is *not* to be taken as a metaphysical or ontological invariant, but as a flexible, historical fold that warrants our scrutiny. This view of words and things can be seen as part of his critical encounter with Heidegger—at least if we accept

Gilles Deleuze's contention that, on this issue, Foucault was parting ways with certain phenomenological presuppositions that Heidegger purportedly held. As Deleuze summarizes in his Foucault book:

> In Heidegger and Merleau-Ponty, Light opens up a speaking no less than a seeing, as if signification haunted the visible which in turn murmured meaning. This cannot be so in Foucault, for whom the light-Being refers only to visibilities, and language-Being to statements.[44]

Although Deleuze is reflecting on the Foucauldian project as a whole, his remarks are pertinent to the character of an episteme in *The Order of Things*. For Foucault states at the outset of the study that he is interested in exposing and exploring "that less apparent syntax which causes words and things (next to and also opposite one another) to 'hold together.'"[45] The book's French title—*Les mots et les choses*—thus attests to one of the key features of an episteme, that the fold between words and things is specific to and is first established within a given epistemic constellation.

According to Foucault, in the Renaissance words were part of the Order of Creation, woven amidst and marking the similitudes of things. In the classical age language retreats into the mind of the subject as the signifying "medium" that represents the tables of identities and differences. And in modernity language becomes unmoored from representation, leaving representation in need of deeper grounds, with language becoming dispersed in culture, even manifesting beyond the episteme as the counterdiscourse of literature. For his part, Heidegger engages in creative retrievals of past understandings of the being of language, as with his meditations on ancient Greek logos. But these musings on the essence of language are by no means as explicitly historicist as Foucault's, and often sound a transepochal and normative understanding of language's essence. One can readily imagine Foucault seeing his own analyses of words and things as complexifying and advancing beyond the Heideggerian project.

Foucault takes an additional step. Not only does he see the relation between words and things as a historical variable, but so, too, the "schema" of time and space. An episteme, Foucault contends, exhibits the *experience* of time and space characteristic of a culture.[46] Now Heidegger, for his part, in the late lecture "Time and Being," did speak of time-space, but in a different register than does Foucault, and as part of an autocritique of section 70 of *Being and Time*, where he had tried to derive spatiality from temporality. As he states in the lecture:

> With this presencing, there opens up what we call time-space. But with the word "time" we no longer mean the succession of nows. Accordingly, time-space no longer means merely the distance between two now-points of calculated time. . . . Time-space now is the name for the openness which opens up in the mutual self-extending of futural approach, past and present. This openness exclusively and primarily provides the space in which space as we usually know it can unfold.[47]

Heidegger is here positing a more general model of the Opening of Being. The time-space he is speaking of is "before" ordinary time and space. In contrast Foucault's discussions in *The Order of Things* would seem directed in the main to the more everyday senses of these terms.

For Foucault, then, a "schema" of time and space is integral to the operations of a given episteme. In the Renaissance the Order of Creation is eternal, hence fundamentally spatial. Time unfolds as the duration of the human knower tracing out the correspondences of the text of the world. One can begin anywhere and end anywhere, begin at any time and end at any time, starting either with things or with words, since they mutually imply and inform God's Order. Knowing in the Renaissance is an infinite task, open ended, a weak form of knowledge. In the classical age Order is what the human knower has to reconstitute. God's created Order is no longer immediately apparent in the world, having been dispersed by time, requiring the knowing subject to represent and cognitively reform the order of things. Time is both what has disrupted the Order of creation and the condition that permits the subject to restore facets of this Order in the tables of identities and differences. Representation in modernity, however, undergoes a crisis, leading to a decisive "mutation of Order into History."[48] God is dead; things are no longer products of Creation, evacuating any sense of a preestablished Order of things. Time, which in the classical episteme dispersed the Order of Creation, now penetrates to the essence of things, with the consequence that empiricities are doubly temporal, emerging historically in analogical succession and performing functions as organic structures. The narrative plot of Foucault's history turns on the epistemological break between the premodern predominance of space and Order and the modern irreducibility of time and History. Modernity is a distinctive chapter in the history of the Same. Knowing now motors the incessant *order-ing* and *reorder-ing* of things, constituting Man—the subject and object of knowledge—as "a mode of being . . . always open, never finally delimited, yet constantly transversed."[49] Said otherwise, with the transition from Order to History—from a presumed metaphysical totality to a restless knowing that is effectively totalizing—the history of the Same reaches a kind of terminus where there is no longer ready access to an "outside" beyond the epistemic grids that define and constitute human being as Man.

By radically historicizing the relation between words and things as well as the "schema" of time and space, Foucault does indeed distance archaeological analysis from the history of Being. And in doing so he ends up offering an interpretation of modern experience and existence that parallels and complements what Heidegger viewed as the fate of the subject in the "circuits" of Enframing *(Gestell)*:

> The subject-object relation thus reaches, for the first time, its pure "relational," i.e., ordering, character in which both the subject and the object are sucked up as standing-reserves. That does not mean that the subject-object relation vanishes, but rather the opposite: it now attains to its most extreme dominance, which is predetermined from out of Enframing. It becomes a standing-reserve to be commanded and set in order.[50]

Here we meet the issue, explored by Béatrice Han in her excellent contribution to this volume, of the modern character of finitude.

The Foucault of *The Order of Things* and the Heidegger of later writings like the Bremen lectures see modern finitude as conditioned by and caught within totalizing networks that objectify Man through the ways of knowing (Foucault) or disclose human being as a mere resource always already on call for the demands of the "System" (Heidegger). The issue for both authors is *not* primarily a conceptual prob lem for philosophy, and certainly not a problem of epistemological self-grounding or self-justification (as we have seen, Foucault seems to suggest that his own archaeological project cannot account for itself in any complete way, without this necessarily being some sort of defect). With important and significant differences of concern and emphasis, the common "problem" for these two thinkers might be summarized as how, given modern conditions of finitude, we might achieve something like radical (Foucault) or authentic (Heidegger) transcendence of such all-defining, totalizing processes.

In the Bremen lectures, Heidegger suggests that we poetically attune to the ancient Greek sendings of Being, so to disclose ourselves in the fourfold as mortals, thereby opening ourselves up to Being and

Time, ungrounding our self-interpretations in the acknowledgment of the being-towards death of self and others. And this creative retrieval is to be achieved through the saving power of art—which can poetically bring forth earth, sky, mortals, and immortals as these are granted and folded together within the Open.[51] Similarly, in the essay "Thought from the Outside," published in the same year as *The Order of Things,* Foucault suggests that it is through the modern counterdiscourse of literature, as exemplified in the writings of Blanchot, that we have a path to move beyond the dictates of the modern episteme. The "I speak" of literature, unlike the epistemic "I think" (with its diremption from the "I am"), effaces rather than constitutes the speaking-writing subject, effecting the "death" of the "I" who is Man himself. Nor is this effacement nihilistic, but on the contrary realizes a profound wakefulness that is itself a radical *self*-forgetting:

> This [self-] forgetting, however, should not be confused with the scatteredness of distraction or the slumber of vigilance; it is a wakefulness so alert, so lucid, so new, that it is a good-bye to night and a pure opening onto a day to come. In this respect forgetting is extreme attentiveness—so extreme that it effaces any singular face that might present itself to it. . . . It is a forgetting that the wait remains a waiting: an acute attention to what is radically new, with no bond of resemblance [hence transgressing the Same] or continuity with anything else (the newness of the wait drawn outside of itself and freed from the past [hence transgressing History]; attention to what is most profoundly old (for deep down the wait has never stopped waiting).[52]

Literature's voiding of the "I" realizes an almost mystical, contemplative awareness that transcends constitution as a self or subject.[53] Like the later Heidegger, albeit in a distinctive manner, the Foucault of the mid-1960s looks to the literary arts as a means of transcending modern finitude.

Having worked out his engagement with the history of Being in *The Order of Things,* Foucault quickly ventured into new lines of thought informed by what he had learned in this critical encounter with Heidegger, leaving behind forever the analysis of epistemes. He would likewise soon drop the proposal of literature as a "way out," only to return toward the end of his life to the modernist theme of art's redemptive power, reconfigured anew as the aesthetics of existence.[54]

Notes

1. Michel Foucault, "Truth, Power, Self: An Interview with Michel Foucault, October 25, 1982," in *Technologies of Self: Seminar with Michel Foucault,* ed. Luther H.

Martin, Huck Gutman, and Patrick H. Hutton (Amherst: University of Massachusetts Press, 1988), 12–13.

2. Michel Foucault, "The Return of Morality," in *Politics, Philosophy, Culture: Interview and Other Writings, 1977–1984* (New York and London: Routledge, 1988), 250.

3. Foucault credited Dreyfus and Rabinow for being the first to note the influence of Heidegger upon his thought: "I was surprised when two of my friends in Berkeley wrote something about me and said that Heidegger was influential [Hubert L. Dreyfus and Paul Rabinow, *Michel Foucault: Beyond Structuralism and Hermeneutics* (Chicago: University of Chicago Press, 1982)]. Of course it was quite true, but no one in France has ever perceived it" ("Truth, Power, Self," 12–13). Besides the groundbreaking commentaries of Dreyfus and Rabinow, there is the fundamental study by Rainer Forst that demonstrates how Heideggerian themes, especially those from *Being and Time,* repeatedly inform Foucault's work throughout ("Endlichkeit Freiheit Individualität: Die Sorge um das Selbst bei Heidegger und Foucault," in *Ethos der Moderne: Foucaults Kritik der Aufklärung,* ed. Eva Erdmann, Rainer Forst, and Axel Honneth [Frankfurt and New York: Campus, 1990], 146–86; cf. R. Kevin Hill's "Foucault's Critique of Heidegger," *Philosophy Today* 34 [winter 1989]: 334–41, which argues that the early archaeological works are a critique of *Being and Time*). For a recent full-length study on Heidegger and Foucault, see Lee Joseph Braver, "A Thing of This World: Anti-Realism and Epistemology in Heidegger and Foucault" (Ph.D. diss., Emory University, 1999).

4. For example, see Jürgen Habermas, *The Philosophical Discourse of Modernity: Twelve Lectures,* trans. Frederick Lawrence (Cambridge, Mass.: MIT Press, 1987), 266; and Stephen David Ross, "Modernity and the Misrepresentation of Representation," in *Dialectic and Narrative,* ed. Thomas R. Flynn and Dalia Judovitz (Albany: State University of New York Press, 1993), 139–40.

5. Martin Heidegger, *Nietzsche,* 4 vols., ed. David Farrell Krell (San Francisco: Harper and Row, 1987), 3:20.

6. See Gary Gutting, *Michel Foucault's Archaeology of Scientific Reason* (Cambridge, England, and New York: Cambridge University Press, 1989); see also Peter Dews, "Foucault and the French Tradition of Historical Epistemology," in *The Limits of Disenchantment: Essays on Contemporary European Philosophy* (London and New York: Verso, 1995), 39–58.

7. Michel Foucault, *The Order of Things: An Archaeology of the Human Sciences* (New York: Random House, 1973), xxiv.

8. Ibid.

9. One of Foucault's principal questions is: "What historical a priori provided the starting-point from which it was possible to define the great checkerboard of distinct identities established against the confused, undefined, faceless and, as it were, indifferent background of differences?" (ibid). For critical evaluation of the concept of a "historical a priori" as it is variously formulated in Foucault's oeuvre, see Béatrice Han, *L'ontologie manquée de Michel Foucault: Entre l'historique et le transcendental* (Grenoble: Jérôme Millon, 1998).

10. Foucault, *The Order of Things,* xxii.

11. Ibid., xxi.

12. See Heidegger, *Nietzsche,* 2:189; 3:22; and 4:164.

13. Heidegger, "The Question Concerning Technology," in *The Question Concerning Technology and Other Essays,* trans. William Lovitt (New York: Harper and Row, 1977), 13. See also, idem, *Nietzsche,* vol. 1, *The Will to Power as Art,* 57.

14. On *Verwindung* (contra *Überwindung*) in Heidegger's "overcoming" of metaphysics, see Gianni Vattimo, "Nihilism and the Post-Modern in Philosophy," in *The End of Modernity* (Baltimore: The Johns Hopkins University Press, 1985), 164, 171–80.

15. Heidegger, *Nietzsche,* 4:162.

16. Ibid., 163.

17. Heidegger, *Discourse on Thinking*, trans. John M. Anderson and E. Hans Freund (New York: Harper and Row, 1966), 79.

18. Ibid., 241. See also idem, *Identity and Difference*, trans. Joan Stambaugh (New York: Harper and Row, 1969), 45.

19. Heidegger, *Nietzsche*, 2:186.

20. Ibid., 3:69.

21. Ibid., 3:83.

22. Foucault, *The Order of Things*, xx–xxi. For an important reading of the book's preface that diverges from the interpretation I shall be offering, see Han, *L'ontologie manquée de Michel Foucault*, 92–103.

23. Heidegger, *Nietzsche*, 3:43–44.

24. Heidegger, "The Age of the World Picture" and "Science and Reflection," in *The Question Concerning Technology*, 115–82.

25. Heidegger, *Nietzsche*, 3:43.

26. Ibid., 1:35–36.

27. See the discussions of *Gelessenheit* ("releasement" in Heidegger, *Discourse on Thinking*).

28. Idem, *Nietzsche*, 3:23.

29. Foucault, *The Order of Things*, 307.

30. Gary Gutting, in his very important and invaluable book on Foucault's archaeology of scientific reason, notes: "But far more important is the fact that Foucault's extension of the history of concepts [via the notion of an episteme] undermines the privileged role of disciplines in the history of thought and knowledge. For Bachelard and Canguilhelm, each particular domain of knowledge (e.g., chemistry, biology) emerged at some point from prescientific confusion and has, since that point, developed progressively as a unified body of scientific knowledge. There may be sharp conceptual breaks, but subsequent concepts are rectifications of earlier ones and contain them as special cases of a broader and more adequate explanation of the world. Accordingly, the history of science is written from the normative standpoint of current science, which provides the historian with standards for judging past scientific work by the extent to which it is preserved in today's science. For Foucault, however, the possibility of the entire conceptual development of any discipline is based on deeper concepts, shared by other disciplines, and themselves subject to transformations over time that are not controlled by any discipline" (Gutting, *Michel Foucault's Archaeology of Scientific Reason*, 219). Foucault took this one step further. Not only does he regard an episteme as regulating the various regional sciences but also as governing higher-order reflection, a view that (as I have attempted to show) has its precedent in Heidegger's Nietzsche lectures.

31. Michel Foucault, "Philosophy and the Death of God," in *Religion and Culture*, ed. Jerome R. Carrette (New York: Routledge, 1999), 86. The essay was originally published under the title "Que'est-ce qu'un philosophie?" See idem, *Dits et écrits 1954–1988*, ed. Daniel Defert and François Ewald, 4 volumes (Paris: Gallimard, 1994), 1:552–53.

32. On the place of philosophical reflection in the modern episteme, see Foucault, *The Order of Things*, 347.

33. Foucault, *The Order of Things*, 322–28 ("The 'Cogito' and the Unthought").

34. See Heidegger, *Nietzsche*, 1:4, 67–68. For comparable articulations of this theme, see idem, *Nietzsche*, 3:189–90, and 4:151–52, 207, 211.

35. Ibid., 68.

36. Foucault, *The Order of Things*, 323.

37. Ibid., 325.

38. Ibid., 328–35 ("The Retreat and Return of the Origin"). On Foucault's criticism

of Heidegger, see Hubert L. Dreyfus and Paul Rabinow, *Michel Foucault: Beyond Structuralism and Hermeneutics,* 2d. ed. (Chicago: The University of Chicago Press, 1983), 38–41; and Gutting, *Michel Foucault's Archaeology of Scientific Reason,* 223.

39. Foucault, *The Order of Things,* 307

40. Ibid., xxi.

41. Ibid., 219.

42. Ibid., 221; see also 217–18.

43. Foucault developed the notion of discursive practices in his 1969 methodological tract *The Archaeology of Knowledge.* In the 1970 foreword to the English edition of *The Order of Things* he redescribed the episteme-project in terms of this new theory of discourse. For discussion about Foucault's periodic redescription of his previous work in light of his current project, see my "Critical Reproblemization: Foucault and the Task of Modern Philosophy," *Radical Philosophy* 91 (September–October 1998): 19–21.

44. Gilles Deleuze, *Foucault,* trans. Seán Hand (Minneapolis: University of Minnesota Press, 1988), 111.

Deleuze's invocation of a language-Being and a light-Being suggests an ontology that is not incompatible with Foucault's own passing remarks in *The Order of Things* about the epistemic imposition of order upon a pregiven chaos—itself a formulation very close to that in chapter 11 of Heidegger's third Nietzsche lecture, titled "Knowing as Schematizing a Chaos in Accordance with Practical Need." In the subsequent chapter, "The Concept of 'Chaos,'" Heidegger explains that "*[c]haos is the name for a peculiar preliminary projection of the world as a whole and for the governance of that world.* . . . The fundamental experience of the world as 'chaos' has its roots here [in the perspective of animals, animality, and biologism]. But since the body is for Nietzsche a structure of dominance, 'chaos' cannot mean a turbulent jumble. Rather, it means the concealment of unmastered richness in the becoming and streaming of the world as a whole" (*Nietzsche,* 3:80, italics mine; see also 3:92).

In *The Order of Things,* order and chaos are by no means centered on animality and the body. But chaos understood as the "concealment of unmastered richness" does seem to be in accord with the upshot of Foucault's "ontological commitments," at least as far as these can be teased out of the text. Cf. Han, *L'ontologie manquée.*

45. Foucault, *The Order of Things,* xviii.

46. Ibid., xxi, and in the case of modernity, 321 and 333. This formulation has a neo-Kantian ring to it (for Foucault's creative appropriation and redeployment of the Kantian notions of "transcendental aesthetic" and "transcendental dialectic," see ibid., 319). It calls to mind works like Ernst Cassirer's *Philosophy of Symbolic Form*—and indeed, in 1966, the same year as the publication of *Les mots et les choses,* Foucault reviewed in glowing terms the French translation of Cassirer's *Philosophy of Enlightenment,* concluding that "this book . . . founds the possibility of a new history of thought" ("Une histoire restée muette," in *Dits et écrits,* 1:549).

47. Martin Heidegger, "Time and Being," in *On Time and Being,* trans. Joan Stambaugh (New York: Harper and Row, 1972), 14.

48. Foucault, *The Order of Things,* 220.

49. Ibid., 322.

50. Heidegger, "Science and Reflection," in *Questions Concerning Technology,* 173.

51. Heidegger, "The Thing," in *Poetry, Language, Thought,* trans. Albert Hofstadter (New York: Harper and Row, 1971), 178–80. Toward the end of his life Heidegger expressed doubts as to the viability of this creative retrieval of the ancient Greek understanding of Being as a way of "overcoming" modern world-disclosure.

52. Michel Foucault, *Maurice Blanchot: The Thought from the Outside,* trans. Brian Massumi (New York: Zone Books, 1990), 56–57. Many of the effects of literature, as

expounded in the Blanchot essay, would seem to be precise counterpoints to facets of the modern episteme as defined in *The Order of Things*—for example, literature as a forgetting of the past (and hence a self-forgetting) would contrast philosophy's function in the modern episteme as the Memory of thought having a history (the latter constituting and sustaining the "I think").

53. Foucault's description of the effacement of the subject as a heightening of attentiveness, as a wakefulness, as a forgetting of the past, as a calm nonanticipatory and always present waiting—this account has much in common with the highest levels of spiritual realization in the world's wisdom traditions, for which see Ken Wilber, *A Brief History of Everything*, 2d ed. (Boston: Shambhala, 2000), 198 ff.

54. Foucault's ethical project of practices of self is a creative and brilliant return to and reworking of Heideggerian themes from Division II of *Being and Time*, themes that Foucault had previously explored in his earliest publications. See Michael Schwartz, "Repetition and Ethics in Late Foucault," *Telos* 117 (fall 1999): 113–32.

Reading Genealogy as Historical Ontology

Stuart Elden

What is genealogy? This seemingly simple question rarely seems to receive an appropriate answer. What does it mean when Foucault suggests that, were he being pretentious, he would say he was writing a genealogy of modern morals?[1] Do we simply follow this back to Nietzsche and characterize Foucault as a Nietzschean genealogist? What would that mean? This chapter suggests that Foucault's work has been largely appropriated as a kind of historical sociology, albeit with interest in his theoretical pronouncements on issues such as discourse, power, and the body. It argues that such a reading makes Foucault, despite the protestations of the academy, far too much of an orthodox historian. Though I do not wish to dispute the importance of this discipline, or the worth of works in the field of historical sociology, I do think it is too narrow a view of what Foucault is actually doing. Rather I argue that Foucault's project can be thought of in terms of historical ontology, and that this is the best way to see genealogy. This is pursued through a reading of Foucault's work in the light of Kant, Nietzsche and, most centrally, Heidegger.[2]

Historical Sociology

Historical sociology is not simply sociology with an awareness of the historical dimension, nor history with an account of social context.

Rather, as has been made clear in a number of important studies, it is much more about an issue or problematic of structuring, something that forces the two disciplines of history and sociology to rethink what they are about and, in so doing, to recognize they both have a common project. The awkward version of this thesis is that while history provides the empirical, sociology provides the theory. This is awkward for a number of reasons, most obviously that history has always been informed by theory, whether the historian acknowledged it or not. Gareth Stedman Jones criticizes the worth of the theory he thinks sociology can bring, while Philip Abrams questions the distinction between the disciplines in the first place.[3] For Abrams, in terms of their basic concerns, history and sociology "are and always have been the same thing. Both seek to understand the puzzle of human agency and the process of social structuring, and do it chronologically." Essentially his argument is that the structures of society constrain the acts of those within it, while those within it have made the structures. Of course, this was most famously put by Marx: "[M]en make their own history, but not of their own free will; not under circumstances they themselves have chosen but under the given and inherited circumstances with which they are directly confronted."[4] The division between the diachronous and the synchronous found in structuralism is seen as obsolete; the structures must be examined historically, and so historical sociology is therefore sociology, its very core.[5]

While this gives historical sociology almost unlimited scope, Abrams suggests three areas where it has particular emphasis. The first is the transition to industrialization, particularly from the 1840s on. The second is what he calls micro-history, with emphasis on families, hospitals, workplaces, and the like as arenas of social change. The third is an emphasis on the relations of the agent to society, not in an abstract sense, but in the immediate world of history.[6] This is a change from an earlier period of historical sociology, when it seemed to concentrate on primitive society.[7]

Now, of course, this seems very close to Foucault. Foucault was clearly touched by the structuralist revolution in France, but he retained a historical perspective at all times. *Histoire de la folie, The Birth of the Clinic,* and *The Order of Things* are all in some ways related to structuralism, but are, in practice if not nominally, histories. Similarly his work on space—which unlike most structuralists extends far beyond the use of spatial metaphors—alongside his work on history shows that Foucault can be seen as bridging the diachronic/synchronic divide. The question of agency and the subject is a central one for Foucault, and though a semistructuralist critique of these notions is prevalent at certain periods, he is actually much more interested in their problemization, both in the late sixties and the early eighties, than their abandonment. It is therefore not entirely surprising that some commentators have seen Foucault as contributing to the area of historical sociology. This is especially true for those who see him in a similar lineage as Max Weber.[8]

But my question is, if Foucault was really doing historical sociology, why is this not made clear in his texts? Why did he outline a complex model of archaeology? What is behind the shift to the notion of genealogy, and what relation does this all have to the key figures in the history of philosophy that he orients himself toward? While Foucault's work exhibits elements of what might be called historical sociology, I am concerned that seeing him solely in this way leads to valuable, though limited studies. Are we not in danger of, while celebrating Foucault and pursuing Foucauldian studies, actually neutralizing the acidic bite of his work by slipping it into a potentially anodyne academic category?

Genealogy in Nietzsche

As is well known, in the *Critique of Pure Reason,* Kant distinguishes between analytic and synthetic judgments and a priori and a posteriori ones. The central problem of the first *Critique* becomes "how are synthetic a priori judgements possible?"[9] Kant's search for an answer to this question is his reply to Hume's skepticism: synthetic a priori knowledge allows the foundation of a mathematical system, allows science to proceed by means of experiment, and allows the establishment of a ground for an ethics. Kant answers this question by suggesting that though experience is a *necessary* condition for knowledge, it is not a *sufficient* condition for knowledge. For any knowledge that is not merely an explication of the meaning of something already known—analytic knowledge—some synthesis of experience and reason is necessary. Kant puts this famously as "thoughts without content are empty, intuitions without concepts, blind."[10]

In *Beyond Good and Evil,* Nietzsche comments on this issue. He suggests that Kant's answer to the question "how are synthetic a priori judgements possible?" is "by faculty of a faculty" [Vermöge eines

Vermögens]. These faculties—Kant's perceptual manifold and the categories—continue into his moral thought, with the "discovery" of the categorical imperative. Nietzsche suggests that this is not really an answer, or an explanation, but rather a repetition of the question. It has parallels, he suggests, with the doctor in Molière's play: opium induces sleep "because it contains a sleepy faculty whose nature it is to put the senses to sleep." Nietzsche suggests such replies should remain in comedy, and that therefore we should replace the Kantian question "how are synthetic a priori judgements possible?" by the question "why is belief in such judgements necessary?"[11] This question, I suggest, is the key to understanding the genealogical approach of Nietzsche's work, because it suggests that the structures of knowledge that are taken as absolutes at a particular time are contingent, and that they must be examined historically.

Essentially, therefore, genealogy in Nietzsche can be seen as a historicization of the Kantian question of conditions of possibility.[12] For example, Nietzsche realizes that the declaration that God is dead—by which he means that belief in the Christian God has become unbelievable—is itself not enough: "[I]n former times, one sought to prove that there is no God—today one indicates how the belief that there is a God could arise and how this belief acquired its weight and importance."[13] What needs to be examined is how beliefs and ideas arose and how they developed. Nietzsche's main area of examination with the genealogical approach is morality, and he spends a great deal of time examining how various moral "norms" became accepted, subjecting their conditions of possibility to historical examination.

Even before Foucault's celebrated essay on Nietzsche, which is often seen as the first systematization of genealogy as an approach, I believe that this is a key hook on which to hang the notion. What we take to be the conditions of possibility of the foundation of knowledge is actually a historical question. This explicit historicizing of the Kantian question—to ask why synthetic a priori judgments are necessary—is clearly linked to the project outlined in the second *Untimely Meditation,* where Nietzsche asks how history can serve life. For Nietzsche, history is not capable of objectivity, and where this is aimed for, great harm often results. Instead, history has to be subjective, and therefore historians need to be aware of the uses to which their work is being put. In the preface to this essay, Nietzsche provides a succinct summary of how he sees the use of historical study:

> For I do not know what meaning classical philology would have for our time if not to have an untimely effect within it, that is, to act against the time and so have an effect on the time, to the advantage, it is to be hoped, of a coming time.[14]

In other words, Nietzsche is aware that studying the past allows us to affect the present, and through this, the future. This much was clear from *The Birth of Tragedy;* it is also at play in *On the Genealogy of Morals, The Anti-Christ,* and *The Twilight of the Idols.*

Heidegger on Nietzsche

Heidegger's discussion of the second *Untimely Meditation* in *Being and Time* is, to my mind, one of the most pregnant parts of the book. Though it only lasts a paragraph, it is by far the most sustained reference to Nietzsche in the whole work—surprising, perhaps, given the central role Nietzsche would hold for the later Heidegger. Nietzsche, says Heidegger, "distinguished three kinds of historiography—the monumental, the antiquarian, and the critical—without explicitly pointing out the necessity of this triad or the ground of its unity."[15] In fact, though his later genealogical approach is arguably a fusion of these three types of historiography, Nietzsche never explicitly states that the three *should* be conflated. Given Heidegger's purpose, this joining together is of key importance. "*The threefold character of historiography* [Historie] *is adumbrated in the historicality* [Geschichtlichkeit] *of Dasein* . . . [which] enables us to understand to what extent these three possibilities must be united factically and concretely in any historiography which is authentic" (396). It is important to note the distinction Heidegger draws between *Historie* and *Geschichte. Historie* is, for Heidegger, the writing of history, the discipline; *Geschichte* is history as it actually happens *(geschieht),* the events.

Heidegger reads these three types of historiography as having distinct attitudes to time. The antiquarian approach orients itself to the past, the having been; the monumental to the future; and the critical to the present. In his reading of the last of these Heidegger departs from Nietzsche, for Nietzsche used the critical approach as an orientation to the *past.*[16] As far back as 1922 Heidegger had suggested this: "The *critique* of history is always only the critique of the present."[17] He explains: "Dasein temporalises itself in the way the future and having been are united in the present. . . . As authentic *[eigentliche],* the historiography which is both monumental and antiquarian is necessarily a critique of the 'present.' Authentic historicality is the foundation for the possibility of uniting these three ways of historiography."[18]

Heidegger and the Question of History

Now, although Heidegger clearly recognizes the importance of history, in *Being and Time* it is largely defined as a characteristic of Dasein, rather than as a methodological issue. There are strong reasons for this. First, Husserlian phenomenology was basically ahistorical,[19] perhaps because of Husserl's background in mathematics and logic. Second, as both Kisiel and van Buren have noted, *Being and Time* is a very Kantian book.[20] Krell has argued that for Heidegger, the *history* of philosophy was an "essential counterweight to phenomenology": whereas Husserl had once remarked that he had "forgotten about history," Heidegger never did.[21] And yet, despite the occasional comments indicating the importance of the historical project, the published portions of *Being and Time* do not go nearly far enough, as Heidegger's later work shows.

It is worth drawing out some of the potential implications of *Being and Time.* From the discussion of Newton, it is clear that Dasein and truth are fundamentally linked, that truth is context dependent.[22] This does not mean that truth is only what an individual thinks, but that truth only has a context dependent on the existence of Dasein.[23] Any eternal truths must rest on an eternal immutability to Dasein. It clearly follows from this that if being changes or is historicized, so, too, is truth. It has been remarked by some critics that Heidegger does indeed, in *Being and Time,* suggest such an immutability to Dasein, examining it and its structures as if they were true eternally. Such critics sometimes point to a shift in the later Heidegger toward an understanding of the historical nature of being, of Dasein, which leads to a historicizing of truth.[24]

Immediately after *Being and Time,* Heidegger turned his attention to Kant. In terms of the issues at stake here, the crucial part of this reading is the suggestion that Kant recognizes the ontic/ontological distinction. Heidegger suggests that ontic knowledge is knowledge pertaining to the distinctive nature of beings as such, whereas ontological knowledge is the basis on which any such theory (of ontic knowledge) could be constructed, the a priori conditions for the possibility of such sciences. Heidegger's own exercise as *fundamental ontology* deals with the conditions of possibility not just of the ontic sciences, but of the ontologies that precede and found them. Ontological knowledge provides the a priori conditions for ontic knowledge; it concerns being rather than beings.[25] The predominant strain of Kant interpretation in Heidegger's time was the neo-Kantianism of the Marburg school, which argued that the *Critique of Pure Reason* was a work of epistemology. This view, put forward by Hermann Cohen, Heinrich Rickert, and Paul Natorp, among others, held sway in the late nineteenth and early twentieth centuries. Heidegger, lecturing at Marburg, tackles this interpretation head on: the *Critique of Pure Reason* is a theory of knowledge, but it is not a theory of ontic knowledge (i.e., experience) but rather of ontological knowledge—transcendental philosophy, ontology.[26] Ontic knowledge (of beings) must conform to ontological foundations (being). This is the real meaning of Kant's Copernican revolution: that instead of our knowledge conforming to objects, objects must conform to our knowledge.[27]

What was for Kant the examination of the transcendental possibility of experience becomes in Heidegger's terms an examination of the ontological possibility of the ontic. Heidegger continues, "[W]ith the problem of transcendence, a 'theory of knowledge' is not set in place of metaphysics, but rather the inner possibility of ontology is questioned."[28] Ontology is seen as the laying of the ground for metaphysics as a whole.[29] What is particularly important in this discussion is that Heidegger's reading of the ontic/ontological distinction runs almost parallel to Kant's discussion of synthetic a priori knowledge. The central question of the *Critique of Pure Reason* was "How are synthetic a priori judgements possible?" The central question of *Being and Time* could be rephrased as "How is ontological knowledge possible?"[30] Synthetic a priori knowledge is possible on the basis of the original synthetic unity of the pure productive power of imagination, on the basis of temporality. As temporality is the basic constitution of human Dasein, humans have the possibility of having a pure understanding of being. The understanding of being in general (i.e. ontological knowledge) is possible on the basis of the temporality of Dasein.[31] In Kant, as in *Being and Time,* this is a radically ahistorical question. In Nietzsche—who asks not how synthetic a priori knowledge is possible, but why it is necessary—and the later Heidegger, this question, the problem of metaphysics, or the question of being, is posed historically.[32]

The idea of the history of being does not appear as an explicit theme until later works, though it would appear that the second part of *Being and Time* would have covered some of this area. As it stands, in this early period Heidegger attempts to understand the structures of Dasein, among which is the sense of history. In this attempt his enterprise is thoroughly Kantian, resolutely ahistorical in terms of the approach, and concerned with the conditions of possibility of Dasein. In his later works, Heidegger historicizes these very structures; in the specific case effectively historicizing the sense of history. If in *Being and Time* Heidegger attempts an ontology of history (for which the ground must be Dasein rather than historiography),[33] in his later work he attempts a history of ontology. Historicizing his own Kantian impulses, effectively following Nietzsche, Heidegger becomes a historical ontologist.

We can see this turning in his work by looking at a letter Heidegger sent to Rudolf Bultmann at the very end of 1927, the year *Being and Time* was published. "My work is directed toward a radicalisation of ancient ontology and at the same time toward a universal structuring of this ontology in relation to the region of history."[34] It is only when Heidegger devotes several years to reading, thinking, and writing about Nietzsche and Hölderlin that his thoughts develop and become clear.[35] Crucially, the ontology is no longer universal in relation to the region of history, but is itself historicized as a historical ontology. This means that the de-struction *(Destruktion)* of the tradition is no longer pursued with temporality as the clue, but historically, as a history of being or a historical ontology. Following Kisiel's work, it is possible to suggest that this was the initial direction Heidegger was pursuing, and that *Being and Time* was a side move undertaken and then abandoned. The initial project, as outlined in the Aristotle book introduction, certainly suggests as much: "For philosophical research, the de-structive confrontation *[Auseinandersetzung]* with philosophy's history is not merely an annex for the purposes of illustrating how things were earlier. . . . [it] is rather the authentic path upon which the present must encounter itself in its own basic movements."[36] In contrast to the suggestion at the end of the introduction to *Being and Time,* which stated that part 2 would contain "a phenomenological de-struction of the history of ontology with the problematic of temporality as our clue," toward the end of the actually published book, Heidegger talks of the "historiographical de-struction of the history of philosophy" to follow.[37] Given that part 2 was never published, it is impossible to know what Heidegger would have achieved in it.

Heidegger as Historical Ontologist

In *An Introduction to Metaphysics* there is the first clearly evident use of the historical approach I have argued is implicit in *Being and Time*. As Heidegger states, "[W]e maintain that this preliminary question [about being] and with it the fundamental question of metaphysics are historical questions through and through."[38] He then suggests that even men's relation to history is itself historical: an example of the historicizing of the (in *Being and Time*) ahistorical structures of Dasein. With his regular references to the etymology of key terms, the historical references to the Greek beginnings, and the more oblique allusions to tracing a path of thought, Heidegger allows this historicizing to pervade this and practically all future work. Once again there is a reference to the concurrent nature of the dimensions of time, joining together in the study of history: "History as happening *[Geschichte als Geschehen]* is an acting and being acted upon which pass through the present, which are determined from out of the future, and which take over the past" (48; 44). The importance of the historical for Heidegger's purpose is shown when he sets out his aim of the present study: "1. The determination of the essence of man is never an answer but essentially a question. . . . 2. The asking of this question is historical in the fundamental sense that this questioning first creates history" (149–52; 140–43).

By the time of the Nietzsche lectures Heidegger has realized that his own project of "de-struction *[Destruktion]*, like 'phenomenology' and all hermeneutical-transcendental questions, has not yet been thought in terms of the history of being," and that, fundamentally, though these critical approaches can be useful, these must be used alongside that of history.[39] "History is the history of being *[Die Geschichte ist Geschichte des Seins]*,"[40] says Heidegger, and much of his later work is taken up in an investigation of the history of philosophy that in many ways, like Hegel, though with clearly divergent results, becomes a meditation on the philosophy of history (6.1:404; 2:186). In the third lecture course on Nietzsche, Heidegger reaches the stage it was suggested was implicit in his formulation of the import of Newtonian physics: "In its own being, therefore, truth is historicised" (6.2:231; 3:187). Truth is now seen as historical, as plural. Within this formulation of history and truth, Heidegger also sees the central importance of Nietzsche's idea of power: "In the sense of Nietzsche's interpretation of history, the question asks, what configuration of the will to power was at work here?" (6.2:102; 4:75). So, questions must be asked bearing in mind the historical dimension, and considering the power relations at stake.

This is shown not only in Heidegger's thoughts on Nietzsche, but also in the separate lecture from the same time entitled "The Age of the World Picture." In the Nietzsche lectures, Heidegger makes the link: "Science, for example, knowledge in general, is a configuration of will to power. Thoughtful reflection . . . about knowledge—and science in particular—must make visible what will to power is" (6.1:443; 3:19), and some pages later, "the essence of knowledge, that is, the essence of truth, must be defined in terms of the will to power" (6.1:448; 3:24). This is put into practice in a number of investigations. As David Farrell Krell notes, the investigation of boredom in *The Fundamental Concepts of Metaphysics* is not *Kulturdiagnostik,* phenomenology, or fundamental ontology, but closer to genealogy than anything else.[41] I suggest that it is historical ontology, a term almost synonymous with genealogy. This notion of historical ontology is at work in Heidegger's readings of technology, the housing crisis in postwar Germany, the polis in the early 1940s, and other later concerns.[42] All of these are oriented as critiques of the present. Indeed, in *Being and Time,* Heidegger talks of the "ontological task of constructing a non-deductive genealogy of the different possible ways of being."[43]

Archaeology, Genealogy, Historical Ontology

Now clearly Foucault is indebted to Heidegger. In a work such as this I do not need to rehearse the arguments behind that claim. But how he is indebted to Heidegger is clearly a central issue. What I am suggesting here is that Heidegger's take on Nietzsche, and his attitude to the issue of history is central to what Foucault is doing.

In Foucault's understanding of archaeology, for an *énoncé* to be accepted within a discipline—even before it can be pronounced true or false—it must "fulfil complex and serious demands"; it must be, in Canguilhem's phrase, "within the true."[44] This is an important point, as it proves that a discourse conditions the possibility of all *énoncés*—whether they are true or false. This becomes clearer in the discussion of the "positivity of a discourse" that "characterises its unity throughout time. . . . it defines a limited space of communication. . . . positivity plays the role of what might be called the historical *a priori.*"[45]

Foucault accepts that juxtaposing these two words produces a "rather startling effect," as the standard understanding of a priori is that it is ahistorical, absolute. Foucault's term does not simply mean that the a priori is also endowed with a history; rather he is introducing a notion of pluralism into the history of ideas, in that there have been several a priori structures in various disciplines that conditioned possibilities in those subjects.[46] This bears definite comparison with the understanding of history found in Nietzsche and Heidegger. Foucault's understanding of the historical a priori does not function as "a condition of validity for judgements, but a condition of reality for *énoncés*."[47] In other words, it does not determine their truth, but rather their possibility.

Foucault suggests that "instead of exploring the consciousness/knowledge *[connaissance]*/science axis (which cannot escape subjectivity), archaeology explores the discursive practice/knowledge *[savoir]*/science axis" (239; 183). It is clear that a distinction between *connaissance* and *savoir* is essential, though they are both usually translated as "knowledge" in English. To explain his understanding of these terms, Foucault adds a note to the English edition: "By *connaissance* I mean the relation of the subject to the object and the formal rules that govern it. *Savoir* refers to the conditions that are necessary in a particular period for this or that type of object to be given to *connaissance* and for this or that enunciation to be formulated" (15n). As Foucault had said some years earlier, explaining his aim in *Histoire de la folie:* "[I]t is this *savoir* I wanted to interrogate, as the condition of possibility of *connaissances,* of institutions and of practices."[48] This understanding is close to the distinction Heidegger makes between ontic and ontological knowledge in *Being and Time.* For Heidegger, the question of being is an ontological question, which aims "at ascertaining the *a priori* conditions . . . for the possibility of the sciences which examine entities"—ontic knowledge. It is clear that for Foucault, like Heidegger, the key is *savoir,* or ontological knowledge. What is important is that for Foucault this ontological investigation is historical—it thereby refuses to set universal conditions—something that Heidegger only does in his later works.[49]

Foucault conceives of the historical a priori as a grid *[grille]* structuring possibilities at a given time. In *L'Ordre du discours,* setting out his program for future work he suggests that, in our time, the "regions where the grid is the most constricting *[resserrée],* where the danger spots multiply, are the regions of sexuality and of politics: as if discourse, far from being a transparent or neutral element where sexuality is disarmed and politics pacified, is one of those places where they exercise, in a privileged manner, some of their most formidable powers *[puissances]*."[50] Later in the same piece he gives the example of education, suggesting it is "a political means of sustaining or modifying the appropriation of discourse, with the knowledge and the powers it carries with it . . . following the lines which are marked by distances, oppositions and social struggle" (45–46).

Foucault looks at these questions of politics, sexuality, and education in later works, suggesting that now he is making genealogical studies. With the adoption of the term "genealogy" Foucault becomes more explicitly Nietzschean. Such an influence had always been acknowledged, but is now brought to the fore. In the 1961 preface to *Histoire de la folie* Foucault had likened his study to Nietzsche's *The Birth of Tragedy;* he gave a paper to a colloquium in 1964 entitled "Nietzsche, Freud, Marx," where he clearly identified with the first of these thinkers; and in 1967 he had suggested that his "archaeology owes more to the Nietzschean genealogy than to structuralism properly called."[51] In this period he had also been involved in the French publication of Nietzsche's *Complete Works.*[52] This Nietzschean influence becomes especially pronounced in the 1971 key essay, "Nietzsche, Genealogy, History"—one of Foucault's central theoretical pieces.[53]

Though genealogy is sometimes seen as a replacement for archaeology, it is better to see the two as existing together, as two halves of a complementary approach. Archaeology looks at truth as "a system of ordered procedures for the production, regulation, distribution, circulation, and operation of *énoncés,*" while genealogy sees truth as "linked in a circular relation with systems of power which produce and sustain it, and to effects of power which it induces and which extends it."[54] This shows that, for Foucault, knowledge and power are linked and dependent on each other, but not that they are synonymous: "[T]he exercise of power perpetually creates knowledge and, conversely, knowledge constantly induces effects of power."[55] This obviously bears comparison with Nietzsche—"Knowledge works as a tool of power: Hence it is plain that it increases with every increase of power"—and with Heidegger's discussion of this point in *Nietzsche.*[56] The relation between the knowledge/power dyad is examined in detail in Foucault's future works, though he does realize that this has been the case all along: "When I think back now, I ask myself what else it was that I was talking about, in *Histoire de la folie* or *The Birth of the Clinic*, but power? Yet I'm perfectly aware that I scarcely ever used the word and never had such a field of analyses at my disposal."[57]

Like Nietzsche, Foucault is opposed to some kinds of history, and demands the need for a historical sense. Likewise he is opposed to the tendency toward what Nietzsche called "Egyptianism"—of dehistoricizing, or of tearing things from their true context. There are two potential situations. Either the historical sense is mastered by a "supra-historical point of view, metaphysics can bend it to its own purpose, and, by aligning it to the demands of objective science, it can impose its own 'Egyptianism,'" or, by refusing the certainty of absolutes, "the historical sense can evade metaphysics and become a privileged instrument of genealogy."[58] Genealogy was for Nietzsche a critical history; it was untimely in the sense that it was "acting counter to our time and thereby acting on our time and, let us hope, for the benefit of a time to come."[59] As we have seen, Heidegger's reading of Nietzsche on history made some fundamental points concerning the three modalities of history. These points are central to understanding Foucault's reading of Nietzsche:

> In a sense, genealogy returns to the three modalities of history that Nietzsche recognised in 1874. It returns to them in spite of the objections that Nietzsche raised in the name of the affirmative and creative powers of life. But they are metamorphosed: the veneration of monuments becomes parody; the respect for ancient continuities becomes systematic dissociation; the critique of the injustices of the past by a truth held by men in the present becomes the destruction of the man who maintains knowledge *[connaissance]* by the injustice proper to the will to knowledge *[savoir]*.[60]

Like Heidegger, Foucault sees the three modalities working together, and he follows Heidegger's shift in orienting the critical to the present, rather than the past. Nietzsche's critical history became for Heidegger a critique of the present, a critique that was historicized in Heidegger's later works. For Foucault it becomes a history of the present.[61]

Though Foucault only describes his project in these terms in *Discipline and Punish*, it is clear that it applies to all his work. As he describes his early works: "[I]t is a question of presenting a critique of our own time, based upon retrospective analyses."[62] Such a critique, or history, of our own time, of the present, is exemplified in the advent of the death of man in *The Order of Things;* the history of the modern subject pursued in *The History of Sexuality;* and in Foucault's engagement in debates over psychiatry, penal reform, homosexuality, and various other issues. It also lends an explicitly political tone to his work. Some of the most direct links to present-day issues are found in his interviews and journalism, whereas the analyses in his books tend to end around the middle of the nineteenth century. The attitude to the present is also the topic of Foucault's reflections on Kant's essay "What Is Enlightenment?"

In reading Kant, Foucault returns to the original German. The opening line of Kant's text reads: "Enlightenment *[Aufklärung]* is the exit *[Ausgang]* of man from his self-imposed immaturity *[Unmündigkeit]*."[63] It is important, contends Foucault, that Kant defines *Aufklärung* as "an *Ausgang,* an 'exit,' a 'way out,'" a way out of the present to the future.[64] This present is our immaturity, mentally, spiritually, and physically, and *Aufklärung* will lead us into a new maturity, a modernity. This "point of departure . . . the attitude to modernity" (4:568; 38) needs clarification. Foucault concedes that "modernity is often spoken of as an epoch, or at least as a set of features characteristic of an epoch; situated on a calendar," but wonders "whether we may not envisage modernity rather as an attitude than as a period of history . . . a bit, no doubt, like what the Greeks called an *êthos*" (4:568; 39). This *êthos* is conceived as "a permanent critique of our historical being *[être]* . . . consisting in a critique of what we are saying, thinking and doing, through a historical ontology of ourselves" (4:571–74; 42–45). This project is given greater scope in an interview from around the same time:

> Three domains of genealogy are possible. First, a historical ontology of ourselves in relation to truth through which we constitute ourselves as subjects of knowledge; second, a historical ontology of ourselves in relation to a field of power through which we constitute ourselves as subjects acting on others; third, a historical ontology in relation to ethics through which we constitute ourselves as moral agents. (4:618; 351)

Foucault therefore suggests that Kant founds two great traditions in philosophy. One of these is the project found in the *Critiques,* where he looks for the conditions of true knowledge and asks the question "What is man?" The second is found in "What Is Enlightenment?" The former project was criticized by Foucault in his secondary thesis and *The Order of Things*, but Foucault finds the second more interesting, characterizing it as "an ontology of the present, an ontology of ourselves." Essentially this involves reading the historical Kant against the critical one. This is the tradition Foucault allies himself with, and these two ontologies clearly delineate the research he pursued in the last years of his life—and, indeed, in the description of the three domains of genealogy, his life work.[65]

Reading Foucault in this way underlines the continuity that runs throughout his work. The notion of an ontology of the present is clearly linked to Foucault's general project of a history of limits. Speaking of the *êthos* he sees develop out of the Enlightenment, he conceives it as a limit-attitude:

> We have to move beyond the outside-inside alternative; we have to be at the frontiers. Criticism indeed consists of analysing and reflecting upon limits. . . . The point, in brief, is to transform the critique conducted in the form of a necessary limitation into a practical critique that takes the form of a possible crossing. . . . this criticism is not transcendental, and its goal is not that of making a metaphysics possible: it is genealogical in its design, and archaeological in its method.[66]

This orientation of a historical study to the present, rather than the past, is a theme I find common to Nietzsche, Heidegger, and Foucault—and it is framed by their responses to the Kantian question, "How are synthetic a priori judgments possible?" Taking Nietzsche's response, "Why is belief in such judgements necessary?" as a guiding principle within his genealogical approach, and seeing how Heidegger's response to Kant is crucial to understanding the shift between the published and the unpublished divisions of *Being and Time* and to the development of historical ontology, I have recast Foucault's historical approach as a historical ontology. This characterization of genealogy as historical ontology shows that while Foucault exhibits some common interests with historical sociologists, he is also doing something more fundamental. Foucault is not simply concerned with the question of structure and agency, the realm of micro-history for its own sake, or a particular historical period. Rather, through his investigation of the ontic phenomena of history, he is exposing the metaphysical assumptions behind the systems of thought that condition their possibility.

There is not the space here to show how this would cast the standard readings of Foucault's major works in a new light. It would require us, for example, to read *Discipline and Punish* as a study of the birth of the prison, but in the light of the comment that the "soul is the prison of the body." *Discipline and Punish* is, as Foucault says, "a genealogy of the modern 'soul.'"[67] Likewise, *The History of Sexuality* is not simply an examination of sexuality and subjectivity, but a genealogy of the subject precisely in order to circumvent these notions. All of these works of genealogy can be read as historical ontologies, rather than as historical sociology. Like the later Heidegger—and in, for example, Nietzsche's *The Birth of Tragedy*—these historical ontologies are framed as histories of the present. Noting how Foucault's *connaissance/savoir* distinction parallels Heidegger's ontic/ontological difference allows us to see both the continuity between archaeology and genealogy and the continuity between two of the twentieth century's foremost thinkers.

Notes

1. Michel Foucault, *Dits et écrits 1954–1988*, 4 vols., ed. Daniel Defert and François Ewald (Paris: Gallimard, 1994), 2:753; and *Power/Knowledge: Selected Interviews and Other Writings 1972–77*, ed. Colin Gordon (Brighton: Harvester, 1980), 53.

2. A much more detailed version of the argument here, particularly with regard to the question of space within historical inquiry, is found in Stuart Elden, *Mapping the Present: Heidegger, Foucault, and the Project of a Spatial History* (London: Continuum, 2001).

3. Gareth Stedman Jones, "From Historical Sociology to Theoretic History," in *The British Journal of Sociology* 7, no. 23 (September 1976): 295–305; Philip Abrams, *Historical Sociology* (Ithaca: Cornell University Press, 1982).

4. Karl Marx, *The Eighteenth Brumaire of Louis Napoleon*, in *Surveys from Exile*, vol. 2 of *Political Writings* (Harmondsworth: Penguin, 1973), 146.

5. It is important to note that historical sociology is not the same as social history, for as Harry Elmer Barnes (*Historical Sociology: Its Origins and Development* [New York and London: Garland Publishing Inc., 1984], 71), drawing on his work with Howard Becker, points out, historical sociology "embodies a more theoretical and generalised approach to the history of human society."

6. Abrams, *Historical Sociology*, 7.

7. On this change, see Dennis Smith, *The Rise of Historical Sociology* (Cambridge: Polity Press, 1991).

8. See, for example, John O'Neill, "The Disciplinary Society: From Weber to Foucault," in *The British Journal of Sociology* 37, no. 1 (March 1986): 42–60; Mitchell Dean, *Critical and Effective Histories: Foucault's Methods and Historical Sociology* (London: Routledge, 1994); Arpád Szakolczai, *Max Weber and Michel Foucault: Parallel Life-Works* (Routledge, London and New York, 1998). David Owen's *Maturity and Modernity: Nietzsche, Weber, Foucault and the Ambivalence of Reason* (London: Routledge, 1994) is a useful discussion of many pertinent issues, and indeed his eighth chapter bears a similar title to this discussion. Yet though Owen examines the idea that genealogy is historical ontology, he never discusses Heidegger, and so does not address

what Foucault might mean by this. More generally, see also Stephen Kalberg, *Max Weber's Comparative Historical Sociology* (Cambridge: Polity, 1994).

9. Immanuel Kant, *Critique of Pure Reason*, ed. Vasilis Politis (London: J. M. Dent, 1993), B17.

10. Ibid., A50/B74.

11. Friedrich Nietzsche, *Beyond Good and Evil*, trans. Walter Kaufmann (New York: Vintage, 1966), 11; see also page 4, where Nietzsche suggests that the falsest judgments (which include the synthetic a priori) are, however, necessary, as without them man could not live. It seems clear, though, that Nietzsche realizes that more—historical—investigation is needed.

12. See Owen, *Maturity and Modernity*, 17ff.

13. Friedrich Nietzsche, *The Gay Science*, trans. Walter Kaufmann (New York: Vintage, 1974), 343; and *Daybreak*, trans. R. J. Hollingdale (Cambridge: Cambridge University Press, 1981), 95.

14. Friedrich Nietzsche, *Untimely Meditations*, trans. R. J. Hollingdale (Cambridge: Cambridge University Press, 1983).

15. Martin Heidegger, *Being and Time*, trans. Edward Robinson and John Macquarrie (Oxford: Blackwell, 1962), 396. Page references are to the marginal pagination found in the English and German, which refer to the original text: *Sein und Zeit* (Tübingen: Max Niemeyer, 1967), 11th ed.

16. For a discussion of this, see Charles Guignon, "History and Commitment in the Early Heidegger," in *Heidegger: A Critical Reader*, ed. Hubert L. Dreyfus and Harrison Hall (Oxford: Blackwell, 1992); and David Couzens Hoy, "History, Historicity, and Historiography in *Being and Time*," in *Heidegger and Modern Philosophy*, ed. Michael Murray (New Haven: Yale University Press, 1978).

17. Martin Heidegger, "Phänomenologische Interpretationem zu Aristoteles (Anzeige der hermeneutischen situation)," in *Interpretations Phenomenologiques d'Aristote*, French-German edition (Mauvezin: Trans-Europ-Repress, 1992), 19.

18. Heidegger, *Being and Time*, 397. See Theodore Kisiel, *The Genesis of Heidegger's Being and Time* (Berkeley and Los Angeles: University of California Press, 1993), 254. The translation of *Eigentlichkeit* and related words by "authenticity" is enormously problematic, though there is not the space to discuss this here.

19. Kisiel, *The Genesis of Heidegger's Being and Time*, 360.

20. See ibid. and John van Buren, *The Young Heidegger: Rumor of the Hidden King* (Bloomington: Indiana University Press, 1994).

21. David Farrell Krell, *Intimations of Mortality: Time, Truth, and Finitude in Heidegger's Thinking of Being* (University Park: Pennsylvania State University Press, 1986), 5.

22. Heidegger, *Being and Time*, 227; see also Heidegger, *The Basic Problems of Phenomenology*, trans. Albert Hofstadter (Bloomington: Indiana University Press, 1982), 313–16.

23. Martin Heidegger, *Kant and the Problem of Metaphysics*, trans. Richard Taft (Bloomington: Indiana University Press, 1997), 281–82.

24. See, for example, Hubert Dreyfus's comments in Bryan Magee, *The Great Philosophers* (London: BBC Books, 1987), 269–71; and Dreyfus's *Being-in-the-World* (Cambridge: MIT Press, 1991), 127.

25. Heidegger, *Being and Time*, 11; see also *The Metaphysical Foundations of Logic*, trans. Michael Heim (Bloomington: Indiana University Press, 1984), 195–202.

26. Heidegger, *Kant and the Problem of Metaphysics*, 17; Heidegger, *The Basic Problems of Phenomenology*, 180–81; Heidegger, *Phenomenological Interpretation of*

Kant's Critique of Pure Reason, trans. Parvis Emad and Kenneth Maly (Bloomington: Indiana University Press, 1997), 186. See also Daniel O. Dahlstrom, "Heidegger's Kant Courses at Marburg," in *Reading Heidegger from the Start: Essays in His Earliest Thought,* ed. Theodore Kisiel and John van Buren (Albany: State University of New York Press, 1994). This is hinted at in *Being and Time,* 10–11.

27. Heidegger, *Phenomenological Interpretation,* 55–56; Kant, *Critique of Pure Reason,* Bxvi. This disagreement with neo-Kantianism is the subject of the "Davos Disputation between Ernst Cassirer and Martin Heidegger" (Heidegger, *Kant and the Problem of Metaphysics,* 274–96); the movement is outlined in "On the History of the Philosophical Chair since 1866" (304–11).

28. Heidegger, *Kant and the Problem of Metaphysics,* 16–17.

29. Ibid., 124–25. See also Heidegger, *The Fundamental Concepts of Metaphysics: World, Finitude, Solitude,* trans. William McNeill and Nicholas Walker (Bloomington: Indiana University Press, 1995), 306.

30. See Dahlstrom, "Heidegger's Kant Courses at Marburg," 297.

31. Heidegger, *Phenomenological Interpretation,* 424–25. Heidegger recognizes that as "ontology has for its fundamental discipline the analytic of the Dasein . . . ontology cannot be established in a purely ontological manner. Its possibility is referred back to a being, that is, to something ontical—the Dasein. Ontology has an ontical foundation" (*The Basic Problems of Phenomenology,* 26).

32. Nietzsche, *Beyond Good and Evil,* 11; Heidegger, *Kant and the Problem of Metaphysics,* 249.

33. See Kisiel, *The Genesis of Heidegger's Being and Time,* 326.

34. Martin Heidegger, letter to Rudolf Bultmann, 31 December 1927, quoted in Kisiel, *The Genesis of Heidegger's Being and Time,* 452.

35. On the reading of Hölderlin, see Stuart Elden, "Heidegger's Hölderlin and the Importance of Place," in *Journal of the British Society for Phenomenology* 30, no. 3 (October 1999): 258–74.

36. Heidegger, "Phenomenological Interpretations with Respect to Aristotle," 20–21.

37. Heidegger, *Being and Time,* 39, 392.

38. Heidegger, *Gesamtausgabe* (Frankfurt am Main: Vittorio Klostermann, 1975–), 40:46; and *An Introduction to Metaphysics,* trans. Ralph Mannheim (New Haven: Yale University Press, 1959), 430.

39. Martin Heidegger, *Gesamtausgabe* 6.2: 378; and *The End of Philosophy,* trans. Joan Stambaugh (London: Souvenir Press, 1975), 15.

40. Heidegger, *Gesamtausgabe* 6.2:20; and *Nietzsche,* 4 vols., trans. David Farrell Krell, Frank Capuzzi, and Joan Stambaugh (San Francisco: Harper Collins, 1991), 3:182.

41. David Farrell Krell, *Daimon Life: Heidegger and Life Philosophy* (Bloomington: Indiana University Press, 1992), 109.

42. On the polis, see Stuart Elden, "Rethinking the *Polis:* Implications of Heidegger's Questioning the Political," in *Political Geography* 19, no. 4 (May 2000): 407–22.

43. Heidegger, *Being and Time,* 11.

44. Michel Foucault, *L'Ordre du discours* (Paris: Gallimard, 1970), 35–36.

45. Michel Foucault, *L'Archéologie du savoir* (Paris: Gallimard, 1969), 166–67. Translated by Alan Sheridan as *The Archaeology of Knowledge* (New York: Barnes and Noble, 1972), 126–27.

46. As Colin Gordon ("Foucault in Britain," in *Foucault and Political Reason,* ed. Andrew Barry, Thomas Osborne and Nikolas Rose [London: UCL Press, 1996], 261) suggests, this phrase arouses the "double suspicion of historicism and irrationality," especially within the empirically bound British culture.

47. Foucault, *L'Archéologie du savoir,* 167–69; and *The Archaeology of Knowl-*

edge, 128. On this period of Foucault's thought, see Gilles Deleuze, "A New Archivist," in *Foucault*, trans. Séan Hand (London: Athlone Press, 1988).

48. Michel Foucault, *Dits et écrits* 1:498; *Foucault Live: Interviews 1961–1984*, ed. Sylvère Lotringer (New York: Semiotext[e], 1996), 13.

49. Heidegger, *Being and Time*, 11. On the question of ontology in Foucault, with some of the links to Heidegger, see Béatrice Han, *L'ontologie manquée de Michel Foucault* (Grenoble: Jérôme Millon, 1998).

50. Foucault, *L'Ordre du discours*, 11.

51. Foucault, *Dits et écrits* 1:564–79, 599; and *Foucault Live*, 31.

52. See Foucault, *Dits et écrits*, 1:549–52 and 561–64.

53. It should be noted that while most commentators see this as a crucial essay for understanding Foucault, Mitchell Dean (*Critical and Effective Histories*, 14) suggests that we should remember it is about Nietzsche, and that we should not necessarily equate it with Foucault. It is, however, clear from Foucault's genealogical studies—as he calls them—that the essay is part of a program of future work.

54. Foucault, *Dits et écrits* 3:160; and *The Foucault Reader*, ed. Paul Rabinow (Harmondsworth: Penguin, 1991). A different conception is provided by Philip Barker (*Michel Foucault: Subversions of the Subject* [New York & London: Harvester Wheatsheaf, 1993], 71; and David Owen, *Maturity and Modernity*, 151), who see archaeology as concentrating on the synchronic and genealogy on the diachronic.

55. Foucault, *Dits et écrits* 2:752; *Power/Knowledge*, 52.

56. Friedrich Nietzsche, *The Will to Power*, trans. Walter Kaufmann and R. J. Hollingdale (New York, Vintage, 1968), 480.

57. Foucault, *Dits et écrits* 3:146; and *The Foucault Reader*, 57.

58. Foucault, *Dits et écrits* 2:146–47; and *The Foucault Reader*, 87.

59. Nietzsche, preface to *Untimely Meditations*.

60. Foucault, *Dits et écrits* 2:156; and *The Foucault Reader*, 97.

61. Michel Foucault, *Surveiller et punir—Naissance de la prison* (Paris: Gallimard, 1975), 40. Translated by Alan Sheridan as *Discipline and Punish—The Birth of the Prison* (Harmondsworth: Penguin, 1976), 31.

62. Foucault, *Dits et écrits* 2:183; and *Foucault Live*, 68. As Deleuze (*Foucault*, trans. Seán Hand [London: Athlone Press, 1988], 50), states, "Archaeology does not necessarily refer back to the past. There is an archaeology of the present." See also John Rajchman, *Michel Foucault: The Freedom of Philosophy* (New York: Columbia University Press, 1985), 58; and the posthumously published interview "What Our Present Is," in *Foucault Live*, 407–15.

63. Immanuel Kant, "Beantwortung der Frage: Was ist Aufklärung?" in *Werke: Gesamtausgabe in zehn Bänden* (Leipzig: Modes und Baumann, 1843), 1:111; "An Answer to the Question: What Is Enlightenment?" in *Perpetual Peace and Other Essays On Politics, History and Moral Practice*, trans. Ted Humphrey (Indianapolis: Hackett, 1983), 41.

64. Foucault, *Dits et écrits* 4:564; and *The Foucault Reader*, 34.

65. Foucault, *Dits et écrits* 4:687–88; and *Politics, Philosophy, Culture: Interviews and Other Writings 1977–84*, ed. Lawrence D. Kritzman (London: Routledge, 1990).

66. Foucault, *Dits et écrits* 4:574; and *The Foucault Reader*, 45–46. As Dean, *Critical and Effective Histories*, 20, suggests, "[T]he general context for a consideration of genealogy and archaeology is, then, a third term which they both serve, that of a history of the present." In this context, see also Patrick Baert, "Foucault's History of the Present as Self-Referential Knowledge Acquisition," in *Philosophy and Social Criticism* 24, no. 6 (November 1998): 111–26.

67. Foucault, *Surveiller et punir*, 38–39; and *Discipline and Punish*, 29–30.

The Ethics and Politics of Narrative: Heidegger + Foucault

Leslie Paul Thiele

Despite their many notable differences, Martin Heidegger and Michel Foucault present us with a complementary vision of the philosophical and political dangers of late modernity. The demon that bears its face most clearly to Foucault in Bentham's Panopticon appears to Heidegger in the guise of technology and the hegemonic rule of the "world picture." Both demons threaten us with a totalistically represented and regulated system of thought and behavior whose watchword is disciplinary efficiency. This efficiency—primarily oriented to the accelerated exploitation of resources, foremost of which are "human resources"—comes at the expense of philosophically ecstatic, culturally diverse, and politically spontaneous experiences.

Both the Heideggerian and Foucauldian demons exercise relatively anonymous forms of power. The chief concern is not domination at the hands of a tyrant, but the more insidious and equally despotic grip of subjectification and objectification. The age of the world picture that Heidegger laments is much like the panoptic age that Foucault decries—a time in which human being is both subjectified and objectified to a degree hitherto unknown. Contemporary subjectification is the product of a humanism that identifies the world as the malleable product of the human subject. Worldliness—the notion that human beings are part of a whole, a whole that both escapes and defines us—

is overwhelmed by philosophical and cultural anthropomorphisms. Contemporary objectification is the product of a humanism infatuated with technological control. In the technophilic, disciplinary society, technology has turned upon its agents. We become our own and each others' jailers—or perhaps better said, our own and each others' human resource managers. Heidegger and Foucault insist that our self-made jails are not dungeons of deprivation. They are sites of the extensive and intensive pursuit of heightened productivity and consumption. The world, including its human occupants, has been transformed into a standing reserve. Through our own subjectification and objectification we participate in the maximally efficient use and using up of natural and human resources.

Heidegger engages in ontology as a means of excavating the modes of representation that define this brave new worldview. He targets metaphysics as a form of representational thinking that separates human beings from their world by subjectifying the former and objectifying the latter. Building on these excavations, Foucault supplies us with genealogies of the disciplinary methods that characterize the brave new world. He focuses on the modes of thinking that sustain self- and social surveillance and the history of actions and institutions that generate the internalization of disciplinary power.

Both Heidegger and Foucault despair of any final liberation from representational thought and disciplinary practice. Yet both envision and extol the struggles—philosophical and political—that place the world picture and its disciplinary discourses and institutions in question. Both celebrate, in tragic fashion, the ephemeral freedom that such struggles allow. This freedom is chiefly displayed through releasement, or *Gelassenheit,* for Heidegger. It is displayed through artistic self-creation for Foucault. Heideggerian and Foucauldian freedom fleetingly arises from our nonidentification with and creative resistance to the metaphysical thought, panoptic vision, disciplinary power, and technological control that characterize late modernity.

The complementarity of Heidegger's and Foucault's accounts of modern demons and saving graces should not be too surprising. Foucault's indebtedness to and fascination with Heidegger is well documented.[1] My intent in this chapter is neither to focus on the complementarity of these visions, nor to outline the striking philosophical and political differences that remain in Heidegger's and Foucault's work. Rather, I attempt to make a claim for what at first blush might appear a lost cause.

Despite their originality and intellectual brilliance, Heidegger and Foucault are often castigated as ethico-political dead-ends. They are criticized for their unwillingness or inability to supply the grounds for sound moral and political judgment. Heidegger's embrace of Nazism, in particular, is frequently identified as proof positive that he has little, if anything, to contribute to the ethico-political domain. The standard charge is that his highly abstract form of philosophizing, empyrean ontological vantage point, and depreciation of "das Man" undermines moral principle and political responsibility. From his philosophical heights, it is suggested, Heidegger remained blind to human sufferings, ethical imperatives, and political practicalities. He immunized himself against the moral sensitivity, compassion, and prudence that might have dissuaded him from endorsing and identifying with a brutal regime. Those who embrace his philosophy, critics warn, court similar dangers.

In like fashion, it is held that Foucault dug himself into an equally deep, though ideologically relocated, moral and political hole. Genealogical studies left Foucault convinced of the ubiquity of the disciplinary matrix. There would be no final liberation. The sticky, normalizing webs of power were inescapable and a "hermeneutics of suspicion" quashed any hope of gaining the ethical and political high ground.[2] As such, critics charge, Foucault stripped from us all reason for resistance to unjust power and all hope of legitimating alternative ethico-political institutions. In a Foucauldian world of panoptic power that shapes wants, needs, and selves, critics worry, one would have no justification for fighting and nothing worth fighting for.[3]

In sum, Heidegger's and Foucault's critics suggest that both thinkers undermine the foundations of the practical wisdom needed to ethically and politically navigate late modernity. Despite the brilliance and originality of their thought, arguably the greatest philosopher and the greatest social and political theorist of the twentieth century remain ungrounded ethically and divorced from political responsibility. Critics argue that Heidegger's statements and actions endorsing and defending Nazi authoritarianism and Foucault's radical anarchism, as displayed in his discussions of popular justice with Maoists, demonstrate that neither thinker is capable of supplying us with the resources for sound moral and political judgment.

In the following section, I will revisit these accusations in light of Heidegger's and Foucault's inherent skepticism. I do this to set the stage for my central argument. My thesis is that Heidegger and Foucault do indeed provide us with the resources for prudential thought and action, for *phronesis,* as Aristotle described the preeminent political virtue. If we seek, however, to ground prudence in an axiomatic ethics or a politics of first principles, the cause is indeed lost. Neither Heidegger nor Foucault is willing or able to supply us with a foundation for ethico-political judgment of this nature. Neither thinker proposes or accepts the rule-based capture of moral or political life. Neither Heidegger nor Foucault proposes or accepts a metaphysics that would ground such a deontological systematization. Yet both thinkers remain moral and political philosophers in an important sense. They implicitly highlight the importance of moral and political judgment by providing compelling narratives that foster its cultivation. Making good on this claim will entail a discussion of the capacity of narrative for cultivating ethico-political judgment and an examination of the *phronetic* potential of Heidegger's ontological story and Foucault's genealogical tale.

Political Philosophy and Skeptical Inquiry

Political philosophy investigates, among other things, the ways in which our self-understandings affect or should affect our participation in collective life. Political philosophy also investigates how our collective lives shape and define our self-understandings. How we act toward each other and how we organize our world largely depends on who we think we are. Both Heidegger and Foucault ask the large order question: Who are we at this time of late modernity? To answer this question one must address two distinct but related concerns: the essential nature of human being—the thing that makes us humans and individuals, if indeed such a "thing" exists—and the historical development of the discourses and institutions that form and transform our self-understandings or identities. The concern for the nature of human being, philosophically speaking, demands an ontological investigation. The concern for the historical development of the discourses and institutions that (have) shape(d) our self-understandings and identities is addressed through genealogical forays. Heidegger's ontological investigations and Foucault's genealogical studies are inherently politico-philosophical in this sense.

Traditionally understood, political philosophy is concerned with large order questions (e.g., What is justice? What is liberty? What is equality?), each of which supports countless corollaries (e.g., How should we balance the pursuit of liberty and equality?). The manner in which these quandaries are addressed, at least as much as their substantive content, determines the inquiry to be philosophical in nature. Philosophy, as Heidegger observed, pertains to the "how" of questioning as much as the "what" of questioning. Philosophy is a voyage on uncharted seas where sustained inquiry keeps the ship afloat and in transit. Seldom, if ever, is terra firma reached. Political philosophical thought is inherently an unsettled and unsettling inquiry. It is a tensioned balance between tastes of knowledge grounded in perception, insight, and logic and profound epistemological doubt sustained by our finitude and familiarity with paradox. The siren songs of metaphor masquerading as truth, Nietzsche observed, forever tempt the philosopher. But his experience with their capacity for deception keep him from foundering on the shoals. This understanding of the philosophic project is, I propose, fundamentally Heideggerian and Foucauldian.

Heideggerian and Foucauldian political philosophy is an inherently skeptical enterprise. It is unwilling to pronounce dogmatically about the parts because it knows itself to be ignorant of the whole—indeed ignorant of whether a whole exists. At the same time, political philosophy remains fundamentally insatiable. It is unwilling to rest in the absence of knowledge, or rather, in the absence of the struggle for knowledge. While the questions of political philosophy never produce wholly satisfactory answers, by necessity "we live *some* answer all the time."[4] These lived answers demand ongoing justification—however tentative and ungrounded justification must remain. Unless we are to become dupes of our own biases and socially constructed identities, we cannot stand down from the politico-philosophical quest.

Heidegger writes that philosophy is a form of skepticism in the original Greek sense of the word *skepsis,* which means inquiry. It is an open-ended mode of study that is chary of all claims of truth. Nonetheless, Heidegger insists that skepticism properly speaking cannot deny all knowledge and all efforts to gain knowledge. Such a skepticism would not be philosophy at all but a kind of "sophistry"[5] betrayed by its own dogmatic denial. Likewise, Foucault speaks of avoiding presumptions about underlying truths that would ground knowledge once and for all. "I try to historicize to the utmost in order to leave as little space as possible to the transcendental," he writes. At the same time, Foucault acknowledges that one cannot confirm the nonexistence of transcendental foundations. "I cannot exclude the possibility," he writes, "that one day I will have to confront an irreducible *residuum* which will be, in fact, transcendental."[6] Like Heidegger, Foucault observes that "there is no way that you can say that there is no truth."[7]

The pursuit of knowledge continues unabated for the skeptic. Yet it proceeds with a suspicious eye. There are inherent limitations to—and a price to pay for—the pursuit of knowledge. Charles Scott describes Foucault's efforts in this regard: "Far from the skepticism that argues that nothing is really knowable . . . genealogies embody a sense of the historical limits that define our capacities for knowing and believing. Things are known. But they are known in ways that have considerable social and cultural costs."[8] Both Heidegger and Foucault maintain that there is no legitimate basis for the radical skeptic's conviction that knowledge is impossible or unworthy of pursuit. This sort of skepticism, Heidegger states, consists merely in an "addiction to doubt."[9] The skeptical nature of political philosophical thought, in contrast, is grounded in the imperative of endless inquiry. The point for Heidegger and Foucault is to inquire not in order to sustain doubt, but to doubt that one might better sustain inquiry. At the same time, inquiry is tempered with a sensibility of the ethico-political costs of any "knowledge" that is gained.

Doing political philosophy of this sort might be likened to walking on a tightrope. If vertigo is experienced, a precarious balance may be lost. Falling to one side leaves one mired in apathy, cynicism, and apoliticism. This results when skeptical inquiry degenerates into a radical skepticism, an addictive doubt that denies the value of (the search for) knowledge and undermines the engagements of collective life, which invariably demand commitment (based on tentatively embraced knowledge). Falling to the other side of the tightrope leaves one mired in dogmatic belief or blind activism. Authoritarian ideologies come to serve as stable foundations, or a reactive iconoclasm leads to irresponsible defiance. Apathy, cynicism, and apoliticism, on the one side, and dogmatic authoritarianism or reactive iconoclasm, on the other, are the dangerous consequences of losing one's balance. These states of mind and their corresponding patterns of behavior relieve the vertigo of political philosophical inquiry, but at a prohibitive cost.

It has been argued that Foucault did not so much walk the tightrope of political philosophy as straddle it, at times leaving his readers hopeless and cynical, at times egging them on to an irresponsible monkey-wrenching. For some, the Foucauldian flight from the ubiquitous powers of normalization undermines any defensible normative position. Hopelessness accompanies lost innocence. Cynicism or nihilism become the only alternatives for those who spurn all ethical and political foundations. By refusing to paint a picture of a better future, Foucault is said to undercut the impetus to struggle. Others focus on Foucault's development of a "tool kit" whose contents are to be employed to deconstruct the apparatuses of modern power. Yet the danger remains that Foucault's "hyperactive" tool-kit users will be unprincipled activists, Luddites at best, terrorists at worst. In either case, Foucault provides no overarching theoretical vision. Indeed, Foucault is upfront about his rejection of ethical and political theories and ideals. "I think that to imagine another system is to extend our participation in the present system," Foucault stipulates. "Reject theory and all forms of general discourse. This need for theory is still part of the system we reject."[10] One might worry whether action is meant to take the place of thought.

If Foucault occasionally straddles the tightrope of political philosophy, Heidegger obviously stumbled off it. In the 1930s, Heidegger enclosed himself within an authoritarian system of thought grounded in ontological reifications of a "folk" and its history. Heidegger's historicization of metaphysics led him to believe that a new philosophic epoch was about to be inaugurated. It implicitly called for a philosophical Fuehrer who could put an end to two millennia of ontological forgetting.[11] The temptation for Heidegger to identify himself as this intellectual messiah and to attach himself to an authoritarian social and political movement capable of sustaining cultural renewal proved irresistible. Whether Heidegger ever fully recovered his balance has been the topic of much discussion. Some argue that Heidegger's prerogative for political philosophizing was wholly undermined by his infatuation with folk destiny, salvational gods, and political authority.[12]

Already by 1938, in his *Beiträge zur Philosophie,* Heidegger would admit that an ontological focus on Dasein meant that a "folk can never be a goal or program." He warned here that a people must beware the danger of "becoming caught up in itself and idolizing what are only the conditions *[Bedingungen]* of its existence as its *Absolute*

[Unbedingten]."[13] Despite such veiled recantations, however, Heidegger could never bring himself to declare the folkish idol completely hollow. His celebration of the transcendent destiny of an organic folk is best seen as the last hurrah of metaphysical thought. Echoes of this cheer linger in Heidegger's work to the end. In a letter to Karl Jaspers written in 1950, Heidegger insists of his land and people that "despite death and tears, despite affliction and horror, despite privation and suffering, despite dislocation and banishment, what is happening in this state of *homelessness* is not nothing; *concealed therein is an Advent* whose distant beckoning we may just be able to divine in the faint stirring of the air."[14] Even after the war, then, Heidegger continues to portray himself as a latter-day John the Baptist—betrayed, ignored, and attacked by the powers that be and his chosen people, yet persistent in his prophecy of the Second Coming of Being.

I will not revisit Heidegger's and Foucault's stumblings off the tightrope of political philosophy at greater length here. My primary concern is neither to bury nor praise Heidegger and Foucault as political philosophers, nor even to get them "right" in a biographical or exigetical sense. Rather, I want to make productive use of their thought. The task at hand, therefore, is not to defend Heidegger's and Foucault's skeptical probity against their ideological lapses. The task is to outline the normative resources that remain available in the narratives that Heidegger and Foucault compose. These narratives allow skeptical probity to coexist, perhaps even to thrive, with sound moral judgment. When taken together and creatively combined, Heidegger and Foucault produce a viable (anti)foundation for prudential ethicopolitical life.

The Anemia of First Principles

One might take Heidegger's spurning of metaphysics and Foucault's rejection of theory and all forms of general discourse as confirmation that their work is incapable of fostering sound moral and political judgment. Certainly less skeptical theorists who embrace humanistic ideals have easier recourse to ethical principles that might guide judgment. Yet moral and political theories grounded in axioms and foundational principles—liberal or otherwise—may actually do less to cultivate moral and political judgment than more radical and unsettling narratives. Prudence or *phronesis,* Aristotle points out, is primarily cultivated through experience, not instruction. Such experience may be direct or mediated. The chief form of mediated experience for human beings is narrative. Stories allow us to learn our lessons by way of the experiences of others. "Any fool can learn from his own mistakes," the old adage goes. "It takes a wise man to learn from the mistakes of others." Narrative is ersatz experience. To the extent that we rely on axiomatic theories and forego narrative in our political philosophy, therefore, the cultivation of prudence may be undermined.

Alasdair MacIntyre observes that "I can only answer the question 'What am I to do?' if I can answer the prior question 'Of what story or stories do I find myself a part?' . . . Mythology, in its original sense, is at the heart of things."[15] The quandaries of moral life are typically negotiated by way of reflective mythologizing. We find out what we ought to do by determining what our roles are in a story that concretely embeds us in life. Principles, propositions, and logic have their place in political philosophy to be sure. The effectiveness of these instruments of argumentation, however, largely rests on the appeal of the narratives they supplement and support.

Ethical and political dispositions do not get settled, or even much realigned, with the lever of logic. These dispositions largely develop through the internalization of stories—through identification with characters, themes, and the struggles they depict. Individuals typically find their ethical and political moorings by grounding themselves in narratives whose plots and characters valorize certain relationships and actions while depreciating others. Axiomatic theories and first principles are supportive, not generative, of such moorings. Metaphor and mythology play a greater role than axioms and principled argument in the development of moral character and political community. Narratives serve as the banisters of ethico-political life.

Heidegger observes that human beings are defined by their "thrownness." That is to say, we are always already situated in narratives and these narratives largely define our individual and collective selves and lives. If metaphor and mythology lie at the heart of things, however, they do so not as stories handed down from the heavens and written in stone. Metaphors and mythologies change. Human beings are active story makers and interpretive story tellers. We are never completely without (pre)scripted roles, but neither are we without the relative autonomy to refashion our narrative resources. We can and do alter our characters and adjust plots. We are participants in narratives whose development and outcomes depend in large part on the way we adapt to and transform our roles within them.

I am arguing that practical, moral judgment is not primarily gained through the development and application of metaphysical principles. It is cultivated through our immersion in and transformation of the narratives that chiefly structure our lives. Both Heidegger and Foucault opposed metaphysical moorings. They spurned the axiomatic ethics and systematic politics generated by metaphysical thought. Heidegger developed a grand ontological narrative to replace metaphysics. Foucault produced multiple genealogical tales. Rather than generating a set of analytical statements to define the relationship between power and right, Heidegger and Foucault provide compelling narratives to inform our moral and political judgment and facilitate our prudent navigation of late modern life.

The Narrative Potential of Heideggerian Ontology

Heidegger was a Nazi, and a rather unrepentent one at that. Some suggest Heidegger's Nazism cannot be separated from his philosophy, that indeed the former follows from the latter. The argument, in short, is that Heidegger's political biography pretty well tells the whole story. This position has been rearticulated periodically since the end of the Second World War, each time creating something of an academic row.[16] To be sure, the story of Heidegger's life does not well illustrate an education in sound moral and political judgment, except perhaps as an example of a lesson left unlearned. Yet the story that Heidegger himself tells about human life, about human being in history, can do much to cultivate moral and political judgment. I assert this despite insightful critiques of Heidegger that accuse him of ignoring and eliding *phronesis* as a human potentiality.[17] My argument, then, is not that Heidegger's work explicitly celebrates prudence, but that his philosophical narrative facilitates its cultivation.

Martin Heidegger's writings are best described as timely meditations.[18] Heidegger's philosophy is timely in ways that underline its narrative potential. First, time itself was a central concern of Heidegger's magnum opus, *Being and Time,* and remained of primary importance in his later philosophy. Dasein, Heidegger writes, is the being which is itself its "there." The "Da" of Dasein is not simply a spatial designator, however, but a temporal designator as well. The "there" of human being is not only a worldly place—it is a historical time. As historical beings, humans live *in* time. Human beings are defined by what Heidegger calls finitude, which speaks both to their historical contingency and their mortality. Historicity, understood as a historical self-consciousness and a sense of temporality, is a central category of Heidegger's work.

Second, time is of importance to Heidegger not only because human beings live amidst beings *in* time. Given their philosophic potential, humans also have the opportunity and responsibility to disclose Being *as* time. They are shepherds of Being's timeliness. Ordinarily, time is conceived as the duration that marks the changing appearance of beings. Herein human beings think, speak, and act in the medium of time's passage. Heidegger, in his effort to address the age-old but enduring philosophical query, "What is the Being of being?" conceives time more fundamentally. The Being of being is not a *what* (as metaphysical accounts would have it). The Being of being is more a *how*. How, then, are beings? They are revealed as an upsurgence, as a coming into presence. The Being of beings is temporal. Being is a timely revealing, presencing or emerging into unconcealment.

Third, Heidegger's preoccupation with time figured in Heidegger's own encounter with world history. Heidegger wrote, "The question of how it stands with Being proves to be the question of how it stands with our Being-there in history, the question of whether we *stand* in history or merely stagger."[19] The degree of our openness to temporal Being-in-the-world determines whether we are *truly* living historically, that is, living our historicity with resoluteness. To live historically, Heidegger insists, entails reclaiming ontological questioning as our prerogative and fundamental responsibility.

Fourth, time is central to Heidegger's philosophy because he is concerned with the history of Being *(Seinsgeschichte)*. This history may be understood as the unfolding of human forgetfulness of Being *(Seinsvergessenheit)* over time.

Fifth, Heidegger's philosophy is best described as a timely meditation because it constitutes a progressively critical engagement with Nietzsche, the author of untimely meditations. Nietzsche's effort to be untimely culminates in his thought of the eternal recurrence. Turning the tables on Nietzsche, Heidegger observes a spirit of revenge in the effort to will the eternal recurrence. The attempt to overcome temporal horizons, to undo time's "It was" by way of an imposition of ultimate value on its endless repetition, is perhaps the most sublime resentment yet achieved. But it is resentment nonetheless. Heidegger effectively criticizes Nietzsche for being untimely. To live in the here and now is to let being be. Letting being be entails letting time be. For being is only in time. Fully participating in the timely disclosure of what is, then, allows the greatest celebration of life and being. Nietzsche's effort to *will* the eternal return signifies not the living of one's being in time, but the attempt conceptually to control life's temporal unfolding. Yet human being is thrown, hence it neither sets this unfolding in motion nor overcomes its contingency. To psychologically and philosophically (no less than socially and politically) flee the horizons of one's historical finitude, in other words, is to abandon the task of dwelling in time. By embracing the eternal recurrence, Nietzsche effected this abandonment.

Sixth, Heidegger's sustained confrontation with technology was grounded in his aversion to the war against time evidenced in technology's imperial demand for efficiency. The goal of technology is to achieve given ends—such as the production of energy, artifacts, knowledge, wealth, power, or pleasure—with a minimum expenditure of resources. Foremost among these resources is time itself. Modern technology assails time in its effort to speed through atomic, global, and cosmic space, and by accelerating daily routines and functions. This victory over time bears a price: humanity comes to relate to time chiefly as an obstacle and antagonist. Time becomes a recalcitrant force that demands harnessing. Heidegger defines human being as a dwelling in time, a disclosive being-in-the-word. Human being's "letting-become-present," Heidegger writes, "is nothing other than time itself."[20] Yet one cannot truly dwell *in* time if one orients oneself to it as a hostile force to be overcome or a fleeting externality to be captured and put to work. In fostering an antagonistic orientation to time, technology undermines our efforts to discover and inhabit a worldly home.

Finally, and in summation, Heidegger's philosophy is a timely meditation because Heidegger understood all genuine philosophy to be timely. To do philosophy, Heidegger maintains, is to think historically. Thinking remains firmly grounded in the historical present, in the story that tells us where we are and how we got there. To do philosophy, Heidegger observes, our efforts must be "at once recollective and focused on the present."[21] Indeed, any attempt to achieve an ahistorical thinking is in vain, Heidegger insists, an enterprise as futile as the attempt to jump over one's own shadow.[22] This is not to say that philosophy neglects "eternal questions." It remains fundamentally concerned with the enduring question of Being. But philosophic thought approaches this question by way of the historically mediated relation of human being to Being. It brings us toward "a historical sojourning," calling forth our historic way of being in the world.[23] To think philosophically is to re-collect oneself historically, to live one's historic *there* authentically. Heidegger's philosophy, in this sense, attempts to reconcile human being to its narrative essence. His critique of metaphysics was a resistance to those philosophic efforts that deny the narrative contingency, the temporality, of the human condition by way of an ahistorical, conceptual freezing of Being and human being.

Heidegger's philosophic narrative provides us with multiple converging storylines. To illustrate the narrative potential of his philosophy, I will focus on one subplot—Heidegger's portrayal of the ongoing human quest for conceptual and technological mastery. Effectively, Heidegger's ontological story of human being is the historical tale of a supporting character who seeks to be the protagonist. Human being is, most essentially for Heidegger, the witness of Being. Human being is uniquely gifted with, and uniquely made responsible for, the disclosure of Being. But to disclose Being is not to control Being. Most fundamentally, to be the voice of Being is to be a caretaker of the mystery of Being. Heidegger tells us the story of human being's increasing abandonment of the task of caretaking in its quest for mastery.

Beginning with the Greeks, Heidegger informs us, a unique effort was made to gain conceptual control of Being. Enter the representational thought of Plato, with its designation of the "what" of Being as a form or idea. In time, the attempted mastery of Being in thought finds a counterpart in the attempted mastery of Being in deed. Enter modern technology. Now, the age of the representational "world picture" has also become the age of *Gestell,* the wholesale enframing of the world as a standing reserve awaiting efficient exploitation.

At the denouement of Heidegger's story, we learn, our efforts to gain conceptual and technological control of Being produce a sort of amnesia. As we forget how to let Being be, we also forget how to let human being be. We come to instrumentalize ourselves; we become our own and each others' tools. In the pursuit of mastery, we forget our own identities and responsibilities as witnesses and caretakers and assume the role of technologue.

Having told this story, one might expect Heidegger to embrace an ethical perspective that admonishes us to reclaim our moral responsibilities to each other, as co-witnesses of Being. This does not happen. Indeed, Heidegger spurns ethical discourse. His chary relationship to ethics as a branch of philosophy follows from his critique of the representational nature of most philosophic thought. To the extent that traditional ethics concerns the positing of principles, it seeks conceptual mastery through moral categorization. It partakes of objectification and subjectification. "Through the characterization of something as 'a value,'" Heidegger writes, "what is so valued is robbed of its worth. That is to say, by the assessment of something as a value what is valued is admitted only as an object of man's estimation. But what a thing is in its Being is not exhausted by its being an object. . . . Every valuing, even where it values positively, is a subjectivizing. It does not let beings: be. Rather, valuing lets beings: be valid—solely as the objects of its doing."[24]

Heidegger does not suggest that we abandon our moral predispositions to engage in ontological questioning. But neither should we attempt to escape ontological investigation behind the supposed security and stability of ethical formulae. "Should we not safeguard and secure the existing [ethical] bonds, even if they hold human beings together ever so tenuously and merely for the present?" Heidegger asks. "Certainly," he responds, and goes on to add: "But does this need ever release thought from the task of thinking what still remains principally to be thought, as Being prior to all beings, is their guarantor and their truth?"[25] Morality is not to be abandoned. Before we can sketch out the principles by which we might best live with others, however, we must come to terms with who we are, as witnesses of the mystery of Being, and what our Being-in-the-world-with-others means. For this reason, Heidegger believed that "ethics as a mere doctrine and imperative is helpless unless man first comes to have a different fundamental relation to Being."[26] Establishing this fundamental relation is for Heidegger a type of ethics itself. Expanding the etymology of "ethics" *(ethos)* to indicate not solely a customary way of being with others but a characteristic way of being in the world, Heidegger considers his work an "original ethics."[27] His ontological narrative might then be construed as an ethics—if ethics addresses not simply the customs of the human collective, but the fundamental character of the human condition.

Heidegger understands politics as that activity that safeguards a place for humans to practice an original ethics. He writes that the *polis* should be primarily understood neither as a city *(Stadt)*, nor a state *(Staat)*, but first and foremost as a site or place *(Statt)*. The *polis* is the "site of the historical dwelling of human beings in the midst of beings."[28] Politics, he states, pertains to the ongoing founding and preserving of a public place or site, a realm characterized by the initiating powers of action and the preservative powers of speech. "Unconcealment occurs only when it is achieved by work," Heidegger writes, "the work of the word in poetry, the work of stone in temple and statue, the work of the word in thought, the work of the *polis* as the historical place in which all this is grounded and preserved."[29] The political realm is that haven that preserves thought, speech, and action by creating, securing, and maintaining the space(s) wherein these diverse modes of disclosure may occur. Preserving this public space, the *res publica*, is fundamentally a work not of principle but of prudence—practical wisdom that unites knowledge of the human condition with virtuous action.

To achieve increasing control of one's life and one's world, through conceptual representation and technological force, Heidegger warns, is to transform human life and the world into an extension of the human will. Eventually our lives and world become filled with instrumental power and activity and, simultaneously, drained of all meaning. That is because the stories of our lives become meaningful not because we control their outcome, but because we learn to act authentically in the midst of historical circumstances that we may shape, but ultimately do not create.

The discovery of meaning is, in large part, a receptive (and retrospective) rather than proactive endeavor. The meaning of our lives is discovered at least as much as it is made. With this in mind, Heidegger insists that we cannot "make" the world into our home. Indeed, the force of subjectivist willing often prevents us from finding a home in the world. Heidegger suggests that if we are to discover a home in the world, it will come not by endlessly extending our control over it, but by acknowledging our limits and limiting our grasp. This is Heidegger's understanding of caretaking.

Caretaking is an active endeavor. Yet in many instances, caretaking entails letting things be. In this sense it is an act of prudence, understood as the wise receptivity of one's limits. Heidegger provides a narrative about the death of prudence that ensues from humanity's hubristic, immoderate quest for mastery in all things. The demise of prudence is evident in modernist attempts to philosophize in a totalizing fashion. Heidegger criticizes metaphysics accordingly. The demise of prudence is also evident in those technological efforts to control human beings and nature so as to extort their resources most efficiently.

Heidegger comes up somewhat short in addressing human exploitation. He does, however, outline the dangers inherent in efforts to master nature. He insists that "Man is not the lord of beings. Man is the shepherd of Being" and writes that "Mortals dwell in that they save the earth."[30] He extrapolates the ontic ramifications of this identity: "To save really means to set something free into its own presencing. To save the earth is more than to exploit it or even wear it out. Saving the earth does not master the earth and does not subjugate it, which is merely one step from spoliation."[31] To achieve mastery over the earth, one must presume to comprehend it. According to Heidegger, nature is inexhaustibly mysterious. One of Heidegger's favorite Heraclitean fragments was "Nature loves to hide." However one reveals the natural world, something else remains hidden: relationships of interdependence are left undiscovered; evolutionary legacies unexplored; biological, aesthetic, or physical properties untouched. Once nature is enframed, in contrast, everything equally and inclusively becomes appropriated as standing reserve. Everything is made available for our calculation and assessment, becoming at once "overseeable, controllable, definable, connectable, and explicable."[32] Yet every such attempt to "penetrate" the earth with "calculating importunity," Heidegger insists, will become destructive and, ironically, reveal our inability to disclose the mystery of nature: "This destruction may herald itself under the appearance of mastery and of progress in the form of the technical-scientific objectification of nature, but this mastery nevertheless remains an impotence of will. The earth appears openly cleared as itself only when it is perceived and preserved as that which is by nature undisclosable, that which shrinks from every disclosure and constantly keeps itself closed up."[33] Only when we prudently preserve the earth by restraining our reach may we reclaim our identity as witnesses and caretakers. Heidegger's ontological narrative teaches us prudence by limning its historical decline and outlining the philosophical and practical costs of its absence.

The Narrative Potential of Foucauldian Genealogy

Foucault proposed an aesthetics of existence. He made this proposal in opposition to the late modern alternative: a science of life understood as a domain of knowable laws. An aesthetics of existence is not grounded in axioms or algorithms. It can only be sustained by good judgment. Foucault's aesthetic judgment is inherently moral and political in nature. Its cultivation is facilitated by the genealogical investigation of the struggles that define who we are and what we will become.

In submitting his own entry to the *Dictionnaire des philosophes* toward the end of his career, Foucault summarized his "general project" as a study of "the methods and techniques used in different institutional contexts to act upon the behavior of individuals taken separately or in a group, so as to shape, direct, modify their way of conducting themselves, to impose ends on their inaction or fit it into overall strategies. . . . These power relations characterize the manner in which men are 'governed' by one another. . . . It is a matter of analyzing . . . a historically singular mode of experience in which the subject is objectified for himself and for others through certain specific procedures of 'government.'"[34] Though accurate enough, Foucault's self-description does not address the aspect of his work that many readers find most original and unnerving. Foucault's fame (and infamy) largely stems from his claims concerning the peculiar nature of the "methods and techniques" of governing, that is, the nature of power in late modernity. Power creates the background conditions under which the world comes to be encountered and known. Its methods and techniques are omnipresent and largely anonymous. It is capable of the production of selves and souls, not simply their repression. For Foucault, as for Nietzsche, the individual is molded by power. Corrigible drives, inchoate instincts, and pliable capacities are shaped into something both sociopolitically docile and economically productive. The webs of power constitutive of life insidiously figure in the formation and transformation of our very identities. Though strategies of power create and maintain inequalities and hierarchies of domination, Foucault does not describe us as victimized flies caught in a despotic spider's webs. We are the spiders, and the webs that we co-create become our disciplinary homes.

Foucault describes modern societies as "demonic."[35] Modern societies are demonic in that the individuals composing them are disciplined to think, feel, and act in certain ways, within certain limits. Yet this soulcraft occurs unperceived by the individuals themselves. Subjects are created whose subjection to particular ways of thought and life prove so successful, so thorough, precisely because they have been internalized and accepted as an identity. Power is most effective when it is invisible, when it flows through rather than impacts one, and therefore cannot be resisted. Foucault uncovered this most fecund form of power. His uncanny knack was to make the invisible visible.

That is also the source of his troubles. Fighting invisible monsters is a never-ending task. Foucault is frequently castigated for burdening us with this task while supplying little if any guidance as to how we might carry it out. Critics charge Foucault with stripping us both of reasons to fight (because normalizing power is inescapable in any case) as well as reasons for establishing any limits to fighting (because it is a total war). We are encouraged to resist, but are supplied with no ethics of resistance. In the face of ubiquitous power, resistance becomes a way of life while taking on the same dimensions as the power it combats. One is apt to refuse rules of combat when such ethical standards remain suspect of being yet another ploy of normalizing power. Foucault, critics charge, advocates transgression for its own sake.

At times, Foucault comes pretty close to this position. He acknowledges that "[t]he idea of a morality as obedience to a code of rules is now disappearing, has already disappeared." But Foucault also supplies an alternative: "To this absence of a morality, one responds, or must respond, with a research which is that of an aesthetics of existence."[36] We are encouraged to engage in an aesthetically oriented resistance that is, in its largest sense, self-creative. We are admonished "to create ourselves as a work of art."[37] Self-creation becomes the only effective form of resistance against strategies of power that are themselves productive rather than merely prohibitive. Fire must be fought with fire. This is not a satisfactory response for many who worry that Foucauldian aesthetics amounts to a form of self-absorbed relativism, to "narcissism minus truth."[38] The question is whether Foucauldian individuals—focused as they are on creating themselves as works of art—would display the self-restraint and (minimal) other-directedness that could generate and maintain a just, stable, social order. In other words, how can a Foucauldian aesthetics be melded with a politics of prudence?

Statements about the end of morality notwithstanding, Foucault is not suggesting that we move beyond good and evil. It is a question not of dissolving ethics and escaping all norms, but of reinventing morality. He writes: "I do not think that a society can exist without power relations, if by that one means the strategies by which individuals try to direct and control the conduct of others. The problem, then, is not to try to dissolve them in the utopia of completely transparent communication but to acquire the rules of law, the management techniques, and also the morality, the *ethos*, the practice of the self, that will allow us to play these games of power with as little domination as possible."[39] Foucault wants to reconstitute our ethical relations such that they are governed less by codes of rules and more by an aesthetically oriented care of the self and others. This ethical and aesthetic reconstitution, he suggests, promises a reduction in disciplinary domination.

The problem with moral codes is that they are governed by distinct rationalities. Though claiming objectivity and neutrality, Foucault observes that these rationalities always remain in the service of power. Indeed, they are the chief weapon of power. That is because rationalities help disguise power. They make it less visible. For Foucault, invisible power is the most dangerous kind. The capacity of rationalities to cloak power in principles makes them efficient vehicles of domination. Ethical codes and the rationalities that support them, Foucault suggests, are the Trojan horses that surreptitiously gain entry to our souls . . . and eventually open their doors to forms of domination lying in wait. Foucault takes on the role of Virgil's Cassandra.

Like Nietzsche, Foucault assesses moral codes as "idols." They are approached hammer in hand. The hollowness of their rationalities must be sounded out. That is the task of genealogy. Foucault sees his work as an effort to investigate "forms of rationality: different foundations, different creations, different modifications in which rationalities engender one another, oppose and pursue one another. . . . What reason perceives as *its* necessity, or rather, what different forms of rationality offer as their necessary being, can perfectly well be shown to have a history; and the network of contingencies from which it emerged can be traced."[40] Foucault's genealogies provide narratives of how rationalities, the masks of power, develop. Uncovering their inauspicious origins and the contingencies of their development underlines their artificiality. By displaying the hollowness of rationalities, genealogy facilitates resistance to them. By telling the story of particular rationalities, Foucault makes us chary of their claims over us and apprehensive of the costs involved in adopting alternatives. Genealogy is a schooling in prudence.

Genealogy, we must be clear, is not metanarrative. History is not the product of grand narratives displaying teleological movement. Foucault's genealogical stories are tales of unique, diverse, contingent struggles. Nonetheless, these struggles become organized into coherent, that is to say more or less continuous, patterns of domination, subjectification, and government. With this in mind, one might say that Foucault breaks the metanarrative of reason into countless micronarratives of specific rationalities. These micronarratives illustrate how historically contingent artifices in the service of particular concentrations of power take on the color of ahistorical objectivity.

Foucault's narratives, in this sense, provide us with histories of the present. Because power is in the business of soulcraft, Foucault's narratives effectively provide histories of ourselves. He sets a mirror before us. Yet this mirror does not reflect our "true" selves. Quite the contrary. It reveals our many false selves, our masks. To speak more precisely, it reveals the masks of power, the seamy undersides of the rationalities that we have come to accept as constitutive of our true selves. "Practicing criticism is a matter of making facile gestures difficult," Foucault explains.[41] Foucault's genealogical narratives allow this disruption. They did so for Foucault himself no less than for his readers. He writes: "The way I do my books, I have always conceived them as direct experiences 'tearing me' from myself, to prevent me from always being the same."[42] By constantly changing the self, normalizing power is confronted with a target more difficult to hit. Self-transformation in this context is simply another name for resistance. "The target nowadays," Foucault explains, "is not to discover what we are, but to refuse what we are."[43] This refusal is inherent to the task of an aesthetic self-creation.

One creates oneself as a work of art as an act of intellectual critique and physical resistance to the powers that be, to who we are and what we have become. It is in this creative resistance that freedom is discovered. Foucault calls for resistance to the productive forces of power that manipulate and produce our identities. Freedom today, he maintains, is to be discovered in the ongoing struggle against the techniques of subjectification. Foucault insists that freedom is not something to be secured, like the individual rights and opportunities that

Isaiah Berlin described as negative liberty. Freedom is an activity to be engaged. "Liberty," Foucault insists, "is a *practice*." It must be "exercised."[44] With this in mind, Foucault preferred not to speak of an "essential freedom" to be safeguarded so much as an "agonism" inherent in all social and political relations.[45] With the self no longer given (as the gift of God or nature), freedom becomes manifest only through its "invention." Foucault argues that freedom of the creative self arises only in the social and political arenas wherein our identities become the spoils of battle. His genealogical efforts to destabilize and contest modern modes of subjectification are consequently aimed at giving "new impetus, as far and wide as possible, to the undefined work of freedom."[46]

Foucauldian freedom entails abjuring definitions of the self that prescribe its *telos*. Freedom is found in the construction of a protean self as it evolves by way of the dynamic clash of productive power and resistance. Primarily, this freedom is actualized *in* the struggle of self-creation. As a student of Nietzsche's tragic school of thought, Foucault celebrates this freedom in the seemingly futile and endless attempt to create a self that necessarily remains forever enmeshed in webs of power. Hence Foucault calls for a "hyper- and pessimistic activism."[47] He denies that the aesthetic self can gain complete sovereignty within the webs of contemporary power. Contingency is everywhere in evidence. Citing Nietzsche, Foucault acknowledges that the individual harbors "not an immortal soul but many mortal ones," and that these are "unable to be mastered by the powers of synthesis."[48] But, as with Nietzsche, the tragico-heroic effort is made nonetheless. Foucault encourages us to gain our freedom by moving beyond the "subjected sovereignties" of humanism, beyond "the subject as a pseudosovereign," to a self whose true sovereignty is marked by the absence of inhibitions in the effort to define—and continually redefine—its own identity.[49]

John Rajchman writes that "Foucault's freedom is not liberation, a process with an end. It is not liberty, a possession of each individual person. It is the motor and principle of his skepticism; the endless questioning of constituted experience."[50] That questioning, as we have come to see, is both an act of resistance and (self)creation. It remains chary of standards, yet eager for virtue. It might well be described as a form of prudence arising from lessons learned via genealogical stories of the production of selves as late-modern subjects.

Foucault's liberating questioning is seldom described in terms so tame as practical judgment. Yet the unflagging vigilance, strategic sense, creative resistance, and wariness of ideals espoused by Foucault is very much akin to prudence. Our problem today, Foucault states, "is not that everything is bad, but that everything is dangerous, which is not exactly the same as bad. If everything is dangerous, then we always have something to do. . . . I think that the ethico-political choice we have to make every day is to determine which is the main danger."[51] The ethical and political virtue of understanding and courageously confronting the dangers we face in our daily lives is the virtue prudence.

Importantly, Foucault's narratives cultivate prudence not only by exposing dangerous forms of power and their rational masks. His narratives set *themselves* up for contestation. They solicit prudential interpretation rather than naïve acceptance. As Foucault emphasizes, following Nietzsche, "interpretation is always incomplete. . . . There is nothing absolutely primary to interpret, for after all everything is already interpretation. . . . There is never, if you like, an *interpretandum* that is not already *interpretans,* so that it is as much a relationship of violence as of elucidation that is established in interpretation . . . it can only seize, and violently, an already present interpretation, which it must overthrow, upset, shatter with the blows of a hammer."[52] Foucauldian genealogy is narrative that helps us contest who we are and what we have become. At the same time, it offers itself up, as a partisan among partisans, for contestation. It asks us to take nothing for granted and solicits our suspicion of all claims to objectivity, including any that genealogy might be tempted to allow itself. Ironically, then, Foucauldian narrative might take some credit for the cultivation of the prudence displayed in the cautiousness of Foucault's critics.

An Eclectic Proposal

Foucault prompts us to scramble the matrices of power that condition and constrain us. His object is to proliferate the guerilla struggle against these disciplinary matrices so that we might create ourselves as works of art. Thus Foucault promotes a prudential politics chiefly defined by the aesthetic resistance of beleaguered individuals caught in the apparatuses of normalization. Offered no hope of escape from these apparatuses, yet encouraged not to submit, the individual engages in a deconstructive monkey-wrenching of the system that is at the same time an act of self-invention. Prudence is chiefly displayed in the careful selection of targets, the practical virtue displayed in one's "hyper-active" agonism, and by way of a chary relationship to standards, norms, and their respective rationalities.

The Foucauldian individual pursues freedom as the heroic, albeit tragic task of creative self-mastery in the face of ubiquitous webs of power. Despite Foucault's rejection of the goal of individual sovereignty, the artistic struggle he prescribes bears the appearance of a highly individualistic (if not narcissistic) endeavor. This willful transformation of the self into a work of art harbors subjectivist overtones. One might wield Heidegger against Foucault at this point. Heidegger's ontological insights may be marshaled into a critique of Foucault's ideal of self-invention and its accompanying subjectivist freedom. Heidegger celebrates freedom as a form of guardianship rather than a mastery of the world, the other, or the self.[53] Foucault's aesthete, Heidegger might argue, has simply internalized the technological imperative of production and control. Heidegger advocates, in contrast, the pursuit of freedom as a disclosive "letting-be."

Foucault's valorization of self-invention coupled with his notion of individualized battle against "pastoral power" makes his system of thought resistant to community entanglements. His concern with the panoptic administration of selves fosters wariness of sociopolitical interdependence.[54] That weakens the case for Foucauldian narrative as a schooling in prudence. As understood since ancient times, prudence is the virtue of adroitly navigating our sociopolitical interdependencies. Prudence is the skill of building in a way that preserves what Heidegger called the "with-world." With this in mind, prudence is far from a form of individualized self-invention. Reflecting on the ancient Greeks, Joseph Dunne writes that the *phronetic* individual "can never possess an idea of himself in the way that the craftsman possesses the form of his product; rather than his having any definite 'what' as blueprint for his actions or his life, he becomes and discovers 'who' he is through these actions. And the medium for this becoming through action is not one over which he is ever sovereign master; it is, rather, a network of other people who are also agents and with whom he is bound up in relationships of interdependency."[55] Heidegger's understanding of "being-with-others" and his rejection of the will to mastery provide a sound ontological foundation for the development and exercise of prudence. It may also provide an antidote to the lingering (aesthetic) subjectivism found in Foucault.

At the same time, Foucault's critical focus on domination provides a needed moral orientation, one that is largely absent in Heidegger. Despite Heidegger's assessment of his ontology as an "original ethics," one cannot but rue his lack of concern for the alleviation of oppressive social relationships. In turn, Foucault's micronarratives may provide a better soil for the cultivation of good judgment than Heidegger's grand ontological tale. *Phronesis* or practical wisdom has traditionally been understood as the product of experience. It is enhanced by an acute sense of history. When history is no longer studied for its insights into the (fickle) ways of human being, but becomes instead the recounting of a cosmic fate, it can no longer serve as a schooling in prudence. The problem is that Heidegger came very close to playing the Hegelian game—though he denied it—of identifying world history as a metaphysically ordained script. It is the comprehensiveness and self-enclosure of this historical overview, which Lyotard called "metanarrative," that eroded moral sensitivity.

In his Nietzsche lectures, Heidegger maintained that when viewed "with respect to the duration of the history of Being" ontological forgetfulness may be considered "more hazardous than the crass adventures of a merely brutal will to violence."[56] One cannot excuse the callousness of Heidegger's "merely" in the context of the Nazis' ruthless campaigns. And one suspects that the ontological vantage point from which Heidegger grandly oversees the "history of Being" blinds him to the needs and duties of the here and now. Like Oedipus's, Heidegger's blindness was not unrelated to his vast insight. Heidegger insists, in contrast to Plato, that there exists no temporally transcendent Idea that might gain worldly incarnation. Yet the metaphysical grounding that Plato found in the Forms, Heidegger discovered in the *Volk*.

In many respects, Heidegger set himself up as a Teutonic Moses leading his compatriots out of their enslavement to a Platonic pharaoh. Having ascended the philosophic Sinai to listen directly to Being, Heidegger delivered the redeeming ontological commandments to a forgetful *Volk* below. With the historical destiny of a *Volk* foremost in his mind, concern for mundane questions of morality and politics ebbed. Predictably, the *Volk* refused to listen to Heidegger. They were occupied with the worship of a craven image, the golden calf of technology. One suspects that Heidegger eventually accepted the prophet's fate of being ignored by his own people. As Gadamer reminds us, however, Heidegger's history of philosophy was "burdened with the violence of a thinker who was veritably driven by his own questions and a desire to rediscover himself everywhere."[57] This continual rediscovery lent a tremendous coherence and cogency to Heidegger's thought—at the cost of ethical and political sensibility.

Heidegger's affiliation with Nazism and his shunning of ethics ostensibly militates against my case for (Heideggerian) narrative as a schooling in prudence. Yet, as Hans Sluga ably demonstrates, many of Germany's deontological philosophers fared no better than Heidegger in resisting the allure of Nazism.[58] While only twelve out of about 180 philosophers holding appointments in German universities at the beginning of 1933 were members of the Nazi party, thirty more philosophers, like Heidegger, joined that year and another forty joined in subsequent years. By 1940, almost half of Germany's philosophers were party members. Many of the philosophers who aligned themselves with nationalism were neo-Kantians.

If commitment to deontological rationalism and rule-based ethics did not safeguard Germany's philosophers from fascism, we should not assume that Heidegger's rejection of humanistic perspectives and principles explains his moral and political shortfalls. Indeed, I would argue that Heideggerian narrative, despite its dangers, provides a more nourishing soil for the cultivation of moral and political judgment than a deontological rationalism. That is because Heideggerian narrative, like any story, is more open to interpretation than axiomatic argument. Following Foucault's recommendation, we may "elucidate" the narrative appeal of Heidegger's philosophy while doing "violence" to its metaphysically folkish atavism. Interpreting Heidegger, in other words, demands the exercise of prudence. Heidegger would concur. His lectures on Aristotle developed the theme that *phronesis* was nothing other than hermeneutical virtue itself.[59] Like Foucault's genealogical stories, Heidegger's ontological narratives solicit a prudential reading.

Hayden White writes, "There is no center to Foucault's discourse. It is all surface—and intended to be so. For even more consistently than Nietzsche, Foucault resists the impulse to seek an origin or transcendental subject that would confer any specific meaning on existence. Foucault's discourse is willfully superficial. And this is consistent with the larger purpose of a thinker who wishes to dissolve the distinction between surfaces and depths, to show that wherever this distinction arises it is evidence of the play of organized power and that this distinction is itself the most effective weapon power possesses for hiding its operations."[60] Heidegger, in sharp contrast, often writes as if there are no surfaces. It is all depth. Profound ontological forces are at work everywhere. As Heidegger digs ever deeper, the importance of historical detail and moral context slips through his fingers.

I am suggesting that we might fruitfully combine Foucauldian surface with Heideggerian depth, genealogical insight with ontological wisdom, aesthetic resistance with a disclosive letting-be. Mingling Heidegger + Foucault, we might learn to generate philosophically sustained, historically detailed narratives that are ethically and politically informed. These narratives could then serve readers as ersatz experience, providing fertile soil from which prudence might grow.

Notes

1. Michel Foucault, "Final Interview," *Raritan* 5 (1985): 8–9.

2. See Leslie Paul Thiele, "Reading Nietzsche and Foucault: A Hermeneutics of Suspicion?" *American Political Science Review* 85 (June 1991): 584–91.

3. Jürgen Habermas, "The Genealogical Writing of History: On Some Aporias in Foucault's Theory of Power," *Canadian Journal of Political and Social Theory* 10 (1986): 1–9, 7. See also Nancy Fraser, "Foucault on Modern Power: Empirical Insights and Normative Confusions," *Praxis International* 1 (1981): 272–87.

4. Michael Sandel writes: "Political philosophy seems often to reside at a distance from the world. Principles are one thing, politics another, and even our best efforts to 'live up' to our ideals typically founder on the gap between theory and practice. But if political philosophy is unrealizable in one sense, it is unavoidable in another. This is the sense in which philosophy inhabits the world from the start; our practices and institutions are embodiments of theory. To engage in a political practice is already to stand in relation to theory. For all our uncertainties about ultimate questions of political philosophy—of justice and value and the nature of the good life—the one thing we know is that we live *some* answer all the time." Michael Sandel, "The Procedural Republic and the Unencumbered Self," in *Communitarianism and Individualism*, ed. Shlomo Avineri and Avner de-Shalit (Oxford: Oxford University Press, 1992), 12.

5. Martin Heidegger, *On the Way to Language*, trans. Peter Hertz (New York: Harper and Row, 1971), 72; see also Martin Heidegger, *The Question Concerning Technology and Other Essays*, trans. Wiiliam Lovitt (New York: Harper and Row, 1977), 180; Martin Heidegger, *What Is Called Thinking*, trans. J. Glenn Gray (New York: Harper and Row, 1968), 4.

6. Michel Foucault, *Foucault Live: Interviews, 1966–84*, trans. John Johnston (New York: Semiotext(e), 1989), 79.

7. Michel Foucault, quoted in William Connolly, "The Irony of Interpretation," in *The Politics of Irony*, ed. Daniel W. Conway and John E. Seery (New York: St. Martin's Press, 1992), 144.

8. Scott is describing both Nietzsche and Foucault. Charles E. Scott, *The Question of Ethics: Nietzsche, Foucault, Heidegger* (Bloomington: Indiana University Press), 96.

9. Martin Heidegger, *Hegel's Concept of Experience* (San Francisco: Harper and Row, 1970), 65–66, 73, 110. The Greek Skeptics, as Martha Nussbaum demonstrates, were not all that skeptical about the worthiness of their own teaching or the value of *ataraxia,* or freedom from disturbance, that produced happiness or *eudaimonia.* In these cases, as in situations needful of action, the skeptic would justify his commitments by suggesting that they were based solely on "natural inclination." Yet these inclinations should not be exempted from interrogation, as they remain, in important ways, sociocultural constructs. See Martha C. Nussbaum, *The Therapy of Desire: Theory and Practice in Hellenistic Ethics* (Princeton: Princeton University Press, 1994).

10. Michel Foucault, *Language, Counter-Memory, Practice,* trans. Donald Bouchard and Sherry Simon (Ithaca: Cornell University Press, 1977), 230–31.

11. Not known for self-criticism or retractions, Heidegger eventually acknowledged that there was never a pristine and transparent relation to Being at the Greek beginnings of Western thought. By 1954, he would admit that "that which really gives us food for thought did not turn away from man at some time or other which can be fixed in history—no, what really must be thought keeps itself turned away from man since the beginning" (Heidegger, *What Is Called Thinking?* 7). In his 1962 lecture on "Time and Being," Heidegger would be more specific: neither Homer, other Greek poets, nor everyday Greek speakers used *aletheia* in the sense of unconcealment but also largely understood it as correctness of representation, as *orthotes.* Heidegger thus admits that his earlier assertion about the "essential transformation" of the historical understanding of truth from unconcealment to correctness is "untenable." Martin Heidegger, *On Time and Being,* trans. J. Stambaugh (New York: Harper and Row, 1972), 70.

12. Leo Strauss wrote, "There is no room for political philosophy in Heidegger's work, and this may well be due to the fact that the room in question is occupied by gods or the gods." Leo Strauss, *Studies in Platonic Philosophy* (Chicago: University of Chicago Press, 1983), 30.

13. Martin Heidegger, *Gesamtausgabe* (Frankfurt am Main: Vittorio Klostermann, 1976–89), 65:319, 398.

14. Hugo Ott, *Martin Heidegger: A Political Life,* trans. Allan Blunden (New York: Basic Books, 1993), 24.

15. Alasdair MacIntyre, *After Virtue: A Study in Moral Theory* (Notre Dame: University of Notre Dame Press, 1981), 201. See also Alasdair MacIntyre, *A Short History of Ethics* (New York: Macmillan, 1966), 187.

16. Emil Kettering identifies seven "phases" of the controversy from 1946 to the late 1980s (Guenther Neske and Emil Kettering, *Martin Heidegger and National Socialism: Questions and Answers,* trans. Lisa Harries [New York: Paragon House, 1990], 127–32). Richard Wolin reasserts this position recently, maintaining that "Heidegger's Nazi experience stood in an 'essential' relation to his philosophical project as a whole," and that his "involvement with National Socialism. . . was *rooted in the innermost tendencies of his thought*" (Richard Wolin, *The Politics of Being: The Political Thought of Martin Heidegger* [New York: Columbia University Press, 1990], 8, 66).

17. Central to Heidegger's writing on the technological nature of modern times is his discussion of Aristotle's notion of truth as *aletheia.* In the *Nichomachean Ethics,* Aristotle observes a number of ways in which *aletheia* may present itself to human being. Key to this discussion is Aristotle's treatment of the human capacity of practical wisdom or *phronesis.* For Aristotle, *phronesis* is the intellectual virtue that pertains to *praxis,* just as *techne* is the intellectual virtue that pertains to *poiesis.* This practical capacity is ignored and concealed by Heidegger, who expounds Aristotle as if *techne* and *poiesis* were the only objects of concern, with *poiesis* as the only recourse to those confronted with modern technology. Richard Bernstein believes that Heidegger elides

phronesis and praxis because he disregards the fact of human plurality, and it is *phronesis,* not *sophia* (theoretical wisdom), that acknowledges the ambiguity and contextual idiosyncracies of the human condition. See Richard Bernstein, *The New Constellation: The Ethical-Political Horizons of Modernity/Postmodernity* (Cambridge: MIT Press, 1991).

18. This portion of the chapter reconfigures and expands upon material found in Leslie Paul Thiele, *Timely Meditations: Martin Heidegger and Postmodern Politics* (Princeton University Press, 1995); Leslie Paul Thiele, "Postmodernity and the Routinization of Novelty: Heidegger on Boredom and Technology," *Polity* 29 (summer 1997): 489–517; and Leslie Paul Thiele, "Heidegger, History, and Hermeneutics," *Journal of Modern History* 69 (September 1997): 534–56.

19. Martin Heidegger, *An Introduction to Metaphysics,* trans. Ralph Manheim (New Haven: Yale University Press, 1987), 202.

20. Martin Heidegger, *History of the Concept of Time: Prolegomena,* trans. Theodore Kisiel (Bloomington: Indiana University Press, 1985), 213–14.

21. Martin Heidegger, *The Metaphysical Foundations of Logic,* trans. Michael Heim (Bloomington: Indiana University Press, 1984), 9.

22. Heidegger, *Way to Language,* 39; Heidegger, *Introduction to Metaphysics,* 199; Martin Heidegger *Schelling's Treatise on the Essence of Human Freedom,* trans. J. Stambaugh (Athens: Ohio University Press, 1985), 11.

23. Heidegger, *Question Concerning Technology,* 180–81.

24. Martin Heidegger, *Basic Writings* (New York: Harper and Row, 1977), 228.

25. Ibid., 232.

26. Heidegger, *What Is Called Thinking?* 89.

27. Heidegger, *Basic Writings,* 234–35.

28. Heidegger, *Gesamtausgabe,* 53:100–1.

29. Heidegger, *Introduction to Metaphysics,* 191.

30. Heidegger, *Basic Writings,* 221.

31. Martin Heidegger, *Poetry, Language and Thought,* trans. Albert Hofstadter (New York: Harper and Row, 1971), 150.

32. Martin Heidegger, "Heidegger's Letter to the Boss' Daughter," *Telos* 77 (fall 1988), 126.

33. Heidegger, *Poetry, Language and Thought,* 47.

34. Michel Foucault, *Aesthetics, Method, and Epistemology,* vol. 2, ed. James Faubion, trans. Robert Hurley et al. (New York: The New Press, 1998), 463.

35. Michel Foucault, *Politics, Philosophy, Culture: Interviews and Other Writings, 1977–1984,* ed. Lawrence Kritzman (New York: Routledge, 1988), 52.

36. Foucault, *Foucault Live,* 311.

37. Michel Foucault, "On the Genealogy of Ethics: An Overview of Work in Progress," in *Michel Foucault: Beyond Structuralism and Hermeneutics,* ed. Hubert Dreyfus and Paul Rabinow, 2d ed. (Chicago: University of Chicago Press, 1983), 237.

38. Ronald Beiner, *Philosophy in a Time of Lost Spirit: Essays on Contemporary Theory* (Toronto: University of Toronto Press, 1997), 78.

39. Michel Foucault, *Ethics,* vol. 1, ed. James Faubion, trans. Robert Hurley et al. (New York: The New Press, 1998), 298.

40. Foucault, *Politics, Philosophy, Culture,* 28–29, 37. See also Michel Foucault, *Power/Knowledge: Selected Interviews and Other Writings, 1972–1977* (New York: Pantheon Books, 1980), 164.

41. Foucault, *Politics, Philosophy, Culture,* 155.

42. Quoted in John S. Ransom, *Foucault's Discipline: The Politics of Subjectivity* (Durham: Duke University Press, 1997), 55.

43. Michel Foucault, "The Subject and Power," in Dreyfus and Rabinow, *Beyond Structuralism and Hermeneutics,* 216.

44. Michel Foucault, *The Foucault Reader,* ed. Paul Rabinow (New York: Pantheon, 1984), 245.

45. Foucault, "The Subject and Power," 222.

46. Foucault, *Politics, Philosophy, Culture,* 46.

47. Foucault, "On the Genealogy of Ethics," 232.

48. Foucault, *Politics, Philosophy, Culture,* 94.

49. Foucault, *Language, Counter-Memory, Practice,* 221–22.

50. John Rajchman, *Michel Foucault: The Freedom of Philosophy* (New York: Columbia University Press, 1985), 7.

51. Foucault, "On the Genealogy of Ethics," 232.

52. Michel Foucault, "Nietzsche, Freud, Marx," *Critical Texts* 3 (1986): 3–5.

53. See Leslie Paul Thiele, "Heidegger on Freedom: Political Not Metaphysical." *American Political Science Review* 88 (June 1994): 278–91.

54. See Michel Foucault, "Governmentality," in *Ideology and Consciousness* 6 (1979): 5–21; Michel Foucault, "Omnes et Singulatum: Towards a Critique of 'Political Reason,'" in *The Tanner Lectures on Human Values,* vol. 2, ed. Sterling McMurrin (Salt Lake City: University of Utah Press), 1981.

55. Joseph Dunne, *Back to the Rough Ground: "Phronesis" and "Techne" in Modern Philosophy and in Aristotle* (Notre Dame: University of Notre Dame Press, 1993), 244, 263.

56. Martin Heidegger, *Nietzsche,* vol. 4, *Nihilism,* trans. Frank Capuzzi and David Krell (New York: Harper and Row, 1982), 247.

57. Hans-Georg Gadamer, *Heidegger's Ways,* trans. John Stanley (Albany: State University of New York Press, 1994), 165.

58. Hans Sluga, *Heidegger's Crisis: Philosophy and Politics in Nazi Germany* (Cambridge: Harvard University Press, 1993).

59. Gadamer, *Heidegger's Ways,* 141.

60. Hayden White, *The Content of the Form: Narrative Discourse and Historical Representation* (Baltimore: The Johns Hopkins University Press, 1987), 105.

Heidegger, Foucault, and the "Empire of the Gaze": Thinking the Territorialization of Knowledge

William V. Spanos

Victor Farías's careless identification of Heidegger's thought with Nazism in *Heidegger et le nazisme* (1987) has not only been enthusiastically endorsed by European and American humanist scholars who adhere to the philosophical tradition that Heidegger's discourse exists in part to interrogate. Its scandalization of the question has compelled many of those radical thinkers on the Left whose thought Heidegger had catalyzed to distance themselves from his work or to "admit" that its overdetermination of *die Seinsfrage* (the question of being) rendered it indifferent to history and politics, or even complicit with political totalitarianism. As a consequence of this multiply situated initiative to delegitimize Heidegger's ontological approach to the question of modernity, "Heidegger" and "Heideggerianism," which had been foundational in the discourse and practice of emancipation at least since the end of World War II, has been more or less marginalized by the Left in favor of more historical and sociopolitical perspectives, more specifically, by a number of discourses—new historicism, cultural studies, feminism, neo-Marxism, postcolonialism—that by and large derive their problematic from a certain (disciplinary) reading of Michel Foucault. To risk an oversimplification for the sake of focalizing the question this essay addresses, it might be said synecdochically that, increasingly since the publication of Farías's book, "Heidegger" and

"Foucault" have come to be represented by the Left as incommensurably opposed to one another, indeed, as a binary opposition in which the latter has been privileged over the former.

This binarist representation is not simply a distortion of the relationship between Heidegger's and Foucault's thought; more important, it is politically disabling. This becomes especially evident when one reconstellates Heidegger and Foucault into a post–cold war context. This is the era that the deputies of the "triumphant" liberal capitalist culture, utterly indifferent to Heidegger's proleptic announcement of the fulfillment of the (techno)logical economy of modernity in the terrible banality of the "age of the world picture," have euphorically represented as "the end of history," that is, as the fulfillment of the (onto)logical economy of the Western logos.[1] Against this tacit hierarchical binary, I want to argue that Heidegger's ontological and Foucault's sociopolitical orientation toward post-Enlightenment modernity "belong together," not in a dialogic harmony, but in strife, that their destructive and genealogical discourses are most productively understood if they are read in terms of Heidegger's *Auseinandersetzung*: as *polemos* that *always already* opens out (dis-closes what is *latent* but in some degree or other invisible to each's discourse) rather than closes down by way of a decisive victory of one over the other.[2]

To put it provisionally, they "belong together," on the one hand, because both their discourses have their point of departure in the recognition that the identity of the West is grounded in the complicity of knowledge with power. I mean, more specifically, that they are in some degree or other attuned to the way the West, since the Roman colonization (technologization) of Greek thought, but especially in the post-Enlightenment period, 1) has privileged vision in knowledge production; 2) has reified—or, more precisely, territorialized—differential and relational living processes; 3) has naturalized a socially constituted hierarchical binary logic (Being/nothing or time; Identity/difference; the One/the many; Truth/Falsehood) *and* its corollary metaphorics (Light/dark or shadow); Center/periphery, Clearing/wilderness, Culture/savagery, the Improved/the unimproved, and so on; and 4) has concealed the complicity of this relay of knowledge-producing assumptions with power over alterity in all its manifestations: has rendered, that is, its disciplinary and/or imperial essence invisible. They are "in strife," on the other hand, because their discourses remain vestigially disciplinary. Heidegger's overdetermination of *die Seinsfrage* (and his consequent minimization of the historically specific manifestations of the ontotheological tradition) in his confrontation with modernity blinds him in some disabling degree to the sociopolitical imperatives latent in his de-structive thinking. Foucault's overdetermination of the question of sociopolitical power (and his consequent minimization, by way of emphasizing the uniqueness of the Enlightenment episteme, of the continuity of the Western tradition) blinds him, in turn, in some disabling degree, to the ontological imperatives latent in his critical genealogical thinking.

To put it alternatively, "Heidegger" and "Foucault" belong together because they both, if only in a resonantly *symptomatic* way, reject the West's seductively disarming disciplinary orientation toward knowledge production (and the base/superstructure model informing it) in favor of a thinking that perceives the being into which they inquire as relational: as a lateral relay or continuum of "sites"—from being and the subject as such all the way across to domestic and global sociopolitics—that, however unevenly developed in any historically specific moment, are indissolubly related. They are in strife because each fails to adequately adhere to their antidisciplinary commitment to relationality and thus perceive and to think the adjacent sites disclosed by their respective overdeterminations. Tearing Heidegger's and Foucault's discourses out of the contexts in which they have hitherto been imbedded, especially since Farías's book, and reconstellating them into each other's orbit will disclose this paradoxical relationship. It will also disclose the positive possibilities for a more adequate critique of the present, post–cold war occasion: what I have elsewhere referred to as the fulfillment of the logical economy of the Occident in the *Pax Metaphysica,* which is simultaneously the *Pax Americana.*[3]

Heidegger's Critique of Ontological and Epistemological Imperialism

Reconstellated into Foucault's discursive orbit, Heidegger's texts undergo an estrangement that enables us to look elsewhere for evidence concerning the relationship between his thought and his politics than to those sedimented and deeply worn places habitually prescribed not only by traditional Heideggerians and their humanist critics, but by neo-Heideggerians as well. Indeed, the positive possibilities of Heidegger's destructive hermeneutics are evident, however minimally thought in terms of their historical specificity, at several prominent, yet largely overlooked, sites in Heidegger's seamless texts, especially those written after his realization in 1934 that the Nazi project to which he had committed his intellectual energies in the period of the Rectorship was itself "caught up in the consummation of nihilism."[4] These circulate above all around Heidegger's curiously neglected but insistently reiterated genealogical argument that the identity of Europe, *both* philosophical *and* political, has its origins not in ancient Greek culture, as it has been massively claimed since the Enlightenment, but in the Roman colonization of Greek thinking.

Thus, for example, in "Letter on Humanism," written after the war in 1947, Heidegger extends his ontological/epistemological genealogy of the "truth" of modernity in *Being and Time*—the truth of "presuppositionless" or disinterested inquiry—to disclose its affiliation to a coercive cultural politics. He shows that it was the epochal Roman translation of the Greek *a-letheia* to *veritas* that gave birth to the general concept of truth that has determined knowledge production (including that of institutions of learning) in the onto-theological tradition at large, especially—and contrary to modern apologists who trace its origins to Greek thought—in post-Enlightenment modernity. In so doing, as I will show, Heidegger implicates the discourse of modern humanism and the sociopolitical practices of democratic/humanist states with Rome's imperial project.

According to Heidegger's genealogy of humanist (anthropo-logical) truth in essays such as "The Essence of Truth" and "The Origin of the Work of Art," which follow immediately from the existential analytic of *Being and Time,* the decisive event in the historical process of the Occident's self-representation occurred when the Romans translated the Greek understanding of truth as *a-letheia* (unconcealment) to *veritas (adaequatio intellectus et rei),* which, whether understood as "the correspondence of the matter to knowledge" or "the correspondence of knowledge to the matter" has "continually in view a conforming to . . . and hence think[s] truth as *correctness (Richtigkeit).*"[5] The epochal turning point occurred, that is, when the Romans began to think temporal being, which the Greeks thought in-the-midst, from a transcendental perspective: when, that is, they technologized the originative thinking of the Greeks. "Beneath the seemingly literal and thus faithful translation," Heidegger reiterates, "there is concealed . . . a *trans*lation of Greek experience into a different way of thinking."

Roman thought emphatically and insistently "*takes over the Greek words without a corresponding, equally original experience of what they say, without the Greek word.* The rootlessness of Western thought begins with this translation."[6] Henceforth, and increasingly, "the ontology which . . . has thus arisen has deteriorated to a tradition in which it gets reduced to something self-evident—merely material for reworking, as it was for Hegel." Greek ontology thus uprooted becomes "a fixed body of doctrine,"[7] a "free-floating"—and, as Heidegger's insistent emphasis on deterioration suggests, banalized—discourse, that, remote from the historicity of being-in-the-world, nevertheless *determines* history from that remoteness.[8]

Truth as *veritas,* in other words, involves the transformation of the un-centered—originative and errant[9]—thinking of the Greeks into a secondary and derivative—and calculative—mode of inquiry, in which the *ratio,* the principle that identity is the condition for the possibility of difference, is determinative. It is a logocentric technology that begins inquiry into the differential/relational phenomena (objects and events) disseminated by a temporality "grounded" in Nothing *(das Nichts)* from the *end.* To invoke the visual metaphorics underlying Heidegger's differentiation between *a-letheia* and *veritas*—the metaphorical relay that, as I will suggest, brings his interrogation of humanist modernity into convergence with Foucault's various archaeologies of the "gaze"—inquiry understood as the adequation of mind and thing proceeds from *after* or *above (meta-ta-physica),* i.e., retrospectively: from a teleological or fixed transcendental vantage point. In thus privileging the invisible surveying eye, this all-encompassing, i.e., global, mode of knowledge production has as its ultimate purpose the coercion of difference into the circumference of the Self-Identical Circle. The center spatializes/reifies time in order to "comprehend" the elusive flow of the differences it disseminates: not simply to "know" them, but as the Latin etymology suggests, "to take hold" *(prehendere)* or "to manage" *(manus),* i.e., to dominate, pacify, and utilize their force. The comportment toward phenomena is thus that of the *commanding eye,* or, to invoke Foucault's sociopolitical vocabulary, the panoptic gaze. It is a visual comportment that represents the force of difference as that which Truth is not—as *false (falsum)*—and thus as a threat to Truth that must be domesticated or pacified at all costs: willfully reduced to the Same in the name of this justice. To anticipate a metaphorics that will become prominent—and literal—in Heidegger's later, more politically, if not historically, conscious, account of the Roman origins of European modernity (in all the manifestations of its being), the meta-physical gaze determining knowledge production in modernity flattens out the differential dynamics of the being into which one inquires into a territory: a supervised space to be conquered, mapped, classified, and colonized. It is, in other words, a "disciplinary," or more inclusively, an "imperial" gaze.

From this genealogy of the "Truth" of humanist modernity, which discloses its origins in the Roman translation of the Greek *a-letheia* to *veritas,* the hermeneutic circle (repetition) to the *circulus vitiosus* (Recollection), and serves to pacify the force of that "other" that is "outside" the boundary limits of the centered circle, Heidegger proceeds in "Letter on Humanism" to implicate this Romanized concept of "Truth" (and its imperialist binarist logic) explicitly with modern cultural production—specifically *paedeia*—and implicitly with the modern Western state:

> *Humanitas,* explicitly so called, was first considered and striven for in the age of the Roman Republic. *Homo humanus* was opposed to *homo barbarus.* Homo humanus here means the Romans, who exalted and honored Roman *virtus* through the "embodiment" of the *paideia* [education] taken over from the Greeks. These were the Greeks of the Hellenistic age, whose culture was acquired in the schools of philosophy. It was concerned with *eruditio et institutio in bonas artes* [scholarship and training in good conduct]. *Paideia* thus understood was translated as *humanitas.* The genuine *romanitas* of *homo romanus* consisted in such *humanitas.* We encounter the first humanism in Rome: it therefore remains [to this day] in essence a specifically Roman phenomenon.[10]

In this very decisive but largely overlooked passage, Heidegger ostensibly restricts the genealogy of modernity to the indissoluble complicity between humanist ontology and humanist pedagogy: the logocentrism (and its will to power) informing Roman *veritas* also informs the Roman *paedeia.* Truth or knowledge production in the anthropological tradition are, however unevenly developed, coextensive. But if this essay is read in the historically specific context in which it was written—the catastrophe of Europe precipitated by the Third Reich—a further extension in the relay of power informing the discourse and practice of humanist modernity announces itself, one that implicates truth and knowledge production with the disciplinary politics of imperialism. Clearly, what Heidegger is saying here is not simply that the "disinterested truth" and the "liberal" cultural apparatuses of the post-Enlightenment tradition (humanism) have their origins in a Roman pedagogical technology designed to produce "Romans" *(homo Romanus)*, a "manly" citizenry, which, as the *"embodiment"* of a *paedeia* that "exalted and honored Roman *virtus*" (manly/powerful/good, as the etymological history of this word makes clear) would constitute a disciplined—or, in Foucault's terms, "useful and docile"—collective of individuals. As the resonant binary opposition between *homo humanus,* which "here means the Romans," and *homo barbarus* makes evident, the ultimate purpose of the logocentric Roman *veritas* and its *paedeia* was the production of a disciplined, efficient, and dependable army of citizens under the aegis of a metropolitan state committed to the achievement of the hegemonic empire.

To put this genealogy in terms of the metaphorics of the centered circle privileged by the humanist tradition, the self-present subject as interpellated citizen/soldier produced by the discourse of *veritas* and its *paedeia* became the structural model of the *Civitas.* Just as the self-identical humanist *anthropologos* justifies the territorialization of knowledge and the domestication by "cultivation" of the differential "provincial" (ultimately from *pro-vincere*: "before being conquered") energies of immature and deviant youth, so the self-present "Metropolis" justifies the colonization of the barbarian energies of the provincial ("lowly") peoples, who, as "Other," "threaten" to turn its "civilized" space back into a wilderness. It is no accident that the English words "culture" and "cultivate" privileged by this humanist tradition, especially since the Enlightenment, are cognates of "colonize," which derives from the Latin *colere* ("to cultivate," "plant"), *colonus* ("tiller," "cultivator," "planter," "settler"), or, more tellingly, *agricola* ("cultivator of the *agr[i]os* or wild earth"), and that these derive their essential ideological meaning from their binary opposites: *silva* ("forest"; i.e., "uncultivated wilderness") and *silvestris* ("savage," literally, "of the forest").[11]

Heidegger's genealogy of modern humanism, in sum, discloses that the ideological reduction and codification by the Romans of the "errancy" and "prodigality" of originative (aletheiological) Greek thinking—their *circumscription, cultivation,* and *colonization* of the truth as always already *a-letheic*—gave rise not simply to its disciplinary educational project (the *Studia Humanitatis*), but also legitimized the Romans' imperial will to power over the peripheral and lowly—provincial—"barbarians." To put this alternatively, the Roman translation of Greek thinking enabled in a fundamental way the Roman "*imperium sine fine*" (as Virgil puts it in the *Aeneid*), which goes by the duplicitous name of the *Pax Romana*.

It is, according to Heidegger's genealogy, this indissoluble relay of repressions at the sites of the subject, knowledge and cultural production, the earth, and the City, a relay enabled by the *idealization* of meta-physical thinking in the image of the circle, the center of which is both inside and outside (above), that constitutes the origins of the discourse and practice of the modern West.[12] The circle and the affiliated white metaphors constellated around its center—the polarities of Light/darkness, High/low, Prelapsarian/fallen, True/false, Beauty/ugliness, Perfection/crudity, Normality/deviance, Plantation/wilderness, Direction/errancy, Citizen/savage, Inhabitant/nomad, and so on—are *polyvalent* in their material applications. To put Heidegger's *Destruktion* of the discourse, cultural institutions, and sociopolitical practices of humanist modernity in terms of the legacy, not of "classical" Greece, but of imperial Rome, is to indicate how near, however more generalized, it is not only to Michel Foucault's genealogy of the modern disciplinary society, but also to the imperial society that Foucault did not quite think, but made possible for Edward Said and the host of postcolonial critics Said has influenced. I mean, specifically, the "panoptic" society eventually precipitated by an "Enlightenment" that, according to a certain constant in Foucault's genealogical discourse, deliberately appropriated the Roman model (specifically, the structure of the military camp) to articulate its disciplinary epistemology, pedagogy, and cultural agenda, as well as its domestic and international politics.

In my interpretation of the historically resonant passage from "Letter on Humanism" quoted above, I have, admittedly, drawn a "political" thematic from Heidegger's philosophical discourse that, in suggesting its affiliation with a fundamental political motif in Foucault, is no doubt in excess of what he actually "says" about the Roman provenance of modern humanism and what he implies about the "disciplinary"/"imperial" character of the post–World War II historical conjuncture his text addresses. It may be objected, therefore, that this interpretation constitutes an apologetic reading. That the political content I have thematized is justified by Heidegger's discourse at this historically specific moment, indeed, with the exception of the period of the Rectorship, by his discourse at large, is further borne witness to by the seminar on the Parmenides fragments he gave in 1942–43, significantly after his resignation as Rector of Freiburg University, but considerably before his "Letter on Humanism."

This is not the occasion for a full analysis of what surely ought to be (but isn't) one of the central texts in the debate over the question of the relationship between Heidegger's philosophical discourse and Nazi politics. Keeping in mind what I have said above about Heidegger's identification of *homo Romanus* with *homo humanus,* it will suffice for my general purpose to comment on a crucial passage from the *Parmenides* that traces the origins of the "imperial" politics of Western modernity—and, as the "we" suggests, of Nazi Germany?—back to the Roman "translation" of the Greek *aletheia* as *veritas,* or, more precisely, of the *pseudos,* the counterterm of *aletheia,* as *falsum,* the counterterm of *veritas.* For this synecdochical passage not only implicates all three sites of the indissoluble relay I have thematized: the discourse of *veritas* (the true versus the false), the *paedeia* understood as *eruditio et institutio in bonas artes* (the disciplinary pedagogy devoted to scholarship and training in good conduct), and the *imperium sine fine* (the global imperial project). It also brings into visible play the hidden binarist visual metaphorics encoded in them—the panoptic gaze, light, spatialized time, heights, directionality, and so on—that are privileged over the appetitive senses and the metaphorics to which they have given rise—darkness, temporality, lowness, fallenness, errancy—and the indissolubly related figure of the centered circle that is privileged over the periphery. In so doing, this passage constitutes a remarkable, if highly generalized prefiguration of Foucault's genealogy of the relationship between truth and power in modernity, specifically—and most suggestively—his exposure of the "repressive hypothesis," which informs the "liberal" discursive practices of the post-Enlightenment and enables the disciplinary society.

Heidegger's analysis of the Roman provenance of and the indissoluble relationship between the modern Western understanding of truth, knowledge, and imperial power in the *Parmenides* has its point of departure in the Roman concept of truth, which was predicated on a doctrinaire metaphysical orientation toward being. This, as we have seen, is the reduced truth—*veritas*—that the Romans, in the name of certainty, constructed and naturalized by splitting and hierarchizing the earlier, more originative—and erratic—Greek understanding of truth *(a-letheia),* in which its negative (*pseudos*: "dissembling") was perceived, not, like the Roman negative of *veritas, falsum,* as an antithetical negative, but as *belonging* "positively" with the "positive": "The essence of negativity [for the Greeks] is nothing negative, but neither is it only something 'positive.' The distinction between the positive and the negative does not suffice to grasp what is essential, to which the non-essence belongs. The essence of the false is not something 'false.'"[13] Whereas in the earlier texts I have cited it is the "truth" of metaphysics that Heidegger destructures, in the *Parmenides* it is the "false" (Latin, *falsum*), the counterterm of "truth" understood as the correspondence of mind and thing. But the purpose is the same: the disclosure of the will to power over alterity that informs this perennially privileged binary logic. Now, however, the destruction of the Roman reduction of *pseudos* to *falsum* will disclose the will to power informing this logic to be, literally, a polyvalent imperial will to power. What should not be overlooked in Heidegger's analysis of the Roman *falsum* is *the indissolubly double register* of his commentary: the fact that he is talking about knowledge production (truth) *and* imperial practice at the same time: in Foucault's phrase, the "regime of truth."

In the first phase of Heidegger's inquiry into the relationship between metaphysical perception, knowledge production, and imperialism, he traced the origins of the Roman *falsum* back to the Greek *sfallo* ("to overthrow, bring to a downfall, fell, make totter"). But this, according to the directive inhering in the stem following the privative prefix of *a-letheia,* was *not* for the Greeks the counter-essence of their concept of truth. By way of demonstrating that the Romans represented being as a domain or territory to be mastered, Heidegger suggests that this forced etymology, which enabled them to circumvent the Greek *pseudo,* which he shows is affiliated with the *lathos* ("concealment") that constitutes the stem of *aletheia,* was intended to put the truth (of being)—and its binary opposite, the false—at the service of the *imperium*:

> The essential domain which prevails for the deployment of the Roman *falsum* is that of the "*imperium*" and of the "imperial." We take these words in their strict and original sense. "*Imperium*" means "command" *[Befehl]*. . . . In passing through French [a Romance language], *Befehlen* [originally "to entrust to sheltering"] became

> "to command," more precisely, it became the Roman *imperare*—*im-perare* = to install *[enrichten]*, to take preliminary measures, that is, *prae-cipere*, to occupy in advance and by so doing to have the "possessed" as domain *[Gebiet]*, to dominate over it *[darüber gebieten]*. The *imperium* is the domain that founds itself on the basis of the order *[Gebot]*, and under whose dominion the others are subject. The *imperium* is the command *[Befehl]* in the sense of the disposing order. Command, thus understood, is the essential ground of domination *[Herrschaft]*, not at all only its consequence, and not only a form of its exercise. . . . No god of the Greeks . . . is a god who [like the god of the Judeo-Christian tradition] commands, but rather a god who shows, who indicates. The Roman "*numen*," by which the Roman gods are characterized, signifies by contrast "injunction" *[Geheiss]* and "will" *[Wille]* and has the character of command. The "numinous," in the strict sense, never concerns the essence of the Greek gods, that is, the gods who have their essence in the realm of *aletheia*. In the essential domain of "command" belongs the Roman "justice," *ius*. The word is attached to *jubeo:* to enjoin *[heissen]*, by injunction *[Geheiss]* to have done and to determine acts and gestures. Command is the essential ground of domination *[Herrschaft]* and of "being in the right" and "to have the right," understood in the Roman sense. As a result *iustitia* has an altogether different essential ground than *dike*, which has its essence in *aletheia*. (*P*, 58; 40)

In this remarkably resonant passage, Heidegger points to the affiliation of the word *prae-ciperes*, which possesses the same stem as the Latinate words "conceive," "concept," "capture" (from *capere*, "to take"), with "metaphysics": that is, between the epistemological act of grasping and mastering the flow which has been reified and the perception of being from the end or, what is the same thing, from above: panoptically, as it were. It is an affiliation that reduces being to a spatial totality, a *territory* "to be occupied in advance." Further, as Heidegger suggests in identifying the command with the Roman *ius/jubeo*, which he translates with the German verb *heissen*, "to enjoin, command, bid, order, direct," but also "to name, call, denominate," the passage constitutes a remarkable prefiguration of Althusser's analysis of ideology as the "interpellation (or 'hailing') of the individual as (subjected) subject by an 'Absolute Subject.'"[14] It is an analysis that, as I will show, is taken over by Foucault in his genealogy of the "free" individual celebrated by bourgeois democracy.

In keeping with this insight into the affiliation between knowledge and power, the second phase of Heidegger's analysis invokes the visual metaphorics informing metaphysical inquiry to demonstrate that the false, as a fundamental dimension of commanding, is related to *over-seeing*, or, to suggest the continuity between Heidegger's thought and Foucault's, *sur*veillance:

> To commanding as the essential foundation of sovereignty belongs "being on high" [or "above" *(Obensein)*]. That is only possible through constant surmounting *[Überhohung]* in relation to others, who are thus the inferiors *[Ünteren]*. In the surmounting, in turn, resides the constant ability to oversee [super-vise and dominate] *[Ubersehen-konnen]*. We say "to oversee something," which means "to master it *[beherrschen]*." (*P;* 59; 40–41)

This oversight of an absolute subject is not, as it is assumed in the prevailing discourse of Western knowledge production, a matter of the failure of attention. It is the proper form of vision understood as enframement *(Gestell)*.[15] Seeing, in the onto-theological tradition, is not passive reception of that which it perceives. It is an *action* or discursive *praxis*: "To this commanding view, which includes surmounting, belongs a constant 'being-on-the-lookout' *[Auf-der-Lauer-liegen]*. That is the form of all action that oversees [dominates from the gaze], but that holds to itself, in Roman the *actio* of the *actus*." And this reifying oversight that, in *putting* every thing/time it sees [the spatial and temporal detail] in its "proper" *place,* is an action, implicates it essentially in the disciplinary/imperial project:

> The commanding overseeing is the dominating vision which is expressed in the often cited phrase of Caesar: *veni, vidi, vici*—I came, I *oversaw [ubersah]*, I conquered. Victory is already nothing but the consequence of the Caesarian gaze that dominates *[Obersehens]* and the seeing *[Sehens]* which has the character of *actio*. The essence of the *imperium* reposes in the *actus* of constant action. The imperial *actio* of the constant surmounting over others implies that the others, in the case where they raise themselves to a comparable or even identical height to command, will be brought down—in Roman: *fallere* (participle: *falsum*). The "bringing-to-fall" *[das Zu-Fall-bringen]* belongs necessarily to the domain of the imperial. (*P,* 59; 41)

After establishing the literal identity of metaphysical ontology, over-seeing or sur-veillance, and imperial domination of the inferior "Other," Heidegger goes on in the last and most resonantly contemporary—and Foucauldian—phase of his meditation on the provenance of the Western idea of the false to distinguish between two kinds of imperial practice: on the one hand, a primitive and implicitly uneconomical and inefficient (i.e., politically resistible) imperialism and, on the other, a fully articulated ("proper") and, as the reference to its "greatness" suggests, highly economical, efficient, productive, and virtually invulnerable imperialism. It should not be overlooked that this developed, polyvalent form of imperialism is deeply inscribed by the metaphorics of vision and the affiliated figure of the circle:

> The "bringing-to-fall" can be accomplished in a "direct" assault *[Ansturm]* and an overthrowing [*Niederwerfen*: literally, "throwing down"]. But the other can also be brought to fall by being outflanked *[Um-gehen]* and tripped up from behind. The "bringing-to-fall" is now the way of deceptive circumvention *[Hinter-gehen]*. . . . Considered from the outside, going behind the back is a complicated, circumstantial and thus mediate "bringing-to-fall" as opposed to an immediate overthrowing. In this way, what is brought to fall does not thereby become annihilated, but in a certain manner redressed within the boundaries *[in den Grenzen]* which are staked out by the dominators. (*P*, 59; 41)

In thematizing this developed imperial practice's textualization (mediation) of power—its harnessing of the truth to domination—the distinction Heidegger articulates cannot but recall Foucault's (and Edward Said's) differentiation between power relations in the ancien régime and in the Enlightenment. More specifically, it points proleptically to Foucault's enabling disclosure of the complicity of the microcosmic table or map—the advanced *structural* model of knowledge production that develops out of the earlier and more generalized spatialization and territorialization of a recalcitrantly volatile being—with the colonization and administration of the "Other":

> This "staking out" *[Abstecken]* is called in Roman: *pango,* whence the word *pax,* peace. This, thought imperially, is the firmly established condition of what has been brought to fall. In truth, the bringing-to-fall in the sense of deception and outflanking is not the mediate and derived imperial *actio* but the imperial *actio* proper. It is not in war, but in the *fallere* of deceptive outflanking *[hintergehenden Umgehens]* and its appropriation to the service of dominion that the proper and "great" trait of the imperial reveals itself. . . . In the Roman *fallere*—to bring-to-fall—as a going around resides deceit; the *falsum* is the insidiously deceptive: "the false.". . . The Greek *pseudos,* through its translation into the Roman *falsum,* is *trans*ferred [über*gesetzt*] into the imperial Roman domain of the bringing-to fall. (*P*, 60; 41)

The end of the pursuit of knowledge, according to this developed, post-Enlightenment form of imperial practice, is to produce peace.

But this peace will be achieved only by the total colonization and administration of the "Other." Theory (understood as a mode of inquiry that territorializes time and privileges seeing, *theoria*) and imperial practice become coterminous. In the "age of the world picture," which constitutes the fulfillment of the spatializing logic of Occidental enframement *(Ge-stell),* the *Pax Metaphysica is* the *Pax Romana.* This, finally, is what Heidegger means when, in alluding to the West's claim that its origins lie in classical Greece, he says, "[W]e today still see the Greek world with Roman eyes—and indeed not solely within historiographical research into ancient Greece but also, and this is the only decisive thing, within the historical metaphysical dialogue of the modern world with that of the ancients. . . . [W]e think the Greek *polis* and the 'political' in a totally un-Greek fashion. We think the political as Romans, i.e., imperially" (*P,* 67; 43).

The relay in this extraordinary meditation on the complicity of Roman Truth (and Falsehood), Roman cultural production, and Roman politics, which is determined by the "white" metaphorics of the supervisory gaze and the transcendental center, is too obvious to need further elaboration. What should not be overlooked, however, is that Heidegger's *Parmenides,* like Foucault's *Discipline and Punish,* is not intended as a history of the past as such, but a "history of the present."[16] It constitutes a *genealogy* of *modern* power relations. Specifically, it discloses that the "strong" discursive practices of what he calls "humanism" in his postwar "Letter" has its origins, not in Greek thought, as it is assumed in modernity by and large, but in the circular (anthropo)logic, the disciplinary pedagogy, and the imperial practice of Rome. It is no accident that Heidegger concludes his meditation by carefully distinguishing between two kinds of domination that, nevertheless, have a single (metaphysical) origin. One kind of power over the "fallen" "Other" operates directly (is "immediate") and is thus visible; the other operates by indirection or detour *(Hintergehung)*—is "mediate"—and is thus invisible. The "bringing-to-fall" can be accomplished by means of a "direct" assault, i.e., repressive conquest; or it can be achieved by *discursive practices* that seem deceptively benign. But what is crucial is not simply that they are both determined by a fixed center that is above or beyond the reach of the free play of criticism, but also, and above all, that it is the latter—specifically, the discourse enabled by the Roman *veritas/falsum* opposition—that characterizes the developed form of "imperial" domination. However generalized Heidegger's formulation, we are not far here from Foucault's poststructuralist interrogation of power relations in modernity, specifically, as we shall see, his analysis of the "repressive hypothesis" determining the disciplinary practices of postmonarchical humanist society.

Indeed, if we conflate the passages from the lectures on the *Parmenides* and "Letter on Humanism" referring to the Roman reduction of Greek thinking, we arrive at the following Foucauldian proposition: Truth and power, knowledge production and repression are not external to each other (as they are all too duplicitously assumed to be in the discursive practices of humanism), but continuous and complicitous with each other. The violence that accompanies overt imperialism is not incommensurate with, but latent in, the Truth of humanism. In a remarkable parallel with Foucault, the benign discursive practices that humanism substitutes for "immediate overthrowing" in the name of "peace" collectively constitute an oppressive "regime of truth."

The reconstellation of Heidegger's thought into Foucault's more radical discursive orbit yields the following narrative about the course of Western history: the inaugural tendency of the grave "Romanized" metaphysical eye to *"over-look"* distracting or disconcerting "deviations"—what Heidegger calls the "ontological difference" and Foucault "the singular event" or "extra-being"[17]—from the Archimedean vantage point of a Transcendental Signified in behalf of Truth, inevitably, however erratically and unevenly, became in time completely internalized. In the age of the "Enlightenment," it took the form of a willful, indeed, *mono*-maniacal and totalizing obsession of instrumental rationality to territorialize, name, classify, comprehend, administer, and control the disruptive mystery of difference. This movement, in turn, precipitated the transformation of "over-sight" into a generalized, calculative, "reformist" cultural and sociopolitical strategy of *sur-veillance* or *super-vision* that, according to Foucault, constitutes the essence of the modern disciplinary society (and, according to Said and other "postcolonial" critics Foucault has influenced, of postcolonial colonialism). To put this narrative in the related spatial terms of geo-metry, the centered circle (the figure of Truth/Beauty/Perfection theorized by the post-Socratics and, according to Heidegger, practiced by the Romans), came to be understood and utilized in and by the modern world of liberal capitalist democracy as the *discreet and polyvalently productive* figure not only of cultural, but of sociopolitical power.

This is not to say that in overdetermining the (scientifically and technologically organized) sociopolitical site, the post-Enlightenment occasion has rendered Heidegger's ontological destruction of modernity irrelevant for critique in favor of a Foucauldian genealogy of discipline. However uneven the distribution of power in the present historical occasion, the ontological and the sociopolitical constitute an indissoluble relay. Insofar as Heidegger's destruction emphasizes the ontological construction of modernity (its ancient "philosophical" ground) it is, as we have seen, a limited agency of critical practice. But insofar as Foucault (and other contemporary worldly critics) emphasizes its sociopolitical construction (and its modern "scientific/technological" ground), it, too, constitutes a limited agency of critique, especially in the post–cold war context, which has borne witness to a triumphant neo-Hegelian, that is, metaphysical, announcement of the end of history and the globalization of technological thinking. The circular/panoptic technology of power that characterizes modernity, in other words, is *both* ontological *and* sociopolitical. And it has as its calculative end the coercive "re-formation"—in the name of the Logo-/Euro-centric sociopolitical Norm (the guardian eye)—of "de-formed" or "de-viant" (or "fallen")—ec-centric or er-ratic—forces all along the indissoluble continuum of being: temporal, linguistic, ecological, sexual, racial, and sociopolitical. What needs to be emphasized provisionally is that the planetary technology of power informing the discourse and practice of Western modernity is not simply the consequence of the rise of the scientific/technological episteme of the Enlightenment as Foucault's genealogy might suggest. Nor, on the other hand, is it simply the consequence of "philosophy," as Heidegger's discourse all too insistently affirms. It is, rather, as a reading of Heidegger with Foucault or Foucault with Heidegger suggests, the consequence of both. An *Auseinandersetzung* between their discourses will show that the overdetermined sciences and the "residual" humanities—the "Two Cultures"—which the dominant culture strategically represents as adversaries, a *querrelle des modernes et anciens*—are, in fact, different but affiliated instruments of the *anthropo-logos,* i.e., the discourse of Man, and thus complicitous not simply with the Late Capitalist West's (neo)imperial project of planetary domination, but with its ominous banalization of terror.

Foucault's Critique of Cultural and Sociopolitical Imperialism

It is not the explicit intention of Michel Foucault's genealogical analysis of the theory and practice of post-Enlightenment humanist society to extend the scope of Heidegger's destructive hermeneutics to the site of sociopolitics. Indeed, Foucault apparently rejects an understanding of Western history as a continuous narrative—a progressive onto-theological tradition—in favor of one characterized by ruptures. But in his last interview before his untimely death, Foucault said this about his relationship to Heidegger's thought:

> For me Heidegger has always been the essential philosopher. I began by reading Hegel, then Marx, and I set out to read Heidegger in 1951 or 1952; then in 1952 or 1953 . . . I read Nietzsche. I still have here the notes that I took when I was reading Heidegger. . . . And they are much more important than the ones I took on Hegel and Marx. My entire philosophical development was determined by my reading of Heidegger. . . . My knowledge of Nietzsche certainly is better than my knowledge of Heidegger. Nevertheless, these are the two fundamental experiences I have had. . . . I had tried to read Nietzsche in the fifties but Nietzsche alone did not appeal to me—whereas Nietzsche and Heidegger: that was a philosophical shock.[18]

This statement in and of itself says nothing, of course, about the specific relationship between Foucault's and Heidegger's discourses. But if it is remembered that the "very small article on Nietzsche" to which Foucault refers in the interview was "Nietzsche, Genealogy, History" (1971), this teasing "aside" in his discussion of the hitherto unacknowledged influence of Heidegger on his thought activates a resonance that demands but has not received adequate attention. For this pivotal essay in the itinerary of Foucault's thought locates the enabling source of Nietzsche's critique of modern Western historiography, culture, and sociopolitics at precisely the site where Heidegger's does: the distanced visualist, i.e., "meta-physical," perspective from which humanist historiography is enabled to accommodate and reduce the differential dynamics of historicity to the subsuming principle of Identity:

> Nietzsche's criticism, beginning with the second of the *Untimely Meditations*, always questions the form of history that reintroduces (and always assumes) a suprahistorical perspective: a history whose function is to compose the finally reduced diversity of time into a

> totality fully closed upon itself; a history that always encourages subjective recognitions and attributes a form of reconciliation to all the displacements of the past; a history whose perspective on all that precedes it implies the end of time, a completed development. The historian's history finds its support outside of time and pretends to base its judgments on an apocalyptic objectivity. This is only possible, however, because of its belief in eternal truth, the immortality of the soul, and the nature of consciousness as always identical to itself. Once the historical sense is mastered by a suprahistorical perspective, metaphysics can bend it to its own purpose and, by aligning it to the demands of objective science, it can impose its own "Egyptianism."[19]

In focusing on Nietzsche's exposure of the "Egyptianism"—the will to power over difference—inscribed in the *suprahistorical* perspective of humanist historiography, Foucault's essay also enables his epoch-making genealogy of modern knowledge/power relations, the aptly titled *Surveiller et punir* (1975),[20] which discloses the origins of Western modernity's disciplinary/hegemonic "microphysics of power" in the panoptic technology precipitated by the obsessive quest for enlightenment by the Enlightenment.

A reconstellation of Foucault's *Surveiller et punir* (and the earlier texts it restructures, especially *Madness and Civilization* and *The Birth of the Clinic*) into the context of Heidegger's disclosure of the founding metaphorics informing and determining the "truth" achieved by the discourse of knowledge production in the Western tradition will go far to establish the affiliation between Heidegger's destruction of the philosophical discourse of the onto-theological tradition and Foucault's genealogy of the "discursive practices" of the Enlightenment. I am referring to the spatialization or territorialization of being that precipitates the Light/darkness opposition or, what has always been another version of the same figural constellation, the Centered Circle/periphery, which privileges the first term as the symbol of Beauty, Perfection, and Civilization, and thus justifies the "conquest" and "colonization" of the "inferior" second. More important, such a reconstellation will also suggest a theory of knowledge/power relations that overcomes the disabling disciplinary tendencies of each discourse, a theory that is more adequate than either for a critique of modernity. By modernity, I do not simply mean what Foucault calls the "regime of Truth" (and Gramsci, "hegemony"), the discursive practice that has internalized visible manifestations of state power by putting the "Truth" (Identity) of "disinterested inquiry" in a binary adversarial opposition against the "false" (difference). Following the directive suggested by Heidegger's *Parmenides* lectures, I also mean that global "regime of Truth" (increasingly called the *Pax Americana* by postcolonial critics such as Edward Said and Gayatri Spivak) that has internalized the visible manifestations of international power by putting the white, civilized, technologically developed West in a binary adversarial opposition against the "Third World": the colored, barbarian, errant, undeveloped, and "strife-riven" East and South.

Taking their point of departure from his critique of the concept of progress, Foucault's commentators have represented the origins of the disciplinary society to lie in an epistemic rupture that precipitated the Enlightenment. They take as axiomatic what in his genealogy is, in fact, only an emphasis:

> This business about discontinuity has always rather bewildered me. . . . My problem was not at all to say, "*Voilà,* long live discontinuity, we are in the discontinuous and a good thing too," but to pose the question, "How is it that at certain moments and in certain orders of knowledge, there are sudden take-offs, these hastenings of evolution, these transformations which fail to correspond to the calm, continuist image that is normally accredited?"[21]

In thus interpreting Foucault's apparent rejection of the continuist understanding of Western history as an affirmation of historical discontinuity, Foucault's commentators have also gone far to crystallize as dogma a corollary tendency in his discourse: the separation of traditional "philosophy" (i.e., the truth discourse of classical humanism) and the post-Enlightenment empirical sciences. As a result of this disciplinary partitioning, they have, among other things, overlooked the symptoms that point to the affinities between Foucault's genealogy of the disciplinary society and Heidegger's destruction of the ontotheological tradition. To retrieve these critically resonant affinities, therefore, it will be necessary to extricate *Surveiller et punir* from the interpretive matrix in which it has hitherto been imbedded and to reconstellate it into the "Heideggerian" context, focusing especially on what has been overlooked, necessarily, by commentary grounded on the assumption that modernity begins with an epistemic break occurring in the eighteenth century. I am referring to those marginal but insistently recurrent occasions in Foucault's text that refer to a history of the figuration of being (the "site" of knowledge production) as a (conquerable) territory, specifically, as a centered circle presided over by the panoptic gaze (and the will to power over difference inscribed in this metaphorics) that long precedes its consummation and overdetermination in the Enlightenment and after. These occasions suggest the affiliative relationship between Heidegger's and Foucault's discourses; they also implicate the "Two Cultures" in the establishment, legitimation, and reproduction of the disciplinary society and its global allotrope, the global empire.[22]

Foucault is remarkably persuasive in suggesting that the supervisory schema emerging as something like, if not absolutely, an epistemic break in the Enlightenment, has determined and continues increasingly to invest every facet of life in the modern West, from the everyday lives of ordinary men and women (what Heidegger would call *das Man*) through pedagogy, cultural and material production to the history-making agendas of those who administer civil and political societies. What I am suggesting by way of reconstellating Foucault's historically specific discourse within the larger framework of Heidegger's interrogation of "philosophy" (the ontotheological tradition at large), however, is that this practically polyvalent schema long precedes the historical juncture in which Foucault apparently locates it. It is, as the affiliation of Foucault's and Heidegger's "Nietzschean" rhetoric suggests, a latent possibility of the "suprahistorical" metaphysical mode of inquiry: of the binary Light/darkness opposition inaugurated by post-Socratic Greek philosophy (Plato, for example, in the "Allegory of the Cave") and decisively codified by the official intellectuals of republican and imperial Rome. I am also suggesting, by way of thematizing what Heidegger left unsaid, that this disciplinary super-visory schema came to be theorized and practiced considerably earlier, however experimentally, however underdeveloped in execution, than the Enlightenment.

To locate the emergence of the supervisory schema, as Foucault tends to do, in the Enlightenment as such is to suggest that the repressive ideology informing its ostensibly "benign" purposes is coincidental with the emergence of instrumental reason, empirical science, the classificatory table, modern cartography, applied technology, the bourgeois class, and capitalism. It is, as the so-called "Two Cultures" debate in the 1960s bears witness, a context from which liberal humanists can all too easily disengage their "poetic" anthropology from complicity in the production of the disciplinary society and the colonial empire. This distinction collapses, however, when it is seen that the fulfilled supervisory schema can be traced back through the idealized circular cities of the Renaissance to the generalized polyvalent image of Beauty/Perfection privileged by Augustine and, before that, by Vitruvius and Plato and that, as I have suggested by way of invoking the witness of Heidegger's "Letter on Humanism" and his *Parmenides,* it was harnessed politically in the form of the opposition between Center and periphery, Metropolis and provinces, *homo romanus* and *homo barbarus,* to the Roman pursuit of the *imperium sine fine*: the global empire. In other words, to recognize, with Heidegger, the always reconstituted "continuity" of this schema is not simply to realize the profound degree to which the relationship between the *spatial* perception of *temporal* difference and sociopolitical power is inscribed in the Occidental consciousness at large. It also suggests the continuing complicity of the two cultures: modern humanism—its "classical" mode of "disinterested" inquiry, the philosophical and literary texts it privileges, its institutions of knowledge production, and its cultural apparatuses—with the instrumental mode of "objective" inquiry and its disciplinary/imperial technology that Foucault, among other sociopolitical thinkers such as Althusser, Adorno, and Said, overdetermines in his critique of modernity.

According to Foucault's emphasis, then, the relationship between the spatializing eye—"the disciplinary gaze" (*DP,* 170)—and power, supervision, and discipline assumed overt theoretical articulation and practical implementation during the "Enlightenment" or *"Aufklarung"* (the metaphorics are not accidental). This theoretical and practical reality became increasingly prominent thereafter: when, it is important to remember, the "universal" (Occidental) possibilities of humanistic (i.e., disinterested, liberal) cultural practices began to become manifest.[23] The reformers of the spectacularly brutal aristocratic punitive machinery were not essentially committed to humanitarian principles. Their real intention was to formulate and elaborate a more efficient penal system, one that overcame the economic limitations and political vulnerability of penal practices in the ancien régime:

> The true objective of the reform movement, even in its most general formulations, was not so much to establish a new "right" to punish based on more equitable principles [than those governing the practice of the *ancien régime*], as to set up a new "economy" of power to punish, to assure its better distribution, so that it should be neither

> too concentrated at certain privileged points, nor too divided between opposing authorities; so that it should be distributed in homogeneous circuits capable of operating everywhere, in a continuous way, down to the finest grain of the social body. The reform of criminal law must be read as a strategy for the rearrangement of the power to punish, according to modalities that render it more regular, more effective, more constant and more detailed in its effects; in short, which increase its effects while diminishing its economic cost . . . and its political cost. (*DP*, 80–81)

What the early reformers of the Enlightenment were ultimately searching for was not a penal system that, in opposition to the arbitrary brutality of punishment in the ancien régime, acknowledged the otherness of the antisocial others. It was, rather, a system that would diminish the economic wastefulness of the indiscriminate irregularities and, equally important, the political visibility of the earlier use of power, a system that would internalize, distribute, and saturate power in and throughout the body politic to increase productivity of "knowledge" (cultural capital) as well as capital goods and to decrease the threat of revolt to which an identifiable power—a *visible* sovereign center—is necessarily exposed. They were, in short, seeking a *generalized and generalizable system*—a microcosm, a table, a map, as it were—capable of annulling the "force" of the alienated "Other" and producing the "peace" of "docile and useful bodies": what Heidegger, in invoking the dynamics of enframement, refers to as "disposable reserve." As Foucault puts the fully developed agenda of the post-Enlightenment:

> The historical moment of the disciplines was a moment when an art of the human body was born, which was directed not only at the growth of its skills, nor at the intensification of its subjection, but at the formation of a relation that in the mechanism itself makes it more obedient as it becomes more useful, and conversely. . . . This discipline produces subjects and practical bodies, "docile" bodies. Discipline increases the forces of the body (in economic terms of utility) and diminishes these same forces (in political terms of obedience). In short, it dissociates power from the body; on the one hand, it turns it into an "aptitude," a "capacity," which it seeks to increase; on the other hand, it reverses the course of the energy, the power that might result from it, and turns it into a relation of strict subjection. If economic exploitation separates the force and the products of labor, let us say that disciplinary coercion established in the body the constricting link between an increased aptitude and an increased domination. (*DP*, 138)

In their search for such a "new 'economy' of the power to punish," the reformers were inevitably guided by the photological semiotic network developed and privileged by the Enlightenment. The episteme's overdetermined valorization of the eye and its light and the discriminating technology of optics to which it gave rise—"the telescope, the lens and the light beam, which were an integral part of the new physics and cosmology" (*DP*, 170)—made these reformers increasingly aware of the relationship between enlightenment—making visible, particular, knowable, and measurable the obscure, fluid, amorphous, and always wasteful and threatening "Other"—and power. They thus sought after a sophisticated design/apparatus the economy of which could organize and apply visible space for the purpose of achieving optimal disciplinary supervision of and productivity from the individualized multiplicity enclosed within its well-lighted and pacified parameters.

There is no doubt, as Foucault remarks, that the "obscure art of light and visibility was preparing a new knowledge of man" that was to culminate in the disciplinary society (*DP*, 170–71). But the historically specific density of Foucault's genealogy—especially its emphasis on the new science of optics and its technology—should not obscure the legacy these humanist reformers inherited from the onto-theological tradition, above all, that variation of optics inscribed in the theology of Calvinist Protestantism. It is no accident that the "reformatories"—from the Rasphuis of Amsterdam (1596) through the penitentiary at Gloucester (England) to the Walnut Street Prison (in Philadelphia, 1790) that provided architectural models for the disciplinary prison (as well as the analogous insane asylum) culminating in Bentham's Panopticon—were largely Protestant in origin (the latter instituted "under the direct influence of the Quakers") (*DP*, 124). Despite Foucault's minimization of significant reference, it is quite clear that, however overdetermined, the Enlightenment's war of reason (the *ratio*) against "wastefulness" (and de-viance or er-rancy) in behalf of sociopolitical and economic economy (duty and utility) coincides with the Calvinist/Protestant work ethic, which, according to Max Weber, gave rise to the "spirit of Capitalism." This was the ethic rationalized and enabled by the circular doctrine of predestination, by, that is, the austere pro*vid*ential history that, as the etymology suggests, was the project of the absolutely hidden, inscrutable, and supervisory eye of the Calvinist God. In Weber's telling words, it was the "transcendental being," "beyond the reach of human understanding," who, by his "quite incomprehensible decrees has decided the fate of every individual and regulated the tiniest details of the cosmos from eternity."[24] Foucault, in fact, alludes to this resonant continuity between the eye of the Calvinist *Theo-logos* that, in accounting even for the fall of a sparrow, makes every singular thing and event accountable, and the later *Anthropo-logos* that, in the accommodation and surveillance of detail (difference) by way of the invention of the table and the map, makes it serve the hegemonic purposes of the dominant culture (Identity):

> The classical age did not initiate ["the utilitarian rationalization of detail in moral accountability and political control"]; rather it accelerated it, changed its scale, gave it precise instruments, and perhaps found some echoes for it in the calculation of the infinitely small or in the description of the most detailed characteristics of natural beings. In any case, "detail" had long been a category of theology and asceticism: every detail is important since in the sight of God no immensity is greater than a detail, all minutiae of Christian education, of scholastic or military pedagogy, all forms of "training" found their place easily enough. For the disciplined man, as for the true believer, no detail is unimportant, but not so much for the meaning that it conceals within it as for the hold it provides for the power that wished to seize it. (DP, 140)[25]

What lay more immediately at hand as architectural/methodological models for these "observatories" were, significantly, the insane asylum, the medical clinic, the workshop, the elementary classroom, and, above all, the military camp. In these spaces, as in the medieval plague town (*DP*, 147), time was territorialized, enclosed, partitioned, serialized, functionalized, and thus immobilized or frozen. It was, that is, arranged to achieve optimal supervision under "the scrupulously 'classificatory' eye of the master" (*DP*, 17)[26] of a prolific and proliferating temporal world assumed to be naturally deviant—or, on another level, "prodigal" or "fallen" and "dispersed." It was a spatializing economy, in short, designed to eliminate confusion and waste by rechanneling the irregular force of living bodies from the vantage point of a preestablished judgmental norm: a regularizing *logos* or center elsewhere, as it were.[27] In the perfect military camp (the model was, not accidentally, that of the Roman imperial legions):

> power would be exercised solely through exact observation; each gaze would form a part of the overall functioning of power . . . the

> geometry of paths, the number and distribution of tents, the orientation of their entrance, the disposition of files and ranks were exactly defined; the network of gazes that supervised one another was laid down. . . . The camp is the *diagram of a power* that acts by means of *general visibility.* For a long time this model of the camp *or at least its underlying principle* was found in urban development in the construction of working-class housing estates, hospitals, asylums, prisons, schools: the spatial "nesting" of hierarchical surveillance. (*DP,* 171–72)

Thus, a whole "new" spatial problematic emerges: that of an architecture that would assure the pacifying ends of discipline by rendering those errant or nomadic "deviants" on whom power acted visible to the super-visory gaze. It was to be "an architecture that is no longer built simply to be seen (as with the ostentation of palaces), or to observe the external space (cf. the geometry of fortresses)." Its spatial economy was designed, rather, "to permit an internal, articulated, and detailed control—to render visible those who are inside it." More generally, it was "an architecture that would operate to transform individuals: to act on those it shelters, to provide a hold on their conduct, to carry the effects of power right to them, to make it possible to know them, to alter them. Stones can make people docile and knowable" (*DP,* 172).

"The [Roman] camp is a *diagram* of power": I emphasize provisionally the abstraction that Foucault's rhetorical focus on the effects of the specific military camp's structure might deflect attention from. Reconstellated into the context of Heidegger's thematization of the will to power informing the perennially privileged but naturalized metaphors of vision and the centered circle, Foucault's account of the origin of such modern disciplinary architectural experiments undergoes a telling metamorphosis. It discloses, in fact, how deeply, however more complex its articulation, the affiliation between spatial or, in Foucault's Nietzschean terms, "suprahistorical," perception—perception *meta-ta-physica*—and power, Being and time, Center and periphery, was inscribed as an "underlying principle" of Western thinking by the time of the Enlightenment. This was the historical conjuncture, it should be remarked, that in Great Britain was characterized by the politically troubling dislocation and unhoming of the traditional peasantry precipitated by the predations of the enclosure movement, the geopolitical equivalent of the classificatory table. It was inevitable, however ironic, therefore, that the "quest" of the emergent bourgeois culture of that demographically volatile age for such a functional economy of space—a productive economy that would serve both as agency of surveillance and correction (reformation and pacification) according to the anthropological Norm—would culminate at the end of the century in an architectural model of the ideal prison that epitomized *in practice* the operation and effects vis à vis the differences that time disseminates of the territorializing gaze of logocentric thinking. I mean precisely the distancing/reifying panoramic gaze that, according to Heidegger's story, informs the ontotheological philosophical tradition at large: its ontology (metaphysics), its epistemology (truth as *adaequatio intellectus et rei*), its pedagogy *(eruditio et institutio in bonas artes),* its affiliated symbolic figurations (the centered circle and the commanding gaze), and, not least, its end: the imperial *pax.* It was inevitable, in other words, that the Enlightenment, as its very name suggests, should "discover" an architectural model for reforming and normalizing sociopolitical "deviants," one in which military surveillance becomes *sur*-veillance, supervision, *super-vision.*

Nor is it accidental that this particular structural model should have been inferred from the Western philosophical tradition by a bourgeois humanist of the English Enlightenment who, in the context of the social dislocations produced by the deterritorializing/reterritorialization effects on the peasantry of the enclosure movement,[28] contributed significantly not only to the advance of technology, industrialization, and capitalism, but also to the detemporalizing and reifying cultural momentum that culminated in what Heidegger tellingly calls the "age of the world picture" and the consequent reduction of being in all its manifestations to "disposable reserve." It was inevitable, to put it alternatively, that this specific architectural trope should have been inferred by a thinker who brought the tradition beginning with the Romans' institutionalization of the gaze (*veritas:* the adequation of mind and thing), the re-collective memory, and, by extension, the binary spatial logic of the hierarchized polis, to its fulfillment—and, according to Heidegger, its end. I am referring, of course, to the utilitarian philosopher Jeremy Bentham and his "Panopticon" or "Inspection House," which laid the ground for the production of the disciplinary (and colonialist) society. This was the centered/circular architectural structure that drew the territorializing/disciplinary machinery of knowledge production into absolute symmetry with the super-vision that reformed and "normalized" errancy, that is, with the policing enabled by the binary metaphorics that privileged light over darkness and space over time. It was the dedifferentiating differentiating structure that brought into affiliation the panoptic gaze and the microcosmic figure of the centered circle—now, with the rise of empirical science, differentiated into the "taxonomic table"—with the "'evolutive' time of genesis," the "examination," and so forth, and the partitioned spatial economy of the presiding public institutions articulated during the eighteenth century (the hospital, the insane asylum, the workhouse, the military camp, the classroom).

Since Foucault's account of the Panopticon has become well known by this time, there is no need to rehearse its description here. It will suffice to say that the intention of his analysis of its circular structural economy is to foreground Bentham's "guiding principle": "that power should be visible and unverifiable" (*DP*, 201). "The Panopticon," Foucault writes, "is a machine for dissociating the seeing/being seen dyad: in the peripheric ring, one is totally seen, without ever seeing; in the central tower, one sees everything without ever being seen" (*DP*, 201–2). It would induce in the errant inmates as its primary effect "a state of conscious and permanent visibility that assures the automatic functioning of power. So to arrange things that the surveillance is permanent in its effects, even if it is discontinuous in its action; that the perfection of power should tend to render its actual exercise unnecessary; that this architectural apparatus should be a machine for creating and sustaining a power relation *independent of the person who exercises it*; in short, that the inmates should be caught up in a power situation of which they are themselves the bearers" (*DP*, 201, my emphasis).

In other words, the totalizing geometric structure of Bentham's Panopticon was designed to transform or re-collect the threatening force of *any* amorphous and errant constituency of the nation into unitary "conformity" and predictable regularity. Its end was to produce a collective of discreet and thus knowable individuals who would eventually take their *proper* place in the Identical and Self-Present national Whole—who would, that is, becomes subjected (or colonized) subjects. Like Heidegger's ventriloquized *das Man*—the collective "They" whose speech and acts are determined by "the way things are publicly interpreted"—Bentham's deviants would themselves become the tautological transmitters of the normative power that renders them docile and useful instruments of the dominant cultural and sociopolitical orders. Behind this particular disciplinary practice of the post-Enlightenment, it should now be evident (even though Foucault does not overtly refer to them), lies what Heidegger's destruction of the onto-theological tradition discloses to be the enabling and perennial principle and figurative corollaries of Western metaphysical thinking at large: 1) *the principle that Identity is the condition for the possibility of difference and not the other way around*; 2) the transcendental/imperial Eye (and its light), which this founding principle must necessarily privilege; and 3) the metaphorics of the centered circle, which it precipitates to do its discreetly colonizing and pacifying work.

What I am suggesting in this reconstellating of Foucault's *Surveiller et punir* into the matrix of Heidegger's interrogation of the ontotheological tradition, in short, is that Bentham's Panopticon does not constitute a historical rupture. Rather, it brings to momentary fulfillment *in a particular practice* the coercive potential always already *latent* in the "oversight" of the metaphysical thinking that constitutes the foundation of the identity of Europe *and,* by way of this identifiable excess, makes explicit (visible) the coercive disciplinary genealogy of the "disinterested" or "objective" discursive practices of modern "liberal democratic" (humanist) societies.

A reading of Foucault's text that is indifferent to the *Seinsfrage* (the question of being, which constitutes the point of departure of Heidegger's destruction of the onto-theological tradition) might raise the objection that Bentham's Panopticon represents a historically specific institution: the reformatory prison that emerges to prominence at the beginning of the nineteenth century. But such an interpretation is what Foucault's genealogy insistently resists. This is suggested by several passages already quoted from *Surveiller et punir* that disclose (often inadvertently) the degree to which the generalized disciplinary model—the *figure* of the centered circle—had been inscribed, long before Bentham's historical occasion, in the knowledge-producing, social, and political institutions of the West. As I have provisionally remarked, it is also suggested by Foucault's insistent, however muted, reference to the *principle underlying* the concrete architectural instance: the Roman military camp, we recall, is a "*diagram* of power that acts by means of general visibility." But this essential affiliation between Bentham's Panopticon and the metaphysical tradition at large is most decisively thematized in Foucault's analysis of Bentham's Panopticon itself. There, he shows that Bentham himself conceived of his historically specific "inspection house" as a *generalized* structural model that was separable from any concrete and particular practice:

> [The Panopticon] is the *diagram of a mechanism of power reduced to its ideal form; its functioning, abstracted from any obstacle, resistance or friction, must be represented in a pure architectural and optical system:* it is in fact a *figure* of political technology that may and must be *detached* from any specific use.
>
> *It is polyvalent in its application;* it serves to reform prisoners, but also to treat patients, to instruct school children, to confine the insane, to put beggars and idlers to work. Whenever one is dealing with a multiplicity of individuals on whom a task or a particular form of behavior must be imposed, the *panoptic schema* may be used. It is—necessary modifications apart—applicable "to all establishments whatsoever, in which, within a space not too large to be covered or commanded by buildings, a number of persons are meant to be kept under inspection." (*DP,* 205–6, my emphasis)[29]

Bentham's Panopticon, in other words, is not the historically specific effect of an epistemic rupture that bears witness to the sudden emergence of the positivist scientific worldview as such. It represents, rather, an overdetermined and highly developed instance of the multiple practical uses to which the traditional polyvalent panoptic diagram enabled by metaphysics—and mediated by the inscription of the imperial Roman prototype into the culture of the revolutionary age[30]—was put in the post-Enlightenment, when the transcendental eye was compelled to descend into the world in the form of the empirical or "objective" gaze, when, that is, the earlier generalized and "empty" space it projected was transformed into the gridded and individuated table. The prominence that Foucault gives to the panoptic penal institution should not obscure the fact that, however unevenly, this ancient diagram, now differentiated to accommodate the smallest detail, was simultaneously being applied to other institutional discourses and practices as diverse as medicine, psychiatry, economics, hermeneutics, education, literature, literary criticism, and other modes of cultural production. Not least, though Foucault does not refer to it overtly in *Discipline and Punish,* it was also being applied to the discourse and practice of cartography (Mercator's projection) and colonialism, a discourse and practice, not incidentally, that Edward Said explores in *Orientalism,* which was inspired by *Discipline and Punish.*[31] I invoke this globalization of Foucault's genealogy of the disciplinary society to recall Heidegger's location of the origins of Europe in Rome and his identification of its (metaphysical territorializing) mind with modern Western imperialism.

In the end, given the compellingness of its totalizing binarist logical economy, this "polyvalent diagram of a mechanism of power reduced to its ideal form" would utterly obscure all the material signs of its genealogy and power to become the naturalized, all-encompassing, and comprehensive "truth of being," the truth of the free subject of liberal democracy that concealed the hegemonic "panopticism" of the "disciplinary society": "The movement from a schema of exceptional discipline [the Panopticon] to one of generalized surveillance [panopticism] rests in a historical transformation." This was "the gradual extension of the mechanisms of discipline throughout the seventeenth and eighteenth centuries, their spread throughout the whole social body." The result of this totalizing extension and internalization of the panoptic gaze was not only "the formation of what might be called in general the disciplinary society" (*DP*, 209), but also, as Heidegger's theoretical discourse maintains and Said's postcolonial discourse bears witness, of the imperial society.

Reconstellated into the "Heideggerian" matrix, the usual "political" reading of Foucault's genealogical analysis of the modern disciplinary society undergoes a radical metamorphosis. The post-Enlightenment historical process, which, according to Foucault, bears witness to the internalization of the panoptic technological mechanism and the centered circle (the humanist figure of Truth/Beauty/Perfection) in the "soul" of the body politic at large suddenly appears remarkably like Heidegger's history of Western thought, the logical economy of which begins with the Roman reduction of an always already originative Greek truth *(a-letheia)* to a derivative/calculative truth *(veritas)* and comes to its end in the planetary triumph of technological thought: the "Age of the World Picture." This is the age in which anthropo-logical re-presentation in its instrumental modality comes to traverse the entire lateral continuum of being, from the representation of being itself, through language and cultural production, to national and international political formations. In the end, it could be said, it is not so much the panoptic prison, the hospital, the asylum, the classroom, the factory, as such that are Foucault's primary concern as it is the repressive *panoptic schema* that, masquerading as the objective pursuit of knowledge, informs these practical institutions and that has become totalized in the present age as the "panoptic*ism*" of the disciplinary/imperial society. That is to say, it is the totalized "*regime* of truth," the end of whose logical economy is the reduction—or, better, the colonization of the force of human being—to a "useful and docile body." It is, I suggest, this insight into the dominion of the *ratio,* largely activated by the ubiquity in the period of the French Enlightenment, of what Foucault calls "the Roman reference" (*DP,* 169), this recognition of the indissoluble relation between Western thought and practice (truth and power) that affiliates Foucault's genealogy of the disciplinary society with Heidegger's genealogy of the age of the world picture. I mean specifically, as I have been suggesting, the truth of enframement *(Ge-stell)* that has as its inevitable end the reduction of the force of being in its totality, including human being, to a regulated mindlessness: to "disposable reserve." It will not be an exaggeration, especially if we are attuned to the operations of Enlightenment thinking in both the domestic and the international spheres, to say that the ultimate agenda of the emergent bourgeois reformers was to bring the *Pax* of this "world picture" into being, but in such a way as to conceal the fact that this peace, like the *Pax Romana,* has as its essential purpose the colonization, administration, and exploitation of the Other all across the continuum of being, from thinking itself to the practices of nationhood and colonialism.

What the reconstellation of Foucault's thought into the context of Heidegger's unexpectedly reveals, in short, is that it is not exclusively the painful effects of a repressive political power that Foucault is intent on disclosing; it is also, as it is more focally in Heidegger's discourse, the apparently irreversible *global* momentum, undertaken in the name of a triumphant objective reason and its freedom, towards the colonization of the human mind: its reduction to a calculative instrument that, in *seeing* and *occupying* being *in advance* (metaphysically), for the purpose of comprehending and utilizing "it," must eventually become utterly indifferent to the differential life that is not seeable and speakable.

Thus, there is a massive Western momentum toward the banalization of thinking—a thinking that, according to Heidegger and Foucault, reduces being to "disposable reserve" or a "docile and useful body" in behalf of a "productive" peace—to which both Foucault's genealogy of the modern "panoptic disciplinary society" and Heidegger's destruction of the modern "age of the world picture" point. And, if that is the case, then it is also their awareness of the imminent global triumph of this thoughtless thinking, which results in the routinization of practical violence, that instigates their recognition of the urgency of rethinking thinking and its legacy. More specifically, it is their awareness of the pending total colonization and pacification of the mind of humanity by the calculative and leveling instrumentalism that provides the directive of this urgent project. To rethink thinking in the age of the world picture, their genealogies imply, means to think *positively* the shadowy "Other" *of*—that belongs to—the light of this "triumphant" Occidental discourse. It means, in other words, to think the radical difference that Heidegger in "What Is Metaphysics?" names "the Nothing," that modern instrumental reason "will have nothing to do with," and Foucault terms, in *Madness and Civilization,* the "irreducible" life of "unreason": the specter that paradoxically has been precipitated precisely by the fulfillment—the coming to its end—of the visualist/panoptic thought of the West and that now haunts its banalizing hegemony.

Heidegger, Foucault, and the Repressive Hypothesis

Let me now summarize Foucault's historically specific analysis of the transformation of power relations that took place between the period of the ancien régime and the post-Enlightenment in the rhetoric he introduces in volume 1 of *The History of Sexuality,* which follows immediately after *Surveiller et punir.* The bourgeois humanist "reformers" of the Age of the Enlightenment seized the opportunity afforded by the delegitimation of monarchical uses of power—the arbitrary, overt, visible employment of force by a sovereign agent that was economically wasteful and politically vulnerable—to elaborate in the name of justice a far more subtle system of coercion grounded in the "repressive hypothesis." This "new" view of power relations, according to Foucault, represents power in essentially negational terms: as "prohibition, censorship and denial": "repression" pure and simple.[32] In so doing, it authorizes and instigates, rather than restricts, the discourse of truth (the will to knowledge). Indeed, it renders (the production of) "truth" (its pacifying light) the essential agency of deliverance from power's negative (evil) effects (its strife-riven darkness).[33] Reconstellated into the Heideggerian matrix, this post-Enlightenment version of power becomes the privileged means of bringing universal peace (the *Pax Romana,* as it were) to a volatile world, a world that the dominant culture represents as being in perpetual strife.

Foucault's point, of course, is that the "repressive hypothesis" on which the relations between truth and power in modernity rests is a seductive *deception*—a strategic construction of the dominant culture and sociopolitical order that is given the tempting semblance of being naturally derived—that must be exposed. In representing power as purely negative, external, and essentially in opposition to truth, post-Enlightenment humanists also represented the discourse of truth (and justice) as essentially benign: *disinterested* and thus "liberal," "emancipatory," "ameliorative," and, not least, "irenic." In fact, this bourgeois humanist truth discourse is—precisely in its ability to produce detailed knowledge (of the Other)—complicitous with power. It is a compelling ruse of the dominant culture that, in Gramsci's phrase, is intended to evoke "spontaneous consent" from those differential constituencies on which power is practiced: "We must cease once and for all to describe the effects of power in negative terms. . . . In fact, power produces; it produces reality; it produces domains of objects and rituals of truth. The individual and the knowledge that may be gained of him belong to this production" (*DP,* 194). And again: "[T]he notion of repression is quite inadequate for capturing what is precisely the productive aspect of power. . . . If power were never anything but repressive, if it never did anything but say no, do you really think one would be brought to obey it?"[34]

Despite Foucault's overdetermination of the rhetoric of "rupture," "break," "mutation," his analysis of the "repressive hypothesis" suggests, on the contrary, that the transition from the ancien régime to the disciplinary society of liberal capitalist democracy accomplished by the Enlightenment humanists was not finally a radical departure. Rather, to invoke Heidegger's tripartite division of the history of Western philosophy, the onto-theo-logical tradition, it entailed the substitution of one center for another. In the age of monarchs, the determining and repressive center elsewhere or "eye of power" (the *theologos* that sanctioned the sovereign king's direct use of spectacular force to punish or discourage deviation—and to conquer and exploit the "new worlds") was *visible,* identifiable, and thus vulnerable to critique or insurrection (as the French Revolution bears witness). In the post-Enlightenment, on the other hand, the commanding/supervisory gaze (the *anthropologos*) of the bourgeois humanist reformers (and their colonialist counterparts) became increasingly *invisible* (internalized) as the objectifying and banalizing effects of its power spread throughout the capillary network of the social body. Put alternatively, the center of the ancien régime was not abandoned; it was *mediated.* The immediate and visible center, that is, was rendered a "center elsewhere" that at the same time operated invisibly *in* the ever-expanding circumferential world, reducing the mind to calculative instrument and the body to useful and docile mechanism. This difference-in-continuity is, in fact, the enabling thesis of Foucault's genealogy of truth/power relations inscribed in the related site of the discursive practices of sexuality in modernity: "At bottom, despite the differences in epochs and objectives, this representation of power has remained under the spell of monarchy. In political thought and analysis, we still have not cut off the head of the king."[35]

In thus bringing to explicitness the affiliated naturalized tropes of the centered circle and the supervisory gaze, which according to Foucault, inform the humanist "ruse of the repressive hypothesis" and its leveling "peace," we cannot help but recall Heidegger's neglected genealogy of truth/power relations as these have been increasingly elaborated in and by Western civilization. I am primarily recalling the distinction he makes, by way of thinking the implications for knowledge/power of that Roman territorialization of the knowledge of being, between an older, "immediate" Western imperialism, which applied force against the "Other" directly, and its developed, fulfilled, and proper form, a mediate or "neo"-imperialism, as it were, that accomplished the hegemonic end—the *pax*—of empire by means of the ruse of the discourse of Truth understood as *adaequatio intellectus et rei.* The "bringing-to-fall" can be accomplished in a "direct" assault *[Ansturm]* and an overthrowing *[Niederwerfen].* But the other can also be brought-to-fall by being outflanked and tripped from behind. Considered from the outside, going behind the back is a complicated, circumstantial and thus mediate "bringing-to-fall" as opposed to an immediate overthrowing. In this way, what is brought-to-fall does not thereby become annihilated, but in a certain manner redressed within the boundaries that are staked out by the dominators. This "staking out" *(Abstecken)* is called in Roman *pango,* whence the word *pax* is peace. In truth the bringing-to-fall in the sense of deception and outflanking is not the mediate and derived imperial *actio,* but the imperial *actio* proper. It is not in war, but in the *fallere* of deceptive outflanking *(hintergehenden Umgehens)* and its appropriation to the service of dominion that the proper and "great" trait of the imperial reveals itself.[36] It is, it will be recalled, this "mediate" *hintergehenden Umgehens*—the ruse enabled by the "naturalization" of the imperial center and the invisible commanding gaze (the *Übersehen-konnen*) in the "truth discourse" of humanist modernity—that, according to Heidegger, has facilitated the "Europeanization of the planet"[37] in the technocratic "age of the world picture," and the establishment of the *Pax Europa/Americana* that ensues from the total transformation of the temporality of being—the differences that time disseminates—to a territorialized and "staked out" spatial totality in which things and events have been reduced to expendable stockpile.

Despite Heidegger's generalization of its sociopolitical implications, this *hintergehenden Umgehens* clearly bears a striking resemblance to Foucault's analysis of the ruse of the "repressive hypothesis," which was enabled not simply by the Enlightenment's rendering of the visible center elsewhere/panoptic gaze of the sovereign king invisible, but also by its ontologically prior spatialization of being, that is, *by its reduction of knowledge to a material and gridded space* to be "conquered" and "settled." This is precisely the point Heidegger makes in the *Parmenides,* when he implicates the Romans' epochal reduction of the Greek *pseudos* to *falsum* in behalf of its imperial/colonial project with their indissolubly related reduction of the Greek *gea* to *terra:* "For the Romans . . . the earth, *tellus, terra,* is dry, the land as distinct from the sea; this distinction differentiates that upon which construction, settlement, and installation are possible from those places where they are impossible. *Terra* becomes *territorium,* land of settlement as realm of command. In the Roman *terra* [which refers to both the literal earth and to the knowledge of being] can be heard an imperial accent, completely foreign to the Greek *gea* and *ge.*"[38]

This, I suggest, especially if it is thought in terms of the pervasiveness of the "Roman reference" in his genealogy of the "disciplinary society," is also the point Foucault makes in an important but neglected interview following the publication of *Surveiller et punir* conducted by the editors of the journal *Herodote,* who would apply his analysis of modern knowledge/power relations to the unduly neglected discourse of geography. To their suggestion that this discourse "grew up in the shadow of the military" and is thus informed by naturalized "spatial metaphors [that] are equally geographical and strategic"—

"The *region* of the geographers is the military region (from *regere*, to command), a *province* is a conquered territory (from *vincere*)"—Foucault responds (in a way that anticipates Edward Said's interrogation of the discursive practices of Orientalism):

> Once knowledge can be analyzed in terms of region, domain, implantation, displacement, transposition [all pertaining to the practice and effects of planting colonies], one is able to capture the process by which knowledge functions as a form of power and disseminates the effects of power. There is an administration of knowledge, a politics of knowledge, relations of power which pass via knowledge and which, if one tries to transcribe them, lead one to consider forms of domination designated by such notions of field, region and territory. *And the politico-strategic term is an indication of how the military and the administration actually come to inscribe themselves both on a material soil and within forms of discourse.*[39]

The end of the logical economy of this double inscription, is, like the end of that epochal territorialization of being that, according to Heidegger's genealogy of the truth discourse of modernity at large, enabled the Romans to put knowledge production (the "truth") in the service of their imperial project: the *Pax* that, in representing itself as the benign light of the truth, deflects attention away from the repressive darkness that belongs to it.

By this dark end of the light of truth, I am not simply referring to the total colonization of the "Other" of Being in all its particular manifestations—the reduction of its differential force to "useful and docile body" or to "disposable reserve." Following Heidegger's version of this reduction, I am also referring to its necessarily deethicized concomitant: the banalization of thought and the leveling and standardization of violence against whatever, in its refusal to be accommodated, presents itself as an obstacle to this deadly, "benignly productive" logic. In both Heidegger and Foucault, the "peace" that is the ultimate end of the binarist logic of instrumental reason is a living death.

This knowledge of the insidious way in which knowledge works in modernity, is, I suggest, the real legacy of Heidegger and Foucault to the present, so-called postcolonial age, the age that has borne witness to the planetary "triumph" of technology or, to use more current rhetoric, to the globalization of the instrumental thinking informing the late or consumer capitalist polity, which represents itself as the

New World Order. Or, rather, it is this dark knowledge, precipitated by the dislocation of their thought from the sedimented partial contexts in which they have been hitherto embedded and reconstellated into each other's orbit, that renders what they have to say about knowledge and power in the "age of the world picture" or, alternatively, of "panopticism," eminently useful as a diagnostic and critique of this global regime of truth, which now represents itself in euphoric eschatological terms: the end of history and the advent of the New World Order.

But this joint legacy is not restricted to a negative function. In its *symptomatic* recognition of the be*ing* of the relay of spectral contradictions precipitated by the fulfillment of the instrumentalist metaphysical logic of modernity—the *non*-beings *of* its Truth, from the ontological nothing and the identityless subject through the madman, the female, the person of color, and the homosexual to the refugee—the person who has been unhomed by the depredations of Western colonialism—this legacy also bequeaths the present age a productive directive. It points urgently to the need to think positively this spectral relay that refuses to be accommodated to and therefore haunts the panoptic vision of the New World Order. It calls us to ask: What would a thinking be like that retrieves the nonbeing(s) that the thinking of being in the West will have nothing to do with? What would a political *praxis* of "specters" be like, a *praxis* that acknowledges the differential being—the identityless identity—of those whom the political thought and practice of the West has perennially represented as nonbeing?

Notes

1. Francis Fukuyama, *The End of History and the Last Man* (New York: The Free Press, 1993). See also Richard Haass, *The Reluctant Sheriff: The United States after the Cold War* (New York: Council on Foreign Relations, 1997).

2. Martin Heidegger, *Introduction to Metaphysics*, trans. Ralph Manheim (New Haven: Yale University Press, 1959), 62.

3. William V. Spanos, *America's Shadow: An Anatomy of Empire* (Minneapolis: University of Minnesota Press, 2000).

4. Martin Heidegger, "The Rectorate 1933/34: Facts and Thoughts," trans. Karsten Harries, *Review of Metaphysics* 38, no. 3 (March 1985), 498.

5. Martin Heidegger, "On the Essence of Truth," trans. John Sallis, in *Basic Writings*, ed. David Farrell Krell (New York: Harper and Row, 1993), 118.

6. Martin Heidegger, "The Origin of the Work of Art," trans. Albert Hofstadter, *Basic Writings*, 149.

7. Martin Heidegger, *Being and Time,* trans. John Macquarrie and Edward Robinson (New York and Evanston: Harper and Row, 1962), 43.

8. Some suggestion of the crudeness of Victor Farías's anecdotal approach to the question of Heidegger's complicity with Nazism is suggested by his reductive attribution of Heidegger's "massive reservations about the so-called 'Latin' or 'Roman'" to "a radical xenophobia" that is "typical of a [German] tradition for which Abraham a Sancta Clara [the seventeenth century German monk whose virulent anti-Semitism, according to Farías, was a decisive influence on Heidegger throughout his life] was exemplary." Victor Farías, *Heidegger and Nazism,* trans. Paul Burrill and Gabriel R. Ricci (Philadelphia: Temple University Press, 1989), 223.

9. I derive the word "errant" from Heidegger's discussion of "errancy" in "On the Essence of Truth" (*Basic Writings,* 132–35), and use it throughout this essay with the ironic intention of thematizing its etymology: from the Latin *errare,* "to wander without direction," i.e., "to stray from the *ratio.*"

10. Martin Heidegger, "Letter on Humanism," trans. Frank A. Capuzzi, *Basic Writings,* 224. This is admittedly a problematic genealogy, the controversial character of which is exacerbated by its extreme generality. The two aspects of its content that will be challenged by humanists in the Arnoldian tradition are its differentiation between the cultures of classical Greece and Rome, which have been invariably elided into the "Greco-Roman" age or simply "antiquity" since the Renaissance; and, especially, its location of the origins of modern humanism in Rome, rather than Greece, where it has been located since the revival of classical Greek studies inaugurated by Winckelmann in Germany at the end of the eighteenth century. I cannot address these issues in this limited space. For an extended qualified defense of Heidegger's genealogy, which also introduces Martin Bernal's location of the origins of the modern humanist representation of Western history in the "Aryan model" constructed by the German classicists of the eighteenth and early nineteenth centuries, see chapter 2, "Culture and Colonization: The Imperial Imperatives of the Centered Circle," in my book, *America's Shadow: An Anatomy of Empire.*

11. As I have shown in *America's Shadow,* this binarist system of naturalized ("white") metaphors, based on the assumed superiority of those who cultivated the earth on which they dwelled over those "nomadic" or "wandering" tribes that did not, pervades the discursive history of European and American imperialism up to the very present, as the binary between "developed" and "underdeveloped" nations testifies. And it has become a prominent topic of postcolonial criticism. See, for example, Peter Hulme, *Colonial Encounters: Europe and the Native Caribbean, 1492–1797* (London: Methuen, 1986); and Mary Louise Pratt, *Imperial Eyes: Travel Writing and Transculturation* (London: Routledge, 1992). What, however, is missing, and I submit, disabling, in these commentaries is the Roman provenance of this metaphorics. A notable exception is Richard Waswo, *The Founding Legend of Western Civilization: From Virgil to Vietnam* (Hanover, N.H.: Wesleyan University Press, 1997).

12. As I have shown more fully in *The End of Education* (Minneapolis: University of Minnesota Press, 1993), the Roman rhetoric that represents the disciplinary violence of education and the sociopolitical violence of colonialism in terms of "Culture" and the establishment of "Universal Peace" informs the discourse and practice of imperialist projects throughout the history of the Occident. I am not simply referring to those sanctioned by the *theologos* mediated by the Roman imperial model: for example, the projects of the Holy Roman Emperors and, from a different, i.e., Calvinist, representation of the *theologos,* of the American Puritans. See Sacvan Bercovitch, *The American Jeremiad* (Madison: University of Wisconsin Press, 1978) and my essay, "De-struction and the Critique of Ideology," in *Repetitions: The Postmodern Occasion in Literature*

and Culture (Baton Rouge: Louisiana State University Press, 1987), 282–84. I am also referring to those justified on anthropological grounds (the projects of Napoleonic France, Victorian England, and, less overtly, the modern United States. See my discussion of the discourse of the *Pax Britannica* and the *Pax Americana* in *America's Shadow.*

13. Martin Heidegger, *Parmenides,* vol. 54 of *Gesamtsausgabe* (Frankfurt am Main: Vittorio Klostermann, 1982), 67, my translation. The English translation is *Parmenides,* trans. Andre Schuwer and Richard Rojcewicz (Bloomington: University of Indiana Press, 1992). Subsequent citations will abbreviate *Parmenides* as *P* and include paginations from both the German original and English translation in parentheses.

14. Louis Althusser, "Ideology and Ideological State (Notes Towards an Investigation)," in *Lenin and Philosophy and Other Essays,* trans. Ben Brewster (New York: Monthly Review Press, 1971), 180–81. Behind Althusser's formulation of the subjected subject of Capitalism is, of course, Lacan's formulation of the subject of post-Freudian psychoanalysis; ahead of Althusser is Foucault's formulation of the subject of the disciplinary society. Is it exorbitant to say that Heidegger's formulation of the subject of humanism stands as a "point of departure" for this chain?

15. Martin Heidegger, "The Question Concerning Technology," in *The Question Concerning Technology and Other Essays,* trans. William Lovitt (New York: Harper and Row, 1977), 17–21. Just as Heidegger's understanding of the subject anticipates Althusser's interpellated subject, so also his understanding of "enframement" *(Ge-stell)* anticipates Althusser's "problematic," especially as its implications for sight are articulated in "From *Capital* to Marx's Philosophy," in *Reading Capital,* Louis Althusser and Etienne Balibar (London: Verso, 1970), 24–28. See also Spanos, "Althusser's 'Problematic' in the Context of The Vietnam War: Towards a Spectral Politics," *Rethinking Marxism* 10, no. 3 (fall 1998): 1–21.

16. Michel Foucault, *Discipline and Punish: The Birth of the Prison,* trans. Alan Sheridan (New York: Pantheon, 1977), 31.

17. Michel Foucault, "Theatrum Philosophicum," in *Language, Counter-Memory, Practice: Selected Essays and Interviews,* ed. Donald F. Bouchard, trans. Donald F. Bouchard and Sherry Simon (Ithaca: Cornell University Press, 1977), 168, 170.

18. Michel Foucault, "Final Interview, " *Raritan* 5, no. 1 (summer, 1985), 8–9.

19. Michel Foucault, "Nietzsche, Genealogy, History," in *Language, Counter-Memory, Practice,* 152. The paradox that this "Egyptianism" is also an "Apollonianism" should not be overlooked.

20. Michel Foucault, *Surveiller et punir: Naissance de la prison* (Paris: Editions Gallimard, 1975). In Alan Sheridan's English translation, *Discipline and Punish: The Birth of the Prison* (New York: Pantheon, 1977; hereafter cited as *DP*), the title obscures the crucial relationship between visual perception and power and thus diverts the reader from making the connection between the metaphysical tradition (and the cultural apparatuses to which it has given rise) and sociopolitical power, i.e. from the affiliative relationship between Foucault's and Heidegger's discourses.

21. Michel Foucault, "Truth and Power," in *Power/Knowledge: Selected Interviews and Other Writings, 1972–1977,* ed. Colin Gordon (New York: Pantheon, 1980), 112; my emphasis.

22. For an influential example of this distorting limitation of Foucault's genealogy of the panoptic gaze to the post-Enlightenment and his critique to empirical science, see Martin Jay's unsympathetic essay, "In the Empire of the Gaze: Foucault's Denigration of Vision in Twentieth-Century French Thought," in *Foucault: A Critical Reader,* ed. David Couzens Hoy (Oxford: Basil Blackwell, 1986). Jay delimits the context of Foucault's analysis of the gaze to the modern French interrogation of visualism and the

origins of this French initiative to Bergson's critique of science as the "spatialization of time" *(durée réele)*. It thus obscures the affinities of Foucault's "denigration of vision" with Heidegger's and the larger (historical) context it is the purpose of this essay to thematize: that which understands the ideological continuity between the "objectivity" of empirical science and the "disinterestedness" of "lyrical" humanism. Jay widens the context of this modern "denigration" of visual perception in his magisterial, but deeply flawed *Downcast Eyes: The Denigration of Vision in Twentieth-Century Thought* (Berkeley and Los Angeles: University of California Press, 1993).

23. From Foucault's demystified perspective, as from Heidegger's, the term "Enlightenment" assumes an ironic significance. The emphasis on the spatializing eye, which, in fact, deliberately forgets or conceals temporal being for the sake of power over "it," becomes not simply a blindness, but a blinding insight. For a similar critique of the Enlightenment, see Max Horkheimer and Theodore Adorno, *Dialectic of the Enlightenment*, trans. John Cumming (New York: Herder and Herder, 1972).

24. Max Weber, *The Protestant Ethic and the Spirit of Capitalism*, trans. Talcott Parsons (New York: Scribners, 1958), 104–5.

25. This Calvinist ontology that compels the accommodation of the smallest detail to the inscrutable providential design of God was not, as Foucault seems to imply, restricted to the space of the nation. It was also applied to global space. This is specifically evident in the American Puritans' "errand-in-the-['New World'] wilderness" and its secularized counterpart, the post-Revolutionary imperial discourse of Manifest Destiny. It is also evident, if more generally, in the colonial discourse of Elizabethan and Augustan Britain. Daniel Defoe's *Robinson Crusoe* bears synecdochical witness to this.

26. Though Foucault is referring here specifically to Jean Baptiste de la Salle's "dream of the ideal classroom in *Conduite des ecoles chretiennes*" (B.N. Ms. 11759), it is clear that the reference is intended to apply to other disciplinary institutions as well.

27. According to Foucault, "the power of the Norm appears" when the emergent disciplines combined with "other powers—Law, the Word *(Parole)*, and the Text, Tradition"—and with surveillance to become fundamental to the pedagogical economy of power in modern society: "The Normal is established as a principle of coercion in teaching with the introduction of a standardized education and the establishment of the *écoles normales* [teacher training colleges]. . . . Like surveillance and with it, normalization becomes one of the great instruments of power at the end of the classical age" (*DP*, 184; see also 192).

28. See Robert Marzec, "Enclosures, Colonization, and the English Novel: Inhabiting Land in the British Empire" (Ph.D. diss., State University of New York at Binghamton, 2000). Using Gilles Deleuze and Félix Guattari's treatise on "Nomadology" in *A Thousand Plateaus: Capitalism and Schizophrenia* (trans. Brian Massumi [Minneapolis: University of Minnesota Press, 1987]) as a point of departure Marzec has productively explored the momentous literary, cultural, and sociopolitical effects of the decisive demographic transformation precipitated by the enclosure movement in Britain in the period of the Enlightenment.

29. Using Bentham's own words, Foucault underscores the polyvalency of this Panoptic schema: "It is a way of obtaining from power 'in hitherto unexampled quantity,' 'a great and new instrument of government.' . . ; its great excellence consists in the great strength it is capable of giving to *any* institution it may be thought proper to apply it to" (*DP*, 206–7).

30. Foucault, "Nietzsche, Genealogy, History," 100.

31. Though Foucault, following Bentham, emphasizes the domestic sociopolitical scene in *Discipline and Punish*, he is not unaware of the applicability of the panoptic

mechanism to imperial theory and practice. See, for example, his references to the Napoleonic empire, most notably on pages 168–69.

32. Michel Foucault, *The History of Sexuality*, vol. 1, *An Introduction*, trans. Robert Hurley (New York: Pantheon Books, 1978), 10. For Foucault's generalization of the "repressive hypothesis" to include other sociopolitical sites besides the sexual, i.e., his recognition of its polyvalency, see also "Truth and Power," 109–33.

33. For a succinct account of Foucault's understanding of the repressive hypothesis, see Hubert L. Dreyfuss and Paul Rabinow, *Michel Foucault: Beyond Structuralism and Hermeneutics* (Chicago: University of Chicago Press, 1982), 129–30.

34. Michel Foucault, "Truth and Power," 119.

35. Michel Foucault, *The History of Sexuality* 1: 88–89. See also "Truth and Power," 121.

36. Should the convergence I am suggesting sound like a perverse imposition on Foucault's texts, let me retrieve a largely overlooked dimension of his genealogy of European modernity, which, though he subordinates it to his immediate focus on the emergent technologies of discipline (the discourse of detail, the table, the examination, anatomy, and so forth), nevertheless informs them through and through. I am referring to what Foucault calls "the Roman reference" (briefly remarked above in my citation of the military camp as a source of the panoptic diagram): the fact that the Age of the Enlightenment was also an age that modeled its cultural, military, and sociopolitical self-image on Roman (not Greek) antiquity. "One should not forget," Foucault writes, in invoking the synecdochical example of the "pyramidal" supervisory structure of the French Jesuit colleges, "that, generally speaking, the Roman model, at the Enlightenment, played a dual role; in its republican aspect, it was the very embodiment of liberty; in its military aspect, it was the ideal schema of discipline. The Rome of the eighteenth century and of the Revolution was the Rome of the Senate, but it was also that of the legion; it was the Rome of the Forum but it was also that of the camps" (*DP*, 146).

37. Martin Heidegger, "A Dialogue on Language (Between a Japanese and an Inquirer)", trans. Peter D. Hertz, in *On the Way to Language* (New York: Harper and Row, 1971), 15. See also, Heidegger, "The End of Philosophy and the Task of Thinking," in *Basic Writings:* "The end of philosophy proves to be the triumph of the manipulable arrangement of a scientific-technological world and of the social order proper to this world. The end of philosophy means the beginning of the world civilization based upon Western European thinking" (377).

38. Heidegger, *Parmenides*, 60.

39. Michel Foucault, "Questions on Geography," in *Power/Knowledge*, 69; my emphasis. The parallel between this genealogy of the discourse of geography and Heidegger's should not be overlooked. As I have suggested elsewhere, the interlocutors' comment that this discourse "grew up in the shadow of the military" is very likely a reference to the complicity of the Roman or Romanized Greek geographies—those of Pliny, Strabo, Diodorus Siculus, and so on—with the Roman imperial project. See Spanos, "Culture and Colonization: The Imperial Imperatives of the Centered Circle," in *America's Shadow: An Anatomy of Empire*, 64–125. See also Claude Nicolet, *Space, Geography, and Politics in the Early Roman Empire* (Ann Arbor: University of Michigan Press, 1991).

Heidegger, Foucault, and the Askeses of Self-Transformation

Edith Wyschogrod

Heidegger and Foucault can be envisioned as thinkers of emancipatory askeses, disciplines of liberation in which each may be seen as engaged in the freeing of knowledge and truth from embedding contexts of repressive epistemological constraints and their ancillary ethical implications, a freeing through which a certain release is attained.[1] Deconstructive techniques in which historical accretions are not merely jettisoned but reenvisioned are deployed by Heidegger to deliver the relation of Being and beings into what he calls a concealing-revealing and by Foucault to uncover the disguises truth wears by bringing to light the strategic power relations that generate the practices of knowledge, politics, and culture.

Foucault insists that philosophy "was and continues to be an 'ascesis,' *askesis,* that thinking is a self-transformative exercise" (*UP,* 9).[2] Distinguished from asceticism understood as the renunciation of pleasure, the term *askesis* is interpreted by Foucault as a mode of self-transformative freedom. Applied to Heidegger, askesis in this sense can be envisaged as a disciplined questioning of the meaning of Being, language, and truth, when applied to Foucault as a probing of strategies for the formation and reinvention of self. In a succinct statement of the direction such a project might take and in which issues of sex and gender figure, Foucault proclaims:

> The *askesis* is a work one performs upon oneself in order to transform oneself or make the self appear that happily one never attains. Can that be our problem today? We've rid ourselves of asceticism. Yet it's up to us to advance into a homosexual *askesis* that would make us work on ourselves and invent, I do not say discover, a manner of being that is still improbable. (*FL*, 206)[3]

Although the perspective of this statement seems to veer drastically from that of Heidegger's thought, insofar as Foucault is engaged in a Nietzsche-like reversal, he remains comprehensible in Heideggerian terms: the meaning of Being experienced as Spirit is inverted and Being is seen as corporeality. As Otto Pöggeler notes, for Heidegger "this metaphysical interpretation [of Being as Spirit] is upended when (in Nietzsche) the body becomes the guiding thread."[4]

For Foucault, repressive self-formation is an expression of what he calls technologies of the self, modes of imposing thought conformations upon corporeality, especially in its sexual expressions. Foucault concedes that there are preferable modes of configuring, but no egress from the necessity for an askesis or discipline of self-formation.[5] Similarly for Heidegger thought cannot escape the thinking of Being even when Being is manifested in calculative representation, its current mode of disclosure, one that constitutes a clear and present danger in which, however, there can be found a saving power. Heidegger's questioning of the essence of technology is a questioning that is already *unterwegs* (underway) to deliverance. Through a discipline of silence and listening presaged in his earliest work and elaborated in his later descriptions of the essence of technology and the shaping of the artwork, we may encounter the incalculable that cannot be represented.

I shall, in my analysis, pursue these lines of inquiry by envisioning each thinker as questioner of the other. Rather than engaging in an exercise in intellectual history, influences upon and shifts within their thought will be mentioned only when relevant to the larger narrative.[6] I discuss first the meaning of questioning as a point of orientation, a questioning that includes both existential involvement and distancing from the question.[7] I turn next to Heidegger's interrogation of Western philosophy's articulation of Being and truth and to Foucault's approaches to philosophical discourse, archaeological as the exhuming of the rules of conceptual and social practices and genealogical as a tracking of regulations and protocols that govern the modern subject's self-transformations. Neither approach will be conceived as a method (a term already tainted by virtue of its relation to the being of the modern subject), but rather as a purifying activity, an emancipatory askesis.

I then consider several modes of askesis as pathways: the paths of thinking, of the appropriation of death and sexuality and of shaping the body through the practices of medicine and art. In each case, work and thought are not severed, but rather *melete* (Latin *meditatio*) and *gymnasia* (to train oneself) can be seen to interact, to work in tandem as dynamic aspects of self-formation.[8]

Exhibiting an Askesis as the Askesis of Exhibiting

Despite the dearth of extended commentary about Heidegger by Foucault, it is no secret that he considered Heidegger's thought significant for the formation of his own. As early as in his 1955 comments on Ludwig Binswanger, Foucault proclaims the advantages of Binswanger's appropriation of Heidegger for psychoanalysis over a purely Freudian description of psychic life. More important, Foucault discovers in the later Heidegger the view that human beings are constituted by historical practices, thereby linking Heidegger's depiction of the oblivion of Being to his own archaeological method as an exhuming of the epistemic, social, and political practices that enable a given science or discipline to be seen as true.[9]

Conceding both indebtedness and suspicion, Foucault contrasts his own work, "[t]he precise domain of [which] is what I should call technologies . . . discourses about the subject," with Heidegger's interest in the formation of the object. For Heidegger it is as "an increasing obsession with *techne* as the only way to arrive at an understanding of objects that the West lost touch with Being." Identifying his own enterprise as a reversal of Heidegger's, Foucault proclaims: "Let's turn the question around and ask which techniques and practices form the Western concept of the subject, giving it its characteristic split of truth and error, freedom and constraint" (*RC*, 161 n. 4).[10] Yet Foucault's allegation that Heidegger is inattentive to the subject neglects the focus in *Sein und Zeit* upon uncovering the obscuring of the being we ourselves are.[11] Foucault's point, however, is not to discover a more primordial ground concealed by the cognitive subject, but to bring to the fore the political implications of self-formation.

In something like the manner in which Vedic religions speak of wiping away mind-obscuring karma, Heidegger hopes to illuminate the ways in which truth has been covered over and encrypted. Speaking of his inquiry as "build[ing] a way, a way of thinking" (*QCT,* 5) that is to bring about the experiencing of the essence of technology, he warns that we are caught up in what is merely instrumental, technology's effort to take hold of itself in an act of willful mastery.[12] Deconstructing the notion of instrumentality demands an understanding of the means-end relation, of cause and effect, that Heidegger in a Nietzsche-like move unmasks as a relation of indebtedness, one that is not to be interpreted in moral terms, but rather as a thinking of what has heretofore remained unthought in the essence of technology. Indebtedness and responsibility are given new meaning as a letting come forth into presence. Thus, significations that have piggybacked on one another are peeled away and the bringing forth of that which presences into appearance is brought to light. Neither an askesis of repristinization nor a nostalgic willing back, the process Heidegger describes, is an undoing of technology as mastery that is at once deconstructive and salvific. Such questioning elicits the meaning of bringing-forth that is a "moving freely in revealing *(das Entbergen),*" a term derived from *bergen,* to rescue, and leads back to the much commented upon term *aleutheia,* unconcealment. In the present context, bringing-forth may be read (boldly) as an askesis of cognitive liberation.

Foucault questions not the ontological conditions that make it possible for there to be philosophical practices at all, but rather how and why at any given time something can be said, but not some other thing. He proceeds by interrogating what he calls an archive, "the mass of things spoken in a culture, conserved, valorized, reused, repeated and transformed." He goes on to say that "[t]he 'archive' appears then as a kind of great practice of discourse, a practice which has its rules, its conditions, its functioning and its effects" (*FL,* 58). In proceeding archaeologically, Foucault attempts to understand the rules of formation governing the human sciences, not in a quest for origins, but rather in an effort to uncover a site where he hopes to find the rules and protocols that render possible the existence of the matrix from which thought emerges, in short of the archive.

Without abandoning archaeology when dealing with the subject as a locus of corporeal activities, Foucault initiates inquiry with a current social or political question, thereby introducing genealogical concerns. Such an analysis is located at the point where an archaeology of problematizations and a genealogy of practices intersect (*UP,* 12–13).

This strategy will be seen to yield an account that shifts from the rule-governed care of the self in the Greco-Roman world to later Christian practices of confession and penitential ritual, a history of progressive etiolation that moves from a disciplined corporeal erotics to a discourse of chastity.

On the face of it, Foucault might ask, is Heidegger's quest not also genealogical, but in the pejorative sense of seeking to return to origins, thereby distinguishing it from his own? Does Heidegger not use such phrases as "that which endures primally out of the earliest beginning"? It can be replied, however, that when Heidegger interrogates the essence of technology, there is no intent to reveal a ground or primordium, but rather to heed what has been said and is now no longer said by philosophy. To bring to the fore what cannot now be said, one must first grasp the current mode of Being's revelation, a mode Heidegger calls Enframing *(Gestell)*. In the mode of Enframing, beings manifest themselves as standing-reserve and Being reveals itself as a storehouse of energy that is stockpiled in order to be managed. Heidegger states repeatedly that he is not a Romantic who seeks to revive the pretechnological past, but rather he hopes to free thought from the ontological entrapment of the Gestell (*QCT*, 22). In Foucauldian terms, Enframing expresses power. Like Foucault, Heidegger recognizes in the contemporary will to truth a will to control whose very essence is unfreedom. Thus an emancipatory askesis must somehow be will-less insofar as "the essence of freedom cannot originally be connected with the will or even with the causality of human willing." Instead, it is as "the happening of revealing, i.e., of truth, that freedom stands in the closest and most intimate kinship" (*QCT*, 25).

Thought's Way: How Thinking Exculpates

Heidegger is careful to maintain that thought's way is not the knowledge of philosophy's history as an account of conceptual change, that the meaning of concepts continues to withdraw from us unless we first know who we ourselves are.[13] Philosophizing "is a questioning in which we inquire into beings as a whole and inquire in such a way that in so doing we ourselves, the questioners, are thereby also included in the question, placed into question" (*FCM*, 9). Unlike the inquiries of the special sciences, such questioning involves the repertoire of all the self's comportments in its world relations, a questioning that itself constitutes a discipline.

For Heidegger, thinking is a transformative art, one that radically changes the way in which the meaning of Being is understood. Metaphysics or philosophizing that takes the meaning of Being as self-evident presencing must be overcome, not bypassed or leapt over. Thinking must engage in the arduous task of passing through the history of metaphysics by thinking what is unthought in it, its concealed ground, Being or *Seyn* (Heidegger's occasional archaism) as distinguished from the truth of beings. This task is not an academic exercise, but an intense struggle, a recasting of thinking so as to free thinking to experience the truth of Being. Thus, Heidegger insists, even if metaphysical questioning is comprehensive, "[n]o, matter how extensively we are concerned *about it*, everything remains a misunderstanding unless we are *gripped* by such questioning. . . . Although we have spoken *of* philosophy, we have not yet spoken *from out of it*" (*FCM*, 57).

Genuine questioning is not to be confused with an inquiry into phenomena as an interrogation of present being, but is rather a questioning "without why." Contrasting the why of aetiological inquiry with the questioning that seeks the because of an abyss-al ground, Heidegger alludes to the mystical tradition of Angelus Silesius, for whom the rose *is* simply because it *is*. Thus Heidegger writes: "The because which wards off every accounting for and every why, names the simple plain lying before that is without why, upon which everything depends, everything rests."[14]

An askesis, and especially one of questioning, it could be argued, would self-destruct without rules for combatting errancy. But if Heidegger implies that erring consists in making "the why" the origin of thought, does he not thereby put forth a rule for erring? However, the why cannot be interpreted in this way for, were this the case, thought would be trapped by the self-reflexive paradox of the why itself, by the presumption that an explanatory why can be given for rejecting the why. Such an account would already reflect the view that truth is correctness, the possibility of a correspondence between question and answer, that statements mirror states of affairs just as they are.

In his account of truth as correspondence, Heidegger maintains that as a condition of presentness, there is that which stands in contrast to the present being, that is, in contrast to the thing, and is placed over and against us. The appearing of the thing can be seen as a traversing of this opposition. The thing's appearing, or crossing over into presence, occurs within an opening whose openness is not created by presenting itself but is prior to it, an openness that is free to take on the strictures of presenting. Thus, "Freedom is setting oneself free for what is manifest in the open, as letting the being be."[15]

If the thinking of Being is without why, "a highly errant . . . matter," may we then conclude that thought is an askesis of nihilism, of the "lawless caprice" pinpointed by Nietzsche from which the true has vanished (*PLT,* 186)?[16] In a statement whose mood suggests an empassioned quietism, Heidegger, in a 1950 letter to a student, writes: "To think Being means to respond to the appeal of its presencing, an appeal both revealed and veiled" (*PLT,* 185). Reminiscent of the voices of Silesius and Eckhart so familiar to the early Heidegger, thinking is said to demand "long concentration and constant testing of its hearing" if the respondent to the appeal of Being is not to go astray. What must also be thought in this context is the absence of God and the divinities whose fullness now exists in the manner of not being, a "no longer" which is itself "a not-yet" (*PLT,* 184). Heidegger's response is not one of despair, but rather can be envisioned as an askesis for what he calls a destitute time: "learning the craft of thinking, unswerving, yet erring" (*PLT,* 186).

For Foucault philosophy in the positive sense is a stepping back in order to detach oneself from received views of truth. As an activity directed to transforming conceptual frameworks and accepted values, to philosophize is both to "think otherwise" and "to do something else."[17] Whereas for Heidegger, thinking-questioning interrogates the history of metaphysics, Foucault turns instead to "a history of 'ethics,'" understood as an account of the rules of self-formation "that enable an individual to fashion himself into a subject of ethical conduct" (*UP,* 251). Yet, in a move reminiscent of Heideggerian questioning, Foucault disavows the history of mentalities and of ideas as constituting thought. As distinguished from representations that accompany behavior and from attitudes that ground it, inquiry is to problematize, to step back from modes of acting and place them in question: "Thought is freedom in relation to what one does, the motion by which one detaches oneself from it, establishes it as an object and reflects on it as a problem" (*E,* 17).[18] Problematization defamiliarizes its object by eliciting the conditions that render a political, social, or cultural object possible and to which those engaged in its practices are likely to be oblivious.

Foucault does not hesitate to name such philosophizing as thought's critical inspection of itself, an askesis, a getting free of oneself: "The living substance of philosophy," was and continues to be "an 'ascesis,' *askesis,* an exercise of oneself in the activity of thought" (*UP,* 9). In so doing, the "truth games" played out in specific technologies of the self are exposed. It is not the manipulation of things and signs that principally concerns Foucault, but the technology of self he identifies as conduct-regulating, a technology of power that determines individual behavior and makes possible the individual's submission to domination. Eschewing straightforward determinism, Foucault acknowledges those technologies of the self that enable individuals alone or with the aid of others to alter themselves, to effect radical changes "upon their own bodies, and souls, thought, conduct, and way of being, so as to transform themselves in order to attain a certain state of happiness, purity, wisdom, perfection or immortality" (*TS,* 18).

Ars Erotica, Artes Moriendi: The Ways of Sex and Death

Before they can consider the thought formations in which sex and death are configured as human constructs, it is crucial for Heidegger and Foucault to disentangle them from the view that they are natural processes. What is meant by nature must be thematized in that a category mistake in this regard might convey the misleading view that the purpose of a liberating askesis is a return to nature.

Although inferences about human sexuality as a natural process might be drawn by attending to what Heidegger means by world, there is no specific discussion of sexual being in his major works as there is, for example, of motility.[19] It could be surmised that one among many possible explanations for such reticence stems from a worry about reviving the suppositions of an Aristotelian biology, according to which human sexuality is linked to animal nature, a position that Heidegger would unequivocally reject.

In depicting the being of animals, Heidegger focuses on the distinction between having a world and the privation of world: the animal is "poor in world" whereas human beings are world forming. Disavowing any hierarchical assessment of the difference, Heidegger offers this graphic example: "When we say the lizard is lying on a rock, we ought to cross out the word rock. . . . whatever the lizard is lying on is given *in some way* for the lizard and yet is not known to the lizard as rock" (*FCM,* 197). Heidegger contrasts *behavior,* a term applied to animals as "captivated," as impelled by drives *(Trieben),* with *comportment*, a term that refers to the human way of being as inhabiting a world. Animals live in an environment in which they struggle to maintain themselves against a "disinhibiting ring," an environmental encircling that triggers its behavior (*FCM*, 253–54). Described privatively, animal being is lived as a withholding of the ability to take something as something. It is not, however, as a contrast between animal disinhibition *(Enthemmung)* and human life as existence in a meaning-laden world or between animal reproduction and human sexuality that Heidegger turns to explicate the meaning of human being, but rather to human mortality. "Because captivation belongs to the essence of the animal, the animal cannot die in the sense in which dying is ascribed to human beings but can only come to an end" (*FCM*, 267).

Were one to view Heidegger's account of mortality in *Being and Time* through the lens of Foucault, it might be seen as an exhumation of Dasein's finitude as a fundamental possibility of its existence that Dasein must take upon itself as an askesis in the interest of liberating itself from socially constructed views. Dasein, the being that one is, is an entity distinguished by the fact that Being is an issue for it. For Foucault, the modern subject must be released from the conceptual and institutional practices, the sexual politics that form it, whereas for Heidegger, the self is "liberated" when it transforms everyday existence into clarified existence to become the Dasein it is by exposing its death as its ownmost potentiality for Being. Each Dasein must take on this possibility for itself: no one can die for one. What is at stake is the very Being-in-the-World of the Dasein. Its death is the possibility of no-longer-being-able-to-be-there. As its ownmost possibility, "Dasein cannot outstrip the possibility of death. Death is the possibility of the absolute impossibility of Dasein," revealed to it not cognitively, but through anxiety (*BT*, 294).[20] Such anxiety is not a failing of Dasein, but a basic mood grounded in a fundamental comportment, that of Care *(Sorge)*.

To uncover one's mortality is not yet to grasp the manner in which it is camouflaged in everyday existence. Just as, for Foucault, the sexual discourses entrenched in Western thought exhibit modes of flight from the intensities of pleasure, so, for Heidegger, the public interpretation of death or the They-self, *Das Man*, tranquillizes Dasein in the face of death. Does not everyone after all die, it is asked? But the fact that death occurs is only empirically certain and not yet existentially decisive. That which brings Dasein out of its evasiveness, Heidegger designates a call *(Ruf)* of conscience *(des Gewissens)*, a summoning of the Dasein from its lostness in the They-self. The Dasein must respond by gathering itself together so that it can assume its own death. First, a primordial being-guilty that prepares one for anxiety must be dislodged from the sense of moral guilt bound up with the Kantian view of conscience. Heidegger calls this new state of mind resoluteness, "a reticent self-projection upon one's 'ownmost being-guilty,' in which one is ready for anxiety" (*BT,* 343). Resoluteness is not an act of abstract willing, but always determines what is possible at a specifiable moment.

Yet to grasp becoming ready for anxiety is no simple matter. Just as the Dasein must distinguish the interpretation of death by the They-self that lulls it into tranquillity from the resolute appropriation of its own death, so, too, it must be alert to the difference between the affect of fear, an awaiting or a feeling threatened in the face of something, and anxiety. The latter is not concerned with anything definite, but is a mood that disengages one from the world and renders impossible the projecting of oneself upon some potentiality for Being that depends on some specific object of concern. The disclosure of this impossibility is not intended to lead to despair, but rather to reveal what is already there and for which one has anxiety, namely Dasein itself (*BT,* 393).

Unlike the drifting of fear from one worldly possibility to another and that is lived as a present that one can neither hold on to nor repeat, anxiety has its own mode of temporality. It brings one up against one's thrownness as a *repeatable* possibility. "The character of having-been is constitutive for . . . anxiety; and bringing one face to face with repeatability is the specific ecstatical mode of this character" (*BT,* 394). Although anxiety is grounded in the pastness of its repeatability, it must be recalled that it is resoluteness that makes anxiety possible and that the mode of temporalization of resoluteness is future in that resoluteness is lived as an anticipation of Dasein's death. Thus a temporal complexity is intrinsic to an askesis driven by mortality: Dasein in the pastness of anxiety repeats, reappropriates its future mortality in resoluteness. As in the lives of the saints in late antiquity who are freed from worldliness by withdrawal and meditation upon death, anxiety liberates the Dasein from concern with the world.[21] That anxiety thus understood is perceived as liberating is explicitly stated: "Anxiety liberates [Dasein] *from* possibilities that count for nothing" (*BT,* 395).

As is the case with death for Heidegger, for Foucault the truth of sexuality cannot be liberated by understanding sexuality as a "natural" process. "It is not through sexuality that we communicate with the orderly and pleasingly profane world of animals; rather sexuality is a fissure . . . which marks the limit within us and designates us as a limit" (*RC*, 58). Instead (glossing the thought of Georges Bataille), Foucault argues that what gives sexuality its unique character is its power to profane in a world from which, paradoxically, the sacred has already been evacuated. The sacred is reconstructed as an empty form, one that does not revert to natural being but rather proclaims the death of God.[22] What may be disguised as a discourse of natural animality is unmasked as theological discourse expressing the absence of God.

Transgression thus understood involves limit, the line it crosses ever so briefly, the "narrow zone where it displays the flash of its passage" (*RC*, 60). Without a limit to breach, transgression would not exist and, if the limit were illusory, transgression would have nothing to violate. Limit as limit must return to the uncrossable. It would be "a reductive exercise," as Jeremy R. Carrette believes, to subsume Foucault's efforts to grasp the complexities of his own gay sexuality in terms of "limit experience" (*RC*, 19). Instead, the value of limit-experience lies in its enabling the subject to think itself without entrapment (*RC*, 23). Transgression is neither a dialectical overcoming, nor a triumph over limits but a nonpositive affirmation that propels being to its limit. The circular path in which it moves leads to the claim that we are becoming more Greek. Yet this circular return to what Foucault calls a homeland (*RC*, 62) cannot be identified with Heidegger's valorization of home that is embedded in an autochthony that would resolve oppositions.

Linked to the imbrication of sacred and profane, to a limit that is exposed in the ontological void left by the death of God, sexuality is tamed by a language that has become a juridical discourse without a divine lawgiver. Foucault's efforts at deconstructing this change indicate a step toward inventing forward-looking contemporary social practices that would intensify pleasure. Freedom today, he insists, is not a matter of unleashing desire, which, in any case, is always already expressed in sexual practices, but of escaping deceptively emancipatory strategies, formulaic views of sexuality such as that of the pure sexual encounter. Thus when Foucault speaks of homosexuality as liberating, his remarks are not directed toward establishing a new gay profile, but rather as a move toward defining a new way of life, "[as] an historic occasion to reopen affective and relational virtualities not so much through the [homosexual's] intrinsic qualities but, due to the biases against the position that he occupies" (*FL*, 207). The problem is not that of enhancing self-knowledge, but rather of establishing a new nexus of relations that Foucault prefers to call friendship (*FL*, 204). Xenophon's account of filia as conversing, confiding, rejoicing, or commiserating together into old age can be said to capture this view (*UP*, 201).

Shaping the Body: From Medicine to Artwork

In accordance with the regimen of studying the "arts of oneself, the aesthetics of existence," Foucault maintains, the self is not only a work of conceptual formation but can be shaped as a work of art (*E*, 207). The expression "technology of the self" is to be understood in relation to the term *techne* in its primordial Greek meaning as a "practice," a knowing how or *savoir faire* in the sense of an art (*UP*, 62). But is there not a difficulty in conflating philosophical thought with art in the process of self-formation? Had Heidegger not warned against identifying art as well as religion with philosophy?

To understand Heidegger's reservations, it is important to see that he does not contest the necessity of encountering art and religion along the way in the quest for revealing the true, but rather their exploitation, their interpretation as tools in the interest of philosophizing (*FCM*, 2–3). Thus Heidegger (like Foucault) does not hesitate to invoke the Greek use of *techne* in depicting the crossing over from truth to the work, proclaiming, "There was a time when the bringing-forth of the true into the beautiful was called *techne*. And the *poeisis* of the fine arts was also called *techne*" (*QCT*, 34).

Lest the difference between philosophy and art be mistakenly imagined to reflect the distinction between thought as somehow passive and the effort that creates an object as active, it is worth noting that only in speaking *about* philosophy do we remain quiescent. "What is decisive, however, is that we emerge from this dealing with . . . *and take action within metaphysics itself*" (ellipsis in original) (*FCM*, 57). Philosophy as a listening-questioning is not a sinking into lethargy, but an activity of a special kind, a fundamental attunement as a presupposition for thinking and acting. Heidegger speaks not of affective or cognitive ascertaining, but rather of "letting whatever is sleeping *become wakeful*" (*FCM*, 60). Reminiscent of the words of Bach's cantata, "*Wachet auf ruft uns die Stimme,*" conscience issues a wake-up call. In a perhaps unguarded Heideggerian moment, Foucault concludes that critical thinking must "bring an idea to life . . . light fires, watch the grass grow, listen to the wind, catch the sea-foam in the breeze and scatter it. It would multiply not judgments, but signs of existence; it would summon them, drag them from their sleep."[23]

If art, like philosophy, is to constitute an awakening, Foucault believes that the artistic shaping of the self must issue in new forms of conduct (*UP*, 13). In tracking the history of this shaping, he describes the body in the classical period as the locus of pleasure and the truth of the body as constructed by medical practices. Conceived not only as a fund of knowledge designed for the cure of disease, medicine was also envisaged as a collection of rules specifying dietary and gymnastic regimens that determined how one was to live. The discourse of medicine was intended to forestall death by creating the body as a work that would be immortal, yet constrained by the corruptible matter that nature uses. Although Foucault does not make the connection, such a conception of the body bears comparison with the received view of the artwork as a passport to immortality.[24] Foucault notes that the Greek physician Galen's account of sexuality situates sexuality in the context of death and immortality. To overcome the corruptibility of the body, "nature had to place the principle of a force, an extraordinary dynamis in the body and soul of the living creature."[25] Galen concludes that pleasure is not incidental to sexual acts, but is imprinted in the body in a way that is irresistible and that, through the circulation of fluids and pneuma generated by sexual activity, the entire body is involved.

Foucault continually wrestles with the question of why Western thought aims to determine the truth about sex rather than to invent ways to intensify sexual pleasure. How, he asks, is an *ars erotica* in this culture to be released from its embedding in a *scientia sexualis?* In reaching for this desideratum he notices that Eastern societies "[define] . . . an art which would be an art of producing, through sexual relations or with the sexual organ, the type of pleasure that one seeks to make the most intense, the strongest, or as long-lasting as possible" (*RC*, 119). At the same time, he maintains that his analyses are not aimed at excoriating historical practices to revert to a priorly selected default position, but rather to track the ways in which the control of pleasure shapes the subject in the hope of inventing an askesis, at once disciplined and transgressive, that maximizes rather than represses pleasure.[26]

Foucault's diachronic narrative of sexual practices can be seen as moving from care of the self as self-knowledge, from the classical *gnothi seauton* (know yourself), to the era of early Christianity, when the self is interpreted in terms of renunciation of the world and sex. What is crucial in this trajectory is the intervening step of transformation from an erotics that recognizes the freedom of the other to a philosophical askesis as a quest for truth, "[an] 'asceticism' [that] was not a means of disqualifying the love of boys [but] a means of . . . giving it shape and form, of valorizing it" (*UP*, 245). Corporeality is configured as a progressive etiolation of the body as ancient rules for care of the self give way to later configurations.

Thus in *Alcibiades I,* Socrates persuades Alcibiades to submit to him in a relationship that is essentially pedagogical and in which concern for the self is still bound up with erotic and political practices. Care of the self is envisaged as tendence of the soul construed not as substance, but as activity and as requiring attention to the divine element in itself. In the second century, attention is still paid to older medical accounts of corporeality, but at the same time, a shift from the Platonic culture of dialogue to one of listening to truth and to oneself could be discerned, an attentiveness to self that is designed to uncover failures of strategy rather than moral flaws (*TS*, 34; *RC*, 128). In mining the texts of this period, Foucault finds a new apprehensiveness with respect to the effects of the abuse of pleasure on body and soul, a stress on conjugal relations and wariness with regard to the love of boys (*CS*, 39).

The link of self-formation to faith in early Christianity necessitated more abstemious protocols of self-purification.[27] Foucault refers to *exomologesis,* a term whose Christian meanings include a complex of penitential exercises such as fasting and sexual abstinence. Unlike the Stoic view that truth about the self is learned by memorizing rules, Foucault stresses that Christian *exomologesis* is a dramatic, not a verbal behavior: "Penance is not nominal but theatrical. . . . It rubs out the sin yet reveals the sinner" (*E*, 244). By contrast, *exagoreusis* is the self-renunciatory analysis and disclosure of one's thoughts to another so that the pedagogical relations of the ancient world become in monastic life a rule of total obedience to one's director (*E*, 246).

Foucault discovers in John Cassian's complex theory of vices according to which all vices are connected, the special importance of fornication. Even the defeat of a vice may not reflect a spiritual victory if its fall generates a presumptuousness that allows a new vice to erupt. In a structure of paired vices, fornication is tied to greed in that both involve the body. Fornication as a sin of the body must be fought not only mentally, but by "mortifying the flesh by vigils, fast and back-breaking labor" (*RC*, 190). Unlike the appetite for food, the sexual appetite is not needed to maintain life and thus can be resisted. Yet far from discussing actual sexual relations, Cassian describes the fight for chastity as an askesis whose success is measured in terms of the monk's unresponsiveness to various forms of temptation. What is to be fought is a concupiscent volition that may even infiltrate dreams, and whose exercise leads to pollution. It is no longer a question of bodily restraint, but rather of expunging images from the mind. Foucault notes in Augustine an obsession with the involuntary acts of the body, with libido or the autonomous movements of the sexual organs, organs that do not obey the will's commands (*E*, 182–83).

It should be clear that Foucault writes no ordinary history. In conformity with his stress on modes of stylization, he is less interested in determining the *reason* for the escalation of sexual prohibitions than the *manner* in which sex is given up and the body shaped. Thus it is not merely the transfer from actual to internalized prohibition, from outside to inside, but the development of new techniques, the birth of a desexualized technology of self that concerns Foucault (*RC*, 195–97).

Circumspect as Heidegger remains with regard to sexuality, it is noteworthy that some "conceptual threads" in his religion courses of 1920–21 can be seen as premonitory of Foucault's more open and robust discussion of various forms of Christian asceticism. To be sure, Heidegger does not attend to the minutiae of ritual practices but, in elaborating Christian themes, he attempts even in these early lectures to offer as the starting point of inquiry descriptions of factical transactions with the circumambient world, the world in which Christians found themselves.[28] It is in this context that the fissuring of self by sexuality makes a brief appearance. In his comments on Augustine's description of the self, Heidegger maintains that the despair that would engulf Augustine is mitigated by hope grounded in divine mercy. He notes, however, that the trade-off for this gift is continence. Thus Heidegger: "The righteous man must therefore be examined, tested and proven in his private parts, in his secrets, that is in his heart (inner reflection) and in his loins."[29]

To uncover the meaning of shaping for Heidegger, one must turn not to sexuality, but to what may seem far removed, his analysis of the origin of the artwork *(Kunstwerk)*. Heidegger notes that the inquiry into the origin of the work is already question-begging since to interrogate art by turning to the artwork presupposes that we know what art is. It is useful, he suggests, to begin with the thingly nature of the work, since the artwork is in some sense a thing. But the thing must be released from received views of it, especially from the view that thingliness is a fusion of matter and form, a view that is often misleadingly applied to the artwork as a composite of inert material substructure and specific shape. Instead, the work is an event, a happening, one in which, through the work's disclosure of what and how a thing is, a world opens, and is made to abide. It is important for the issue of self-formation to grasp the meaning of world in that world and human existence cannot be thought separately. Thus Heidegger:

> World is never an object . . . [but] the ever non-objective to which we are subject as long as the paths of birth and death, blessing and curse keep us transported into Being. Wherever those decisions of our history that relate to our very being are made, taken up and abandoned by us, go unrecognized, and are rediscovered by new inquiry, there the world worlds. (*PLT,* 44–45)

In another seemingly paradoxical claim, Heidegger insists that the artist is not showcased in the artwork, but is a passageway for the work. Yet Heidegger also holds that the work does not merely happen, but is created or brought forth through the *techne* that is art by the *technites,* the artist. An effort is made to resolve this difficulty by maintaining that creation is "causing something to emerge as a thing that has been brought forth" (*PLT,* 60). It is not the artist, but Art that is the origin of the work.

A further disclosure of art's ambiguity manifests itself in its truth as preservation. Far from reflecting a mere static persistence, preservation is active as the setting-forth of truth. Creation of the artwork entails "the fixing in place of a self-establishing truth in the figure bringing forth the unconcealedness of what is," but the work has an ongoing life. The setting-to-work of truth also means the bringing of "work-being into movement and happening as preservation" (*PLT,* 71). Art then is the becoming and happening of truth as creation and preservation. Far from merely reproducing a visible entity, art is a fixing in place of the becoming and happening of truth (*PL,* 36). Even if beings dissemble, this deception is also a condition for bringing to the fore the opposition of concealing and revealing in the occurring of truth in the artwork (*PLT,* 54–55).

In defiance of what a Heideggerian reading of the body might allow, can these doublings themselves not be set to work to expose the body in all of its thingliness and the work of the self as a bringing of this corporeality cogently into the open? If the art hidden in nature can be brought forth in the artwork, as Heidegger alleges, can the body not be thought anew as a unique work shaped by a *techne* in which artist and artwork constitute a single site, a body that is both one's ownmost and a being for the other, inside and outside itself, a eucharistic body, as it were, that exhibits and shrinks from its sacrality, one in which the history of corporeality is encrypted? Heidegger is hardly likely to view such an askesis with favor. Yet does one not in making the body one's own in acts of creation and preservation uncover pointers that, for those who understand, bring about a transformation of themselves?

Notes

1. See Otto Pöggeler, *Martin Heidegger's Path of Thinking,* trans. Daniel Magurshek and Sigmund Barber (Atlantic Highlands, N.J.: Humanities Press International, 1989), 191.

2. Michel Foucault, *The Use of Pleasure,* vol. 2 of *The History of Sexuality,* trans. Robert Hurley (New York: Pantheon Books, 1985), 9. Hereafter cited in the text as *UP.*

3. Michel Foucault, *Foucault Live (Interviews 1966–84),* trans. John Johnston, ed. Sylvère Lotringer (New York: Semiotext(e), 1989), 206. Hereafter cited in the text as *FL.*

4. Pöggeler, *Martin Heidegger's Path of Thinking,* 210.

5. In the interest of imagining Heidegger in engagement with Foucault, I use the term *self-formation* in relation to the thought of both. It should be noted, as Theodore Kisiel (*The Genesis of Heidegger's "Being and Time"* [Berkeley and Los Angeles: University of California Press, 1993]) warns, that the compound self-world used in the lectures of 1919–20 and 1925 to mean "the origin of the around world and with-world" through which one has oneself is abandoned in *Being and Time* (510). Kisiel sees this abandonment as reflecting Heidegger's move to the "transcendence of the world to original temporality" (388).

6. For an excellent brief account of changes in Foucault's thought and informed suggestions for further reading, see Mark Poster, "Foucault and the Problem of Self-Consciousness," in *Foucault and the Critique of Institutions,* ed. John D. Caputo and Mark Yount (University Park, Penn.: Pennsylvania State University Press, 1993), 63–80.

Heidegger bibliographies abound. The work of Theodore Kisiel contains selected bibliographic references.

7. Theodore Kisiel in *The Genesis of Heidegger's "Being and Time"* pinpoints the difference between formalized inquiry and existential asking. In the former the "trivial question . . . of *ens commune* [is that of] a remote I and not the distressed question of *ens proprium* of a fully engaged I" (513 n.13).

8. *Melete* is a term used in rhetoric to indicate the "work of preparing a discourse" or "an improvisation"; *gymnasia* is an activity in a real situation including sexual abstinence and physical privation. See Michel Foucault, *Technologies of the Self: A Seminar with Michel Foucault,* ed. Luther H. Martin, Huck Gutman, and Patrick H. Hutton (Amherst, Mass.: The University of Massachusetts Press, 1988), 36–37. Hereafter cited in the text as *TS.*

9. For a description of these changes see Hubert Dreyfus's preface to Michel Foucault, *Mental Illness and Psychology* (Berkeley and Los Angeles: University of California Press, 1962), esp. xxv–xl.

10. These comments are found in "About the beginning of the hermeneutics of the self (1980)," transcribed by Thomas Keenan and Mark Blasius, in Michel Foucault, *Religion and Culture,* ed. Jeremy R. Carrette (New York: Routledge, 1999). Hereafter cited in the text as *RC.*

11. For an account of the young Heidegger's interest in the medieval roots of "an attunement to the immediate life of subjectivity," see Theodore Kisiel, *The Genesis of Heidegger's "Being and Time,"* 81.

12. Martin Heidegger, *The Question Concerning Technology and Other Essays,* trans. William Lovitt (New York: Harper and Row, 1977, 5). Hereafter cited in the text as *QCT.*

13. Martin Heidegger, *The Fundamental Concepts of Metaphysics: World, Finitude, Solitude,* trans. William McNeill and Nicholas Walker (Bloomington: Indiana University Press, 1995), 4. Hereafter cited in the text as *FCM.*

14. Pöggeler, *Martin Heidegger's Path of Thinking,* 126.

15. Ibid., 76.

16. Martin Heidegger, *Poetry, Language, Thought,* trans. Albert Hofstadter (New York: Harper and Row, 1971), 186. Hereafter cited in the text as *PLT.*

17. Michel Foucault, "The Masked Philosopher," in *Politics, Philosophy, Culture: Interviews and Other Writings,* (New York: Routledge, 1988), 330.

18. Michel Foucault, *Ethics, Subjectivity and Truth,* vol. 1 of *Essential Works of Foucault 1954–1984,* ed. Paul Rabinow, trans. Robert Hurley (New York: The New Press, 1997), 117. Hereafter cited in the text as *E.*

19. Michael David Levin concedes in "The Ontological Dimension of Embodiment," in *The Body,* ed. Donn Welton (Blackwell: Oxford 1999), that "[d]iscussion about seeing and hearing, posture and gesture, bearing and handling are not regarded as discussions about the body" (127). But Levin concludes that "caring is contingent upon openness to what is other and the extent of such opennness to alterity is the measure of . . . the ontological dimension of our embodiment" (146).

20. Martin Heidegger, *Being and Time,* trans. John Macquarrie and Edward Robinson (New York: Harper and Row, 1962), 294. Hereafter cited in the text as *BT.*

21. Accounts of the young Heidegger's relation to the Christian mystical tradition now abound. Among them are Theodore Kisiel's work already cited; John van Buren, *The Young Heidegger: Rumors of the Hidden King* (Bloomington: Indiana University Press, 1994); John D. Caputo, *The Mystical Element in Heidegger's Thought* (New York: Fordham University Press, 1986); and Thomas Sheehan, "Heidegger's Early Years:

Fragments for a Philosophical Biography," in *Heidegger, The Man and the Thinker,* ed. Thomas Sheehan (Chicago: Precedent Press, 1981), 3–19.

22. For an account of premodern transgressiveness as a violation of limits established by ecclesiastic authority, see my *Saints and Postmodernism: Revisioning Moral Philosophy* (Chicago: University of Chicago Press, 1990), 12–13.

23. Foucault, "The Masked Philosopher," 326.

24. For a discussion of medicine in the classical period, see Michel Foucault, *The Care of the Self,* vol. 3 of *The History of Sexuality,* trans. Robert Hurley (New York, Random House, 1988), 99–104. Hereafter cited in the text as *CS.*

25. Ibid., 106.

26. The useful expression "ethical heuristic" is coined by James Faubion to describe this and related constructions of the subject.

27. In a severely critical reading of the biographical relevance of Foucault's descriptions of mystical experience found in James Miller in the *Passion of Michel Foucault* (London: Harper Collins, 1993), Jeremy R. Carrette argues that Miller conflates Foucault's accounts of Christian mysticism with his sexual practices in an effort to effect a "normalizing judgment" of Foucault. See *RC,* 13–24.

28. Heidegger's way of proceeding is explicated in his winter semester 1920–21 lectures in the *Phänomenologie des Religiosen Leben,* Gesamtausgabe, Band 60 (Frankfurt am Main: Vittorio Klostermann, 1995), erster Teil.

29. Kisiel, *The Genesis of Heidegger's "Being and Time,"* 200–1.

From Foucault to Heidegger: A One-Way Ticket?

Rudi Visker

Dasein, Heidegger says, stands in the truth. And not only that: it stands equiprimordially both in the truth and the untruth. Or in a later formulation on which the "Turning" has already stamped its seal: the untruth is "older" or "more primordial" than the truth itself, Dasein must be in the untruth to be in the truth.[1] Mendel, on the other hand, as we read in Foucault, lies outside the truth: what he says gets lost in the tumultuous space of a "wild exteriority," where those are referred whose speech does not conform to the rules that the "discursive police" of their discipline set down.[2]

Mendel produced, if we are to believe Foucault, "true statements, but wasn't involved 'within the true' of the biological discourse of his time" (*OD*, 61). Because Mendel lies outside of the truth, what he says can only take monstrous and grotesque forms, and this deformation makes it impossible for his speech to warm itself at the hearth of the biological discourse of his time. Mendel lies in the untruth, and that means that he—for a time, at least—irrevocably falls outside the truth. Dasein, on the other hand, cannot do without the untruth if it wants to see or have something to say in the light of the truth. Like Mendel, it cannot separate itself from the untruth, but unlike Mendel, it can only be related to the truth because it is already related to the untruth.

As one can see, we have barely begun and already we find ourselves confused by the truth. In the truth, but also in the untruth; in the untruth and just because of that, also in the truth; in the untruth, and therefore not in the truth—imagine the mess that the convergence of two Heidegger quotations and a page from Foucault could cause for the conclusions by an author of a comparative study on the truth in Heidegger and Foucault. If our author is not already totally put out of joint by "the truth" or discouraged by this surplus of truth, he would probably find himself admitting that Heidegger and Foucault, though clearly related to each other, finally are not speaking about the same thing. Naturally, he would hasten to add that this does not prevent them from having had their say and that therefore both of them seem to have part of the truth on their side. But if someone would find the truth of Heidegger more attractive because it digs deeper and thus seems to be able to incorporate certain thoughts of Foucault, he should not forget the fact that this mixing and matching has a price and is only partial. And the same warning holds for those who remark very subtly that the communication distortion, which broke off this posthumous dialogue, seems to indicate that it is Foucault's position that is the most reasonable because, as our author's extensive comparative study itself has shown, both Heidegger and Foucault find themselves—not unlike Mendel—outside the order of truth to which the other belongs. But here our imaginary author would strongly object, he is not prepared to give up rationality itself—imagine that—and he refers to further investigations that are necessary to solve the problems that arise here. Investigations, for example, concerning the relation between Foucault and Nietzsche; for after all, Foucault himself in one of his last interviews pointed out, did he not, that the whole of his philosophical development was defined by Heidegger, but that Nietzsche took the upper hand?[3]

I should apologize for having let myself go and not having been able to resist the temptation of making a caricature of a genre that is still practiced with much zeal, in my discipline at least. But it is understood, of course, that my sarcasm in this had a ritual and exorcising function: I wanted to prevent a discourse from forcing itself upon me that, with the fatality I sketched, would stray into some superficial parallels and meaningless conclusions on the so-called Heideggerian background of Foucault. I wanted to avoid, in the midst of a movement from Heidegger to Foucault, being touched on the shoulder by a connective word that would ask me to slow down my speed and would demand more objectivity. Therefore, I will not devote this essay to Heidegger "and" Foucault. Let us leave the connectives to those who lack the imagination to come up with better titles and less boring subjects. Let us leave the "ands" and the "ors" to those who still mix up philosophy with the history of ideas and whose doxographic bias prevents them from seeing that the name of an author is always hanging between invisible quotation marks that indicate that this name only represents a field of problems in texts that resist domestication by any uniting instance whatsoever. In other words, let us not look for parallels between Foucault "and" Heidegger, but let us concentrate instead on the hesitations and rifts in their texts, and let us listen with a third ear, as it were, to the oppressed moments in those texts, moments that (for some reason or other, and it is important to know which ones) were not accessible to the biographical individuals who put their signatures on them. Instead of searching, in the tradition of a comparative study, for parallels between Foucault and Heidegger, I would rather establish where those texts already deconstruct themselves, in the hope of finding, where those cracks do not fit together, the entrance to the secret tunnel that will allow us to sneak out from the Foucauldian orders of truth and to make our way to the alethic machinery Heidegger was constructing from the waters of the river *Lethe*.

"Foucault": The Order of Truth

When it was mentioned earlier that Mendel fell outside the order of truth, yet made true statements, one of the central theoretical or quasi-theoretical concepts of Foucault was introduced—the notion of order—as well as the embarrassment in which Foucault found himself precisely on the basis of this notion. Strictly speaking, the definition that Foucault gives to the order of truth does not allow him to call Mendel a "true monster" or to assert that "it is always possible that one speaks the truth in the space of a 'wild exteriority'" (*OD*, 61) that lies outside the ruling order of truth. Mendel was a monster—and not a *true* monster—because he spoke about objects, used methods, and worked within a theoretical horizon, none of which were reconcilable with the biology of his time. What Mendel had to say was neither true nor false, because it did not primarily find itself "within the true" or within the order of truth. Every scientific discourse lays down such an order of truth, acknowledges within those limits true or false statements, and in doing so excludes in the same movement a whole teratology of knowledge outside its limits. Discourse is not something other than this order of truth, something that only subsequently proceeds with fixing that order. Discourse is this order itself; it is "the difference between what can be said correctly . . . and what is said" (*Réponse,* 863).[4] That not everything "that can be said correctly in a certain period according to the laws of logic or grammar is effectively said" (*AK,* 44–45, 118–19)[5] shows that an active instance is at work here that is of another nature than a logical or linguistic one. Consider Aldrovandi, for example, who in the middle of the seventeenth century, in his *Historia serpentum et draconum,* in all earnestness, not only extensively covers anatomy, nature and habits, coitus and generation, movements and diet of the serpent, but with no less detail situates that animal in mythology, fables, allegories, and mysteries, covers the proverbs and historical facts about it, and furthermore gives descriptions of the gods to which it is dedicated, of its use in medicine and human diet, of the different meanings of the name itself, of its synonyms and etymologies. All of this may sound strange to us, but it was in strict accordance with the discursive regime of the Renaissance, which involved, among other things, a certain conception of language that determined what could and should be said, how it had to happen, in which order, and what it was to be about.[6] For the same sorts of reasons, what is at first sight the unreasonable refusal of eighteenth-century anatomical pathology to use microscopes or other optical techniques becomes understandable only if one remembers that the type of visibility that was accepted at that time and imposed upon those who wanted to participate in this discipline was modeled after everyday perception: "a *de iure* visibility . . . and not . . . a natural invisibility that is forced, for a certain time, by a technique of an artificially multiplied gaze."[7] From examples of this kind, which could be supported by many others, Foucault does not conclude that the discursive regimes of which we speak suffer from a nearsightedness due to artificial limitations that they impose on themselves. On the contrary, these restrictions seem more like positive conditions of possibility that enabled something to happen in the Renaissance or in the classical period that was different from what could be said, done, or happen, in other periods. Discourse is not only incomplete and limited; it is an essentially incomplete and limited space.[8] It is no accident that speech is subject to a rarefaction by discourse. It has to be subject to it, in order not to fall into chaos. Chaos that not only arises by lack of ordering principles, but also, as one can already read in Merleau-Ponty, by a surplus of ordering rules: *Endlichkeit,* human finitude shows itself in man's dependency on a *Verendlichung* (de-finition); and when this finite ordering falls away or is multiplied, the only thing that remains for man is the panic with which, for example, the victim of color amnesia who carefully sorted out all of the red ribbons throws the whole stack into disorder when he comes upon a soft-red variation and then goes for the soft-yellow ones.[9] The astonishment at first, the vexation finally, with which one spontaneously looks upon this spectacle that endures for hours is not different from the involuntary smile on our faces when listening to Aldrovandi's enumerations. They testify to a certain blindness to the fact that the question—How is that possible there?—properly contains the answer in itself. "That there" is possible in the same way as the "this here" that makes us pose the question: it is possible on the basis of the fact that "speaking consists of doing something which is something different than giving expression to what one thinks or translating what one already knows, and is also something different than letting the structure of a language function" (*AK,* 209). Speaking is an instance of a discourse, that is to say, of a practice that does not allow itself to be reduced to a function of referral or expression. Such a discourse, for example, does something more and something different than documenting the originality of thinking subjects; it binds them to a set of rules that enables their thought and originality. Discourse is not—and this is well known—the effect of a subject, but—and this is less well known—it does not dismiss the subject that participates in it, and to a certain extent is formed by it, from his subjectivity.[10] The kind of speech that Foucault talks about, the speech of the truth, is painful and laborious; it is not at all an automatism that is regulated discursively. It is not because one finds oneself "inside the true" that one speaks the truth, but one can only pronounce something that can be judged in terms of true-false when one finds oneself "inside the true" and submits one's propositions to "certain conditions which are stricter and more complex than [what one usually understands by] the pure and simple truth" (*OD,* 60). There is no truth so pure that it would not be discursively defined. Hence, the definition Foucault gives of "truth"—and he places "truth" between quotation marks: "'by truth' I do not mean the ensemble of truths which are to be discovered and accepted but rather the ensemble of rules according to which the true and the false are separated."[11] There is no truth outside discourse. Discourse is "truth" itself. Or again: for Foucault "truth" is discourse.

Or at least: it seems so, or it could have been this way. And problems start here. More precisely: they started here a long time ago. What I have sketched so far could be called Foucault's problematic, that is to say, a systematic field of problems that are at stake in his work. Foucault's text, however, does not solely consist in an articulation of the problems that become possible through that problematic. This problematic is never purely present—not even in the short text about *The Order of the Discourse* that I commented on a moment ago—but it is always in some way concealed or weakened by the resistance Foucault exerts against it as an inner author, by the direction that he wants to take with it, by the problems he has with it.[12] So it is not quite correct, for example, to state that "truth" and "discourse" are the same for Foucault. This applies only to those discourses that already lend themselves to the truth, those that let themselves be led by the distinction true-false. Discourses are not only "dependent" on a set of internal ordering rules that give color in a certain manner to the distinction true-false and fill it in with the palette of a certain discursive regime. They also involve an ordering rule that itself imposes the distinction true-false—a distinction that, according to Foucault, is not at all evident, but has the status of an exclusion mechanism that in principle does not differ from the exclusion mechanism that defines our normality and makes us put the madmen in asylums (*OD*, 53 ff.). In this exclusion mechanism, Foucault sees the expression of a "will to know" or a "will to truth," which he finds suspect, because it can only assert itself on the basis of "a first and continually repeated *forgery* which poses the distinction between true and false" (*RC*, 14).[13] Foucault seems to think that resisting this "truth" is a political business; what's more, it is *the* political business: it is always connected with power, one can never separate truth from politics, but one can form different alliances, and one has to do so, if one does not want to succumb to that "truth" that has installed itself today. The internal as well as the external rules that establish an order of truth are arbitrary and therefore revisable, albeit in a sea of blood—blood other than that to which they owe their appearance. Every "truth" consists in a colonization and pacification that can give way at any moment to the dead anger of the silent war that it temporarily manages to suppress.[14]

As one can see: it is Nietzsche—a certain Nietzsche—who holds the upper hand here.[15] But at what price? Let us concentrate for a moment on the structure of the decision that Foucault imposes here on his problematic. In what sense is the truth "the effect of a *forgery* which carries the name of an opposition between true and false" (*RC,* 14; italics mine)? Is this forgery avoidable? What exactly is counterfeited here? And in the name of what should we resist this? And if a falsification in an improper sense is involved here, if what is meant here is the idea that every "interpretation is at the same time a disclosure and a concealment,"[16] do we have to resist? If there is no order without forgery, without mechanisms of exclusion, if the conditions of possibility for an order are at the same time necessarily the conditions of impossibility that exclude certain things, events, and so forth, from that order, why should we resist? In the name of whom or what, using which comparative principle? What power does Foucault talk about when he connects truth with power, when he says that there is no truth without power? What kind of power is it that is contained in exclusion mechanisms that at the same time make something possible? A power that is both contingent and necessary? Does not Foucault extend the political terrain inaccessibly far by turning every determination—even up to the episteme itself—into a political affair?[17]

The manner in which I have formulated my questions already suggests the answer I would give to them: it is different from the answers one could find in Foucault himself. Foucault has always adopted an ambiguous attitude toward the fact that for an order to be an order, it has to rely on a number of selection and exclusion mechanisms that cannot be left out if an ordering is to establish itself. Without selection and exclusion there is no order—exclusion is, therefore, constitutive and necessary—but every factually realized order is merely the arbitrary fulfillment of these necessary mechanisms: this particular exclusion is, therefore, something contingent and capable of being abolished. But a critique of an order that has to support itself on something that is irrevocably given with this and every other order—the exclusion of other possible orders—has something arbitrary and unsatisfactory about it. One does not get further than the insight that "what is, could also be otherwise,"[18] and one could always expect the answer that, precisely because of that, one has to cling to "what is." All orders are equally good or equally bad because they all exclude, and we lack a criterion to weigh these exclusions against each other: one can no longer judge, in terms of the truth, the rules that establish the distinction between the true and the false, or give color to it in a certain way. At the same time, in the work of Foucault, there seems to be a sort of resistance to allowing the critical pathos that is so characteristic of his work to depend merely upon a political decisionism that acknowledges the mere partiality of the critique it proclaims. This resistance brings "Foucault" at certain moments to the point of abandoning the notion of order: every ordering now becomes unlawful because it violates a sort of primordial self-sufficiency, a "happy limbo of non-identity,"[19] before the rise of orders, of partiality, of identity. Behind the critique on discipline, which is an ordering of the body, but which in the process nevertheless oppresses "the body itself," there appears the dream of a sort of primordial spontaneity of a body that does not have to be bridled by any order—a dream that at the same time and with the same vigor was always denied and criticized by Foucault.[20] This game, in which one hand erases what the other has written, in which the one hand puts quotation marks around "subject," "science," "soul," on the basis of arguments that are deleted by the other hand, the whole of this to and fro that, as I have been able to show in more detail elsewhere,[21] continually deconstructs Foucault's texts, all of this is characteristic of a situation in which a relativism of conditions of validity (and notions like "order" or discourse do not express anything else) finds itself, from the moment that one tries, like Foucault or Lyotard, but unlike Rorty or the later Wittgenstein, to escape from the "conservative" implications that are included in the starting point.[22] Foucault works himself into difficulties, not on the basis of the notion of order, but on the basis of the critique that he attaches to it. Universalistic positions attempt to exempt the critique from arbitrariness by abandoning the notion of order itself and directing themselves to a common ground that precedes orders or to an all-encompassing horizon that binds the phenomenal orders by installing itself in the high altitudes of formal universality. Now, the interesting point with Heidegger is that he belongs neither to such "modernists," nor to the "postmodernists." Heidegger does not abandon the notion of order, but deepens it and gives the process of ordering a name that, after everything that has been said about Mendel, cannot come as a great surprise: *a-letheia*.

"Heidegger": The Ordering of Truth

Aletheia, as you know, is the groundword for Heidegger, a word that fascinated him from the beginning and gradually demanded all of his attention; like the idea in Plato, so *aletheia* in Heidegger is a kind of condensation of all philosophical questions that preoccupy him, something that keeps these questions open and gives them direction by remaining itself a question.[23] *Aletheia* thus confronts us with a question here, not with an answer, and surely not with the kind of answer that could be decided on the basis of a purely etymological discussion (this does not mean that this discussion has no relevance—I will return to this). Heidegger is not first and foremost concerned with making sure that from now on *aletheia* is no longer translated as "the truth," but by "the unconcealed" or "the undisguised" or "the *undistortedness*" and that one merely adopts one of these translations. The whole discussion of the translation of a single—albeit important—Greek word only makes sense insofar as the traditional conception of truth that is the basis of the usual translation (*aletheia* = truth of judgment) is questioned. The conclusion of this discussion is not dependent on Heidegger's being right to discern an *alpha-privativum* in the word *a-letheia,* but on his being able to show that the primary locus of the truth is not, as it is generally accepted, the judgment and that the presence of the truth still presupposes something other than agreement, correspondence, or *homoiosis* between a proposition and that with which it deals.

Heidegger's argument concerning the derivation of the truth of judgment is in itself very simple. Something must already be, in one way or another, dis-covered or disclosed if a proposition is to be made about it. In *Being and Time,* this "being-discovered" refers to Dasein, which can discover beings because it is a being-in-the-world, and not a consciousness enclosed upon itself that has still to build a bridge to the world. However, because Dasein is not solely discovering *(entdeckend)* but is also prone to having itself be guided by what "One" says or talks about, beings about which a statement is made do not always appear the way they are, but only the way they appear to be (*BT,* § 44b). In the latter case, Heidegger sees the conditions of possibility for an untrue statement. True statements, on the contrary, presuppose that Dasein does not allow itself to be guided by the ruling opinions, but is now in its *own* authentic way discovering, and not fleeing from the openness *(Erschlossenheit)* that belongs to the structure of its Being. Dasein has always to incorporate what has been discovered, against the appearances and distortions into which it is tempted by the "they." Dasein has to assure itself of its "own" discoveries and of its "own" discovering power. Thus, *a-letheia* is "a robbery" that temporarily dismisses the concealment and triumphs over the appearance (*BT,* 265). The beings, time and again, have to be protected against the false appearance of concealment, against the *lethe* that covers up the original intuitions of truth and leaves it in the realm of idle talk. The way in which Heidegger reads the *alpha-privativum* here makes clear the price that *Being and Time* has to pay to ground the truth of judgment on a transcendental (Dasein's) truth: the ontological status of appearance can only be related to the fallenness of Dasein.[24] Later on, Heidegger will continually try to acknowledge in the appearance more than merely a "false appearance" and connect it with the happening of Being. From this attempt, in which Heidegger's so-called "Turning" is executed, there slowly results a different reading of the hyphen in *a-letheia*: the *lethe,* concealing or concealment, now belongs to the core of *aletheia* and can never be fully abolished from it. It is not only that disclosure never manages to dispense with concealment, but also that it needs it—*phusis kruptesthai philei*: Being can only let its Being and beings come to unconcealment on the basis of a fundamental relation to concealment.[25] Formulated more simply: if there is to be something seen, something said, or if something is to occur, then that which brings about this possibility and starts us on this way[26] has to withdraw with humility instead of attracting attention to itself. Being "is" this withdrawal; it establishes a kind of openness, in which beings can appear, by remaining in the background. The "essance" of Being "is" a *withdrawal,* a *Seinsentzug.*[27]

This is not the place to go into the complex structure of the "Turning." This could only be the object of a slow and patient dissection of Heidegger's texts, and an analysis of the role the hyphen plays in them, starting with *Being and Time,* which, as I have suggested, finds itself shipwrecked on this very hyphen, for reasons I cannot reveal for the moment. Let me attempt instead to highlight the risk of the "Turning" by looking at its effect and at the same time protect the terminology of the later Heidegger from a possible misunderstanding.

To speak about "Being that withdraws" does not signify that Heidegger finally turns Being into a substantive again and that he overlooks the ontological difference in a *temporalized philosophy of origins* (Habermas)[28] that displaces the initiative from Dasein to Being and opens the floodgates to irrationality? Not at all. On the contrary, Heidegger tries to understand history and gain insight into the fact that reason and truth appear to have a history. For the later Heidegger the existence of Newton's laws is not solely dependent on the fact that there is Dasein, which allows them by its sheer existence to be "true" in a meaningful way (*BT*, § 44c). Newton's laws also presuppose that beings have already appeared in a certain way or in a certain light, that they are explained in a certain way—bound up with a certain mathematical conception of nature that differs, for example, from the Aristotelian conception and on the basis of which Newtonian science can only see and observe the beings as such. Before the "Turning" Heidegger brings the truth of judgment back to a more original discovery of beings and connects this discovery to an even more original disclosure that comes from Dasein. After the "Turning," *aletheia* points not only in the direction of the unconcealment of beings, but also to an openness *("Offenheit")* of a different kind, a finite frame in which beings can be set free. Such a frame still presupposes the freedom of Dasein, but it is not dependent on it. On the contrary, it is allotted to Dasein: *"es ist das ihm Zugeschickte,"*[29] that within which it must keep itself or that to which it has to relate itself: *"viewed as Dasein (i.e., with respect to his ec-static condition), man [can] only [be], by reaching outwards out of himself to that which is totally other than he himself, namely the clearing of Being"* (*VS*, 124/386). Dasein is no longer itself the "clearing" *(lichtung)*, but lies *in* a clearing that no longer refers to the light of a *"lumen naturale,"* but to an openness or a leeway in which light can play its game with its shadows.[30] Dasein not only dis-covers beings, it is also the one to which the Being of beings reveals itself. One sees how, after a long detour, we arrive at some basic insights of Foucault, but also how we have progressed to a position that can no longer become entangled in "Foucault's" problems. To be sure there is no truth without Dasein; but that "there is" truth is not solely a matter of Dasein. "There is" an order of truth, an "openness" *(Offenheit)* or a *"clearing"* that is not simply limited or delimited by something that remains hidden—but by something that hides and withdraws itself. "Truth" refers not simply to an order of truth *(Unverborgenes)*, but also to an ordering of truth *(Entbergung)*. The essance of truth is not a concept, but a happening: "Truth 'is' ['essances'], it is . . . the constituting force for all the true and the false, which are searched for, which are fought and suffered for."[31] Against Foucault, who merely concludes that orders of truth exist and that truth has a history, Heidegger tries to introduce a terminology that enables us to think the *order* of truth (the *"Gelichtete"*) out of its ordering (the *"Lichtung"*), to conceive of the history of truth by way of the "happening," the "essencing" of truth. Like Foucault, Heidegger speaks of a "decision" that establishes what is to be considered as true and also what can be rejected and thrown aside as untrue.[32] But while Foucault concludes that the truth is what "we struggle for" and relates this "to the power we attempt to make our own" (*OD*, 53), Heidegger relates this decision to a battle that occurs in the core of truth itself, insofar as the unconcealment is fundamentally related to a concealment and a concealing it can never simply leave behind. But the sound of this struggle goes unheard in the fury of the battle that people fight for the truth. For Heidegger, the *"struggle between those who are in power and those who want to come to power"*[33] brings the human being into a position that turns him away from the Being of truth and alienates man vis-à-vis the *Open.*[34] To turn truth into a political situation like Foucault wants to do means for Heidegger to give in to the *Will to Will* and to prepare for the triumph of nihilism. Against the background of this threat, Heidegger's interest in the "question of truth" becomes understandable: he wants to prepare a *"re-volution of the whole of human Being"* by showing that man's Being is dependent on the ruling conception of the Being of truth, a conception that, as is well known, Heidegger wanted to fundamentally question.[35] For Heidegger, what is at stake in the problem of truth, therefore, is not something logical or epistemological, but ethical: what he is questioning is the "ethos," which must correspond to a "relativism of conditions of validity."

But let us not be misguided. It would be too beautiful if all or even part of Heidegger's writings would now suddenly appear to be an attempt to answer the problem that we have been discussing here, if they would consist of nothing more than one massive and solid answer to our questions. Let us not forget that the work of Heidegger consists of a multitude of layers and that it involves a whole series of parallelograms of forces that, like the blades of a propeller, are put into a certain angle to one another by the internal author known to us as "Heidegger." But if this is true, there is nothing here that forbids us from changing the angles if necessary. And, indeed, we will see that such a change might be necessary. I will briefly mention three problems that are important for our problematic because in these problems the parallelism until now suggested between "Foucault" and "Heidegger" breaks down. The first two problems form obstacles, the third is the springboard that will prepare us for the jump from "Foucault" to "Heidegger."

First problem. Until now I have silently presupposed that Heideggerian *aletheia,* like Foucauldian "Truth," forms a condition of possibility for truth in the usual sense, a kind of frame that allows us to speak in a certain manner in terms of truth and falsehood. But is this so? What is, in fact, the relation between *aletheia* and *adaequatio* (truth of judgment)? If a simple deepening of the problem of truth were the concern here, if *aletheia* would be a more original "truth" that makes possible the truth of judgment, then where are we to place the *pathos* with which Heidegger calls *"correctness" (Richtigkeit)* an error *(Irrtum)* (cf. *GA* 45, 31, and passim) and presents the history of truth as a genealogy of these errors in terms of a history of "decay"?[36] What prevents us from holding on to the conception of *adaequatio* and grounding it in *aletheia*? Why does Heidegger have this remarkable symphathy (I did not say nostalgia) for the Greeks, to whom the original locus of truth was not the truth of judgment but the beings themselves? Does this sympathy have something to do with the fact that the Greeks recognized, along with the truth of judgment, truth as the unconcealment of what is? And might the decline (since the Greeks) have something to do with the fact that this duality of truth gave way exclusively to the correspondence theory? Where does this "decline" originate? Here Heidegger hesitates; and one can say, without exaggeration, that the work of Heidegger is this hesitation.[37] Many passages seem to point to the fact that the Greek *homoiosis* is itself the root of the decline: metaphysics starts here (Plato and Aristotle), or at least—first hesitation—it can start from this point. The possibility for the decline, where the *homoiosis* becomes independent, is already inscribed in the origin. But—second hesitation—that origin is itself already in a certain decline because it is corruptible and impure. Behind this origin lies yet another origin, the pre-Platonic start of Greek philosophy, where truth was conceived of as *aletheia,* unconcealment, and *homoiosis* had not yet made its appearance. But even this origin—and this is a third hesitation, to which I will return later—was not totally "in order" because the Greek experience of *aletheia* here is not quite the experience it should be or could be.

The problem, therefore, is the relation between *aletheia* and *adaequatio*. For Heidegger, this relation was surely not one of a simple condition of possibility. To the contrary, *aletheia* and correctness are sometimes (I do not say always) presented as competing conceptions of truth: *aletheia* or *orthotes*.[38] This problem has an interesting corollary in the fact that its formulation is dependent on Heidegger's analysis of the different positions that human beings took or had to take on the grounds of the different essances of the truth, and it has also something to do with the whole of the Heideggerian discourse on the essance or "ethos" of the human being. For Heidegger, the Greeks were receptive,[39] their apprehension is an allowing-to-bring-forth *(Hervorbringen-lassen)* of something that already arises by itself *(antikeimenon, ob-icere)* from concealment and looks upon the human being. The Greeks were not representing subjects who acknowledge objects only on the basis of representations that allow them to appear. They did not present themselves as a "scene" where beings have to (re)present themselves, and where they have to be pictures.[40] All of this is well known. But do we have to follow Heidegger here? To be honest, I do not know what to think about it. Does not the word "scene" by itself already point to Heidegger's resistance to mimesis, and to his mistrust or suspicion of every form of displacement of appearance to a place other than its original one?[41] The whole discussion that arises here on the essance of the human being should be analyzed with the utmost care. Does not Heidegger become the victim of a sort of subject-phobia that turns itself not only against the (re)presenting subject but also against every form of subjectivity that is something more or different from a perceiving (but not responsive) receptivity? To be sure, the Heideggerian apprehension *(Vernehmen)* is not a passivity; it is a *Hervorbringen-lassen,* an *Entsprechen,* co-respondence.[42] But it is the sort of *Entsprechen* that can and must do full justice to that to which it *directs* itself (implicit *homoiosis,* but not in the sense of representation). It is a kind of answer that fully absorbs the question; it is a kind of *Entsprechen* that allows that which already arises out of itself to express itself—better still, to impress itself on the wax receptacle it proposes; it is a *legein* in the sense of a bringing together that takes over and publishes something that is already ordered itself, a bringing together that ex-presses without imposing itself on what it ex-presses. In short, what we have here seems to be a receptivity without response that, as Michel Haar formulates it, turns man into a "man without qualities"[43]—pure *da* or pure *ex,* pure ex-istence. And one can and has to question whether some of the qualities that fall away here—a certain closing or being closed, a kind of impurity—are not ascribed too quickly by Heidegger to the inauthentic. All of the problems that surround this topic in *Being and Time,* specifically in section 44, return here and should be analyzed. But before developing that, I think it might be helpful to formulate the caution or reservation that I express here in another manner, by approaching this problem in yet another way that will confront us again with Heidegger's resistance to *mimesis.*

Second Problem. *Alethes kai on:*[44] the idea that what is true or what is disclosed are beings themselves, repeatedly makes Heidegger translate *aletheia* by *un-distortedness (Un-verstelltheit)*: beings are "true" *(apseudos)* if they can appear as they really are, namely *unverstellt,* un-distorted and un-displaced. But what is the relation between this "ontic" truth or *aletheia* as the *Un-verstelltheit* of *beings* to which Heidegger affords long and painstaking analyses (see, e.g., *GA* 54)—and the "ontological" truth or *aletheia* as *Lichtung inmitten des Seienden* (*GA* 45, 190), "clearing" that, as we have seen, is not a being itself, is not dependent on it, but, on the contrary, allows beings to appear. Can one say that the clearing, like Foucault's "order," "does violence to things" (*OD,* 67) by only allowing them to appear in a certain way, or is the *"clearing"* itself characterized by a sort of receptivity with a structure analogous to the one of *apprehension (Vernehmen)*? Of course, Heidegger warns us that we should not understand the *"clearing"* as a simple *"throwing-light-on" (belichten)* but as an *"allowing to be present" (Anwesen-lassen)*—but what is the structure of this allowing? At first sight the notion of *"undistortedness"* might seem appropriate to characterize the ontic *aletheia.* But since this *aletheia* never stands apart from the *clearing,* the use of this notion becomes somewhat problematic to say the least, as it seems to suggest that there is an ontic truth, a way of appearing for beings *as they are,* regardless of the clearing involved. But if this is to be the case, then the ontological truth threatens to be regulated by the ontic truth.[45] We touch here on an important and anything but abstract problem—we even find traces of it in a certain obscurity or overdetermination of the Heideggerian analysis of the En-framing *(Ge-stell).* Is saying that the

Rhine, once guided through the gates of a hydroelectric plant, does not appear as a river anymore, only dependent on Heidegger's analysis of the "challenging-forth" character of the En-framing?[46] And what can we say about the door that one can no longer open with a doorknob, but that opens with an electric eye? Should we say that it is like an airplane, only a part of the standing reserve *(Bestand)*? Why do we stumble here on such a remarkable neglect of the concrete phenomenological analysis of the technical object; on this hardly repressed depreciation of certain technical media (movies as "experience" *[Erlebnis]*—surely not a compliment)?[47] Whence the strange paradigmatics of the examples that Heidegger chooses (the field, the windmill, the wooden bridge), whence this antiproductionism that only wishes to acknowledge a pro-duction (the *Hervorbringen-lassen*)? Can we, for example, refer to a pro-duction in order to clarify the "relation" (in the above-mentioned sense) between "homosexuality" and the *Clearing* that allows it to exist?[48] The perplexity in which these questions leave us should not be taken as a sign of our superiority, for we do not yet know the answers to these questions, and we would not even be able to pose them were it not for Heidegger. In addition, the questions we cannot but raise here are precisely those questions that keep Heidegger's texts themselves in motion—texts we have hardly begun to analyze here. But as always, it is far better to have some unanswered questions than to have plenty of unquestioned answers. And we should keep to these questions if we care to understand in some way the role and status of the problem of "Greece" in Heidegger's work. That a nostalgia was never present in it, but at most a sympathy, that Heidegger, in the same pages in which he sketches the "decline" that started with Plato, time and time again qualifies that he sees no fault in this decline, but a certain necessity—all of this indicates how intricate the problem remains as long as Heidegger clings to a certain explanation of the Greek experience on the basis of (but not exclusively on the basis of) a questionable etymology. Not that these problems are simplified when Heidegger abandons this explanation—and now thinks that *aletheia,* unconcealment, "was originally [this means already with the Greeks] experienced only as *orthotes* as the correctness of representations and statements" (which means, among other things, that "the assertion about the essential transformation of truth, that is, from unconcealment to correctness, is also untenable").[49] With this third problem, which, as I said, is no longer an obstacle to us, the whole balance of forces changes and it becomes possible to relate the problem of *ethos* to that of *aletheia*.

Gaming into A-letheia

Let us return to the structure of our discussion. I have shown how Foucault saw himself confronted with the choice of either turning every order into an authentic order by accepting exclusion as being constitutive or condemning every order to inauthenticity by appealing to a pre-ordinal self-sufficiency and interpreting the exclusion as a mere effect of power. In the first case, a convincing critique of any given order seems to be impossible; the only thing that can be said is that "everything could also have been otherwise." In the second case, every order becomes alienating and again one has no reason to adhere to Foucault's critique of orders. In both cases, Foucault does not succeed in doing what he claims to do: to give a critique of a distinct order that is specific enough to prevent it from becoming trivial by being just as applicable to every other order. The only way out for Foucault would have consisted in developing a critique that does not question the being-of-an-order because of what it left unrealized (other possible orders) or because of the violence it did to the things it had to order (a pure pre-ordinality, the wild spontaneity of the body or insanity "itself") in order to be an order. How would such a critique look if it were to question, not the ordinality as such, but a specific ordinality? A possible answer could run as follows: it could try to show that certain orders tend to forget or veil the fact that they are an order and on this basis claim an authority that does not properly belong to them. But why should an order not forget or fail to recognize that it is an order? With such questions we have already placed ourselves beyond the boundaries of what for the sake of convenience we referred to as "Foucault." With such questions we already found ourselves in "Heidegger." And we might as well profit from our new position and rephrase our problem in the terms of "Heidegger." A Heideggerian reformulation of our problem would run as follows: What is the "relation" between an order and the occurrence of the order itself? In terms of the example we have concentrated on: between the order of truth and the being or becoming of truth? In other words, what call do we get from the occurrence of the truth? Which comportment or "attitude" is expected of us? Until now, I have only tried to make it acceptable that formulating this question in Heideggerian terms makes sense, and that the answer to this question could clarify a problem that could, in a legitimate way, be transposed from "Foucault" to "Heidegger." Now I shall try to indicate concisely the shape of a possible answer on the basis of "Heidegger," although it should be clear from the discussion of the first two problems that such an answer cannot be unequivocably found in the texts of Heidegger themselves, even less so when a third problem, as we shall see in a moment, is going to add itself to all of the difficulties I have just mentioned.

That Heidegger's sympathy for Greece never led to a call for a *retour à la Grèce* has something to do with the fact that the Greeks had experienced *aletheia,* were philosophically busy with it, but were busy with it in such a way that they never questioned *aletheia* as such. The Greeks, Heidegger says time and again, never thought *aletheia.* Not that he thought ill of them for that. That they never got further than the insight that what "is" is the "unconcealed," that they never questioned unconcealedness itself is not their shortcoming, but perhaps their greatness. It was the destiny of the Greeks to focus on beings as they are, on beings in their unconcealedness and by doing so to begin philosophy; if they had questioned further they would have "abandoned their proper task" (*GA* 45, 137). Nevertheless, for a long time, Heidegger saw in this *not-questioning-further* the reason for the decay in the history of truth as it moved from *aletheia* to correctness. It therefore seemed necessary for him to write a genealogy of the truth to get in touch with the "new element" in the Greek "beginning," an element that carries with it the possibility of another "beginning." Hegel is never mentioned here, but without his influence, which Heidegger would obviously want to defend himself against, it is difficult to understand what could be meant here by the "hidden law of the beginning" *(verbogenes Gesetz des Anfangs)* or "inner law of the beginning" *(inneres Gesetz des Anfangs)* and so forth.[50] Whatever there is of this—and the problems that arise here are certainly not unimportant, if only because they will annoy those of our contemporaries who think they can escape Hegel's long shadow by retiring to the artificial light of their Heidegger library—since the Greeks in their time did not think *aletheia* through to the end, Heidegger is convinced that he can only turn around the history of truth and prepare for a "complete reversal of human Being" (*Umwälzung des ganzen menschlichen Seins*—see note 35) by now attempting to do what they did not do before and did not have to do: to question *aletheia* as such.

But if the Greeks, standing in the midst of *aletheia,* were satisfied by this without questioning its status, then why will we have to do something more and something different? The question seems all the more valid since Heidegger himself, in order to show that the Greeks in no way failed, pointed out that the Greek experience of truth was, in a certain sense, dependent on a forgetting of the occurrence of truth itself. To bring to light what lies within a "clearing," this "clearing" has first to shine forth itself and then shine upon what lies within it; but it cannot and may not become that which keeps our attention. "The clearing, the *aletheia* must in a certain sense be overlooked" (*GA* 45, 147).

Now it is no longer difficult to understand that it became less and less important for Heidegger to hold on to the thesis of the appearance and the immediate disappearance of the truth *(aletheia)* in Greece. One understands why he no longer wanted to make a point of this etymological question. For is not what has just been said about the Greeks valid for every experience? Does not every experience find its possibility in something that is concealed and that precisely conceals itself at the same moment when we, lingering in the "clearing" that opens up the beings for us and makes them accessible, lose ourselves in these beings? Is it not precisely the case that we must "lose ourselves" with the beings and occupy ourselves with them if we want to see what is offered to us by this *"clearing"*? Does not the Being of truth (verbally) have to escape from us, if we are to be capable of formulating our truths? Does not *aletheia* always, for essential reasons, "have to be overlooked"? In other words, the Being of truth would not extract itself only factually and according to the "law" of the "beginning" from Greek experience; it could not do otherwise than extract itself from this and every other experience. *Aletheia* is not something that might appear in an age and attract all the attention of this age; it is that which allows an age to happen, it is "epochality" itself.[51] That which is experienced or thought is that which is present, not presence as such. That which is present claims our attention, not the presence and the *"clearing"* or *aletheia* that allows it to be present.[52] The ordering of truth or the occurrence of truth retreats so that truth can occur and appear in an ordered way. In Heidegger's terms: "With regard to beings, Being is that which shows and makes visible without showing or becoming visible itself."[53] That Being "is" finite in a transitive sense, that it always and necessarily retreats, also entails that there is never a "clearing of presence" as such, but always a clearing of presence concealing itself.[54]

Does this mean that we can do nothing more than forget Being, than forget the ordering of truth—and that we can just leave it at that? Has all the pathos with which Heidegger spoke of an "Overcoming" of metaphysics then been in vain? Misplaced perhaps? Not at all. But the situation becomes considerably more complicated, or to be more exact—since a train of thought is in consideration here that could not at every moment measure its own pace—it now becomes possible to get a clear sense of the complexity that has always been there and to gain insight into its difficulties.

The later Heidegger's discussion with metaphysics was never merely about metaphysics' forgetting of Being, but about the fact that metaphysics showed itself unable to think Being in such a way that this forgetting became an essential part of it. The "overcoming of metaphysics" does not mean leaving metaphysics behind, but abandoning the metaphysical explanation of metaphysics. The "awakening from the oblivion of Being" that the "step back" is to prepare for does not aim, according to Heidegger, at "an extinguishing of the oblivion of Being," but at placing oneself in it and standing within it.[55] What is at stake here is not an escape from the oblivion of Being, but an attempt to make this forgetfulness accessible to experience. What could this mean?

As we have seen, one cannot in a certain sense but forget Being. And this oblivion is not merely a human affair, something one can do or cannot do. Man can only see and act on the basis of a blind spot; he can only deal with beings by not dealing with Being as such; he can only live off the gift of the "There is" *(Es gibt)* by overlooking the giving itself;[56] almost like someone who can only be captivated by the blue of the sky by forgetting the "blue-ing" *(das Blauen)* of that sky (*GA* 34, 187). Being is, therefore, nothing more than the forgetting of Being itself. It is because Being merely "is," "works," "occurs," by keeping itself in the background, because it can merely let beings be by retreating that it is itself forgotten. It is the default of Being *(Ausbleiben des Seins)* that makes possible the omission of the default of Being *(Auslassen des Ausbleibens des Seins)*.[57] But things are even more complicated. That Being withdraws itself seems, for Heidegger, connected not only with the fact that the "clearing" has to step back in favor of what can blossom in that openness, but also with the fact that the "clearing" is finite itself; that it is dependent on a lack of openness or a darkness from which it gains its openness: there never is or can be a total *a-letheia,* but only a *lethe* or concealment that, in a certain sense, is older than the disclosure that arises out of the opposition. And it is this "concealment" that, because of the structure of disclosure itself, is hidden again. In *On the Essence of Truth,* one of Heidegger's most difficult texts, he calls this concealing of the concealed the "mystery."[58] Man has to relate himself to this "mystery," or to be more exact, since he is always already related to it, he has to relate to it in a certain way, according to a certain *ethos.* And here we have finally localized the problem that has occupied us for all of this time: What is the structure of this *ethos*?

The essence of truth is an unconcealment that at the same time conceals itself. And because this unconcealment has necessarily to fall back upon a concealment that is concealed along with the concealing of the unconcealment, truth has something to do with a "secret."[59] "Truth," in the sense of *aletheia,* is therefore, as it were, an occurrence that digs holes that we can only attempt to fill in with our little truths. From these small truths, man borrows measures that give him a direction. But in this he forgets the basis for this measure-taking itself and the essence or occurrence from where the possibility of this measure-taking is handed to him. He forgets the *Mass-gabe* and starts to posit himself as the measure-giver. He insists upon what is accessible for him and thinks that he is the one who made it accessible. Man shuts himself off from the "mystery," he "errs," he goes astray. But, Heidegger says, man always goes astray; this is his condition, and not something that can be left behind. And yet, man may not shut himself off from the "mystery." Therein lies the paradox: on the basis of his existential condition, Dasein forgets (cannot but forget) the essence of the truth, loses himself (cannot but lose himself) in his truths, and, nonetheless, Heidegger still expects from him an *"openness to the mystery"* (*MA,* 55). Can Heidegger still think something like that? Can Heidegger think an "openness" that does not undo the "closedness" that leads one astray? An "openness" that does not have anything to do with being put on the right track, again because there is no "right" track (how could the "clearing" that makes "correctness" possible be "right" or "correct" itself?), but an "openness" that would have to deal with the experience of erring *as* erring, with a going astray that knows that it is doing so, but cannot help but do so? What could such an openness still mean—if not precisely a certain comportment, an *ethos*? But what, then, is the structure of the *ethos* that Heidegger wants to articulate here against the limits of his own thinking?

"Openness for the mystery"—the question is unclear, but it can gain clarity *ex negativo.* What does this *not* mean? In any case, not that man has to become the pure *Da* of *Sein,* pure ek-sistence. For man is also in-sistence, he insists in the "erring"; and this "fallenness," says Heidegger, is a "natural condition of Dasein" (*VS,* 100/362) that cannot be tamed or domesticated by any culture. We are, of course, familiar with his thesis of the existentiality of the "fallenness" from our reading of *Being and Time,* but it seems that only on the basis of his changed conception of truth—truth that can never expel the untruth, the *lethe*; truth that is essentially finite and historical—that Heidegger can take it seriously (or should have to be able to do so, because it is not at all clear that he has done this—I will return to that). *Being and Time* still held on, as we have seen, to a strict opposition between truth and untruth or appearance. The possibility of a pure truth was grounded in the existential possibility of an authentic openness—*Erschlossenheit im Modus der Eigentlichkeit*—against which an inauthentic disclosure remains stuck in appearances, remains "closedness." This existentiell alternative disrupted, went against the grain of the results of the existential analysis, which made the "fallenness" into a structure of the Being of Dasein, or at least imposed a certain reading of it by seeing in it a kind of *in principle* removable "conformism."[60] Dasein may lie equiprimordially in the truth and the un-truth: it can only be "closed" because it was first "open" and thus because it stands (ontologically) "first" in the truth.

This conflict between the requirements of an existentiell analysis and the results of the existential analysis[61] could not or should not be able to arise in the later Heidegger. Dasein does not stand first in the truth, but in the untruth. It "errs" and has always turned its back upon Being. Even more: it has to turn its back upon Being to be able to stand in the truth Being founds.

This experience of having to turn our backs to "something" that in its turn turns (and in a sense *has* to turn) its back to us, this double chiasm of faith and unfaithfulness is not a comfortable position. It is the structure of finitude itself. A finitude that leaves one without the comfort of a rule or a law that tells us how to cope with it. One should not deny this finitude, but at the same time one would still be denying it by affirming it triumphantly. The experience of this finitude—of our being in the "erring"—is an "experience" that in a certain sense always "forgets" what it has "learned" but a moment ago. It is the *experience* of a not-being-able (to be pure ek-sistence) and of a not-being-able-to-do-otherwise (than lose oneself in in-sistence) *at the same time*; an *experience* that never allows for the acquiescence that finitude is what it is (e.g., "since we are all insistent"), an experience one has to cope with, or "to bear" without hope of an "overcoming." One has to *relate* oneself *to* a finitude that one cannot escape. And this relation itself is marked by finitude; it never allows for a tenured position, but at best sends us off with an unclear, barely readable assignment.

Twice Heidegger tried to read this assignment and to translate it. The first time he spoke of a releasement *(Gelassenheit)* and (among other things) meant by it a simultaneous yes and no to the technical world. This attitude, Heidegger says, has to "save the essance of the human being," an essance that is under the threat of being captivated, bewitched, dazzled, beguiled, warped, confused, and laid waste by the oncoming technological revolution in the atomic age (*MA*, 56 and 54). But this spell can be broken. "We can use technical devices and yet at the same time, when we use them in a responsible way, keep ourselves so free from them that we can let go of them at any moment. But we can leave these instruments for what they are, as something that has nothing to do with our innermost and most proper core" (*MA*, 54, translation modified).

Something that has nothing to do with our innermost and most proper core—this central presupposition at the same time makes it difficult to understand why and how Heidegger can claim in the same breath that technical, calculating thinking has its own legitimate place alongside contemplative thinking (*MA*, 46). How can something that has nothing to do with our essential Being have its own legitimate place? And if it has its place, is it not then because the "innermost essance" of the human being does not have the purity that Heidegger wanted it to have? Rather, is not this essance ambivalent, in the way in which Heidegger himself taught us: related to being, "taken into account by a sense, which man did not invent or make," but nevertheless incapable of enduring the impeccable purity of this relation? Is it not precisely this duality that prevents humanity from jumping from the familiar ground of beings to that which has no bottom, to the bottomlessness of Being (*GA* 54, 223)? If Being is bottomless, a permanently shifting bottom full of holes, a bottom that never supports, and if beings are and can only be "a supporting bottom" by forgetting Being, then can man ever have a relation to the abysmal ground of Being without "representing" this ground to himself? If representational thinking is legitimate because something in the essance of human beings keeps them from the purity of ek-sisting, something that brings them to the point of still wanting to ground the groundless ground that Being is, can one then still leave these technical objects for what they are, as something that has nothing to do with our innermost and most proper core? And, if not, can one still follow Heidegger when he tries for the second time to read the inscription that occupies us here as a "without why"?[62] Can man, like the Rose of Silesius, play without why? "Being," Heidegger says, "as what grounds has no ground itself; it plays the game as the abyss, which delivers to us Being and ground as a destiny" (188). And he adds a further question to this, although I am not sure whether he formulated it in the same spirit with which we did and with the uncertainty that befalls us here: "[T]he question remains, whether we and how we when we hear the movements of this game, will play along and join the game."[63] What would it mean if this human game were out of joint? What does it mean for man to "play" or to "game," and is there something in the essance of technology, in the search for grounds, that distorts the structure of human games? With these questions, which in a way are still and at the same time no longer questions of Heidegger, I would like to end this journey between the continent "Foucault," and the continent "Heidegger," without knowing quite where we have arrived. But I have the impression that this was not a single journey nor an *aller-retour,* but that it was a ride on the carousel of thought, the core of which displaced itself after some agitation. For is not the question that moved us along in these last questions the same one with which we began? What keeps us from Being is not an exclusion that we can avoid, but neither is it something we can resign ourselves to. Man is finite and he cannot do without the "violence" that tears him from his ecstasy; he has to walk the erring path allotted to him without despairing and without irony, at the most with the "silent smile"[64] of someone who, by gaming perhaps, has learned that this violence cannot be avoided, and that he has to endure its inescapabilility. Man can at most incorporate this violence into an *ethos* that in some way detaches him from himself, but that at the same time remains fragile, always receptive to the seduction of whatever promises to free him from this fragility, of whatever tempts him into fully ek-sisting or into fully in-sisting. And this could be the reason why technology is dangerous and even, as Heidegger says, the "supreme danger"[65]: it tempts us to give up this fragile tension between an existence we are incapable of and an insistence we cannot but give in to. Technology takes the place of the onto-theological God, who keeps recovering from a death that was announced to us a long time ago. And in the shadow of this ever-returning God, Zarathustra's last man finds himself standing on a firm technological ground. For does he not know how to cope with his finitude? Did he not invent one technique after another to apply to himself? To perfect himself? To bear what is "otherwise than self"? This is the man—and the God—Nietzsche warned us about, and this man, I would wager, is not as moribund as he seemed when we first saw his "face drawn in the sand at the edge of the sea" (*OT*, 387) and mistook it for a sign of his imminent death. For "man" is yet to die; and as with the Golem, only the hand of a child riding the high tides of the alethic seas might be able to erase what should have disappeared a long time ago.

Notes

This text was originally published in *Research in Phenomenology* 21 (1991). A Dutch version of this text appears in *Tijdschrift voor Filosofie* 53, no. 3 (September 1991). I wish to thank David Bowen for producing a first draft of the English text, which I have subsequently rewritten with the help of Greg Renner.

1. See the introduction by Alphonse De Waelhens and Walter Biemel to their translation of *Vom Wesen der Wahrheit* (Martin Heidegger, *De l'essence de la verité* [Paris: Vrin, 1948], 44–45). For the difference from *Being and Time* (trans. John Macquarrie and Edward Robinson [Oxford: Basil Blackwell, 1988], hereafter cited as *BT*), see *BT* § 44b.

2. For Foucault's discussion of Mendel, see his "The Order of Discourse," in *Untying the Text: A Post-Structuralist Reader*, ed. Robert Young (London: Routledge & Kegan Paul, 1981), 60–61; hereafter referred to as *OD*.

3. Michel Foucault, "Le retour de la morale," in *Les Nouvelles Littéraires*, June 28–July 5, 1984, 40.

4. Michel Foucault, "Réponse à une question," *Esprit* 36, no. 5 (1968); hereafter cited as *Réponse*.

5. Ibid. and Michel Foucault, *The Archaeology of Knowledge* (London: Tavistock, 1977), 44–45, 118–19; hereafter cited as *AK*.

6. See Michel Foucault, *The Order of Things: An Archaeology of the Human Sciences* (London: Tavistock, 1970), 17–45 on the *episteme* of the Renaissance; for Aldrovandi, see 39. Hereafter cited as *OT*.

7. Michel Foucault, *Naissance de la clinique. Une archaeologie du regard médical* (Paris: Presses Universitaires de France, 1983), 171.

8. Foucault, *AK*, 67, 110; and *Réponse*, 861.

9. Maurice Merleau-Ponty, *Phénoménologie de la perception* (Paris: Gallimard, 1945), 205, and the allusion to this passage in Foucault, *OT,* xviii.

10. Foucault, *AK,* 209: "These positivities are not so much limitations imposed on the initiative of the subjects as the field in which that initiative is articulated (without however, constituting its centre)."

11. Michel Foucault, "Truth and Power," in *Power/Knowledge: Selected Interviews and Other Writings (1972–1977),* ed. Colin Gordon (New York: Pantheon Books, 1980), 132.

12. I have developed this notion of an "inner author" in the first two sections of my "Can Genealogy Be Critical? A Somewhat Unromantic Look at Nietzsche and Foucault," *Man and World* 23, no. 4 (1990), especially 442.

13. Michel Foucault, *Résumé des cours. 1970–1982* (Paris: Gallimard, 1989), my emphasis. Hereafter referred to as *RC.*

14. See the two lectures of January 1976, published in German as *Vom Licht des Krieges zu Geburt des Geschichte* (Berlin: Merve, 1986).

15. Foucault, "Truth and Power," 133: "It's not a matter of emancipating truth from every system of power (which would be a chimera, for truth is already power), but of detaching the power of truth from the forms of hegemony, social, economic and cultural, within which it operates at the present time. The political question, to sum up, is not error, illusion, alienated consciousness or ideology; it is truth itself. Hence the importance of Nietzsche."

16. Samuel IJsseling, "Nietzsche en de Rhetorica," in *Tijdschrift voor Filosofie* 35, no. 4 (1973): 798.

17. For such a critique see Peter Dews, "The *Nouvelle Philosophie* and Foucault," in *Towards a Critique of Foucault,* ed. Michael Gane (London: Routledge & Kegan Paul, 1986), 82.

18. Paul Veyne uses this expression in his sympathetic description of Foucault's project ("Foucault révolutionne l'histoire," in *Comment on écrit l'histoire* [Paris: Seuil, 1978], 204).

19. Michel Foucault, introduction to *Herculine Barbin: Being the Recently Discovered Memoirs of a Nineteenth-Century Hermaphrodite,* trans. Richard McDougall (New York: Pantheon Books, 1980), xiii.

20. For expressions such as "the body in itself," which one can find in *Surveiller et punir* and *La volonté de savoir* (though not in the English translations!), see my book, *Michel Foucault: Genealogy as Critique* (London and New York: Verso, 1995). For a brief comment, see Visker, "Can Geneology Be Critical?"

21. See my "Foucaults Aufführungszeichen. Eine Gegenwissenschaft?" in *Spiele der Wahrheit. Michel Foucaults Denken,* ed. Bernhard Waldenfels and François Ewald (Frankfurt a. Main: Suhrkamp, 1991), 298–319.

22. The qualification "conservative" is not meant to have a political connotation here.

23. See Martin Heidegger, *Vom Wesen der Wahrheit. Zur Platons Höhlengleichnis und Theätet, Gesamtausgabe,* vol. 34 (Frankfurt a. Main: Vittorio Klostermann, 1988), 172–73. This was Heidegger's Freiburg lecture course, winter term 1931–32. Hereafter *GA* will be used to designate volumes of the Heidegger *Gesamtausgabe.*

24. I follow here Jean-François Courtine, "Phénoménologie et vérité," in *Heidegger et l'idée de la phénoménologie,* Franco Volpi et al. (Phaenomenologica 108) (Dordrecht: Kluwer, 1988), 81–106.

25. See Martin Heidegger, "Aletheia (Heraclitus, Fragment B16)," in *Early Greek Thinking* (San Francisco: Harper and Row, 1984), 113ff.; and *GA* 34, 92–93.

26. "Auf einem Weg des Entbergens bringen" is an expression Heidegger frequently

uses in his essay, "The Question Concerning Technology," in *Basic Writings* (New York: Harper & Row, 1977). Hereafter referred to as *BW.*

27. Following Levinas I write "essance" to refer to the verbal character of Heidegger's "*Wesen.*"

28. See Jürgen Habermas, *The Philosophical Discourse of Modernity: Twelve Lectures* (Cambridge: Polity Press, 1987), 153.

29. Martin Heidegger, *Vier Seminare* (Frankfurt a. Main: Vittorio Klostermann, 1977), 125, and *GA* 15, 387. Hereafter cited as *VS* followed by page number, slash, and the corresponding page in *GA.*

30. See Martin Heidegger, *The End of Philosophy and the Task of Thinking: "The lumen naturale,* the light of reason . . . does concern the clearing, but so little does it form it that it needs it in order to be able to illuminate what is present in the clearing" (*BW,* 386, translation modified).

31. Martin Heidegger, *Grundfragen der Philosophie. Ausgewählte "Probleme" der Logik,* Freiburg lecture course, winter term 1937–38 (*GA* 45, 44).

32. Martin Heidegger, "Plato's Doctrine of Truth," in *Philosophy in the Twentieth Century: An Anthology,* vol. 2, ed. William Barrett and Henry D. Aiken (New York: Random House, 1962), 269, translation modified.

33. Martin Heidegger, "Overcoming Metaphysics," in *The End of Philosophy* (Norwich: Souvenir Press, 1975), 102.

34. Martin Heidegger, *Parmenides.* This was Heidegger's Freiburg lecture course for the winter term 1942–43 (*GA* 54, 44): "weil im Offenen des Seins allein auch das Unverborgene des Seienden erscheinen kann und erscheint, hält sich der Mensch zunächst, und unversehens dann ständig, nur an das Seiende. Er vergisst das Sein und lernt in solchem Vergessen nur das eine: die Verkennung des Seins und die Entfremdung gegen das Offene."

35. See Heidegger, *GA* 34, 323–24: "Unser Fragen nach dem Wesen der Wahrheit ist kein überflüssiger Nachtrag, sondern das Vortragen unseres Wollens und Daseins in ganz andere Bahnen und Bezirke . . . dieser Wandel des Wesens der Wahrheit in die *Umwälzung des ganzen menschlichen Seins,* an deren Beginn wir stehen" (my emphases); and *GA* 45, 214: "In der hier gestellten Wahrheitsfrage gilt es nicht nur eine Abänderung des bisherigen Begriffes der Wahrheit, nicht eine Ergänzung der geläufigen Vorstellung, es gilt eine *Verwandlung des Menschseins* selbst . . . die Verrückung des Menschseins aus seinem bisherigen Standort—oder besser seiner Standortlosigkeit—in den Grund seines Wesens, *der Gründer und Wahrer der Wahrheit des Seyns zu werden.*"

36. Heidegger himself uses the word "decay" *(Verfall),* e.g., in *GA* 34, 181: "auf dem Wege eines Verfallens [ist] der Begriff des 'Denkens' und der 'ratio' enstanden," and passim in *GA* 45 and *GA* 54. I will return to the difficulties and peculiarities that characterize Heidegger's use of this expression.

37. In what follows I comment on Heidegger, *GA* 45, 100–12, and passim.

38. Compare, for example, what is said in Heidegger, *GA* 45, 99, with the remark on the next page, where Heidegger evokes an age "in which the conception of truth as correctness was still foreign to the Greeks; in which rather the original experience of truth as unconcealedness held its sway" (my translation). It seems as if the introduction of *homoiosis* not only has been possible *on the basis of* this original experience of truth, but that it also *corrupted* this experience. With *homoiosis* we have the beginning of a series of *de iure* superfluous supplements to an original experience of truth that (*de iure* again) also could have existed without these supplements and indeed has done so. At the same time, however, Heidegger seems to be trying to link this corruption of the origin to its "corruptability." See my comments in the preceding paragraph.

39. Heidegger, *GA* 45, 139; and "The Age of the World Picture," in *The Question Concerning Technology and Other Essays* (New York: Harper and Row, 1977), 131.

40. Ibid., 132.

41. For this characterization of mimesis as "appearance in another place," see "Heidegger and Mimesis" by Samuel IJsseling in *Mimesis. Over schijn en zijn* (Baarn: Ambo, 1990), 47–60.

42. See Martin Heidegger, *Der Satz vom Grund* (Pfullingen: Neske, 1986), 88: "Unser Vernehmen ist in sich ein Entsprechen."

43. "La pauvreté de l'*Homo humanus* ou l'homme sans facultés" is the title of the second part of Michael Haar's brilliant book, *Heidegger et l'essence de l'homme* (Grenoble: Millon, 1990), translated as *Heidegger and the Essence of Man,* trans. William McNeill (Albany: State University of New York Press, 1993).

44. See Heidegger, *GA* 45, 118, where Heidegger explains that the Greek "*kai*" should be taken here in an explicative sense: "im Sinne von 'und das will sagen.'"

45. This seems to be the problem Phillipe Lacoue-Labarthe discusses in "Typographie," in *Mimesis des articulations* (Aubier: Flammarion, 1975), 165–270.

46. Martin Heidegger, "The Question Concerning Technology," in *BW,* 297ff.

47. See Martin Heidegger, "Memorial Address," in *Discourse on Thinking* (New York: Harper and Row, 1966), 48: "Week after week the movies carry them off into uncommon, but often merely common, realms of the imagination, and give *the illusion of a world that is no world*" (my emphases).

48. For Foucault the "appearance" of homosexuality should not be viewed as a "pro-duction" but as a production. See my analysis in *Michel Foucault: Genealogy as Critique* (London, New York: Verso, 1995), 66–71, 76–87.

49. Heidegger, *The End of Philosophy,* 390.

50. For these expressions, see Heidegger, *GA* 45, 37, 48, and passim. For Hegel/Heidegger, see Michael Haar, *Le chant de la terre. Heidegger et les assises de l'histoire de l'être* (Paris: Editions de l'Herne, 1985), 141–60. Translated as *The Song of the Earth: Heidegger and the Grounds of the History of Being,* trans. Reginald Lilly (Bloomington: Indiana University Press, 1993).

51. See John Caputo, "Demythologizing Heidegger: *Aletheia* and the History of Being," in *Review of Metaphysics* 41 (1988): 519–46.

52. Martin Heidegger, "Time and Being," in *On Time and Being* (New York: Harper and Row, 1972), 12–13.

53. Martin Heidegger, "Summary of a Seminar on the Lecture 'Time and Being,'" in *On Time and Being,* 36.

54. Heidegger, *Identity and Difference* (New York: Harper and Row, 1969), 64; and *The End of Philosophy,* 391.

55. Heidegger, "Summary of a Seminar on the Lecture 'Time and Being,'" 30.

56. Heidegger, *Time and Being,* 8; and *Vier Seminaire,* 102/364.

57. I follow here *Die Seinsgeschichtliche Bestimmung des Nihilismus (1944–46)* in Heidegger, *Nietzsche,* vol. 2 (Pfullingen: Neske, 1961), 335–98. Translated as *Nietzsche,* vol. 4, trans. David Farrell Krell (San Francisco: Harper and Row, 1982), 197–250, in particular 246.

58. Martin Heidegger, *On the Essence of Truth,* § 6 ("Untruth as Concealing"), in *BW,* 132ff.

59. See Jean-Louis Chretien, "La réserve de l'être," in *Cahier de l'Herne. Heidegger* (Paris: L'Herne [Biblio/Essais], 1983), 233–60. In what follows I comment on § 6 and 7 of Heidegger, *On the Essence of Truth.*

60. I borrow the expression "conformism" from a recent lecture course by Rudolf Bernet on *Being and Time.*

61. For an analysis of this conflict, see the first chapter of my *Truth and Singularity: Taking Foucault into Phenomenology* (Phaenomenological nr. 155) (Dordrecht, Boston, London: Kluwer, 1999), 23–46. And my more recent attempt to come to terms with conflict: "In Respectful Contempt: Heidegger, Appropriation, Facticity," in *Appropriating Heidegger*, ed. James E. Faulconer and Mark A. Wrathall (Cambridge: Cambridge University Press), 137–54, esp. 142ff.

62. Heidegger, *Der Satz vom Grund*, 101 and passim.

63. In rendering "*Sätze*," which is, of course, strictly untranslatable (it could, among other things, also mean "bounces"), by "movements" (in the musical sense of the term), I follow Reginald Lilly in his translation of *The Principle of Reason*; see Martin Heidegger, *The Principle of Reason* (Bloomington: Indiana University Press, 1991).

64. I borrow this image from my colleague Herman De Dijn, "Spinoza: rationist én mysticus?" in *De Uil van Minerva* 6, no. 1 (1989–90): 42.

65. Heidegger, "The Question Concerning Technology," 308.

Lightness of Mind and Density in the Thought of Heidegger and Foucault

Charles E. Scott

In his *Introduction to Metaphysics* Heidegger prepares the way in his first lecture for his listeners to understand what he means by *Geist* and a people's spirit. He speaks of the earth's and its inhabitants' place in the universe.[1] He points out that when we view our planetary home in terms of astrophysics and astronomy, it looks so miniscule in its spatial context as to obliterate any sense of significance that a person might attach to it. It is simply too tiny in all ways to count for much. In such a perspective, the earth's inhabitants also seem useless, utterly without cosmological meaning. Our times and efforts, like imperceptible waves of light, blink out of nothing to nothing, evaporated in the moment of energy that produced them. Nothing like *Geist* appears before such a view. What appears in such a construction seems more like mere expenditures of force in rapidly passing shapes, rather like a particle in a moving cloud on a distant horizon. Nor do the formation and articulation of such knowledge themselves bear much witness to *Geist.* They lack awareness of the ways of life and thought that they comprise and to which they give rise. This knowledge composes a kind of objectivity that has little sense for its own event or for its basis in the very questionableness of *life* that it embodies.

Spirit, Heidegger says, happens as we experience the questionableness of our lives and their meaning. We happen in the attunement to our lives as we recoil from and to our uncertainty—when we happen as the recoil of uncertainty—uncertainty so profound that it can call appropriately for no knowledge to dispel it. We embody a questionableness that appears to happen as its own manifestation, not as the manifestation of anything else, and meaning is found in this coming out and uncovering of our lives' unavoidable, alert, self-articulating, highly productive, and caring fragility. No matter where we are in the universe, no matter our comparative dimensions, we *are* in question, and in that is everything that matters.

You can see immediately how complicated and dense spirit *(Geist)* is in this context. Heidegger's use of the word does not suggest something that is reducible to anything else—not to fleshly matter or to an activity that is produced or caused by something else or to a point of view (such as a true way of viewing the world) or to something found like something else, or to anything that can be properly accounted as an object of knowledge. He is clear that *Geist* is not a subjectivity or subjectivity in general. And although he sounds close to identifying *Geist* with a specific culture's specially gifted insight and self-expression (i.e., the whole of the ancient Greek tradition and that of the German language), such a culture's gift now would be found in its knowledge that it has lost touch with what is rightfully most important to it. For *Geist,* as Heidegger thinks of it, seems to be a kind of happening in which its own loss figures its presence—and *that* is dense. It is dense in the sense that as he considers *Geist* in the context of the question of being he is considering an occurrence whose very eventfulness is without a basis—although this being without a basis (being in question) is at least like a basis in the sense that being without a basis is as basic as things ever get. At this point *Geist* seems like a word that means neither heavy nor light, neither solid nor porous, neither subject nor object. I am thinking of *dense* in this sense: in this language I am up against something that I cannot exactly conceptualize or see through or walk through or reach through or around or understand in the luminosity of grammar and common sense. At times I am tempted to say that if the Greek tradition and the German language are specially gifted, in some way that (I am informed by Heidegger) must be utterly foreign to me because of my disadvantage of being neither Greek nor German, I am not sure that I would want to credit the gift of this quandary to their advantage. (When people confront this aspect of Heidegger's opinions they might be cheered by recalling Nietzsche's observation in *Ecce Homo* that the German spirit is the creation of distressed intestines.) On the other hand, I do see and sympathize with Heidegger's observation that the question of being is as basic as things get, that we have no basis at all for contending over whether life itself (being) will survive, that being happens as the coming to pass of each and all things, and that when I said a little whimsically that we do not know whether life itself will survive, the "survive" does not make much sense. I think that Heidegger is talking about something that is dense in a way that I can appreciate (even *if* this knowledge, if it is a knowledge, composes the special gift of people in the traditions of German and classical Greek), and I would like to think of this density in terms of physicality (a word that I will say more about) and also think of it in connection with the function of the metaphor of space as Foucault works with it in *The Order of Things*. I want to think of a kind of density about which we would not want to talk by reference to matter or materiality, a density that, while demonstrably dense, is opposed neither to luminosity nor lightness. And I would like to go on this voyage of thought for the purpose of exploring and refiguring, if only slightly, the way we often think of bodies. Physicality, the question of being, and space will comprise the words around which this exploration will take its bearings.

Heidegger had several purposes when he contextualized *Geist* by the question of being in his 1936 summer lectures in which he introduced students to metaphysical thought. He wanted to counter with maximal energy a growing menace, one by which the question of language was losing what remained of its force in European cultures. By concerning themselves primarily with beings and issues that could be resolved, proved, answered, produced, used, and communicated with relative ease, people were losing a sensibility not only for the unresolvable, dark, and opaque strangeness of life's event, but also losing their sense for the astonishing opacity of language and thought when that strangeness pervades the meanings and references of things as they appear in particular linguistic and thoughtful enactments. Although this menace arrives with special emphasis in Russian and North American influence, it has been around for a long time, been around, indeed, within those two favorite cultures, and it is found by Heidegger's eyes in every faculty in the German universities. Heidegger, in fact, had little more patience with that pedantry that flourishes in German academies than many North Americans and Russians do, and he was strongly predisposed to blow the whole ship of German academics, including the "new" interpretations of Nietzsche, out of the water and start over with what he considered to be a more authentic curriculum—and all of that in the name of *Geist*! This approach to revolution by means of lectures and teaching might not be politics as a labor organizer or party fund-raiser is inclined to think of it, but we would find from Heidegger, I think, if we put him and those politicians in a debate, that their opinion in this case is due to the fact that they are not all that familiar with *Geist* and might even embody, especially in their politics, unwittingly its antagonist in the form of low-minded insensitivity to the lives they lead. *Geist,* the question of being, and a certain astonishment in and before life's questionability are terribly important political foci for Heidegger because, as he saw it, informed opinion was well on its way to thinking that scientific knowledge can tell us more truth about our world than anything else can and to thinking that the value of lives comes down to a matter of serviceability, solutions for problems, and truths that can be understood objectively or commonsensically. All of this suggests to me that he wanted to reactivate in our most lively sensibility a sense of density right where there is common sense and pragmatic, methodological clarity. "It" is not as clear as we tend to think it is when "it" means the occurrence of life.

Another purpose that Heidegger had in mind in these lectures was to join the question of being with a renewed understanding of what the Greek word *phusis* said and named. Even though the Latin translation of *phusis, natura,* suggests coming to birth, Heidegger is dissatisfied with it and its various cognates in Western languages. This word has a history that suggests the tensions in our knowledge of bodies that I want to highlight and that Heidegger wants to address. On the one hand *phusis* speaks of vital force. On the other, it names a created being in its essential character. In both of these senses it has been considered a synonym for being. And in yet a third connotation, *phusis* has been used to name creation as a whole. Amid these differences of nuance I note especially that between vital force and essential character. I believe that I can put the point by asking if the "inner fire" (an image some Stoics used for vital force) has a nature, in the sense of "composed by invariant principles" that define it? Does *phusis* as the springing up of life happen in a reasonable way? Or does *phusis* suggest a springing up of life that is already going on in one way or another when we think that it is either an occurrence according to principle or it isn't? Is *phusis,* in other words, nonrational and a basis for reasonable occurrences rather than happening under rational jurisdiction? If it were nonrational, it probably would be forever escaping rational grasp and frustrating reasonable people while at the same time suggesting, in an absence of principled universality or a status of any perceptible kind, that the rising up and passage of life does not necessarily happen in any definitive way, that our recognized necessities compose, strangely and perhaps irritatingly, only specific happenings of *phusis* and neither *phusis* "as such" nor a grasp of *phusis* "as such." I am approaching the possibility that *phusis* has more to do with the springing up of the image of nature as we usually visualize nature than it has to do with "having" the nature that an image or an idea might require it to have. Or, to speak in a way more like Heidegger spoke, *phusis* is best contextualized by the words "ontological difference" to indicate that *phusis* is not a being or a kind of being at all. That would mean that *phusis* names nothing specific at the same time that it names life's coming to pass.

I see no reason why *nature* could not also refer to birthing and coming to be and not to any kind of definitive structure so that we might say that it is the nature of things to come to pass. It can certainly name the way life is life, and in its sense of disposition and inherence, *nature* can mean the inevitability of the way something is given to be: birthing and dying, we could say, are in the nature of things. Nature is like *phusis* in connoting both animation and identifying form. But I expect that *nature* is too firmly tied to images of invariant definitions to allow conveniently for reference to nothing in particular that seems always to occur in happenings and in some vague sense lies behind and in all mentation, lies in and behind mentations not as a defined, rational predisposition, but as an indefinable sway that does not even suggest its own necessity beyond the locality of specific occurrences—a sway that seems to suggest that we need to rethink our own thinking in its inability to bring such density to thought. It might well be that *phusis* has the advantage of sounding more foreign and less ordinary than *nature* and that, in spite of the stresses of definition that it shares with *natura,* it has the further advantage of not suggesting quite so strongly as *nature* does its own permanence (if it were an "it"). And it has the third advantage of pointing toward the word *physicality,* about which this discussion is and about which I will say more in a moment.

The "second" complexity in the history of *phusis* that I noted above comes to the fore when we see that the word can name created beings in their essential specificity as a group or it can name life in general. It can name, in other words, beings as a whole and being as such, and in such naming it names the happening of lives or life's happening. This ability of the word in association with its suggestion of difference from anything that has a "nature" allows it, at least in Heidegger's language, to say that whatever is, as *is* (in being at all), happens beyond the reach of definitive grasp and that whatever happens happens in coming to pass. In happening, things do not bring to realization anything subject to definition.

When I think of *Geist, phusis,* and our tiny, tiny planet in this context, I am inclined to say that our spiritual *(geistige)* lives, as Heidegger thinks of them, have to do with perceiving things in pervasive awareness of the fragility of their and our lives, that something like fragility has within it, at least in "spiritual" events, a recoiling movement—a doubling dimension—in which whatever appears and the apprehending occurrence find indwelling connection: fragility in things (or inherent uncertainty in their being, or, the questionableness of being) doubles back in the apprehension and shines through every appearing thing, provides a sense of relatedness in this fragility, and provides no sense of permanence. People react differently to such manifestations. They might care for things-in-their-fragility with profound empathy for them in the passing quality of their lives. They might be moved by a sense of beauty before the rising and fading animations of living things with all their hues and diversity. They might wish to find ways to present life to themselves with a good bit more permanence than is plainly apparent. (I think of this last option as one way to affirm a perceived realm of life and, if not to exaggerate it, at least to give it supporting images of deathless, or at least possibly deathless permanence.) However we react, the physicality of *Geist* on Heidegger's account—its *phusis*—appears as an enlivening dimension for people, no matter how painful or happy its manifestations might be, in the appearing of whatever appears, and in those appearances people often find interest and meaning in relation to everything around them without concern for the relative size or "objective" importance of their locality.

In addition to showing that size and permanence are not only not everything, as far as meaning is concerned, but also are inconsequential for meaning in our lives, Heidegger further suggests, largely by indirection in the introductory lectures, that the ways we give order to appearances and answer to the orders we find among them are highly consequential for our sense of life, our spirit. The ways a culture finds order, expression and meaning with things comprise a large measure of the identity and particularity of their appearing. When we know things, for example, primarily by means of their functions and uses, their fragility is figured by their liability to breakage, malfunctioning, or contextual inappropriateness (their being unsuitable and valueless in many contexts). Or if things are determined by size, countable time, and metric distance (like, in Heidegger's example, the relative size of the Earth and its inhabitants), their fragility is measured in comparative terms (lasts more time than . . . has less mass and energy than . . . has more or less force on other objects than . . .). When such ways of knowing come to define and order a people, they compose a thoroughly obscuring texture before what Heidegger identifies as an inherited Western spirit of fragility and question, and most things seem to happen pretty much objectively or subjectively and without much indication of their own eventful, immeasurable, thoroughly questionable, dense lives. Our orders of life and knowledge more or less make manifest the sense of immeasurable fragility and questionableness in the lineages of our being and more or less give moment to astonishment before the occurrences of lives, no matter whether we approve of them in their details. I take this to mean that the ways by which the emerging or springing up orders of our cultural lives as they come to their own forms and endure for a time composes our physicality. The forms of things and their collections, as we live with and by them, define our lives and the locale of our physicality. And the ways we live with things *in* their appearing composes the physicality of our *Geist,* the full interconnected range of lineages, regulations, feelings, languages, and thought.

By translating *phusis* as physicality[2] I have in mind a tranfiguration of the issue of bodies and their density. The word has the considerable disadvantage of not usually connoting flesh, an issue to which I will return toward the end of this discussion. But in Heidegger's thought *phusis,* and hence *physicality,* also has the considerable advantage of suggesting physical, bodily life, animation, bodiliness: the springing up of life in the ways in which we constitute our lives. I have pointed out that when arising, persisting, passage are conceived in the obscure light of the question of being we confront "something" dense—really dense in the sense that there is nothing there clearly to focus on or to see through or to pass through or to understand objectively, and yet "there" in a pervasive sense of happening-without-finality-or-inevitable-continuation. And such density "defines" (in a sense of defines that I cannot satisfactorily define because we're not talking about any thing, much less about something that has a defineable structure) physicality (bodily life). I do not know if such density is more or less dense than traditional notions of flesh say that flesh is, but I have reached a point of not caring about the comparison. What I do want to determine in time is whether I can refer sensibly to physicality, in contexts of bleeding, hunger, suffering, laughter, touching—whether I can find an expressible, sensuous order among such things—so that this image of physicality and its density does not distract us from fleshly existence while it expands our horizons for thinking about body and spirit in ways more satisfactory than those we usually have available to us. *And* I would like to think of orders as composing locales of physicality; I would like to think of orders in a way that complements rather than departs from sensuousness. But for now I wish to do no more than to follow the bend and move toward an image of physicality that is without a suggestion of permanence while it embodies (Heidegger's word here is "say" *[sagt]*) a spirit enlivened by the *question* of being and enlivened in such a way that the word, "physicality," means that question in the word's contextual life. In that case we would confront an instance in which the question of being is embodied and could ask about what it might mean in daily physical life. If this approach were to work out, the approach's own life would embody what it addresses, and it would constitute a recoiling movement that could articulate love as well as desire, and other basic moods and feelings within its own sensuousness.

To develop this thought further, I turn to some aspects of Foucault's thought, aspects I find to be in concert with significant aspects of Heidegger's thinking in striking ways, given their considerable differences in style, lineage, and problematization. In this part of the discussion I will emphasize what happens—and I put this awkwardly now to stress a probability—in the arising and persisting of Foucault's thought in *The Order of Things*. I would like to be alert to a certain physicality in this work as I consider some of his study's implications for thinking about physicality.

An aspect of *The Order of Things* that is important for this discussion is found through two of its leading questions: how have orders arisen in our lineage, and how might we characterize the meaning and persistence of things in those orders? Putting the question this way allows me to underscore the importance of things' coming to appear in various orders as well as the importance of the appearing of different orders. When there are differences among dominant orders, *différences* (or *breaks* or *cesurae*) refers to an exteriority vis á vis the orders, an outside that gives the orders and things in them to appear in their differentiations. "Appearing in their differentiations" here means that whatever defines an order and whatever status and value an order gives to things have validity that is limited by the order's own identity, by *its* difference. The phrase also means that Foucault is giving emphasis to processes of appearing in orders and to the limits and boundaries that define the integrity of a body of appearances and the regions of their appearing. The knowledge he wants to develop in this book seems predisposed to descriptions, not to descriptions that look for some kind of pure origination that justifies their truth, but rather descriptions that embody a knowledge that their accuracy is based on the very lineage that they describe—*and* based as well on a quite determined departure from major aspects of that lineage. The differences among orders and their various departures not only from other orders but from themselves—the differences that define conflicts and transformations among, as well as within, orders—are elaborated by Foucault by means of the metaphor of space. As this part of the discussion unfolds I will bring space and physicality into a close proximity of meaning in order to think of physical space and hence of physical times in a context of both luminosity and density. If this effort succeeds, I will have taken a step toward seeing a concurrent contribution that Heidegger and Foucault make toward an understanding of worldly, historical, social, and disclosing bodies.

Nature can name something essential in the origin of things that unfolds over a period of time. Knowledge of the unfolding, in continuous reference to its essential origin, can show, in this way of thinking of nature, an internal law of formation: if you know that law you have a pretty good handle on the truth—the nature—of whatever is developing; and in the case of conceptions of Nature writ large, you can in principle know the universal truth of everything that comes to rational disclosure. This conception of *phusis,* in other words, is one that finds constitutive of the springing up of life a definitive essence in that animation, and that knowledge just about has to be writ large because, as a conveyor of essential truth, it becomes such a momentous and lasting event: it becomes knowledge of being itself! And with this knowledge a person can understand the place of any particular order with respect to the laws of formation (the *phusis*) that govern all orders and ordering. *Phusis* is conceived as the Nature of all ordering and may properly receive the name of the Originary Order of orders.

It seems clear in many recent orders of knowing that the nature (or Nature) of all appearing things is found in the principle and laws of subjectivity, whether subjectivity is universal and necessary in its laws and principles or culturally or physiologically determined in its laws and principles. While *The Order of Things* can be read within this context and as presenting a theory of historicized subjectivity, I believe that a more considered reading of that book will find that the function in it of the metaphor of space combined with the archaeological/genealogical accounts of orders of knowledge serves the observation that subjectivity derives from orders and not the reverse. To contextualize this observation, I shall return to Heidegger to see how he destabilizes subjectivity's priority by means of giving an account of the lineage of this prioritization. That should give us a basis for seeing in Foucault's thought an alternative to a position that privileges a historicized subjectivity. In this process of exposition, perhaps the viability will emerge of understanding thought and language as events of *phusis* that are not primarily composed either of principles or of some form of subjectivity. This move is preparatory to considering the metaphor of space in Foucault's discourse with emphasis on its density and luminosity.

One primary way by which Heidegger subverts the priority of subjectivity in *Introduction to Metaphysics* as well as in many other of his works is by addressing the lineage of that priority's development. In particular, in *Introduction to Metaphysics,* he shows that in the thought of Parmenides and Heraclitus *phusis* occurs with a sense of life's arising and enduring and without a sense that it is definable by principles. I use the word *sense* here because of Heidegger's claim that in their thought the language of life's fragility—the language that arises from the sense that life itself is in danger and thus arises in the question of being—their language did not come to a fully developed conceptual expression. Their thought and language are prephilosophical in that sense; they know the world through a language that arose with experiences of the possibility that life might always bring as part of its happening destruction and death and that the very event of life might itself always be in jeopardy, that life as such might be subject to the destruction that it brings with the rising up and endurance of things.[3] This prephilosophical sense is textured by a close affiliation of the jeopardized rising up and enduring of things with their unhiddenness—with their clear opacity as they happen and make passing differences.[4] This joining of the sensed fragility of being—its questionableness in Heidegger's terms—and the unhiddenness of things is the setting that, he finds, gives to Western intelligence an impulse away from the dominance of subjectivity for an understanding of beings in their appearing lives. In their language, things come to appear in their *phusis,* not because of the event of some agency, but in an unfolding—an unconcealing—that brings with the arising a limited enduring of things and no other basis than the event of unfolding. This sensibility was no easier to bring to conceptual clarity then than it is now, and it is one that we can at best engage with as much allowance as possible for its difference from our very capacity for disciplined conceptualization. For our capacity for disciplined conceptualization arose with historical endurance in the Greek aspect of our tradition through concerted efforts to think in the astonishment, uncertainty, and incipient thought that permeates their sensibility. This strange nonthing, *phusis*! "It" appears as things come to appear, but "it" never seems to be captured by any definitive appearance. It's not as though *phusis* were something too big to fit into a finite mold or mode. It's rather that *phusis* comes to pass as appearing. And it's not as though *phusis* were something in which all appearing things participate. It's rather that there is neither a subject nor an object behind the occurrence of subjects and objects, nothing there to be defined in the occurrence of things as things appear in the utter commonality of appearing. What it is the same for all existing things as far as their existing is concerned is not an existing being at all. "It's" called *phusis.* So, whatever we are going to say about *phusis* with reference to this sensibility, we are not going to say that it is characterized by any kind of agency. Heidegger says that "it" is the happening of appearing, of unconcealing, that "it" is like the happening of an infinitive in the moods, modes, and voices of verbs, that it's the shining of what shines. But its lack of any it-quality and any character of agency leaves us perplexed when we attempt to think this thought in a disciplined way.

The aspect of Heidegger's account of the early Greek sense of *phusis* that I want to emphasize here points to its departure from those conceptions of nature that compose an image of a process defined by an original, purposive origin or that is sufficiently defined in principle by a series of interconnecting causes. The sense of *phusis* that Heidegger is attempting to bring to thought does not require that causal connections be denied. Far from such a requirement, one may well find all manner of causal complexes that stretch far beyond observational grasp. But such complexes do not address what I have called a sensed fragility of living as such. That things happen, that they arise and endure for a time, that their living seems to require their dying, that complexes of causation happen at all—that appearing *occurs*, however it might occur in uncountable instances—*that* is the puzzlement that gives rise to a provocative mood that we call wonder or astonishment and that, Heidegger says descriptively, gave rise to efforts of understanding that we think of as philosophy in the Greek lineage. The sense is that the occurring of life as the appearing of things is not properly subject to explanation, that just where we might connect things by reference to something—be it law or agency—that means continuation of life, just "there" no definable or describable being happens.

This boggling point has so often been given in our Western tradition's determined focus by efforts of explanation, or by images of time-transcending participation in a being that holds things together, gifted by images of meaning that seam things together into a whole that the early Greek sense that gave impetus to thought has gone wanting in the thought to which it gave rise. People have posited some kind of order just where the noted sensibility found neither order nor orderer. I can here only note that the question of being, as Heidegger finds it operating in the Greek lineage, defines a limit to explanatory thought as such, that it means an endurance of question and uncertainty as they arose in that lineage, and that question and uncertainty endure as the meaning, the silent motivator, in any search for a way of being that gives transcendental meaning to the occurrence of life. Orders of beings are faced with the withdrawal of meaning in those orders as they provide meaning for the happening of life. Such meanings remain in question *in* the orders that provide assurance for life's continuance.

"I should not like," Foucault wrote in his preface to *The Order of Things,* "the effort I have made in one direction to be taken as a rejection of any other possible approach."[5] With these words and others like them, Foucault articulates his proximity and difference vis á vis Heidegger.[6] He turns away from, of course, any claim that suggests that the formations of orders are under the guidance of Subjectivity or Spirit or Law. But he also states, as a guiding preference, that the knowledge (and the preferences) that guide his work should not function like a formation with universal authority for inclusion and exclusion of other manners of knowing. He is prepared for the knowledge that he presents to make differences, but he is not prepared to move from juxtaposition and encounter with other knowledges and values to justified dominance over them. This caveat by itself does not depose the priority of subjectivity, but it does function as a caution before any predisposition toward an equation of knowledge, certainty, and truth with the privileges and dialectics that can accompany transcendental authorities. From the beginning of this study, its own power is restricted to pointed and contextualized encounters and engagements, and whatever remains in his thought of a traditional inclination to fuse knowledge and Truth is put on notice that such fusion will be subject to something closer to derision than obedience. This order—the order of this study—is without metaphysical comfort, and an expectation of its impermanence and limited jurisdiction constitutes a part of its texture.

There is nothing new in such a caution except, perhaps, its tone and style. It is composed in part of an alternative to the heroic sensibility that often accompanied traditional philosophical efforts, a sensibility to which Heidegger was not immune when he considered the importance of the question of being and his originality in its recall (not to mention the heroic status, to which I have referred with something less than awe, that he gives to classical Greek culture and the German language). The alternative is an orientation without a hero, without a desire to be a hero or to find one, and with a textured sense that with the demise of a positive sense for anything momentous and transcendental comes the demise of heroism with a positive value: exceptional accomplishments, certainly, but the extraordinary without the trappings of the tradition of the hero and with a sense for both the advantages and disadvantages, the opportunities and the dangers that compose extraordinary events and accomplishments. I suppose that the passage of emotions that constitute recognitions of heroes marks also the passage of emotions that predispose people to worship. But the relevance of that passage here is found in Foucault's declination of transcendental elevation of either the knowledge that he presents, its methods and values, or its subject matter.

I used, of course, "declination" with purpose. I have in mind my reference to Heidegger's saying that *phusis* is to beings as an infinitive is to the inflections of verbs into moods, modes, and voices. In classical grammar inflection and conjugation were seen as a kind of decline from the infinitives, a compromise that takes place when something that is uncompromised (the infinitive in this case) becomes limited and diluted by determinations (like "to be" becoming "we are"). Something unlimited in its purity becomes tainted by the imperfections of specificity.[7] My observation now is that Foucault's turning aside from the complex lineage of heroism in his evaluation of the knowledge and approach that composes his book is at once a spurning of the sense of perfect (or at least near perfect) instance that constitutes the hero. This refusal certainly bears witness to the heroic tradition but it also presents the alternative of a manner of thought and knowledge that are in relation to no model, image, or ideal other than those that compose their own events. This is a preliminary formation of Foucault's concept of locality that he put to work during the 1970s, a fecund one, I believe, in which the appearing, eventful quality of thought, knowledge, and language is accented by reference to nothing criteriological outside of the space defined by them. Knowledge does not fall away from and yet refer by decline to some "higher" or purer, infinitive-like life. The *phusis* of a discourse happens in self-disclosure and suggests its own truth in the dynamic structures of its appearance. It—*phusis*—constitutes the happening of the discourse's life. Or, as Foucault puts it in his preface, "there is order."[8]

This manner of thought, which is so different in style and some of its moods in comparison to Heidegger's, is nonetheless quite attuned in its sensibility to what I consider to be Heidegger's guiding thought: the ground of existence occurs ungroundingly. We need not use this language of grounds if it feels old-fashioned. We might say that the lives of things present no evidence for thinking that some origin or purpose or agency defines them other than those of the limited determinations that compose them and their environments. Putting it that way, though, does not quite approach a relevant and forceful predisposition in Western culture: a predisposition toward thinking with a more or less inchoate image of something that supports life's ephemeral transciency, something grander in scope and design that provides a transcendent context for our events, one that shines (or almost shines) around the edges of known realities, seems to shine enough to inspire belief in Something transcendental, whether It is worshipful or simply magnificent in its splendid range of indifference. When they address this force of predisposition both Heidegger and Foucault find nothing like an entity or meaning, not because they say that Nothing is There, but because they turn to the historical roots of the predisposition and attempt to work descriptively on the traditional predisposition while at the same time turning out of it in the manner in which they describe its lineage—an effort to dispose the force of this predisposition by valorizing other orienting possibilities in our lineage. Such processes give rise to ways of thinking and speaking and to ways whereby things come to appear that are quite different from those spawned by the dominance of the predisposition that is in question. These processes give thought, language, and appearing a different kind of occurrence and hence a different *phusis*.

This turn to history, which in part grows out of nineteenth-century historicism and also turns away from it, is facilitated for Foucault in *The Order of Things* by means of a metaphor of space. In this context Foucault proposes to come "face to face with order in its primary state" and "to show . . . in what way . . . our *culture has made manifest* the existence of order."[9] This basic sense of order and its meaning and the experiences of things in such a sense bring us to something like a site he calls an epistemological field. He elaborates the image of field by the word "envisage"—it is a space of immediate envisagement; it happens as a vision of order as such in at least several spans of time in our Western lineage of knowing (xxi). The field is a site of order for Foucault, though usually order has been taken to rest in itself—not, that is, to occur as an effect of anything and not as a part of transitional and describable processes, not even as *an* order, but as order as such. This would be a sense of order without chaos. The difference between Foucault and this sense of ultimate order is found in Foucault's placing such envisagement temporally and his naming it an episteme. An episteme is "a space of knowledge," but while fundamental senses of order have produced knowledges ruled by orders and connections of identity-governed differentiations, Foucault gives time a priority in his account of knowledge's spaces and introduces by this move something not ordered by Order. In this work of orientation that he carries out in *The Order of Things,* Foucault shows that the operations of an epistemological field have often functioned as a precognitive sense of the ultimacy of order as such, that such fields are temporally placed (they occur in designatable stretches of time that we may call periods and are characterized by the dominance of certain things in many cultural operations), and that their historical temporality, which is marked by all manner of showable lapses, transitions, and mutations in their stretches of *continuity,* leads us to see that "order as such" is quite mortal, quite without pure order, and quite chaotic in its formations. This epistemological space that Foucault calls an episteme is both the origin of many senses of the finality of order and the site whose description destroys such envisagement. By cutting across many historical corners I can say summarily, this study shows that *phusis* functions synonymously with "order" as Foucault thinks it; it, too, is not properly subject to the priority of Order when people speak of it.

The camaraderie of Foucault's thought here with Heidegger's guiding thought is apparent. Not only has he given time a place of primary importance in his metaphor of space (the implications of which I will address in a moment), he has thereby put to work a thought that suggests the inseparability of space and time as he conceives the ungrounding occurrences of grounds in our lineage.

So when Foucault says "there is order," he is, in the context of this book, pointing out the space-time of the "there is," i.e., the space-time of existential happening. Heidegger, too, concerned himself repeatedly with the space-time of the "there is," that is, that space-time of *phusis,* and concerned himself in ways that make impossible a convincing idea of *phusis*—and hence of the "nature of things"—as an ordered, dynamic principled process governed largely by a purposeful logos and by a force of causation.[10] For space-time does not seem to cause its events, and I believe that *The Order of Things* is as much an attempt to come to grips with that possibility as *Being and Time* and many other of Heidegger's works are. Space-time is a thought in which the idea of ungrounding ground comes aborning, and it is one where the strange affiliation of Foucault and Heidegger is most apparent.

I return now to the larger issue of this discussion, density, luminosity, and physicality. You will recall that I would like to bring together those words for the purpose of forming a conception approximate to what has been addressed traditionally as "body." I have highlighted

Foucault's and Heidegger's complementary ways of removing the priority of subjectivity from the organizing values of their thought. I have given emphasis to Heidegger's reconsideration of "nature" by addressing a prephilosophical sensibility concerning the fragility and question of being and by putting in question the images and concepts of nature that arose in the Greek-spawned lineage of Western philosophy. I found significant linkage between Heidegger and Foucault in the emphases they place on the disclosive, "appeariential" arising and passage of things in their orders (an emphasis that accompanies their removal of subjectivity's priority), and I indicated ways in which the thought of ungrounding ground plays a leading role in their thinking. Throughout I valorized the meaning of *phusis* with the intention of indicating that as I discussed these aspects of their thought I addressed the notion of physicality with its implication of luminosity and density.

Both density and luminosity in this context name dimensions (or aspects) of appearing. When appearing is freed from the context of subjectivity, the word can refer to and, in its thought and expression, embody and give to appear things in their presencing, give them to appear—in their rising and enduring for a time, in their coming to pass. Physicality names the happening of things and can mean neither materiality nor ideality in the usual philosophical sense of those words. The physicality of things is found in their coming to appear, or as some Greek writers put it, in the shining of what comes to shine. Appearing or shining is where the deeds, the works, the pragmata of things come to happen: the space of the "where" and the time of "comes to happen" seem inseparable.

Density in this context names the fragility of happening. The occurrence of what occurs does not seem to come from any other "where." Whatever contextualizes the happening of what happens and provides meaning for it appears as no less a happening. There is no defining presence that is transcendent to the happening of things. The imagery shifts from *something* dense, like a wall, or a rock, that one cannot see through; it shifts from something that is so much in itself or to itself that *its* occurrence is not presentable; and it shifts to a non-something that makes vision possible and that lightens.

When we use *light* in its derivation from *leukos* (white) we may speak of a source of light, like a star such as the sun, or to a standard (in the light of which we act), or even to a traffic signal. Or if we use *light* in its derivation from the Old English *leoht,* we may speak of someone's dismounting (he lit from the horse) or arriving by chance (she lit upon a solution) or attacking forcefully (the wrestlers lit into each other), or settling (the fly lit upon the wall). That sense of the word suggests a lightness of weight and movement, a sense that German also carries when one says that the ship *lichtet* its anchor. It can mean that weight is lifted. The words suggest in their differences to relieve of a burden, to happen without heaviness, and to make clear and brighten.

In Foucault's and Heidegger's thought the appearing of things carries these overtones, in their several nuances, of *light*. Things appear in the light of their occurrences. Their coming to pass—their physicality—happens with lightness. They happen both disclosively and without the weight of substantial presence or purpose. Order as such for Foucault happens spatially and temporally, i.e., in seaming stretches of discontinuity and mortality that allow the density of being to shine through—something like the appearing of mere space without preestablished or principled formation *in* the appearing of ordered things in specific orders. And beings occur according to Heidegger's descriptive accounts in the lightness of not-a-being-at-all, in a dense and lightening withdrawal of any possibility for identification, meaning, and continuous presence. For both Heidegger and Foucault, their own interpretations arise in cultural lineages whose traditional explanatory accounts of themselves and their world—their narrative *historia*—bear a dense and usually obscure sense that things continuously appear in a lightness that lingers, but does not provide assurance for any unbroken continuation.

Foucault often valorizes this sense of fragility by his concept of multiple, incompatible differences that compose ordered identities, in combination with his concept of the danger of axiomatic knowledges, ideals, and effective solutions to pressing problems. Values and knowledges may well address effectively specific threats to social vitality, such as poverty, disease, violent dissent, and environmental changes. But the identity-forming measures that instill character and recognition have *within* them severe conflicts that compose the stabilities and hierarchies (e.g., oppression of some of their own constitutive parts, very different forces of desire with contradictory trajectories, experiences of conflicting values that constitute the ordered standards of placement, exchange, and recognitions). He finds danger in the limitations and exclusions that function silently to diminish such conflicts by means of a sense of purchase on Something where definitive presence is established, such as Order as such, Law, or transcendent purpose in Subjectivity, Nature, or Divine Word. In his well-known phrase, such resolutions and establishments are not wrong, but they are dangerous. The danger inheres in the weighty combination of assurance, limitation, and suppressed conflict, much like the quenching of inherent questionableness in the ways in which the question of being is carried out, according to Heidegger, in those concepts of time, space, truth, and reality that constitute the mainstream of Western thought. In such traditional turns of thought and practice the dense lightness of being is made heavy and dark by the values and patterns of thought that fix it into the *historia* of disciplined intelligence and understanding: Western values and concepts have tended to lose attunement with the physicality of their own events, at least with the physicality that seems to have been experienced by some early Greek thinkers. That is a loss, I am saying, the recognition of which is built into Foucault's image of the danger of our best cultural productions, as well as into Heidegger's account of the question of being.

I find, as I noted at the beginning, that this way of thinking brings about a strange combination of density and lightness. The density is not only a matter of Heidegger's choice of words or Foucault's style of writing. It is something that happens in their unburdening movements of thinking. And it is in this movement that I find their thought to exceed considerably the limits of some of Heidegger's *Lederhosen* parochialism and Foucault's preoccupation with relatively recent forms of normalcy and deviation. Nor is the lightness of their work found in values that I can unambiguously affirm. There is, rather, in their thought a movement of unburdening, one that does not destroy values so much as it loosens them—"frees them" would say, I believe, too much—loosens them from the moorings that hold them to tympanic authorities by virtue of which they resist, often with relentless subtlety and obsession, their own mortal placement. The values that function definitively in Heidegger's and Foucault's own styles of intelligence fall no less prey to the dense lightness of their thought than do those values and beliefs more foreign to them. I often lose sight and bearing in the loosening process, as though abandoned for a time in the dark, for I can find in neither philosopher's work a direction toward the function of a master or a director or even a guide for definitive thought, much less one of a seer of mysteries that can bring me to the truth.

Each, I find, is glad to talk. In fact, each might be a little talky, profuse in the ways many remarkable, intellectual people seem to be. Each is accustomed to being heard and has something of the performer in him—although with Heidegger it's a fairly sober performance without the periods of levity that bubble up in Foucault's thought.[11]

But both Foucault and Heidegger address their reader, tell their interpretive stories, describe intentions and dimensions of life that no one else has described or perceived quite so well—described them in the preceptiveness of styles of language and thought that often transform the good sense of current intelligence into the density of a different perceptiveness. My point is that both Heidegger's and Foucault's thought lift the burdens of eternity and universality from thought and allow in the process of thinking the strange (for Western thought) lightness of open encompassment.

I mean by those last two words that sameness is not any specific thing but happens nonetheless, that Heidegger and Foucault are thinking such happening in various figurations of ungrounding ground ("being," "space," "space-time," for example). Each finds open encompassment in the thought and knowledge of Western culture, in the eventful dimension of meanings and in such images of enclosure as Order, Being, and Subjectivity. Each brings important aspects of our tradition to their own crises of falling apart in their designs that call for closed encompassment, and each thinks in and through such crises without requiring, either by knowledge or hope, a solution to the light of being's fragility in the density of existence.

I suppose that most of us have experienced with varying degrees of intensity the disappearance of something real, whether by death, loss of energy, mere silence, collapse of an order, or a simple change of mind. I believe that most of us have felt in such loss some distressed astonishment and a desire to fill what appears to be a vacuum with some kind of connection and meaning. In such experiences of disappearance many of us have wanted to reach out for a connection with something lasting that relativizes the void or to have a significant connection reach out to us—to feel connected and connected in such a way that the vacuum loses its seeming quality of over and finished. In Foucault's and Heidegger's thought, however, it's the connections themselves in which something like absence of presence inheres, and in their thought that dense lightness appears that leaves us unguided in the very things that are most important and that guide us, leaves these things opened by loss, it seems, at their core, like a space of appearance that rises up without a Nature.

That dense lightness can appropriately be called physicality, and Heidegger's and Foucault's thought join in bringing physicality to expression (in, among other ways, Heidegger's thought of the question of being and in Foucault's considerations of order). I expect that bodies are composed of something like preconceptual awareness in their physicality, that they happen as alertnesses with their fragile needs as they, in their needs, move physically with their environments. Bodies seem to know that they require orders. The orders that compose them appear to compose as well an awareness of orders' need. Such need appears to happen no more as a cry of desperation than as a yes to ordering, no less as an urge to exist and flourish than as bodily predisposition toward cooperation for the sake of continuing. Looking on such elemental interests, like the astronomer in Heidegger's image of the universe within the limits of scientific conception and measurement, we might find in this needful struggle nothing more than a blind process without meaning or grounds for hope. Or we might find in Foucault's account of the mutational rising and falling of orders of axiomatic knowledge a mere replication of creature's instinctual drive for survival by means of orders that embody the deathliness that they mean to forestall. But people might also find in Foucault's lightheartedness and in Heidegger's poetic thought—both without images of cosmic saving power or other enormities of universal proportions—a levity that Heidegger could call *geistig* and Foucault might name acceptance of divergence or a freeing of differences.[12] Each philosopher has achieved a singular lightness of mind in spite of many instances of heavy prose and thought, and I find in their achievement a threshold for encountering bodies in terms of physicality that can neither ignore the "materials" of which things are constructed, nor reduce events to those materials and their functions. I have in mind the physicality of things in terms of which the dense lightness of finite occurrences, the incompleteness of any reduction, directs our attitudes and interpretations regarding them.

This approach suggests a lightness of mind that is able, by virtue of its lightness, to encounter people and things less in terms of hierarchies of importance based on heavy foundations and doctrines and more in terms of the needs of the encountered one in *its* nonreducible event, its difference, its entrée to another beginning and another encounter. There is, as far as I can tell, no necessary connection between lightness of mind and any form of compassion or community. But such lightness does seem to be without a need to spend energy to justify or redeem its occurrences and to be able to perceive singular differences with singular clarity in their needful, ongoing occurrences. Such clarity appears to me to make less dangerous compassion and community, to unburden compassion and community of the weight of mythological or settling purpose and justification, and to make possible alertness to dimensions of suffering and its causes that are difficult, if not impossible, to see when our recognitions are in the service of weighty Truth, Nature, or other capital meanings. Such claims appear to close the physicality of things, to fix it in completions of designation, and to make extremely difficult affirmation of events in the midst of their multiple and differential movements toward their continuing and never containable lives.

Notes

1. The following is a gloss on Martin Heidegger's *Einführung in die Metaphysik*, ed. Friedrich-Wilhelm von Herrman, vol. 40 of Heidegger's *Gesamtausgabe* (Frankfurt am Main: Klosterman, 1983), 5 ff.

2. A translation suggested to me by Susan Schoenbohm.

3. See Heidegger, "The Anaximander Fragment" in *Early Greek Thinking*, trans. David Farrell Krell and Frank A. Capuzzi (New York: Harper and Row, 1975), 13 ff.

4. He speaks of this fragility of being also in terms of being's withdrawal and hiddenness. We can read "withdrawal and hiddenness" as referring not primarily to "fragility," but as referring simply to being's ungraspability, its escape from designation and meaning. Being is in question because of its unavailability to intelligence, because of its opacity in its disclosiveness. People simply cannot know "it" or know even whether it is in any sense at all. While I find this a viable reading of Heidegger's interpretation, I will hold the idea of being's withdrawal in close association with the sense that being brings destruction with arising to life in a being's appearance—I will hold together his study of Anaximander and his reading of Heraclitus and Parmenides—as I render the prephilosophical sensibility that gives rise to classical Greek philosophy. Hence, my remarks here concerning *Introduction to Metaphysics* are informed by other of his writings on the pre-Socratics. See especially the essays collected in Heidegger, *Early Greek Thought*.

5. Foucault, *The Order of Things* (New York: Vintage, 1973), xiv.

6. See ibid., xxiii, for example.

7. See Martin Heidegger, *Introduction to Metaphysics*, trans. Richard Polt and Gregory Fried (New Haven: Yale University Press, 2000), chapter 2, especially 68–74.

8. Foucault, *The Order of Things*, xx.

9. Ibid., xx–xxi.

10. See Heidegger's *Beiträge Zur Philosophie*, vol. 65 (1989) of Heidegger's *Gesamtausgabe*, sections 96, 97, and 111.

11. I have seen a photograph of Heidegger when he was "lit up" after a wine evening

with Medard Boss. That side of him tends to be covered over and forgotten in my experience of his writings.

12. See *Language, Counter-Memory, Practice,* trans. Donald F. Bouchard and Sherry Simon (Ithaca: Cornell University Press, 1977), 185, where he writes in a Deleusean mood.

Contributors

HUBERT L. DREYFUS is professor of philosophy at the University of California, Berkeley. He is coauthor of *Michel Foucault: Beyond Structuralism and Hermeneutics* and author of *Being-in-the-World: A Commentary on Heidegger's "Being and Time," Division 1*, and, most recently, *On the Internet.*

STUART ELDEN is a lecturer in political geography at the University of Warwick. He is author of *Mapping the Present: Heidegger, Foucault, and the Project of a Spatial History* and coeditor of *Henri Lefebvre: Key Writings.*

BÉATRICE HAN is a lecturer in philosophy at the University of Essex. She is author of *L'ontologie manquée de Michel Foucault* (translated in English as *Foucault's Critical Project: Between the Transcendental and the Historical*). She is now completing *Transcendence without Religion.*

STEVEN V. HICKS is professor and chair of philosophy at Queens College of the City University of New York. He is author of *International Law and the Possibility of a Just World Order: An Essay on Hegel's Universalism,* and he has written articles on Hegel and Nietzsche. He is the coeditor of *Mythos and Logos: How to Regain the Love of Wisdom* (forthcoming) and is currently working on a project titled *Reading Nietzsche at the Margins.*

LADELLE MCWHORTER is professor of philosophy and women's studies at the University of Richmond. She is editor of *Heidegger and the Earth: Essays in Environmental Philosophy* and author of *Bodies and Pleasures: Foucault and the Politics of Sexual Normalization.*

ALAN MILCHMAN teaches political science at Queens College of the City University of New York. He has coedited (with Alan Rosenberg) *Martin Heidegger and the Holocaust* and *Postmodernism and the Holocaust,* and he has written articles on Max Weber, Ernst Bloch, Heidegger, and Foucault.

ALAN ROSENBERG is associate professor of philosophy at Queens College of the City University of New York. He has coedited *Echoes from the Holocaust: Philosophical Reflections on a Dark Time, Healing Their Wounds: Psychotherapy and Holocaust Survivors,* and *Contemporary Portrayals of Auschwitz: Philosophical Challenges.*

JANA SAWICKI is professor of philosophy and women's studies at Williams College. She is author of *Disciplining Foucault: Feminism, Power, and the Body* and is currently completing a series of essays on Foucault and queer theory.

MICHAEL SCHWARTZ teaches in the Department of Fine Arts at Augusta State University in Georgia. He has published articles on Foucault, as well as on medieval, Renaissance, and contemporary art.

CHARLES E. SCOTT is Edwin Erle Sparks Professor of Philosophy at Pennsylvania State University. He is author of *The Language of Difference; The Question of Ethics: Nietzsche, Foucault, Heidegger; The Time of Memory; The Lives of Things;* and coeditor of *Companion to Heidegger's Contributions to Philosophy.*

WILLIAM V. SPANOS is Distinguished Professor of English at Binghamton University (State University of New York). He is author of *The End of Education: Toward Posthumanism* (Minnesota, 1993),

Heidegger and Criticism: Retrieving the Cultural Politics of Destruction (Minnesota, 1993), and *America's Shadow: An Anatomy of Empire* (Minnesota, 2000).

LESLIE PAUL THIELE is professor of political science at the University of Florida. He is author of *Friedrich Nietzsche and the Politics of the Soul: A Study of Heroic Individualism; Timely Meditations: Martin Heidegger and Postmodern Politics; Thinking Politics: Perspectives in Ancient, Modern, and Postmodern Political Theory;* and *Environmentalism for a New Millennium.*

RUDI VISKER is professor for contemporary continental philosophy at the Institute of Philosophy in Leuven, Belgium. He is author of *Michel Foucault: Genealogy as Critique* and *Truth and Singularity: Taking Foucault into Phenomenology.*

EDITH WYSCHOGROD is J. Newton Rayzor Professor of Philosophy and Religious Thought at Rice University. She is author of *Spirit in Ashes: Hegel, Heidegger, and Man-Made Mass Death; Saints and Postmodernism: Revisioning Moral Philosophy;* and *An Ethics of Remembering: History, Heterology, and the Nameless Others.*

Index

Made in the USA
Monee, IL
24 April 2025

16315006R00207